The Internet and Cor

This book analyses emerging constitutional principles addressing the regulation of the internet at both the national and the supranational level. These principles have arisen from cases involving the protection of fundamental rights. This is the reason why the book explores the topic through the lens of constitutional adjudication, developing an analysis of courts' argumentation.

The volume examines the gradual consolidation of a 'constitutional core' of internet law at the supranational level. It addresses the European Court of Human Rights and the Court of Justice of the European Union case law, before going on to explore Constitutional or Supreme Courts' decisions in individual jurisdictions in Europe and the US. The contributions to the volume discuss the possibility of the 'constitutionalisation' of internet law, calling into question the thesis of the so-called anarchic nature of the internet.

Oreste Pollicino is an Associate Professor of Comparative Law at Bocconi University, Milan, Italy.

Graziella Romeo is an Assistant Professor of Constitutional Law at Bocconi University, Milan, Italy.

Routledge Research in Constitutional Law

This series features thought-provoking and original scholarship on constitutional law and theory. Books explore key topics, themes and questions in the field with a particular emphasis on comparative studies. Where relevant, titles will engage with political and social theory, philosophy and history in order to offer a rounded analysis of constitutions and constitutional law.

Series Editor: David Marrani

Available titles in this series include:

Weak Constitutionalism
Democratic Legitimacy and the Question of Constituent Power
Joel I. Colon-Rios

Engineering Constitutional Change
A Comparative Perspective on Europe, Canada and the USA
Xenophon Contiades

Freedom of Speech
Importing European and US Constitutional Models in Transitional Democracies
Uladzislau Belavusau

Colonial and Post-colonial Constitutionalism in the Commonwealth
Peace, Order and Good Government
Hakeem O. Yusuf

Dynamics in the French Constitution
Decoding French Republican Ideas
David Marrani

Constitutionalism in the Global Realm
A Sociological Approach
Poul F. Kjaer

The Legal Philosophy and Influence of Jeremy Bentham
Essays on 'Of the Limits of the Penal Branch of Jurisprudence'
Edited by Guillaume Tusseau

Forthcoming titles in this series include:

Equal Citizenship, Civil Rights and the Constitution
The Original Sense of the Privileges or Immunities Clause
Christopher R. Green

Accountability and Transparency in the European Union
Marios Costa

The Internet and Constitutional Law

The protection of fundamental rights and constitutional adjudication in Europe

Edited by
Oreste Pollicino and Graziella Romeo

Routledge
Taylor & Francis Group
LONDON AND NEW YORK

First published 2016 by Routledge

2 Park Square, Milton Park, Abingdon, Oxfordshire OX14 4RN
52 Vanderbilt Avenue, New York, NY 10017

Routledge is an imprint of the Taylor & Francis Group, an informa business

First issued in paperback 2020

British Library Cataloguing in Publication Data
A catalogue record for this book is available from the British Library

Library of Congress Cataloging in Publication Data
The internet and constitutional law : the protection of fundamental rights and constitutional adjudication in Europe / Oreste Pollicino and Graziella Romeo.
pages cm. -- (Routledge research in constitutional law)
Includes bibliographical references and index.
ISBN 978-1-138-92498-7 (hbk) -- ISBN 978-1-315-68404-8 (ebk) 1. Human rights--Europe. 2. Internet--Law and legislation--Europe. 3. Judicial review--Europe. 4. Constitutional law--Europe--Cases. I. Pollicino, Oreste, editor. II. Romeo, Graziella, 1981- editor.
KJC5132.I5675 2016
342.408'5--dc23
2015026656

ISBN: 978-1-138-92498-7 (hbk)
ISBN: 978-0-367-59715-3 (pbk)

Typeset in ITC Galliard by
Servis Filmsetting Ltd, Stockport, Cheshire

Contents

PART III
Models of constitutional adjudication on internet issues: a comparative perspective

Note on contributors

Joan Barata Mir is the Principal Adviser to the OSCE Representative on Freedom of the Media and Research Fellow at the Central European University. His writings and research interests include topics such as freedom of expression, media regulation, public service broadcasting, and political and legal media transitions.

Marco Bassini is a Research Fellow at Bocconi University in Milan and a PhD candidate in constitutional law at the University of Verona.

Filippo Fontanelli is Lecturer in International Economic Law at the University of Edinburgh, where he teaches WTO law and public international law. He is a member of the Centre for Judicial Cooperation of the European University Institute of Fiesole (Italy) and routinely provides training sessions to judges and practitioners on matters of EU law and human rights protection in Europe.

András Jóri is a Hungarian attorney, having served as Data Protection Commissioner for Hungary between 2008 and 2011. He is currently active as a consultant, advising authorities in Eastern Europe and the Balkans about how to establish their privacy regime.

Krystyna Kowalik-Bańczyk is Associate Professor at the Institute of Legal Studies of the Polish Academy of Sciences, specialising in general EU law, EU competition law and EU internet law. She holds an LLM in European law from the College of Europe (Bruges) and a DEA from the University of Social Sciences of Toulouse.

Molly K. Land is Professor of Law and Human Rights at the University of Connecticut School of Law and Human Rights Institute. Her research focuses on the intersection of human rights, science, technology and innovation. Her most recent work considers the relationship between innovation systems and the international human right to benefit from scientific progress, as well as the effect of new technologies on human rights fact-finding, advocacy and enforcement.

Gert-Jan Leenknegt is Associate Professor of Constitutional Law at Tilburg Law School, Tilburg University, the Netherlands. His research and teaching concentrate on Dutch, European and comparative constitutional law. He is also the Programme Director for the Major Law in Europe Programme of the University College Tilburg.

Paolo Passaglia is Associate Professor of Comparative Public Law at the University of Pisa and Coordinator of the Comparative Law Area of the Studies and Research Department of the Italian Constitutional Court. His research and teaching are in the fields of constitutional adjudication and comparative constitutional law.

Oreste Pollicino is Associate Professor of Comparative Public Law at Bocconi University, Milan. He was recurring visiting scholar at the Institute of European and Comparative Law, Oxford. He writes on various issues relating to freedom of expression, media law and constitutional adjudication, and he is the author, with G. Martinico, of *The Interaction between Europe's Legal Systems: Judicial Dialogue and the Creation of Supranational Laws* (2012).

Graziella Romeo is Assistant Professor of Constitutional Law at Bocconi University, Milan. She was visiting scholar and guest lecturer at Fordham Law School, New York, where she focused her research interests on fundamental rights and constitutional adjudication.

Jacob Rowbottom is a Fellow of University College, Oxford and Associate Professor at the Faculty of Law, University of Oxford. He writes on various issues relating to freedom of expression, political participation and media law, and is the author of *Democracy Distorted* (2010).

Clare Ryan is a Robina Foundation Human Rights Fellow for the Yale Law School, working at the European Court of Human Rights. She previously served as a visiting assistant professor in the Department of Political Science at Macalester College.

András Sajó is a judge at the European Court of Human Rights, where he has served since 2008. Previously, he served as the Chair of Comparative Constitutional Law at the Central European University in Budapest and as a recurring visiting professor at Cardozo School of Law and New York University Law School. He is a member of the Hungarian Academy of Sciences and the American Law Institute.

Catherine Van de Heyning is a post-doctoral researcher in human rights at the University of Antwerp and lecturer on criminal law at the KHLIM. She practises criminal law at the Antwerp bar.

Introduction

This volume collects contributions originally prepared and discussed in the international conference Internet Law, Fundamental Rights and Constitutional Adjudication, held in October 2014 at Bocconi University, Milan.

The basic statement behind this book project is that internet law needs a constitutional analysis; that is, using models of constitutional adjudication, in both their institutional and argumentative dimension, to explore the law of the Web significantly enhances the state of the art in internet studies.

To take up this challenge, internet-law scholars who are very familiar with the different models of constitutional adjudication have been put together to discuss the issues connected to the relationship between protection of fundamental rights in the digital era and constitutional review, in a comparative context that takes into consideration the domestic dimension and the supranational one.

The theories that have influenced the research carried out in this volume are those related to constitutional adjudication, which essentially aim at explaining how judges decide cases and how judges ought to decide cases.[1]

The first part of the volume addresses the theoretical framework surrounding Internet studies and the specific issues connected to the jurisdiction conundrum.

More precisely, with regard to the theoretical relevant landscape, András Sajó and Clare Ryan analyse the issues of judicial reasoning in cases involving new technologies, covering the framing activity, which consists in making sense of the internet in a way that enables judges to use traditional legal categories or to face the problem of translating old categories in a new language.

In connection to the jurisdiction conundrum, Catherine Van de Heyning's chapter explores the boundaries of jurisdiction in cybercrime cases from a European perspective, focusing on the problem of identifying potential harms in the Web and exercising jurisdiction in the anarchic world of bit. Finally, Molly K. Land adds the US perspective on both the problem of jurisdiction and the constitutional dimension of Internet issues across the Ocean.

The second part covers the European standards for protection of fundamental rights in the Internet. Joan Barata Mir and Marco Bassini address the European

1 Robert Justin Lipkin, 'Conventionalism, Constitutionalism, and Constitutional Revolutions', (1987–1988) 21 *U.C. Davis L. Rev.* 645.

Court of Human Rights case law underlining recent developments, especially in the area of freedom of expression. Filippo Fontanelli closes the second part of the volume focusing on the Court of Justice of the European Union case law, arguing for the need to reconsider the balancing test in internet-related issues as part of the broader problem of judging in cases in which new technologies are involved.

The third part of the volume is entirely dedicated to domestic constitutional and supreme courts case law, with specific regard to the relationship between the standard of protection of fundamental rights in the internet and the different models of constitutional adjudication. It aims at highlighting the reasoning of these courts in two complementary perspectives: the constitutional dimension of the case law, that is the balancing of rights and interests in the digital era; and more broadly the domestic judges' approach to the internet phenomenon: does it alter the application of existing laws and legal categories?

Jurisdictions, as already mentioned, have been selected on the basis of the model of constitutional adjudication that is performed. Consequently, Paolo Passaglia opens the third part by addressing the case law of courts operating in centralised systems of constitutional adjudication with no direct access to the constitutional courts (Italy and France). András Jori dedicates his chapter to the centralised system of constitutional adjudication with direct access to the constitutional courts (Germany and Central Europe). Krystyna Kowalik focuses on the Polish Constitutional Tribunal, which developed an original understanding of the relationship between law and the internet. Jacob Rowbottom provides an analysis of a 'weak' (that is not Kelsenian) model of constitutional adjudication addressing UK case law. Finally, Gert-Jan Leenknegt develops a study of the Dutch case, which falls under a peculiar constitutional model providing no system of constitutional review of legislation.

The institutional models of constitutional adjudication explain the distinguishing features of the structure of judicial review performed by constitutional and supreme courts. More importantly, they offer a wide overview of the different way in which the protection of fundamental rights can be addressed and ensured.

Ultimately, as it is pointed out in the concluding remarks, the volume challenges the idea that internet law is (only) a highly specialised area of legal studies; it underlines the constitutional dimension of the issues connected to the regulation of the Web and to the protection of rights in the digital era.

1 Judicial reasoning and new technologies

Framing, newness, fundamental rights and the internet

András Sajó and Clare Ryan*

1.1 Introduction

For centuries, judges have struggled to adapt existing law in the face of technological advancement. Both civil law and common law judges confront situations in which technological developments contribute to new social and economic contexts; contexts for which the current legal regime is ill-equipped. When this arises, the judge must first determine whether the technology is indeed new. Does the present case truly fall outside the scope of previous precedent and statute? If so, judges apply metaphors and analogies to the new context so as to make sense of the novel by using the frames of the past.

The act of pouring new wine into old bottles has always been a part of the judicial task – not only for common law development, but also as civil law judges interpret and apply code. There is nothing new in this act of judicial framing. The real challenge comes when judges (or legislators) are confronted with unexpected, unpleasant or ambiguous social and economic consequences of technology. The challenge may be particularly acute when these consequences arise from earlier judicial choices about framing.

The focus of this chapter will be on the complex challenges posed by the internet. Specifically, this chapter will address the interaction between the harms and opportunities of the emerging online world and individual constitutional or human rights. We ask first how judges develop analogies and metaphors to make sense of new technology. We then question whether those frames provide an adequate response to the modern world. We argue that, with regard to individual rights and the internet, a process of reframing is occurring. This reframing has begun to reject traditional rights frames – like freedom of expression.

It is important to note that we are not talking about technological change as such, but rather the interaction between technological change and the relevant social and market reactions to the implications of this change. It is regularly argued that when the current law, or the lack thereof, is insufficient to address

* This chapter is derived in part from a speech given by András Sajó entitled 'Is freedom of expression sustainable in a world of sensitivities?' delivered on 6 December 2014 at the Palais des Académies in Brussels.

present conditions, then it is for the legislature to take appropriate action. This principle surely applies to uncertainties resulting from technological change. But what happens if the legislature is not responding? The judge will decide the case on the basis of laws that are arguably inadequate to handle the new situation. The matter is then further complicated by the application of constitutional or human rights to contexts in which the legal rule governing a technological advancement predates the recognition of the right in question.

When it comes to judicial handling, the subject-matter of litigation is relevant, but of equal importance is the type of court that is supposed to adjudicate. Here we concentrate on apex courts (i.e. constitutional and supreme courts), and also international courts, primarily the European Court of Human Rights. Even at these apex courts, it should be mentioned that rights and fundamental rights-related concerns are only part of the consideration. Risk and economic development are additional considerations, which do play a role in the acceptance of rights restrictions. In other words, the social interest related to the consequences of the technology might give weight to the conventionally recognised grounds for interference.

We have arrived at a point of great tension between existing rights frames and the social reality which creates, and is created by, the internet of the twenty-first century. The first part of this chapter explores judicial framing as a technique for confronting new technology. Next, we examine the ways in which social consequences challenge existing frames. Finally, we demonstrate the ways in which old metaphors are losing their power – including past justifications for values such as freedom of expression.

1.2 Old framing for novel technology

The dilemma of how to balance old norms in new contexts is hardly new, although the scope of its implications may be broader now than in the past. For the continental lawyer the paradigm cases remain, most probably, the French judicial reaction to photography and to the phenomena of industrial accidents. Similarly, the development of liability regimes during the English and American industrial revolutions highlight how integral judicial framing is to the legal reception of technological advancements. Additionally, a classic American case for reframing rights and technology in a socially changing environment came from Justice Brandeis's dissent in the first US Supreme Court case to address wiretapping.

In 1858 it had been five years since Nadar opened his portrait studio in Paris and photography had become commercially available. In that year, a French judge was asked to decide the fate of legally taken photographs of the French actress Rachel on her deathbed. The pictures were taken upon request of her sister for family purposes, but the photographers were forbidden from communicating a copy of them to anyone. Twenty-five copies were put up for sale. The French court ruled that: 'No one may, without the express consent of the family, copy and publish the face of a person on his deathbed, irrespective of the celebrity of the person and the degree of publicity that was attached to the acts of his life. The right to forbid such reproduction in an absolute one.'[1]

Although it was nearly half a century after this case before France codified a general right to personal images, the *Rachel* case is considered to be the beginning of modern personality rights and the right to one's own image. Certainly, it did have an impact on the use of photography (although not on the technology). This case demonstrates that, even in the absence of a civil code rule, the civil law judge was able to determine that the new technology had facilitated the infringement of a heretofore unarticulated individual right.

The second French example is that of no-fault liability. The French Civil Code and French legal doctrine were based on the assumption that fault is the moral base of negligence and legal liability. Therefore, plaintiffs had the burden of proving fault as an element of their claim. In an age of increasingly dangerous industrial equipment, this strict requirement to prove fault wrought evident injustice for victims of industrial accidents (evident, importantly, to judges).

In 1896, the Court of Cassation, invoking Article 1384 of the French Code Civil, held the owners liable for injuries caused by the explosion of a steam engine. The relevant Article had hardly ever been invoked previously; it simply held that a person was responsible for harm caused by objects within their control, but it otherwise appeared to fit within the general negligence regime. However, the French court stated that Article 1384 raises a presumption of fault (*presomption de faute*), which results in shifting the burden of proof (*renversement de la charge de la preuve*) onto the defendant to show that the accident was the result of an uncontrollable event.[2]

This was sheer legal interpretation; applying a new reading to pre-existing statute. The court did not make explicit reference to socio-economic or technological change, although the power of new industrial machinery certainly drove this legal innovation. Rather, the court relied on a relatively open text within the civil code. As Saleilles mentioned in regard to a similar shift in interpretation regarding railway passengers: '*au dela du code civil, mais par le Code civil*'.[3]

The French courts, however, did not apply this innovative legal interpretation to automobile accidents until many decades later. Why? Perhaps out of fear of stifling a nascent industry. More importantly, in the early days, only the wealthy drove automobiles. The courts, despite increasing public frustration with the costs of these dangerous vehicles, refrained from imposing stricter liability on

1 Elizabeth Logeais and Jean-Baptise Schroeder, 'The French right of image: an ambiguous concept protecting the human persona' (1998) 18 *Loyola of Los Angeles Entertainment Law Review* 511, 514 citing T. P. I. Seine (16 June 1858), DPI II 1858, 52.

2 Francis Deak, 'Automobile accidents: a comparative study of the law of liability in Europe' (1931) *University of Pennsylvania Law Review* 271, 274–78.

3 John H. Tucker, Jr, 'Au-Dela du Code Civil, mais par le Code Civil' (1974) 34 *Louisiana Law Review* 957, 957 citing R. Saleilles, *Preface to Gény: Méthode d'Interprétation et Sources en Droit Privé Positive* (1st edn, Paris 1899).

accidents caused by this privileged social class. This stance did not shift until after the First World War.[4]

In the Anglo-American context, the strict liability regime also developed through judicial response to changing technology during the industrial revolution. The United States applied traditionally stringent fault requirements in industrial accidents, justified perhaps by a need to foster growth and encourage entrepreneurial industry. In some cases, however, this default began to erode during the latter part of the nineteenth century. Although there was a pro-industry presumption in legislation and traditional tort rules, as judges perceived the increased dangers of (then) modern technology, and the subsequent injustices created by outdated law in individual cases, they expanded the concept of strict liability into areas that had previously been governed exclusively by a negligence regime.[5] As Lawrence Friedman wrote in reference to this time of legal and industrial change:

> A general pattern may be discerned which is common to the judicial history of many rules of law. The courts enunciate a rule, intending to 'solve' a social problem—that is, they seek to lay down a stable and clear-cut principle by which men can govern their conduct or, alternatively, by which the legal system can govern men. If the rule comports with some kind of social consensus, it will in fact work a solution—that is, it will go unchallenged, or, if challenged, will prevail. Challenges will not usually continue, since the small chance of overturning the rule is not worth the cost of litigation. If, however, the rule is weakened—if courts engraft exceptions to it, for example—then fresh challenges probing new weaknesses will be encouraged.[6]

In the era that Friedman describes, judges increasingly carved out exceptions to the fault rule – conforming to social fairness, rather than strict legal requirement – and, over time, these exceptions eroded the overarching legal frame.

In 1928, Justice Brandeis provided the classic American case for judicial framing in the face of new uses of technology. His dissent in *United States v Olmstead* argued for expanding Fourth Amendment search and seizure protections to telephone wiretapping. The majority held that because listening to a private telephone conversation did not require a physical search or entry into a person's private space, the Fourth Amendment warrant requirements did not apply. Brandeis argued that extending the meaning of the search and seizure protection was warranted, given the changing technology:

4 Francis Deak, 'Automobile accidents: a comparative study of the law of liability in Europe' (n 2) 271, 281–82.

5 See Gary T. Schwartz, 'Tort law and the economy in nineteenth-century America: a reinterpretation' (1981) 90 *Yale Law Journal* 1717.

6 Lawrence M. Friedman and Jack Ladinsky, 'Social change and the law of industrial accidents' (1967) 67 *Columbia Law Review* 50, 59.

> [T]his court has repeatedly sustained the exercise of power by Congress, under various clauses of that instrument, over objects of which the fathers could not have dreamed . . . We have likewise held that general limitations on the powers of government, like those embodied in the due process clauses of the Fifth and Fourteenth Amendments, do not forbid the United States or the states from meeting modern conditions by regulations which 'a century ago, or even half a century ago, probably would have been rejected as arbitrary and oppressive. . . . *Clauses guaranteeing to the individual protection against specific abuses of power, must have a similar capacity of adaptation to a changing world.*[7]

1.3 Framing and the power of metaphors

So what do courts do when they are confronted with a new technology that generates socially contested situations, in particular alleged fundamental rights violations? Compared to the strict liability example, here the stakes are raised. The arguments are elevated to the realm of fundamental and human rights on both sides (users of the technology and its victims). In the fundamental rights context, courts have recourse to constitutional, open text. All things considered, the technology-generated problem will be translated into the traditional legal dilemma of right and non-right: the way it is translated will to some extent determine the answer. For example, if the resulting rights restriction is disproportionate in view of the interest served, it will not be constitutional.

Translation of a technology and its consequences into the legal frame is not automatic. This is particularly evident when the social and normative consequences of the technology are successfully presented as new. Newness in this context means dissatisfaction with the outcomes attributed to existing rules. The mechanism of reframing has two parts: first, one must challenge the existing model by showing the newness of the phenomenon and, second, the phenomena must be fitted into a new frame, which solves the novel problem.

Recognition both of the technology's newness and of the applicable law rely on the same set of techniques for framing. A 'frame' is a cognitive structure designed to facilitate understanding. Reasoning through metaphor enables us to move from a familiar prototype to a new context. When a frame is successful, it allows individuals to use certain words and concepts to evoke other values or concepts: for example, certain ways of describing the internet may evoke a 'privacy' frame, or in others a 'liberty' frame. To refer to George Lakoff's famous study, prototypes and conceptual metaphors are decisive. The metaphor allows for a specific legal move: analogy to existing law. As Lakoff described: 'Abstract thought requires metaphor; almost all abstract thought is metaphorically based on concrete, sensory-motor concepts.'[8] Cognitive scientists over the last several

7 *Olmstead v United States* 277 US 438, 472 (1928) (Brandeis J dissenting, emphasis added).

8 George Lakoff, 'A cognitive scientist looks at *Daubert*' (2005) 95 *American Journal of Public Health* S114, S115.

decades have developed increasingly rich understandings of how 'mostly unconscious correlations in our experience could be the basis for primary conceptual metaphors, which are then combined into complex metaphors'.[9] These studies employ the 'influential approach [of interaction theory, which] has a number of distinguishing features . . . most notable for its assertion that our everyday concepts are structured and molded by a series of cognitive metaphors that all human beings share'.[10]

This is certainly a crucial element in the judicial process of translating something new into the language of past legal models. Judicial framing, as such, is nothing special. It presents the socially constructed shape of judicial reasoning. The new technology may generate decisional uncertainty, in which case framing is uncertain. The applicable constitutional rights and norms are often deliberately vague. So, too, the meaning and implications of a new technology may not be transparent to the judge. As Richard Posner observed: 'The application of a rule to facts is problematic when the facts are incurably uncertain.'[11]

Similarly, with regard to relevant values, one computer scientist-turned-lawyer observed:

> In technology law, the statutes and the technologies are brand new and filled with ambiguity . . . Statutes regulating these ambiguously-specified technologies are passed by technically inexperienced lawmakers, with technical guidance drawn from biased industry representatives, on the one side, and equally biased public interest groups, on the other . . . [Judges] apply the (still largely unlitigated) legal doctrine to the (brand new) facts of a case at hand. This increased judicial flexibility does not necessarily create room for framing . . . however, no one can [be] fully objective and neutral.[12]

In the case of emerging technology, not only is the meaning (and applicability) of a constitutional right uncertain, but even the argument of newness is contested. As Monroe Price so eloquently pointed out, the battle concerning framing starts, or may start, with a battle concerning the newness of technology.[13] If the technology is not so new, or if the consequences are not so new, there is little reason to change existing frames, although there may still be choice among existing frames. For example, even when the technology itself is not new, there may be diverse perspectives on its social consequences. If the technology is new in some important way, then judges may seek new metaphors and analogies to make sense of the change.

9 Mark L. Johnson, 'Mind, metaphor, law' (2007) 58 *Mercer Law Review* 845, 861.

10 Dan Hunter, 'Cyberspace as place and the tragedy of the digital anticommons' (2003) 91 *California Law Review* 439, 469.

11 Richard Posner, *How Judges Think* (Harvard University Press 2008) 176.

12 Chris Riley, 'The rite of rhetoric: cognitive framing in technology law' (2009) 9 *Nevada Law Journal* 495, 504.

13 Monroe E. Price, 'The newness of new technology' (2001) 22 *Cardozo Law Review* 1885, 1889.

The problem with metaphors, said Monroe Price, is that time may be necessary to transcend metaphor.[14] How to get rid of it once it is written into precedent? In the context of the internet legislation, legal academia and the courts mobilised a whole set of analogies based on powerful metaphors: Larry Lessig compared the internet to zoning,[15] whilst Justice O'Connor used the analogy of a land, inhabited by a number of institutions, some of which are purveyors of indecent material.[16] Australian legislation used the same regulatory tools for the internet as it did for broadcasting.[17] Others describe the internet with reference to printing or editing, or considered the providers as libraries and librarians, or similar to billboards. The internet was also considered to be included in existing telecommunications; after all, it is about communication, isn't it – but what kind of telecommunication?[18]

Or, perhaps, none of these metaphors and comparative frames applies; the new context is completely different and unique, and requires new rules. A chosen comparator that reflects relevant technological elements does not necessarily reflect the new technology's social repercussions. If one takes broadcasting as the model for internet regulation, broadcasting may be very different from the internet irrespective of its fundamental technological similarity, depending on the social construction of the technology.

Thus, there are problems with analogies. The real issue is often not the extent to which an allegedly new technology is similar to an existing one, such that the old law shall apply. The issue, at least from a fundamental rights perspective, is that in the search for an analogy only the technology is compared, or only the power of the metaphor is considered. But what is left out is the question of what kind of regulatory considerations emerge from the model that is chosen and whether these regulatory principles are applicable in the allegedly new context.

Courts may become captives of the technology narrative that they have chosen. A technology will then be considered good or bad based on facts attributed to that technology through the existing lens. That the internet increases independent personal information gathering was the factual assumption of a certain narrative. However, there can be an alternative narrative, namely that it makes people even more exposed to hoax and manipulation through orchestrated government propaganda or hidden private advertisement. In both narratives, the lines between technological facts and the related values are blurred.

It is possible to find facts for many (even contradictory) points when it comes to the regulation of a right. When, for example, the issue of least restrictive means arises, courts may make quick assumptions about the availability of the less restrictive technologies. Are those technologies really less restrictive? Are

14 ibid 1894.

15 Lawrence Lessig, 'Reading the constitution in cyberspace' (1996) 45 *Emory Law Journal* 869, 886.

16 *Reno v American Civil Liberties Union* 521 US 844, 886 (1997) (O'Connor J concurring).

17 Geraldine Chin, 'Technological change and the Australian constitution' (2000) 24 *Melbourne University Law Review* 609.

18 See Kevin Werbach, 'Off the hook' (2010) 95 *Cornell Law Review* 535, 541.

they available at a reasonable price? These are hard questions for an apex court. Is computerised filtering of comments less restrictive than notice and take-down? As Lessig rightly predicted in the context of cyberspace: '[C]ourts will, more and more, feel that they can't really say much about what cyberspace is. They will see that their finding affects what they find.'[19]

Moreover, framing may occur at the level of applicable values. Pre-existing values may be formulated at very different levels, as a matter of precedent, rule, standard, principle, fundamental constitutional right or social value. The new technology argument may challenge either the applicable constitutional theme (i.e. free speech is about entertainment, rather than advancement of learning) or confront the existing frame with an unforeseen fact or consequence (i.e. to show that a restriction is necessary).

This analysis is particularly relevant in the constitutional or human rights context, where the issue is argued in fundamental rights terms before a tribunal which understands that its legitimate role is to handle issues in these terms. In such cases, the problems are framed within the existing value system, so that a question of rights might be solved. If reframing occurs at this stage in the judicial process, then a different allocation of values can occur. However, the effect of changing technology is not unidirectional (i.e. the chosen constitutional norm shapes technological change). Pressure arising from the perceived (and often contested) consequences of technology may influence judicial understanding of legal, and even constitutional, values.

Advocates of new constitutional or human rights frames can use the 'new technology' argument to challenge existing frames. This strategy, however, is not without risk. It may be that the new technology argument is too powerful. Its unpredictable novelty is frightening for judges sitting in apex courts. Professional socialisation and peer pressure emphasise conformism in courts. Judges may be reluctant to embrace wholly new frames out of a fear that they might lose legitimacy. For judges, legitimacy is the substitute for physical enforcement power: it is legitimacy that makes the judgment binding, where beliefs replace the power of coercion. All of these elements encourage judges to display prudence, which reflects a reasonable fear. Lessig explained that this prudence 'will yield a relatively passive judiciary, and a relatively deferential attitude toward government intrusion. My sense is that, knowing nothing, or at least not very much, terrified by the threats of which they don't know, these judges will defer to democratic authority.'[20]

Judicial hesitance to prematurely define a new field can be seen in many contexts of emerging technology, such as reproductive technology. The European Court of Human Rights, in *S. H. v Austria*, declining to find a human rights violation, commented that:

19 Lessig, 'Reading the constitution in cyberspace' (n 15) 869, 905.
20 ibid 874.

> The field of artificial procreation is developing particularly fast both from a scientific point of view and in terms of the development of a legal framework for its medical application. It is for this reason that it is particularly difficult to establish a sound basis for assessing the necessity and appropriateness of legislative measures, the consequences of which might become apparent only after a considerable length of time . . . [T]he legislature [has] tried to reconcile the wish to make medically assisted procreation available and the existing unease among large sections of society as to the role and possibilities of modern reproductive medicine, which raises issues of a morally and ethically sensitive nature.[21]

The evident difficulty arises that even where a court, or legislature, refuses to take a position, simply allowing the technology to develop in the absence of clear regulation will also help shape its values, uses and power in the future. So there is a danger, or for others an advantage, in the 'new tech' argument: it encourages the judge to be even more deferential. However, where a social problem persists, if legislatures are slow or reluctant to intervene, the judge may be compelled to decide. In this stressful uncertainty, it will be left, amongst other actors, to judges and lawyers to experiment with metaphors and solutions amongst those existing or imagined. Nevertheless, legal imagination is notoriously weak. Judges find pleasure in declaring that they understand nothing of the world of science and technology as narrated by experts. It is for this very reason that judges will be interested more in the fairness of the legal frame, rather than in the details of a particular technology.

1.4 The early internet

We turn now to the judicial handling of modern technologies, understood as a problem of rights protection, using the internet as our example. When judges first confronted cases involving the internet, they needed to decide whether to create a new 'law of the internet' or import existing frameworks to analyse these novel cases. Not only did the new cases force judges (and legislatures) to create analogies to earlier media (newspapers, bookstores, libraries, broadcasting, etc.), but judges also had to consider the applicability of past constitutional and human rights concepts (privacy, freedom of expression, freedom of assembly, etc.). As Jack Balkin observed: 'Once we shift our focus from the moment of expression to the technological, economic, and social infrastructure that supports and enables expression, we can understand how crucial infrastructure is to the freedoms of speech and press.'[22] However, as the above examples indicate, it is not so much the technology itself but the social problems and social perceptions that pose a challenge to the legal system and to the judge.

21 *S. H. and Others v Austria* [GC] Application no. 57813/00, §§ 103–104 (ECtHR 2011).

22 Jack M. Balkin, 'Old-school/New-school speech regulation' (2014) 127 *Harvard Law Review* 2296, 2301–302.

The internet was opened to commercial interests in the early 1990s in part through amendments to the National Science Foundation's Acceptable Use Policy (which previously had restricted the internet to research and academic purposes).[23] At the same time, the United States Congress authorised distribution of domain names and 'commercial uses' on the web, but did not take a strong position about the applicable legal regime.[24] In other words, the internet was allowed to expand far beyond its previous bounds, although the way in which this new expansive internet would be regulated was left open. Hence the problem. Was pre-existing law applicable, or was the situation so new that it was not applicable?

At the time of the internet's creation, social problems were different from those of today, both in terms of technology and its accessibility. In the early days, for example, there were no images, only words. This is certainly relevant in the choice of the applicable metaphor or analogy. The internet was a very elite, academic matter, not accessible at all, certainly not to children, and hence the problem of pornography was different.

Other early assumptions were taken as accepted truth within the online community; it was believed that the internet was too big and too fast to control, and certainly too big for central government to control. An early popular metaphor for the internet was the Wild West, an unregulated, lawless place where opportunities arose for those brave and clever enough to take advantage of its expansive resources.[25] Indeed, it was a common sentiment that: 'freedom of expression has already received its utmost protection in this new medium [the internet], protection that stems not so much from good regulation as from its non-enforceability online'.[26] This shared understanding among the early, elite user group provided an importance source of information for judges and legislatures.

The dialogue between judges and legislatures developed while the technology and the social context changed rapidly. Legislative intervention arrived in different jurisdictions at different times, and with different frames. In each new round of cases, courts had to decide which metaphor to apply. The image of the unregulated early internet was not static. Over recent decades, courts and legislatures have responded to the social consequences of these early choices.

Today, of course, it seems that the internet is vulnerable to external manipulation, including corporate influence and social media. We do not know what the next round of technological developments (such as the 'Internet of Things') will bring.[27] The development is not only science and market-driven: regulators

23 See Bradford L. Smith, 'The third industrial revolution: policymaking for the internet' (2001) 3 *Columbia Science & Technology Law Review* 1, 25.

24 Developments: V 'The domain name system: a case study of the significance of norms to internet Governance' (1999) 112 *Harvard Law Review* 1657, 1662

25 Alfred C. Yen, 'Western frontier or feudal society? Metaphors and perceptions of cyberspace' (2002) 17 *Berkeley Technology Law Journal* 1207, 1225.

26 Dragos Cucereanu, *Aspects of Regulating Freedom of Expression on the Internet* (Intersentia 2008) 3.

27 See Scott R. Peppet, 'Regulating the internet of things: first steps toward managing discrimination, privacy, security, and consent' (2014) 93 *Texas Law Review* 85.

and existing social norms (see again social media) may set new paths for technological change and control over technology. We turn next to an examination of how these changing conceptions of the internet develop and what it means for constitutional or human rights.

1.5 Judicial analogies and metaphors in the internet age

As we have mentioned, when legislators and judges confront a new (or, at least, new to them) technology, including the internet, they seem to have a number of intellectual tools at their disposal. First, they may claim that there is nothing new in the technology and therefore existing law applies (although, as occurred with Article 1384 of the Code Civil, this might actually indicate a radical change in the law). This is, of course, easier where the concept to be applied is very abstract, as it was in the French case.

Arguably the same technique is used where one says that telecommunications law is reasonably applicable to the internet: 'communication' is a broad enough term. In the United States, for example, the Federal Communications Commission has used the open-ended distinctions between 'telecommunications' and 'information services' to classify aspects of the internet (with important repercussions for the scope of regulatory authority).[28]

A characteristic element of the position that there is nothing new for law in allegedly new technology is represented by Frank Easterbrook:

> I don't know much about cyberspace; what I do know will be outdated in five years (if not five months!); and my predictions about the direction of change are worthless, making any effort to tailor the law to the subject futile. And if I did know something about computer networks, all I could do in discussing 'Property in Cyberspace' would be to isolate the subject from the rest of the law of intellectual property, making the assessment weaker. This leads directly to my principal conclusion: develop a sound law of intellectual property, then apply it to computer networks.[29]

An early example of judicial resistance to new framing came in 1995 with the *Stratton Oakmont* case.[30] In this case, the court's reluctance to recognise newness led it to employ a direct analogy to books and newspapers. The New York court analogised message-board operators to publishers. Therefore, websites that displayed third-party articles and comments were open to the same libel liability as a newspaper or other publisher would be. The New York court was unwilling to

28 See Rob Frieden, 'What do pizza delivery and information services have in common? Lessons from recent judicial and regulatory struggles with convergence' (2006) 32 *Rutgers Computer & Technology Law Journal* 247, 252.

29 Frank H. Easterbrook, 'Cyberspace and the law of the horse' (1996) 11 *University of Chicago Legal Forum* 207, 207.

30 *Stratton Oakmont Inc v Prodigy Services Co.* No. 31063/94, 1995 WL 323710 (NY Sup Ct, 24 May 1995).

see cyberspace as fundamentally different from the physical spaces – bookstores, newspapers and libraries – for which the libel doctrine had been created.

The result in *Stratton Oakmont*, although legally correct, seemed to be socially unacceptable. In the subsequent federal law regulating internet communication, the Communications Decency Act (CDA), third-party providers were explicitly exempted from liability.[31] As such, the legislators, reflecting the desire to protect innovation and expression online, created a powerful safe haven against libel suits. In so doing, the proponents of third-party immunity employed a frame of free expression and technological development. In its findings, Congress noted that 'The Internet and other interactive computer services offer a forum for a true diversity of political discourse, unique opportunities for cultural development, and myriad avenues for intellectual activity . . .' and also emphasised that 'the Internet and other interactive computer services have flourished, to the benefit of all Americans, with a minimum of government regulation'.[32]

The Communications Decency Act goes on to state as one of its purposes: 'to preserve the vibrant and competitive free market that presently exists for the Internet and other interactive computer services, unfettered by Federal or State regulation'.[33] There was little mention at the time of the spectre of unregulated and anonymous commenters 'spreading filth and harassment without consequence' throughout cyberspace. Instead, those opposed to the unregulated internet focused on children.

The legislative intervention reframed certain elements of the conversation – which rights and interests were to be protected – but did not end the legislative–judicial dialogue. The Communications Decency Act also contained strict provisions regarding pornography, which were designed to protect children, but which also restricted adult access. These provisions arose from a frame of morality and were criticised by some as an attempt to turn the internet into Disneyland.[34] Opponents of these provisions, including the American Civil Liberties Union, claimed that the anti-pornography provisions violated the First Amendment.

In cases where fundamental rights are allegedly violated by legislative or judicial interpretation of the law applicable to the new technology, there might be strong pressure to intervene judicially. In the 1997 case of *Reno v ACLU*, the United States Supreme Court intervened to strike down the strict anti-pornography provisions of the CDA. The Court held that:

> The breadth of this content-based restriction of speech imposes an especially heavy burden on the Government to explain why a less restrictive provision would not be as effective as the CDA. It has not done so. The arguments in this Court have referred to possible alternatives such as requiring that

31 *Protection for Private Blocking and Screening of Offensive Material* 47 USC § 230.

32 ibid.

33 ibid.

34 Robert Cannon, 'The legislative history of Senator Exon's Communications Decency Act: regulating barbarians on the information superhighway' (1996) 49 *Federal Communications Law Journal* 51, 80–81.

> indecent material be 'tagged' in a way that facilitates parental control of material coming into their homes, making exceptions for messages with artistic or educational value, providing some tolerance for parental choice, and regulating some portions of the Internet—such as commercial Web sites—differently from others, such as chat rooms. Particularly in the light of the absence of any detailed findings by the Congress, or even hearings addressing the special problems of the CDA, we are persuaded that the CDA is not narrowly tailored if that requirement has any meaning at all.[35]

This holding is important for two reasons – first, because it shows the Court's reliance on the pre-existing free-speech framework and, secondly, because the Court relies on claims about the nature of technology (and which less restrictive means were possible) to make conclusions about rights.

In his early writing on the subject, Larry Lessig was reluctant to allow judges to say what cyberspace shall be.[36] This reluctance was reflected in Justice Stevens's majority opinion in *Reno v ACLU*, in which he declined to extend the full jurisprudence of the broadcast industry to internet regulation. Instead, he explained that:

> [The Supreme Court] observed that '[e]ach medium of expression . . . may present its own problems.' Thus, some of our cases have recognised special justifications for regulation of the broadcast media that are not applicable to other speakers, [due to early government regulation and scarcity] . . . Those factors are not present in cyberspace. Neither before nor after the enactment of the CDA have the vast democratic forums of the Internet been subject to the type of government supervision and regulation that has attended the broadcast industry.[37]

1.6 Challenging the internet's legal frame

Whilst early judicial and legislative analogies may have captured important elements of the emerging internet, today these old frames pose significant problems. First scholars, and now even judges, have begun raising questions about the social and security context in which the internet currently operates and, most importantly, the individual rights involved. The argument follows a common logic: first, that the internet has a social power more threatening and potent than its technological predecessors; secondly, the existing legal frames are inadequate to address these threats; third, the values underlying the current legal frames do not reflect the needs of modern society.

The old values have not disappeared by any means, although some aspects of free speech have been reimagined for the digital age. Jack Balkin, for example, has

35 *Reno v American Civil Liberties Union* 521 US 844, 879 (1997).

36 Lessig, 'Reading the constitution in cyberspace' (n 15) 869.

37 *Reno v American Civil Liberties Union* (n 35) 868–69.

emphasised that '[d]igital technologies highlight the cultural and participatory features of freedom of expression'[38] and that, 'A widely noted and characteristic feature of the digital age is the democratization of information production, and therefore the democratization of opportunities to speak and express one's self'.[39] Anupam Chander defends the internet by arguing that:

> Whatever one's theory of speech, the Internet helped realize speech in ways never before possible. Consider three classic free speech theories: democratic self-governance, marketplace of ideas, and human dignity and self-fulfillment. The theory of 'democratic self-governance' stresses the role of free speech in actualizing society's participation in governance. The Internet not only reduces barriers to participation, it increases the pace of activism and discourse—petitions and protests can be offered with a few keystrokes. Instead of political participation, the 'marketplace of ideas' theory focuses on free speech as a critical vehicle for truth-seeking by ensuring an open forum where ideas compete against each other, furthering human enlightenment.[40]

However, this sort of free-speech optimism is under threat from those who see the dark side of internet freedom.

Brian Leiter uses the term 'cyber-cesspools' to describe parts of the internet that are 'devoted in whole or in part to demeaning, harassing, and humiliating individuals'.[41] Scholars who grapple with freedom of expression and offensive speech on the internet tend to focus on three types of online expression: general racist/sexists/xenophobic/anti-Semitic statements directed at a group of people; attacks targeted at a specific individual (defamatory statements, death threats, threats of sexual violence, etc.); and publication of private information, images or videos (publication of home address, private health information, 'revenge porn', nude photographs, etc.).

General 'hate speech' includes rants, threats and (possibly) even political positions that attack a particular group. Attacks on targeted individuals can be, and often are, also related to gender, race, sexual orientation, religion and so on, although in these cases a particular target has been singled out. Publication of private information, although often treated alongside the aforementioned types of offensive internet speech, presents a rather different situation.

In privacy cases, the information revealed might be true (i.e. not defamatory) and the target of the information might have given the image or information to the poster freely (albeit in a much more intimate context). European commentators in particular tend to emphasise reputational harms or harms to personal

38 Jack M. Balkin, 'Digital speech and democratic culture: a theory of freedom of expression for the information society' (2004) 79 *New York University Law Review* 1, 3.

39 Jack M. Balkin, 'Old-school/New-school speech regulation' (n 22) 2296,2304.

40 Anupam Chander and Uyên P. Lê, 'Free speech' (2015) 100 *Iowa Law Review* 501, 509–10.

41 Brian Leiter, 'Cleaning cyber cesspools: Google and free speech' in Saul Levmore and Martha Nussbaum (eds), *The Offensive Internet* (Harvard University Press 2010) 155.

honour. This focus can certainly be seen in the recent 'right to be forgotten' decision of the Court of Justice of the European Union.[42]

Although a strong voice in American scholarship and popular culture still demands unfettered freedom of speech online, scholars are increasingly taking up a more pro-regulation view. These scholars are the canaries in the mine, seeking out new frames and metaphors. Scholars draw upon feminist theory, hate speech literature, theories of language, social psychology and other legal fields to support various methods for eradicating offensive speech online. Using these disciplines, legal academics are able to reframe the rights at stake in cases involving expression and the internet by rearranging value hierarchies.

Within this frame, scholars argue that the harms associated with internet hate speech and harassment warrant further intervention, even if it means 'chilling' speech. In some ways, this frame is not new, to the extent that it fits within J. S. Mill's 'harm' principle in free speech. Mill argued that: 'The only purpose for which power can be rightfully exercised over any member of a civilized community, against his will, is to prevent harm to others. His own good, either physical or moral, is not a sufficient warrant.'[43] State power may be used to limit individual liberty insofar as such coercion prevents a greater harm than the harm caused by infringing on individual liberty. Therefore, one may argue that the harms caused by attacks in cyberspace justify coercive measures.

Employing the harm principle, some scholars (pushing against the 'newness' of their proposed values) argue that the 'unregulated internet' is already a myth because there are intellectual property, child protection, anti-obscenity and criminal laws that limit speech online.[44] Harm is already a consideration within our legal framework for cyberspace. Therefore, if the law fails to protect targets of hate speech and other offensive speech online, this stems from a failure to recognise the real harms associated with this speech and not with an underlying desire to protect freedom of expression. Put differently, the dominant rights frame simply does not adequately address the harms unique to life online.

According to this perspective, the harms associated with internet speech depend on the nature of the speech in question (targeted at an individual or a group, incitement to violence, revealing private information, etc.). Primarily, scholarship emphasises the harm to victims as psychological distress, loss of physical security, loss of economic and social opportunities and loss of privacy. There are also important harms to the larger community, as this kind of speech spreads false information, encourages extremism and endorses or justifies discrimination and violence.

Of course, all of these effects existed without cyberspace, but the framing exercise once again emphasises the qualitatively and quantitatively different aspects of

42 Case C–131/12 *Google Spain SL, Google Inc v Agencia Española de Protección de Datos (AEPD), Mario Costeja González* Judgment of 13 May 2014 (not yet reported).

43 J. S. Mill, *On Liberty* (first published 1869, Bartleby 1999) 18.

44 See generally Saul Levmore and Martha Nussbaum (eds), *The Offensive Internet* (Harvard University Press 2010).

cyberspace. Anonymity, amplification, permanence and virtual captivity (limited options for exiting situations where harassment occurs) explain why 'the effects of unwilling online embodiment are potentially even more pernicious and long-lasting than real-life harassment'.[45] Proponents of this framework argue for new values to address harms that arise from the newness of the technology.

One key element of this reframing is shifting the focus from the speaker to the addressee. The harms of online speech are more apparent when there is a specific target, although a specific target is not a necessary element of this audience-focused frame. As Martha Nussbaum describes the victim of online attacks: 'not knowing where the abuse is coming from or how to stop it, but affected by it pervasively in her daily activities, she loses agency and employment opportunities'.[46] Scholars cite examples in which people have lost jobs (or job opportunities), have shut down profitable websites and have suffered severe psychological and emotional distress. A commonly cited example is that of Autoadmit.com, where dozens of anonymous posters wrote violent, sexual and defamatory comments about two female students at Yale Law School.[47] Today, stories describing the harms and horrors of internet abuse are commonplace. Pew Research published a survey in November 2014 showing that very large numbers of American internet users claim to have been victim of some form of internet harassment.[48]

Therefore, critics of the current system of online regulation (or lack thereof) push against earlier frames (such as absolute free speech) by showing the social consequences of that framing:

> [H]arms committed in cyberspace are often dismissed as 'not really real,' as they are by their nature not physical, bodily harms. The way this tension plays out in terms of the law's recommended role in cyberspace can yield schizophrenic results: freedom of speech, for example, in cyberspace is 'really real' and must be vigorously protected; harassment in cyberspace is not 'really real' and thus should not be taken very seriously.[49]

However, does internet speech cause harm beyond the individual target of an attack? There, scholars discuss the power of speech – to spread false information, incite group hatred and create a culture in which violence against women and minorities is acceptable and encouraged. In this context, harm may be defined

45 Mary Anne Franks, 'Unwilling avatars: idealism and discrimination in cyberspace' (2011) 20 *Columbia Journal of Gender & Law* 224, 255–56.

46 Martha Nussbaum, 'Objectification and internet misogyny' in Saul Levmore and Martha Nussbaum (eds), *The Offensive Internet* (Harvard University Press 2010) 72.

47 See for example ibid 73. The fact that this case is so frequently cited may suggest that this type of harm is less common than these scholars would like us to believe. A more plausible explanation, however, is that the two women in the *Autoadmit* case filed a lawsuit against the website, which provides researchers with considerable documentation regarding the circumstances of the case – something that is rarely available.

48 Maeve Duggan, 'Online harassment' Pew Research Internet Project (22 October 2014) http://www.pewinternet.org/2014/10/22/online-harassment/ (last accessed 5 August 2015).

49 Mary Anne Franks, 'Unwilling avatars: idealism and discrimination in cyberspace' (n 45) 256.

broadly as 'a series of acts none of which is individually harmful, and it can injure the interests of a group, rather than any identifiable individual'.[50] Speech causes harm by persuading hearers, shaping desires, conditioning hearers, inspiring imitation, constituting subordination and silencing.[51] This perspective ascribes great power to speech, not only as a way of transmitting ideas or information, but as (in itself) an act of power, violence or discrimination.

Apart from emphasising the harms of internet expression, another element of reframing has been to minimise the importance of existing values. Therefore, when balancing speech and other rights, some claim that offensive internet expression is 'low value' speech, which either does not fall under the category of protected speech at all or should not be granted much weight when contrasted with other rights.

Leiter argues that 'cyber cesspools' should, in some cases, be treated like threats, fighting words, obscenity and other unprotected speech. He acknowledges that such treatment will cause increased censorship, which may reduce some valuable speech, but concludes that given the permanence and virulent nature of online 'cyber-cesspools', the law should strike a new balance between free expression and the rights of others.[52]

Cass Sunstein contends that law-makers need to find the optimal level of 'chilling' that encourages truth, rather than convergence on false information, especially given the power of the internet to spread and entrench false rumours.[53] He, along with many others, argues that the truth-producing function of free speech fails online because people are more likely to move towards false (but belief-confirming) information than towards the truth. As he puts it, 'corroboration breeds confidence and confidence breeds extremism'.[54]

For the paternalist regulators there is no reason to frame internet regulation within the presumptions of freedom of expression: that claim makes no sense to them anymore. It has no primacy; there is nothing special about speech. For a while, people more or less accepted wholesale the package of liberal democracy, which includes the not so popular protection of other people's free speech. However, there is increasing unease; the erosion of free speech's value in our society is reaching the tipping point. To use an increasingly more powerful climate change image: the ocean sometimes carries away the beach in grand chunks during a storm, but more often, it is not even perceived.

The same is true for speech rights. The erosion of free speech is dangerous, even for political speech strictly understood, simply because the political, the public and the private are interrelated. A general regulatory power could

50 Ishanti Maitra and Mary Kate McGowan, 'Introduction and overview' in Ishanti Maitra and Mary Kate McGowan (eds), *Speech and Harm: Controversies Over Free Speech* (Oxford University Press 2012) 4.

51 ibid 4–6.

52 Brian Leiter, 'Cleaning cyber cesspools: Google and free speech' (n 41) 155.

53 Cass Sunstein, 'Believing false rumors' in Saul Levmore and Martha Nussbaum (eds), *The Offensive Internet* (Harvard University Press 2010) 91–92.

54 ibid 100.

influence all opinion formation online, as political opinions are formed in private encounters.

1.7 New frames and new values

The new challenges presented by internet filth may force even the unwilling legislator and the judge to reconsider the axiom that speech is a fundamental individual right. The rethinking (and reframing) occurs in a world of heightened sensitivity. The sensitivity, and its relationship with new technology, generates a new frame in which censorship is not only permitted, but also required.

On the one hand, there is nothing new in the uninhibited speech that is so common online. This is the language used in pubs. Pub speech is vulgar and sexually explicit. It has little communicative value; it serves truth only to a limited extent. However, these elements per se do not make it subject to legal intervention in a world based on the assumption that liberty is *the* default. Of course, pub speech uses extremes: personal dislike is often expressed in terms including 'asshole' and 'vermin'. In the social convention (at least the one that exists at the pub level) this is not understood as a factual statement; nor is it a racist offence, except specific circumstances when these amount to fighting words.

One can hear also (if still sober enough) dissatisfaction expressed as 'he'd better drop dead' or 'I'd kill him'. This is seldom understood in that environment as incitement to violence. Some risk-averse people and judges take these utterances seriously, but one does not need to read John Searle to understand the difference between literal sentence meaning and the speaker's meaning.[55] Of course, if there is a known madman among the patrons of the bar who might kill the person who had been described as worthy of death, then the speaker may be held accountable.

On the other hand, the internet situation is slightly different. Anonymity in the internet pub is widespread and the feelings of lack of accountability and interpersonal social control allegedly increase aggression or its display. It is often argued that the absence of personal feedback, together with the lack of empathy caused by deindividuation online, diminishes the social regulatory function of social interactions:

> Dehumanization references the distancing that occurs online as the victim becomes a non-human, while deindividuation explains the tendency to loose one's sense of individual identity when involved in group activities. Coupled, these theories help explain the normative occurrence of aggression online; dehumanization allows the bully to harass without empathy, while deindividuation allows the bully to justify his or her actions through identification with group norms and a propensity towards the extreme.[56]

55 John R. Searle, 'Literal meaning' (1978) 13 *Erkenntnis* 207–24.

56 Stacy M. Chaffin, 'The new playground bullies of cyberspace: online peer sexual harassment' (2008) 51 *Howard Law Journal* 773, 794.

Similarly, Danielle Keats Citron argues that: 'Web 2.0 platforms create a feeling of closeness among like-minded individuals. Online groups affirm each other's negative views, which become more extreme and destructive. Individuals say and do things online they would never consider saying or doing offline because they feel anonymous, even if they write under their real names.'[57]

The US Supreme Court has recently confronted these very issues in the case of *United States v Elonis*, in which the Court was asked to decide what constitutes a threat on social media.[58] The *Elonis* petition for certiorari argues: 'the inherently impersonal nature of online communication makes [it] inherently susceptible to misinterpretation . . . modern media allow personal reflections intended for a small audience (or no audience) to be viewed widely by people who are unfamiliar with the context in which the statements were made and thus who may interpret the statements much differently than the speaker intended'.[59] The well informed *Forbes Magazine* wrote in May of 2014 that 'Elonis's case may be a harbinger of things to come'.[60]

Where a message is accessible to a theoretically large audience, there may well be a couple of unknown madmen in the audience. Is the author of the insulting post liable for creating a risk that the madman will act? To return to an earlier frame, is a car manufacturer liable under product liability if the car causes an accident because of a hole in the road? At first thought the answer might be 'no'; but what if the roads in the country are notoriously dangerous and the manufacturer fails to produce specific brakes or other safety devices? In any event, surely it is the legislator who must find the best allocation of responsibility based on the most efficient method of harm reduction?

Compare this situation with the internet highway and forget for a moment our traditional veneration of free speech. If there are too many madmen waiting for encouragement (especially those with the address of a target available for them), then regulatory intervention might seem prudent. These are the logical steps proposed in scholarship that advocates restrictions of online speech. Their chosen frame is one that emphasises harm – and shifting the costs on online life from the audience to the speaker.

So why is there an emerging socio-cultural willingness to select and aggrandise instances of internet harassment? One element certainly seems to be the increased sensitivity of the contemporary citizen. By sensitivity we mean an increased consideration for the impact of the speech on the audience, where consideration and weight is given to the personal feelings generated by the speech. Of course the sensitivity is not always personal, nor is the perceived attack. The interest of power holders to live above criticism, as well as *jihad* hysteria, are additional ingredients of this potentially lethal cocktail.

57 Danielle Keats Citron, 'Cyber civil rights' (2009) 89 *Boston University Law Review* 61, 83.

58 *Elonis v United States* 134 S Ct 2819 (2014) (petition for writ of certiorari granted).

59 *Elonis v United States*, Petition for a writ of certiorari (filed 14 February 2014) 34.

60 Clay Calvert, Erik Nielsen and Charis E. Kubrin, 'Rap lyrics or true threats? It's time for the High Court to decide' *Forbes* (24 May 2014) http://www.forbes.com/sites/realspin/2014/05/24/rap-lyrics-or-true-threats-its-time-for-the-high-court-to-decide (last accessed 5 August 2015).

Respect for public sensitivity is noticeable in the freedom of expression jurisprudence of the European Court of Human Rights (ECtHR). In *Otto-Preminger v Austria* the Court justified censorship of a controversial film by stating that: 'respect for the religious feelings of believers as guaranteed in Article 9 can legitimately be thought to have been violated by provocative portrayals of objects of religious veneration; and such portrayals can be regarded as malicious violation of the spirit of tolerance, which must also be a feature of democratic society'.[61]

With a heightened sense of sensitivity, one is tempted to accept that the need for democratic deliberation does not justify free-speech protection any longer. People challenge the value, or even the possibility, of informed discourse.[62] It is argued that humans are not autonomous, rational agents capable of the sort of self-expression necessary to create a republic of reasonable citizens. At least, humans online do not display this reasonable self-expression, but instead act as aggressive and narcissistic children. Mill himself has admitted that his theory of free speech applies only to adults. Once the spell is broken and the sacredness of free speech has been destroyed, there is no reason to limit speech restrictions to concrete harms. Nothing remains that would justify the preferential treatment of the speaker; what is needed is a better regulator who will not abuse government and other powers in the protection of the audience. This providential regulator will channel discourse in a way that prevents distortions of rational communication and deliberation.

The cult of sensitivity values the protection of perceived vulnerability over alternative rights and freedoms; security (in the sense of not being disturbed) is the prevailing right. This provides a new frame in which the *bien-pensant* proposes that we view questions of expression and of internet censorship. In an attempt to ensure that no one is offended by attacks on their beliefs or identity, governments are expected to censor speech. Indeed, 'the restrictive interpretation of freedom of speech puts respect for sensitivities . . . into the foreground. . . . The affected person determines what the sensitivity is, since in the end only he or she can feel it.'[63]

Sensitivity discourse prevails in matters concerning religion. As in the *Otto-Preminger* case, arguments that disrespectful speech constitutes a restriction on the free practice of religion have become increasingly common. The same fears, however, facilitate restrictions based on offence in all aspects of identity. The risk that governments will overstep the prevention of real harm is heightened in the online environment, where the capacity for offensive speech is vast, the link between speech and harm is less clear, and regulation must apply *en masse*.

61 *Otto-Preminger-Institut v Austria* (20 September 1994) § 47, Series A no. 295-A, Application no. 13470/87 (1994) 19 EHRR 34, [1994] ECHR 26.

62 See Cass Sunstein, 'Believing false rumors' (n 53), citing social psychology studies demonstrating group and individual behaviour that tends towards extremism, affirming false beliefs, spreading false rumours, etc.

63 András Sajó, 'Countervailing duties as applied to Danish cheese and Danish cartoons' in András Sajó (ed.), *Issues in Constitutional Law: Censorial Sensitivities, Free Speech and Religion in a Fundamentalist World* (Eleven International Publishing 2007) 297.

Whilst advocates for speech regulations online emphasise cases where people have been gravely harmed, they use the fear of such cases to push for much broader censorship. This censorship does not only protect against violence, identity theft, etc, but against 'dignitary' harms or broad, diffuse harms associated with reading comments online that offend one's identity.

1.8 The case for a free-speech frame

In the risk-averse, audience-protecting calculation one should not forget the impact of the restrictive measure chosen. Consider, for example, the Indian Supreme Court advisory issued in 2013 regarding the prosecution of activists for their allegedly defamatory Facebook posts. There, the Court held that only high-level police officials could authorise such prosecutions – thereby acknowledging the broad discretion (and potential for abuse) in a statute that allows law enforcement to decide what constitutes harmful or offensive online communication.[64]

In principle, it looks easy to single out bad guys on the basis of their messages. However, singling out bad views runs into all the objections the free speech doctrine on content discrimination has developed (fallibility, governmental power bias, prejudice stemming from unpopularity). When there is no clear link between speech and harm, there is an inherent risk that content-based regulation, as opposed to regulation based on the actual consequences of speech, will suppress unpopular ideas. Public debate will be manipulated by coercion rather than persuasion.[65]

As Justice Holmes famously observed nearly a century ago: 'as against dangers peculiar to war, as against others, the principle of the right to free-speech is always the same. It is only the present danger of immediate evil or an intent to bring it about that warrants Congress in setting a limit to the expression of opinion where private rights are not concerned. Congress certainly cannot forbid all effort to change the mind of the country.'[66] And of course, content regulation is self-destructive: if you single out one opinion there is nothing to stop others from singling out your right-minded views once you are in the minority.

The consequentialist paradigm shift grounds its perception of harm in problems which are, of course, genuine. What it fails to recognise is that the current high level of protection granted to speech is based on a deliberate social design of ordered liberty. The strong protection of speech stems from the assumption that a tolerant, democratic system cannot exist without free communication. Given the importance of generating ideas and maintaining social communication, speech needs over-protection. If it were treated like other products with externalities, the resulting litigation costs, the possibility of sanctions and so on would

64 A. Vaidyanathan, 'No arrests for Facebook posts without senior cops' permission: Supreme Court' *NDTV* (New Delhi, 16 May 2013) http://www.ndtv.com/article/india/no-arrests-for-facebook-posts-without-senior-cops-permission-supreme-court-367554 (last accessed 5 August 2015).

65 *Turner Broadcast v Federal Communications Commission* 114 S Ct 2445, 2458 (1994).

66 *Abrams v United States* 250 US 616, 628 (1919).

be prohibitive to generate ideas.[67] In that case, the positive externalities flowing from the unrewarded or poorly rewarded generation of ideas would be lost. This is, amongst others, the reason why the right of freedom of expression sides with the speaker and not the audience. In sensitivity-protection, however, priority is given to the feelings of the audience.

There is a strong consequentialist reason for over-protection, which is related to an ultimate social value choice, namely that people would like to live an autonomous life in freedom. It was once assumed that a strong individual free-speech right provides for the best available exchange of ideas and views. Efforts to reframe this right notwithstanding, this assumption remains relevant – even online.

Trusting the state with benevolent censorship in matters of dissent is, irrespective of the actual trust in a society towards the state, a risky matter. The underlying assumption is that we need to trust governmental protective regulation because of the ease with which the human mind can be influenced. The new paternalism, interpreting cognitive science and social psychology data, argues that there is no freedom of choice (will), only easily manipulated people. The advocates of new censorship perceive people through Hobbesian lenses: they are fundamentally brutish. If the problem is hard-wired human fallibility and aggressiveness, how one can hope that in the democratic process the interaction of fallible humans will produce unbiased censors?

The well-meaning internet censors are concerned with alarming phenomena, but fight against a straw man. Contrary to some assumptions, speech is not merely protected because it is an act of the individual's freedom (or even free will) and therefore is, in reality, not a higher right, especially in the absence of overall beneficial consequences. Nor is freedom of expression protected simply because people feel better if they can express themselves – and the more they can speak without constraints, the better they feel. There are better reasons for speech protection than the psychological satisfaction resulting from communicative exhibitionism. If free speech were intended to protect expressive feelings, then the more intense feelings of the offended should prevail. But again, freedom of expression is protected as a social institution. It is protected because of its institutional contribution to a liberal and tolerant social order. One should see the forest of freedom, even where the view is obscured by the trees of insult.

1.9 Conclusion

Early visions of free speech online have given way to increasing acknowledgement that it is no longer a question of whether the internet will be censored, but rather which priorities, interests and values will drive regulation of internet speech. In recent years 'the Internet has increasingly become a tool of censorship, as scores of countries around the world have imposed nationwide filtering regimes to block their citizens' access to various types of Internet speech that they deem

67 Richard A. Posner, 'Free speech in an economic perspective' (1986) 20 *Suffolk University Law Review* 1, 20.

harmful. Instead of trending toward greater freedom, the Internet is now trending toward greater censorship and control . . .'[68] This is true in democracies as well as authoritarian governments. One American innovation scholar observed:

> [W]orried that the early enthusiasm for . . . new technology would be replaced by popular revulsion in the face of its unintended consequences . . . The legal moves . . . in the United States have helped facilitate the 'wow' of the World Wide Web, but they might also usher in the 'yuck.' We need to ensure that in our zeal for promoting Internet enterprise, we do not haphazardly create the conditions for a dystopia.[69]

The social harms associated with online speech have driven many people to react with fear and disgust; challenging the frame which placed online communication into the sphere of strongly protected free speech.

Once free speech is relegated to one interest amongst many, the extraordinary capacity of the online communication sets the stage for more restrictive audience-sensitive frames. As Judge Vajić observed: 'The cardinal role played by the internet in enhancing freedom of speech in a democratic society is counterbalanced by the magnified repercussions of harmful speech especially on privacy and reputations rights in cases of abuse.'[70] Once the magnified perception of harm controls the framework within which the internet is regulated, the past rights models will no longer provide adequate guidance for judges.

There seems to be tremendous pressure on internet freedom: any shift here will have wide-ranging implications on free speech in general and not only because the internet emerges as the most important forum. The right to free speech is subject to erosion in part because of how little people seem to care about the speech rights of others. The malleability of rights-expectations is partly driven by the way in which rights are framed by courts. Courts will be increasingly confronted with difficult questions about how to reconcile their past doctrine with this new reality, but the solutions have not yet been fully articulated. Apex courts around the world – including the European Court of Human Rights – will determine when to embrace a new frame, and when to keep old values and old metaphors alive.

The crucial considerations extend beyond the nature of new technology. Courts must incorporate not only technological change, but also its social and economic context, into their decisions. What are the implications of a new legal frame? Which fundamental rights and values will take precedence? What past understandings of law will serve as precedents? The way that courts approach these complex questions will, to a large extent, shape, and be shaped by, online expression.

68 Dawn C. Nunziato, 'The beginning of the end of internet freedom' (2014) 45 *Georgetown Journal of International Law* 383, 384.

69 Anupam Chander, 'How law made Silicon Valley' (2014) 63 *Emory Law Journal* 639, 689.

70 Nina Vajić, 'The internet and freedom of expression' in Josep Casadevall, Egbert Myjer, Michael O'Boyle and Anna Austin (eds), *Freedom of Expression: Essays in Honour of Nicolas Bratza* (Wolf Legal Publishers 2012) 394.

2 The boundaries of jurisdiction in cybercrime and constitutional protection

The European perspective

Catherine Van de Heyning

2.1 Introduction

In June 2015 the Belgian Privacy Commission, supported by the responsible secretary of state, made worldwide headlines by taking Facebook to court for infringements of Belgian and EU privacy legislation.[1] After several requests to Facebook to alter its tracking system and the use of the data gathered from internet users, the privacy commission responded with proceedings.[2] The decision was applauded by many human rights and consumer organisations, who had warned for many years that data collection, retention and use by telecommunication giants is a serious and increasing threat to the right to privacy on the internet. The *Guardian* commentator Nathalie Haynes stated enthusiastically:

> There's something refreshing about a country that worries about its citizens' privacy, instead of muttering about having nothing to fear if you have nothing to hide, as our government tends to.[3]

Facebook dismissed this move as 'theatrical' and argued that the Belgian authorities lacked jurisdiction to sue a US-based firm with its European headquarters in Ireland.[4] The company held that only the Irish Privacy Commission could

1 Reuters, 'Belgian privacy watchdog takes Facebook to court' (15 June 2015); X, 'Belgium takes Facebook to court over privacy breaches and user tracking' *Guardian* (15 June 2014); S. Schechner and N. Drozdiak, 'Belgium takes Facebook to court over privacy, user tracking' *The Wall Street Journal* (16 June 2015). The Privacy Commission's claim focuses on the tracking by Facebook tracks of internet users (including non-Facebook users) on external websites through the use of 'like' and 'share' buttons. Facebook collects these data for commercial use, e.g. advertising. The procedure is ongoing at the moment of writing and a decision is expected in the fall of 2015. See http://www.privacycommission.be/en (last accessed 31 August 2015).

2 For the document with recommendations to Facebook see Privacy Commission, Recommendation no. 04/2015 of 13 May 2015, 'Own initiative recommendation relating to 1) Facebook, 2) internet and/or Facebook users as well as 3) users and providers of Facebook services, particularly plug-ins' (C0-AR-2015-003) www.privacycommission.be (last accessed 7 August 2015).

3 N. Haynes, 'Hooray for Belgium, fronting up to Facebook' *Guardian* (15 June 2015).

4 'Belgian privacy watchdog takes Facebook to court' *Reuters* (15 June 2015).

undertake such a step.[5] It is to be expected that Facebook will claim that Belgian law does not apply to the firm and the court lacks jurisdiction, given that the data are not processed in Belgium but instead at its European headquarters in Ireland.

In the light of a precedent in France, the objection of Facebook might not hold in court. In March 2015 the French Tribunal de Grande Instance (TGI) of Paris accepted that it had jurisdiction to consider a claim of a French citizen against Facebook.[6] In this case, Facebook also challenged the jurisdiction of the court.[7] The court referred to a provision in French civil law that marks the place of execution of the contract as the default place of jurisdiction for disputes. The TGI held that the contract had been executed in France, given that the general conditions had been accepted on French territory by the claimant.

At the same time, the European Parliament is set to discuss new legislative initiatives in order to improve privacy on the internet and act against the disproportionate collection, retention and use of personal data.[8] After several years during which the protection of privacy on the internet was limited for reasons of international security, cybercrime and economic efficiency, the EU appears to have rediscovered the importance of privacy and data protection. Much cited in that respect is the ECJ's judgment of 2014 on the Data Retention Directive.[9] The Court found the directive to violate EU law, holding that the obligation for internet service providers (ISPs) to collect and retain data constituted a disproportionate infringement of the right to privacy.[10]

5 In the communication between Facebook and the Belgian Privacy Commission that resulted in the Recommendation by the Privacy Commission, Facebook had already claimed that the Commission lacked jurisdiction. See Privacy Commission, Recommendation no. 04/2015 of 13 May 2015 (n 2) paras 11, 13 and 17.

6 Tribunal de Grande Instance de Paris (5 March 2015) www.legalis.net (last accessed 7 August 2015). The French claimant acted against the removal of a suggestive painting by Courbet posted on this wall.

7 In this case, Facebook argued that only American law applied, given that the general conditions of Facebook provide that the courts of California are the competent courts for any civil litigation. In Germany, a claim by users against Facebook before the High Court of Berlin concerning the retention and use of data was also successful: Kammergericht Berlin (24 January 2014) Decision no. 5U42/12 https://www.berlin.de/sen/justiz/gerichte/kg/presse/archiv/2014 0214.1835.394435.html (last accessed 31 August 2015).

8 European Parliament, 'Data protection: parliament's negotiators welcome Council negotiating brief' Press release (15 June 2015) www.europarl.europa.eu (last accessed 7 August 2015).

9 See e.g. the much-cited Safe Harbour Framework between the EU and the US in consequence of which several US companies are considered to comply with the EU Directive on the protection of personal data. See Commission Decision of 26 July 2000 pursuant to Directive 95/46/EC of the European Parliament and of the Council on the adequacy of the protection provided by the safe harbour privacy principles and related frequently asked questions issued by the US Department of Commerce (notified under document number COM(2000) 2441) [2000] OJ L215. The CJEU is yet to decide on the compatibility with EU law at the time of writing (Case C–362/12 *Schrems v Data Protection Commissioner*, pending). The decision was scheduled for 24 June 2015, but has been postponed to a later date.

10 Joined Cases C–293/12 and 594/12 *Digital Rights Ireland Ltd and Seitlinger and Others* [2014] ECR I–0000 (not yet reported); O. Lynskey, 'The Data Retention Directive is incompatible with the rights to privacy and data protection and is invalid in its entirety' (2014) 51 *Common Market*

Several constitutional courts have likewise annulled the domestic legislation implementing the Directive on human rights and constitutional law basis.[11] From the outset, it appears that authorities have taken the decreasing privacy on the internet to heart and decided to act against commercial entities with very strong market positions or quasi-monopolies in cyberspace, at least in Europe.

However, public authorities can easily be reproached for maintaining double standards. On the one hand, they claim that ISPs abuse their economic position and technological expertise for commercial ends to the detriment of privacy rights; on the other hand, judicial authorities regularly force ISPs to cooperate in criminal investigations by transferring traffic and content data. Several ISPs were prosecuted by judicial authorities for refusing to cooperate. These ISPs referred to the protection of privacy and data of their users. ISPs dismiss these claims by holding that the prosecuting state lacks jurisdiction to order the delivery of such data and to prosecute them in case of non-compliance. ISPs operate on a global scale. It can even be questioned whether their virtual platform in cyberspace can even be understood in geographical terms. Their physical territorial presence is mostly limited to a few countries, namely those countries where they have established their headquarters or servers.[12]

Criminals use these ISPs when committing cybercrime, hoping to escape prosecution owing to the difficulties of localising these crimes. They can operate in anonymity behind URL addresses or email accounts in virtual space. As such, in order effectively to combat cybercrime, courts need to settle how traditionally held notions on territorial jurisdiction of a state translate to cyberspace.

Defining jurisdiction in cyberspace is not only of importance for the investigation and prosecution of cybercrime, but also for the protection of constitutional and regional human rights of those persons prosecuted. In principle, constitutional law reaches only as far as the boundaries of the state. Owing to new technologies, judicial authorities can reach into a computer in another state without physically entering that state. In such cases, should judicial authorities still respect procedural rights that apply to searches and seizures on the domestic territory?

This chapter focuses on localising cybercrime and the impact on fundamental rights protection. In particular, the role of ISPs in this regard is highlighted. Section 2.2 considers the role of localising cybercrime from the perspective of effectively combating cybercrime (section 2.2.1) and protecting constitutional

Law Review 1789–811; T. Ojanen, 'Privacy is more than just a seven-letter word: the Court of Justice of the European Union sets constitutional limits on mass surveillance' (2014) 10 *European Constitutional Law Review* 528–41; A. Roberts, 'Privacy, data retention and domination: *Digital Rights Ireland Ltd v Minister for Communications*' (2015) 78 *Modern Law Review* 535–48.

11 Amongst others: Romanian Constitutional Court (8 October 2009), Decision no. 1258 (2010) 47 *Common Market Law Review* 933–41; German Constitutional Court (2 March 2010), Decision nos 1 BvR 256/08, 1 BvR 263/08, 1 BvR 586/081 and BvR 256/08 www.bundesverfassungsgericht.de (last accessed 7 August 2015); or, very recently, Belgian Constitutional Court, Decision no. 84/2015 of 11 June 2015 www.const-court.be (last accessed 7 August 2015).

12 Frequently headquarters of internet firms are located in the US, California and servers placed in Ireland (e.g. Microsoft, Twitter, Dropbox, cloud computing of Amazon, Google and Apple). Owing to its technology and tax-friendly climate, Ireland is an interesting server location for ISPs.

and regional human rights (section 2.2.2). Section 2.3 focuses on international efforts to overcome these jurisdictional disputes and considers its potential impact. Section 2.4 provides the analysis of a case in which the localisation of cybercrime was contested: the Belgian case against Yahoo!, which concerned the cooperation obligation on ISPs with criminal authorities. The case clearly shows the tension between constitutional rights protection and the need for prosecution to redefine jurisdiction in order to combat cybercrime effectively. Section 2.5 concludes the chapter.

2.2 National jurisdiction in cyberspace and constitutional limits

2.2.1 Effectively combating cybercrime

Along with the increasing dependence on internet-related technology, cybercrime[13] is a growing concern for governments.[14] In its 2014 survey on the topic, PriceWaterhouseCoopers contended that one in four firms reported having experienced cybercrime and suffering important financial losses.[15] Governments too frequently fall victim of hackers causing disruption of vital public services and severe damage to their digital networks.[16] Phenomena such as hacking, phishing and spreading viruses are widespread offences committed in cyberspace. National authorities have developed new investigative methods and legislation in order effectively to prosecute such harmful acts. However, owing to the intrinsic trans-border nature of cybercrime, judicial authorities have been confronted with challenges to their jurisdiction to investigate, prosecute and litigate cases of cybercrime based on the traditionally held notion of territoriality defining a state's competence.[17]

13 A generally accepted definition of cybercrime (in the broadest sense) is: 'any illegal behaviour committed by means of, or in relation to, a computer system or network, including such crimes as illegal possession and offering or distributing information by means of a computer system or network'. See Background Paper for the workshop on crimes related to the computer network, 10th UN Congress on the Prevention of Crime and the Treatment of Offenders (2000) A/CONF.187/10. For an exhaustive development of different forms of cybercrime see A. Galicki and D. Havens, 'Computer crimes' (2014) 51 *American Criminal Law Review* 875.

14 In this chapter cybercrime is understood as a generic term for all internet-related acts that are considered harmful for persons, legal entities or public entities. The Cybercrime Convention of the Council of Europe defined four main categories of cybercrimes: computer-related offences, content-related offences, offences dealing with conduct directed against computer systems and processed data and, finally, offences related to intellectual property. Convention on Cybercrime (Budapest, 23 January 2001), CETS no. 185.

15 PricewaterhouseCoopers, 'Economic crime: a threat to business globally' *Global Survey* (2014) www.pwc.com (last accessed 7 August 2015).

16 For a summary of the most notorious cases of government hacking, espionage and internet warfare see KPMG International, 'Issues monitor: cyber crime – a growing challenge for governments' (Report July 2011 vol. 8) 8–9 www.kpmg.com (last accessed 7 August 2015).

17 D. Speer, 'Redefining borders: the challenges of cybercrime' (2000) 34(3) *Crime, Law and Social Change* 259; S. Brenner, 'Cybercrime jurisdiction' (2006) 46 *Crime, Law and Social Change* 189; F. Calderoni, 'The European legal framework on cybercrime: striving for an effective implementation' (2010) 54 *Crime, Law and Social Change* 341.

These challenges to the jurisdiction of judicial authorities might undermine the effectiveness of cybercrime prosecution. If jurisdiction in cyberspace were to be defined too narrowly, many cybercriminals might evade prosecution by using servers in countries that will probably not prosecute these acts. Professor James Boyle makes the point succinctly: 'If the king's writ reaches only as far as the king's sword, then much of the content on the Internet might be presumed to be free from the regulation of any particular sovereign.'[18]

In general, constitutions do not determine the territorial jurisdiction of judicial authorities to examine or litigate criminal acts. These jurisdictional rules can be found in criminal codes or in case law.[19] The territoriality principle is the default rule for jurisdictional competence.[20] This principle implies that criminal jurisdiction is related to the place of the offence and the state on whose territory the crime was committed has jurisdiction to prosecute the offence.[21] Territory is understood in geographical terms, namely the physical territory within the constitutionally or internationally defined borders of the country.[22] It has been questioned whether this traditionally held default rule of jurisdiction was appropriate to determine jurisdiction on cyberspace, given its virtual and not physical nature.[23]

However, the territoriality principle is the preferred basis on which jurisdiction is seised regarding cybercrime offences.[24] For example, when a hacker develops hacking tools on the territory of a state, that state will prosecute him or her for an infringement of criminal law. Given the virtual nature of these offences, many states apply the objective territoriality principle to extend the reach of their jurisdiction.[25] This principle implies that it suffices that the (intended) effects of the actions occurred within the territory of the prosecuting state.

For example, in the case of *Ivanov*, a US court convicted Mr Ivanov for attacking US internet enterprises, including the Connecticut Online Information

18 J. Boyle, 'Foucault in cyberspace: surveillance, sovereignty, and hardwired censors' (1997) 66 *University of Cincinnati Law Review* 179.

19 Certain states have adopted specific provisions in their criminal codes to address the issue of localisation of criminal code. They specify when a crime is considered to have taken place within their boundaries, rendering the judicial authorities competent to adjudicate the crime. See S. Brenner and B. Knoops, 'Approaches to cybercrime jurisdiction' (2004) 4 *Journal of High Technology Law* 15–16.

20 International law does not consider the territoriality principle as the sole valid basis for criminal jurisdiction. The International Court of Justice stated: 'The territoriality of criminal law . . . is not an absolute principle of international law and by no means coincides with territorial sovereignty'; Permanent Court of International Justice (PCIJ), Series A, no. 10 (7 September 1927) 'The case of S.S. Lotus' at 20. Other criteria include active or nationality criminal jurisdiction, passive or victim criminal jurisdiction, protective criminal jurisdiction or universal criminal jurisdiction.

21 R. M. Perkins, 'Territorial principle in criminal law' (1970–1971) 22 *Hastings Law Journal* 1155.

22 G. Urbas, 'Cybercrime, jurisdiction and extradition: the extended reach of cross-border law enforcement' (2012) 16(1) *Journal of Internet Law* 1, 8.

23 A. Weber, 'The Council of Europe's Convention on cybercrime' (2003) 18(1) *Berkeley Technology Law Journal* 425.

24 Urbas, 'Cybercrime, jurisdiction and extradition' (n 22) 10.

25 J. Clough, *Principles of Cybercrime* (Cambridge University Press 2010) 407.

Bureau.[26] It was uncontested that Mr Ivanov was a Russian citizen, residing in Russia and using a computer in Russia at the time the offences were committed. As such, he maintained that the US had no jurisdiction on the basis of the territoriality principle. The judge, however, dismissed the argument, finding that there was jurisdiction for a US court because the 'intended and actual detrimental effects' of his actions in Russia occurred in the US.

The German *Töben* case is a less straightforward use of the effects theory.[27] On an Australian website, German-born Australian citizen Gerald Töben denied the existence of the Holocaust. Such comments are in violation of German criminal law. The German Supreme Court considered that the German courts were competent because the harmful effects of the comments could be felt in Germany, given that the text was addressed to the German public and could be accessed by German citizens from German territory.

The territoriality principle has also been applied to ISPs. Courts have adopted different approaches to this principle to force ISPs to comply with domestic criminal legislation. For example, in France the Tribunal de Grande Instance (TGI) of Paris decided that the possibility to access a website belonging to Yahoo! from French territory provided the court with territorial jurisdiction to adjudicate the ISP. In *LICRA v Yahoo!*, the ISP was prosecuted by French authorities for providing internet access to an online auction service selling Nazi memorabilia in violation of French criminal law.[28] Yahoo! argued that it was not physically present in France and, therefore, the French authorities lacked jurisdiction to prosecute the company in France. However, the TGI maintained that it had jurisdiction to review actions of Yahoo! in France, given that every user of the internet on French territory could buy these items by from Yahoo!. As the company provided its services in France, it was considered to have committed the crime in France.[29]

In addition to the territoriality effect, states might also rely on the nationality or residence of the perpetrator.[30] In the German case of *Bavaria v Felix Somm*, Mr Somm's residence in Germany was considered a sufficient basis to prosecute him

26 US District Court of Connecticut, *USA v Ivanov* 175 F. Supp. 2d 36 (D. Conn. 2003).

27 BGH Urt (12 December 2000) 1 StR 184/00.

28 Tribunal de Grande Instance de Paris (20 May 2000) *UEJF and LICRA v Yahoo ! Inc and Yahoo France* www.legalis.net (last accessed 7 August 2015). Several other authors in this collection discuss this case more extensively. See among others on this case A. Greenberg and H. Marc, 'Return to Lilliput: the *Licra v Yahoo!* case and the regulation of online content in the world market' (2003) 18 *Berkeley Technology Law Journal* 1191; C. Murphy, 'International law and the internet: an ill-suited match – case note on *UEJF & LICRA v Yahoo! Inc*' (2001–2002) 25 *Hastings International & Comparative Law Review* 405. On the constitutional and human rights implications see E. Okoniewski, '*Yahoo! Inc v LICRA*: the French challenge to free expression on the internet' (2002–2003) 18(1) *American University International Law Review* 295.

29 The TGI highlighted that, given that the sites could be accessed in French, Yahoo! was well aware that its site would be used in France.

30 A global survey of UNODC shows that territoriality and nationality/habitual residence are the most common national bases for jurisdiction in cyberspace. UNODC, 'Comprehensive study on cybercrime: February 2013' at 191 www.unodc.org (last accessed 7 August 2015).

in a cybercrime case.[31] At first instance, Mr Somm was found to violate German criminal legislation as the managing director of the ISP CompuServe GmbH for failing to block internet access to child pornographic material. Whilst Mr Somm was a Swiss national and the server was located in the US, jurisdiction was claimed on the basis that Mr Somm as managing partner resided in Germany.[32]

In the above cases, the application of domestic law on the person charged or ISP was disputed as well as the (territorial) jurisdiction. Is it sufficient that a firm's website can be accessed from a computer in a state in order for this website to fall under domestic law of this state (and hence, all other states from which it can be accessed) and to claim that the firm is virtually present in this state? Legal uncertainty regarding jurisdiction in cyberspace does not only affect the adjudication of cases, but also investigations. A public prosecutor is not only limited by the territorial boundaries with regard to his competence to prosecute crimes, but also to conduct investigative acts such as hearings, confiscations or home searches.[33] If the investigating authority of a given country were to conduct such acts on the territory of another state, this would imply a breach of the sovereignty of the other state. This follows from the rules of international law on sovereignty:

> the first and foremost restriction imposed by international law upon a State is that – failing the existence of a permissive rule to the contrary – it may not exercise its power in any form in the territory of another State. In this sense jurisdiction is certainly territorial; it cannot be exercised by a State outside its territory except by virtue of a ermissive rule derived from international custom or from a convention.[34]

31 First instance: Ambtsgericht München (28 July 1998) 8340 Ds 465 Js 173158/95/www.afs-rechtsanwaelte.de. See G. Bender, '*Bavaria v Felix Somm*: the pornography conviction of the former CompuServ manager' (1998) 1 *International Journal of Communications Law and Policy* http://ijclp.net/old_website/1_1998/ijclp_webdoc_14_1_1998.html (last accessed 8 August 2015). On appeal the decision was overturned, finding that the German server merely and automatically transmitted the content from the American mother server without any possibility to block the content. This issue of jurisdiction was not considered. For the appeal see Langericht München I (17 November 1999) 20 Ns 465 Js 173158/95 www.netlaw.de (last accessed 8 August 2015). For an analysis in English see S. Hedley, *The Law of Electronic Commerce and the Internet in the UK and Ireland* (Cavendish Publishing 2006) 142 and Y. Akdeniz, *Internet Child Pornography and the Law: National and International Responses* (Ashgate Publishing 2008) 229–31.

32 In this case the managing partner was prosecuted. However, the court could also have found a basis of jurisdiction in the active criminality principle if it had prosecuted the firm CompuServe GmbH, given that it was an enterprise of German law.

33 It has been highlighted that the investigative jurisdiction is a separate and distinct form of jurisdiction, even though the jurisdiction to investigate and adjudicate are closely connected. The reason for this distinction is that an investigation must not end in a prosecution of the person, as the judicial authorities might decide that there is insufficient evidence. See D. Svantesson and G. Felicity, 'Access to extraterritorial evidence: the Microsoft cloud case and beyond' (2015) 31(4) *Computer Law & Security Review* 478 http://www.sciencedirect.com/science/article/pii/S0267364915000874 (last accessed 8 August 2015).

34 PCIJ, 'The case of S.S. Lotus' (n 20) [18]–[20].

From the perspective of cyber criminality, therefore, it appears elementary to establish where the evidence can be found. When there is a material presence of evidence in the territory of the prosecuting state, cyber criminality does not pose a problem. The investigating authorities can easily confiscate a computer and conduct a search of the soft- and hardware. However, when the evidence is to be found in cyberspace it is less evident to establish how far the competence of a national investigating authority reaches.[35]

For example, does a public prosecutor from New York violate the sovereignty of Japan if he searches files in the cybercloud of a Japanese citizen living in Tokyo? Can a French prosecutor use a server established in Saudi Arabia to gather evidence concerning financial fraud committed by a Turkish citizen committed with his computer in Israel? And can an Argentinian prosecutor force a network provider established in Rwanda to provide the names behind IP addresses on the basis of an Argentinian legal duty to cooperate?

On the one hand, it might be argued that as long as there is no physical presence on the territory of another state, there is no intrusion of the sovereignty of that state. This position would mean that judicial authorities can search and seize documents and data in cyberspace, irrespective of the location of the server, suspect or website. As long as the search or seizure can be conducted from the prosecuting state, the search or seizure does not violate the sovereignty of another state.[36] Such reading can be reconciled with international customary law on sovereignty as these rules are focused on physical presence having been established pre-internet.[37] On the other hand, it could also be argued that virtual presence violates the sovereignty of another state.[38] If a judicial authority wants to search the data of a computer in another state, it cannot simply hack into this computer but will have to request the other state to intervene, or at least require consent.[39]

35 A. Aldesco, 'Demise of anonymity: a constitutional challenge to the Convention on Cybercrime' (2002–2003) 23 *Loyola of Los Angeles Entertainment Law Review* 81, 89–90. For further examples see Urbas, 'Cybercrime, jurisdiction and extradition' (n 22) 8–9.

36 See e.g. S. Young, 'Verdugo in cyberspace boundaries of fourth amendment rights for foreign nationals in cybercrime cases' (2003) 10(1) *Michigan Telecommunications and Technology Law Review* 139, 165–66.

37 It was argued that such trans-border searches are in general not considered to be problematic as the other state in general has an incentive to provide meaningful assistance. See J. Goldsmith, 'The internet and the legitimacy of cross-border searches' (2001) Chicago Public Law and Legal Theory Working Paper No. 16 http://chicagounbound.uchicago.edu/cgi/viewcontent.cgi?article=1316&context=public_law_and_legal_theory (last accessed 8 August 2015).

38 H. Perritt, 'Jurisdiction in cyberspace' (1996) 41 *Villanova Law Review* 82–83; S. Wilske and T. Schiller, 'International jurisdiction in cyberspace: which states may regulate the internet?' (1997) 50 *Federal Communications Law Journal* 174. It is clear that most states still adhere to this concept of sovereignty whereby they shield their (virtual) territory from presence of foreign agents. C. Ram, 'Cybercrime' in N. Boister and R. Currie (eds), *Transnational Criminal Law* (Routledge 2015).

39 See Brenner and Knoops, 'Approaches to cybercrime jurisdiction' (n 19) 23. This seems to be supported in practice whereby states will ask approval or simply inform another state before accessing the virtual territory of that state. See e.g. *United States v Ivanov*, 175 F Supp 2d 367 (D Conn 2001).

The uncertainty regarding these questions frustrates judicial authorities. Transborder investigations are not limited to cybercrime. In cases of general criminal law states are dependent on the willingness of other states to cooperate, for example to provide a warrant for a search on their territory. Such cooperation is mostly restricted, in particular on the basis of the dual criminality principle.[40] States will only cooperate with one another if the crime under scrutiny is punishable in both countries. Such requirement is a serious impediment to the investigation and effective prosecution of cybercrime, given that this field of law is still rather recent and therefore not yet recognised as a crime in other states.[41] In order to facilitate cooperation many states have concluded bilateral treaties (mutual legal assistance treaties or MLATs) in which they detail how and on what conditions they will exchange evidence, extradite suspects or undertake investigative measures. As Urbas correctly stated, the effectiveness of such cooperation is largely dependent on mutual trust through regular contacts between enforcement agencies.[42]

2.2.2 Protection of (constitutional) procedural rights

During the last decade the effectiveness of prosecuting cybercrime has improved. Once the jurisdictional loopholes in the investigation and prosecution of cybercrime had been discovered, domestic actors cooperated to establish international tools of cooperation. New investigative tools were developed, cybercrime provisions adopted in domestic criminal law and international norms established. Whilst the effectiveness of judicial efforts to tackle cybercrime is an ongoing concern, more recently authors have warned that the protection of constitutional – in particular, procedural – rights should not be forgotten.

Several constitutions provide a protection against arbitrary searches and seizures. In general, searches by judicial authorities in network systems are considered virtual searches and equated to physical searches of properties. As such, the same procedural safeguards should apply; for example, a warrant should be provided by a judge sanctioning the search or seizure. Constitutional rights and freedoms limit the interventions by the judicial authorities in this context, including the right to a fair trial, the protection of privacy and home and the peaceful enjoyment of possessions.

In several states these constitutional rights and freedoms have been applied in the context of virtual communication and interaction. Exceptionally, new constitutional rights have been discerned in order to protect the actions of individuals

40 G. Mullan, 'The concept of dual criminality in the context of extraterritorial crimes' (1997) *Criminal Law Forum* 17; Calderoni, 'The European legal framework on cybercrime' (n 17) 342. States apply different notions of this principle. See Council of Europe, European Committee on crime problems, 'Note on dual criminality, in concreto or in abstracto' PC-OC (2012) 02 final.

41 While certain forms of cybercrime are at present adopted in criminal legislation of many countries, specific acts of cybercrime vary significantly. See R. G. Smith, P. Grabosky and G. Urbas, *Cyber Criminals on Trial* (Cambridge University Press 2004), 96; Brenner and Knoops, 'Approaches to cybercrime jurisdiction' (n 19) 7.

42 Urbas, 'Cybercrime, jurisdiction and extradition' (n 22) 9.

on the internet. The German constitutional court argued that individuals in the current context are necessarily active on the internet and that such activity should therefore be protected under the right of personal development entrenched in the German Basic Law.[43] As such, the German constitutional court developed a fundamental right on the confidentiality and integrity of telecommunication systems, protecting individuals against online and remote searches by the police and security forces.[44]

However, the protection of constitutional rights is territorially confined. In general, the protection of the constitution only goes as far as the boundaries of the state.[45] The question is therefore the extent to which people not living in the state are protected against violations of their fundamental rights and freedoms. Furthermore, should judicial authorities still respect constitutional rights and freedoms when investigation crimes in cyberspace? In the United States the question was discussed in relation to the protection of constitutional rights applied to cybercrime, in particular with regard to the Fourth Amendment.[46] This Amendment provides that individuals are secured against unreasonable searches and seizures and that no warrant for a search or seizure shall be issued without probable cause and description of the place to be searched or persons or items to be seized. This Amendment was clearly written from the perspective of physical searches. However, judicial authorities can search a computer or network without having to leave their office, simply by means of their own computer and network.

In several cases American judicial authorities have searched computers abroad and presented the evidence before court. In the case of *Gorshkov*, the court refuted the argument that the evidence gathered by means of internet searches without the use of a warrant should be suppressed, holding that: 'The Fourth Amendment does not apply to the agent's extraterritorial access to computers in Russia and their copying of data contained thereon.'[47]

As such, judicial investigators are not limited by the constitutional amendment when searching networks or computers outside the US, whilst the Fourth Amendment applies when the computer or network can be localised within US

43 German Constitutional Court (27 February 2008) 1 BVR 370/07.

44 ibid para. 201. See on this case R. Weber, 'Internet of things: new security and privacy challenges' (2010) 26 *Computer Law & Security Review* 23–30.

45 Exceptionally, state authority is accepted as criterion for jurisdiction. For example, art 37(1) of the Polish constitution provides that everyone who remains under the authority of Poland enjoys the freedoms and rights ensured by the constitution.

46 See Young, 'Verdugo in cyberspace boundaries of fourth amendment rights for foreign nationals in cybercrime cases' (n 36) 10; S. Brenner and J. Schwerha, 'Transnational evidence gathering and local prosecution of international cybercrime' (2002) 20(3) *John Marshall Journal of Information Technology and Privacy Law* 347; B. Winmill, D. Metcalf and M. Band, 'Cybercrime: issues and challenges in the United States' (2010) 7 *Digital Evidence and Electronic Signature Law Review* 19.

47 *United States v Gorshkov* No. CR00-550C, 2001 WL 1024026 *1, *3 (WD Wash, 23 May 2001). On this case see Brenner and Knoops, 'Approaches to cybercrime jurisdiction' (n 19) 22.

territory. This renders the localisation of a network or server vital for protection of an individual's Fourth Amendment rights in cybercrime investigations.[48]

The Canadian Supreme Court provided that the rights and freedoms of the Charter are to be safeguarded by the Canadian authorities when acting extraterritorially.[49] The majority of judges held in *R v Harrer* that Canadian police are to respect the Charter when they conduct an interrogation in the United States regarding a Canadian offence.[50] The Supreme Court added, however, that the application of the Charter extraterritorially is limited by enforcement. If the state cannot enforce the application of the Charter and is reliant on another state's consent for the enforcement, the Charter does not apply. Applied to constitutional protection against unreasonable searches and seizures, the Court held:

> Searches and seizures, because of their coerciveness and intrusiveness, are by nature vastly different from police interrogations. The power to invade the private sphere of persons and property, and seize personal items and information, is paradigmatic of state sovereignty. These actions can be authorized only by the territorial state. From a theoretical standpoint, the Charter cannot be applied, because its application would necessarily entail an exercise of the enforcement jurisdiction that lies at the heart of territoriality.[51]

Certain jurisdictions have remedied the limited or absent protection of constitutional rights in extraterritorial investigations by providing safeguards for the application of evidence obtained extraterritorially in domestic proceedings. For example, the Belgian Court of Cassation established that domestic courts need to safeguard the possibility for the individual to contest the legitimacy of evidence obtained by foreign judicial authorities (e.g. a search of a foreign computer) in order to protect his or her procedural rights to a fair trial.[52]

This case law was applied to the transcripts of foreign telephone taps and could be applied to taps of online conversations or network searches by foreign judicial authorities. The Canadian Supreme Court held that, whilst the Charter of Rights and Freedoms in principle does not apply to an extraterritorial investigation when

48 Furthermore, several US courts limited the protection of the Fourth Amendment with regard to the duty for ISPs to cooperate with the authorities. These courts stated that users do not have a reasonable expectation of the protection of privacy in the information they provide to ISPs. See Galicki and Havens, 'Computer crimes' (n 13) 875, 884.

49 *R v Harrer* [1995] 3 SCR 562, para. 11, Canadian Supreme Court (19 October 1995); *R v Cook* [1998] 2 SCR 597, para. 46, Canadian Supreme Court (1 January 1998).

50 *R v Harrer*) (n 49) para. 11. The extraterritorial application is thus exceptional. See J. M. Arbour, '*Canada v Khadr*: reflections on the use of international law in the repatriation litigation' (2010) 52 *SCIR* 278–79.

51 *R v Hape* [2007] 2 SCR 292, 2007 SCC 26 para. 87, Canadian Supreme Court (7 June 2007).

52 However, the starting point remains that the domestic courts may assume that evidence obtained abroad by foreign judicial authorities has been collected in a legitimate manner. As such, the domestic courts do not have to review the legitimacy of the evidence ex officio, but only when contested. Court of Cassation (3 April 2012) www.juridat.be (last accessed 7 August 2015).

another state's consent is required for its enforcement, domestic courts may exclude evidence obtained abroad if necessary to preserve a fair trial.[53]

In European countries the ever-increasing prominence of the European Convention on Human Rights (ECHR, or Convention) and the Strasbourg case law, in particular regarding the procedural rights in Article 6 of the ECHR, implies that the determination of jurisdiction of the Convention by the European Court of Human Rights (ECtHR) is of high importance for the protection of fundamental rights on cyberspace. Article 1 of the ECHR provides that the ECHR applies within the jurisdiction of the Member States. In the *Bankovic* case, the ECtHR accepted the territoriality principle as defining 'jurisdiction' under Article 1 of the ECHR.[54]

However, in exceptional circumstances the Court will accept that extraterritorial acts constitute an exercise of the jurisdiction of this state to which the Convention applies. This is the case when the state exercises control and authority over an individual through its agents.[55] In the second place, the ECtHR accepts that the ECHR applies to actions of Member States producing effects outside their territory when the Member State has effective control over the territory of the other Member State.[56]

This case law has been developed in the context of physical acts outside the territory of the Member States. It is unclear how this applied to cyberspace. Would the Strasbourg Court equate searches in the computer located outside the territory of a Member State as an exercise of control and authority over an individual? The issue in such cases is not simply whether the ECHR applies extraterritorially, but whether the Member State acted extraterritorially in the first place. Currently, there is no indication that the Court is willing to develop criteria to address this issue.

The ECtHR provides a wide margin for the Member States to determine their jurisdiction and the limits thereof.[57] If a Member State claims jurisdiction on the basis of nationality or residence of the perpetrator or victim, the ECtHR will not contest this approach. Regarding the Court's case law on the determination of jurisdiction, a report produced by the Council of Europe provided:

> That raises the question, inter alia, of the circumstances in which a court can exercise jurisdiction over a defendant located or domiciled in a country

53 *R v Hape* (n 51) para. 91. The Court held art 7 Charter applicable: 'Everyone has the right to life, liberty and security of the person and the right not to be deprived thereof except in accordance with the principles of fundamental justice.'

54 *Bankovic v Belgium and Others* (2007) 44 EHRR SE5. On the impact of this case on defining jurisdiction see H. Matthew, '*Bankovic v Belgium* and the territorial scope of the European Convention on Human Rights' (2003) 3 *Human Rights Law Review* 1.

55 *Al-Skeini and Others v United Kingdom* (2011) 53 EHRR 18, para. 137. This is obviously the case when an individual is taken into custody (see e.g. *Öcalan v Turkey* (2005) 41 EHRR 985, para. 91), but likewise when agents of the state exercise some public functions with consent of the other state (see e.g. *Bankovic v Belgium and Others* (n 54) para. 71).

56 *Bankovic v Belgium and Others* (n 54) para. 70.

57 In general, the Court will find this decision falls within the ambit of the Member States.

> other than the country in which a complaint has been made about an alleged offence or civil wrong committed over the Internet. That, however, is primarily a question to be answered by the domestic courts applying the relevant principles of private international law on jurisdiction.[58]

For example, in the case of *Premininy*, the Court did not contest the competence of the Russian courts to prosecute the hacking into an online security system of a US bank.[59] In *Perrin*, a French national residing in the UK acted against his conviction for the publication of an article on a US homepage on the basis of the UK Obscene Publications Acts 1959 and 1964.[60] Mr Perrin maintained that owing to the worldwide nature of the internet it was unreasonable to demand publishers to foresee the legal requirements in all individual states where homepages can be accessed. The ECtHR dismissed this argument, finding that owing to the residence of Mr Perrin in the UK the application of the UK Obscene Publications Acts 1959 and 1964 on his publication was sufficient foreseeable. In such cases the ECtHR's jurisprudence on extra-territorial application of the Convention does not come into play, given that the territoriality of these cases is not contested.

Only exceptionally has a Member State's claim of jurisdiction been refuted by the ECtHR. In the case of *Ben El Mahi* the Court held that there was no jurisdictional link between Denmark and the applicants, namely Moroccan citizens living in Morocco and two Moroccan organisations.[61] As such, the Court held that since Denmark had no jurisdiction the Convention did not apply.

The above shows the importance of the localisation of acts of cybercrime and jurisdiction. It is clear that if acts of cybercrime and measures to investigate or prosecute the perpetrators are within a state's domestic borders, constitutional rights and freedoms are better protected.

2.3 International law in cyberspace

2.3.1 Jurisdiction in international law

Given the discrepancy between the territorial approach to legal jurisdiction to prosecute and adjudicate crimes and the global nature of cybercrime, international norms and cooperation in this field were considered vital. The cooperation between Member States based on bilateral agreements (MLATs) or on the basis of international agreements or customary law regarding legal cooperation in criminal cases were regarded as insufficient to tackle the phenomenon of

58 Council of Europe/European Court of Human Rights (Research Division), 'Internet: case-law of the European Court of Human Rights' (2011) www.echr.coe.int (last accessed 7 August 2015).

59 *Premininy v Russia* Application No. 44973/04 (ECtHR, 10 February 2011). E. Lazar, 'Positive obligations of states under the ECHR to protect individuals against unlawful acts on the internet' (2015) 3 *Journal of Law & Administration* 132, 134.

60 *Perrin v UK* Application No. 5446/03 (ECtHR, 18 October 2005).

61 *Ben El Mahi v Denmark* Application no. 5853/06 (ECtHR, 11 December 2006).

cybercrime. Two approaches could have been adopted.[62] First, international law can provide norms standardising offences of cybercrime and investigative tools in order to improve bilateral or multilateral cooperation on cybercrime. Secondly, international norms may address the legal uncertainty regarding jurisdiction of domestic states in cyberspace. The territorial approach to jurisdiction based on territory and physical boundaries could have been readdressed and redefined in the light of cyberspace in order to settle when a country can claim jurisdiction to investigate, prosecute and adjudicate cybercrime.

The most successful international instrument on cybercrime is the Council of Europe's Convention drafted in 2001.[63] The many signatories of the Convention, including non-members of the Council of Europe, and its binding nature rendered this document the most relevant document on the subject on a global scale. The Convention adopted both approaches. In the first place, the Convention provides for offences to be rendered punishable under domestic law and definitions of the relevant terminology. As such, the Convention ensures a harmonisation of domestic legislation of the signatory Member States, ensuring a swifter and more effective cooperation between Member States. For example, many countries require that the offence committed in another country and for which the extradition of a resident is requested by the home state, is also punishable under domestic law. The Convention ensures that this dual criminality principle does not thwart the extradition of suspects.[64]

Secondly, the Convention also provides for rules governing the jurisdiction of states to prosecute cybercrime. Remarkably, the Convention also adopts a traditional approach on jurisdiction, marking territory as the basis for jurisdiction. The Convention does not establish a definition of 'territory'. Article 38 provides that every country should specify what constitutes their territory in the light of the Convention at the signature or deposition of the implementing instrument. As such, the definition of territory in cyberspace remains within the discretion of the signatory states. In addition to territory, the Convention also refers to nationality as a basis for jurisdiction on the condition that either the offence is also punishable in the state in which the offence occurred or no country claims jurisdiction over the offence.

The Convention is by no means a game changer with regard to the legal questions on jurisdiction in cyberspace.[65] The Convention provides a wide margin for the Member States to define territory in the light of cyberspace. As such, either an overlap of territorial competence or a lack of jurisdiction in cyberspace are still possible.[66] In that respect, the Convention does not address jurisdictional com-

62 See Calderoni, 'The European legal framework on cybercrime' (n 17) 343.

63 Convention on Cybercrime (n 14).

64 See Weber, 'The Council of Europe's Convention on Cybercrime' (n 23) 434.

65 See Calderoni, 'The European legal framework on cybercrime' (n 17) 347; Weber, 'The Council of Europe's Convention on Cybercrime' (n 23) 443.

66 The explanatory note of the Convention on Cybercrime (n 14) accepts that more than one Member State will have jurisdiction. The note highlights that it is desirable that Member States choose a single venue for prosecution. However, no conflict rules are provided to address this issue.

plexity in cyberspace from the mindset of the preamble, namely to be conscious of the 'profound changes brought about by the digitalisation, convergence and continuing globalisation of computer networks'. Territoriality, as defined by the Member States, remains the prime basis of jurisdiction.

The Convention will not avoid positive jurisdiction conflicts in which two Member States claim jurisdiction to prosecute a given case of cybercrime.[67] This is not only true for the jurisdiction to adjudicate cybercrime cases, but also for investigative measures. Article 19 of the Convention provides that each Member State is to enact legislation allowing for the search and seizure of computer systems and computer data storage systems in which computer systems may be stored 'in its territory'.

Even though the Convention does not define jurisdiction in cyberspace, it implicitly limits the competence of Member States to adjudicate and investigate cybercrime cases to the territory of the state as defined by these states. The Convention does not provide for a general extraterritorial application of searches and seizures; nor does it suggest that the Convention provides a basis for jurisdiction covering cyberspace in its entirety. Instead, the Convention focuses on cooperation between Member States. For example, Article 31 of the Convention provides that states may request another country to access, seize, secure and disclose data stored on computer systems in the territory of this other country and limits the grounds for the requested state to refuse the transfer of these data.

The Convention accepts one exception to this principled choice in favour of cooperation and jurisdiction based on territoriality. Article 32 of the Convention allows countries without authorisation of another country to access all publicly available stored computer data in cyberspace. As such, the Convention provides for a universal cyberspace jurisdiction for investigative authorities for open source computer data. This provision also allows states to receive data stored in a computer located in another country through a computer system in its own territory, on the condition that it obtains a lawful and voluntary consent of the party who has the lawful authority to disclose the data through that computer system.

In conclusion, the Convention on Cybercrime will not solve jurisdictional issues nor set undisputable boundaries for investigative measures in cyberspace. In that respect, it is a missed opportunity. However, it does provide clues for the domestic courts to delineate jurisdiction. First, the territoriality principle remains the main starting point for defining jurisdiction. Secondly, the Convention on Cybercrime does not provide for a competence to search, collect and seize data on a global scale and, hence, there are limits to the territorial jurisdiction of states in cyberspace, with the exception of open source data. Thirdly, the Convention

The note states that in such instances the Member States are to consult each other to determine the most appropriate venue. See Explanatory note, para. 239.

67 Instead, the Convention on Cybercrime (n 14) relies on cooperation by introducing a consultation mechanism in art 22 para. 55; see Calderoni, 'The European legal framework on cybercrime' (n 17) 347.

on Cybercrime clearly relies on international cooperation and not extraterritorial investigation in order to tackle cybercrime.

Importantly, the Convention on Cybercrime also stresses the importance of the safeguard of human rights. The Convention provides that all powers and procedures established in the Convention are subject to the conditions and safeguards under the domestic (constitutional) law of the Member States and the protection of human rights, in particular those entrenched in the ECHR.[68]

The Convention stresses the importance of judicial and independent supervision and the limitation of the scope and duration of the powers and procedures provided. The Convention does not limit the scope of protection of these rights to certain procedures or jurisdiction. This implies that, even with regard to the competence to collect globally open source data, the protection of fundamental rights applies. As such, the jurisdictional reach of the investigative powers of states under the Convention delineates the reach of the protection of fundamental rights of those under investigation. Nevertheless, the Convention has been criticised for restricting fundamental and constitutional rights, for example with regard to the right to anonymity.[69]

In the European Union, the fight against cybercrime is governed by the Council's Framework Decision on attacks against information systems of 2005[70] and the more recent EU Directive on attacks against information systems of 2013.[71] The directive has a more narrow scope than the framework decision or the Convention. The directive is only applicable with regard to the illegal access to information systems, data interference and interception, as well as to the development, sale or use of tools to commit these offences.[72] Both the framework decision and the directive provide for a dual basis for jurisdiction: the territoriality principle, that is the offences are committed in the territory of the prosecuting state, and the nationality principle, that is the offence is committed by a national of the state.[73]

In addition, these norms specify what is to be understood as the committing of a crime on the territory. First, this is the case if the offender commits the offence when 'physically present' on the territory. Secondly, a Member State can also

68 D. Cangemi, 'Procedural law provisions of the Council of Europe Convention on Cybercrime' (2004) 18(2) *International Review of Law, Computers & Technology* 165, 171.

69 See Aldesco, 'Demise of anonymity' (n 35) 81, 83.

70 Council Framework Decision 2005/222/JHA of 24 February 2005 on attacks against information systems, OJ L69. See further P. De Hert, G. González Fuster and B. Knoops, 'Fighting cybercrime in the two Europes: the added value of the EU Framework Decision and the Council of Europe Convention' (2006) 77(3–4) *International Review of Penal Law* 503 http://www.vub.ac.be/LSTS/pub/Dehert/260.pdf (last accessed 8 August 2015).

71 Directive 2013/40/EU of the European Parliament and the Council of 12 August 2013 on attacks against information systems (Cybercrime Directive) (2013) OJ L218/9.

72 In the fight against cybercrime the EU has developed several initiatives, which are sometimes lacking in coherence. This directive focused only on new forms of cybercrime and is therefore limited in scope. See E. Fahey, 'EU's cybercrime and cyber-security rulemaking: mapping the internal and external dimensions of EU security' (2014) 5(1) *European Journal of Risk Regulation* 46, 52.

73 Council Framework Decision (n 70) art 10 and Cybercrime Directive (n 71) art 12.

claim jurisdiction when the offence is committed against an information system on its territory, irrespective of the physical presence of the offender. Finally, upon informing the EU Commission Member States can also claim jurisdiction if the offender has his or her habitual residence in the territory or the offence is committed for the benefit of a legal person established in the territory. These criteria are clearly more delineating than those held in the Convention.[74] Only the directive refers to the requirement to respect fundamental rights, in particular the protection of privacy and data as entrenched in the Charter of Fundamental Rights of the European Union and the ECHR.[75] As such, it appears that between 2005 and 2013 the focus solely on the effectiveness of combating cybercrime has shifted, taking into account fundamental rights as well.

2.3.2 The cooperation duty of ISPs

International law on cybercrime also provides rules concerning the cooperation duty of ISPs. As mentioned above, many states set out cooperation duties for ISPs with the national judicial authorities in their domestic legislation. ISPs are the prime interceptors, collectors and transmitters of data in cyberspace and are therefore crucial for judicial authorities in order to obtain traffic and content data of criminal activities. However, ISPs regularly refuse to provide data to domestic authorities, claiming that the requesting state lacks jurisdiction. For this reason, it should come as no surprise that cooperation duties of ISPs are also incorporated into the supranational and international rules concerning cybercrime.

Article 18 of the Convention on Cybercrime provides that Member States should introduce a cooperation duty for service providers.[76] Enforcement authorities can compel ISPs to provide data within their possession or control. Given the reference to fundamental rights, in particular the ECHR, in the Convention, this cooperation duty is to be developed with respect for the protection of privacy and data protection.[77] This provision stipulates that the duty to cooperate can only apply to those ISPs 'offering its services in the territory'. If a state requires data stored outside its territory, it will have to rely on the mechanisms of international cooperation. When a Member State concludes that traffic data involved in an investigation concerning cybercrime are stored in a service provider in another country, pursuant to Article 30 of the Convention it should provide a request to the other state to disclose the traffic data to identify that service provider and the path through which the communication was transmitted.[78]

A contrario, this provision suggests that a Member State cannot simply compel service providers in other Member States to provide these traffic data. As such, an

74 De Hert, González Fuster and Knoops, 'Fighting cybercrime in the two Europes' (n 70) 519.

75 Cybercrime Directive (n 71) preamble, paras 29–30.

76 This provision was criticised for not providing sufficient guarantees that the protection of privacy and data are protected. See Aldesco, 'Demise of anonymity' (n 35) 81, 96–97.

77 See also an explicit reference to human rights in view of art 18 of the Convention on Cybercrime (n 14) in the Explanatory note, para. 174.

78 Convention on Cybercrime (n 14) art 30.

ISP should in principle only comply with the rules concerning cooperation with the enforcement authorities and the applicable privacy and data protection legislation of the state where it offers its services. However, neither the Convention nor the Explanatory Note specifies when ISPs are to be regarded as offering services in the territory. As mentioned, the Convention also provides a wide margin for states to define 'territory'. In consequence, orders of states compelling ISPs acting on a global scale to provide data will often result in legal battles on the jurisdiction of a state to issue such order to the ISP.

Even though the Convention does not settle the jurisdiction of states regarding ISPs conclusively, at least the Convention provides for an anchor point to establish jurisdiction, namely 'offering services on the territory'. The EU Data Retention Directive – now annulled – provided a different approach to the cooperation duty of ISPs.[79] The preamble to the directive indicated that one of the purposes of the directive was exactly to avoid that ISPs should be confronted with legal and difficult differences between national provisions concerning data retention for the prevention, investigation, detection and prosecution of criminal offences. The directive had a clear single market objective. As such, the directive focused solely on uniform rules, rather than cooperation between states. This reflected on the approach towards defining the competence of states to order ISPs to cooperate with the national authorities.

In contrast to the Convention, the Data Retention Directive did not refer to territory, but to jurisdiction. Moreover, the point of departure for the cooperation duty was not the offering of services or presence, but the collection of data. Article 3 of the directive provided that the retention duty applies to data generated or processed by ISPs 'within their jurisdiction' in the process of supplying the communication services concerned. Thus, the directive still maintains a margin for the Member States to establish their jurisdiction, but no longer defines competence in the sense of geographical territoriality. In view of the case law of the ECtHR, jurisdiction can be understood as the physical or virtual space in which the state has effective control and authority (section 2.2.2).

Given the annulment of the directive and the annulment by many national (constitutional) courts of its domestic implementation, these criteria will not, however, determine the discussion of jurisdiction over ISPs in the near future.

2.4 Acts of investigation: the Belgian *Yahoo!* decision as case study

As discussed, cybercrime cases are frequently the subject of intense discussions concerning jurisdiction. This is in particular true for the competence of states to

79 Directive 2006/24/EC of the European Parliament and Council of 15 March 2006 on the retention of data generated or processed in connection with the provision of publicly available electronic communications services or of public communications networks and amending Directive 2002/58/EC, OJ L105/54. On 8 April 2014, the Court of Justice of the European Union declared Directive 2006/24/EC invalid for violating fundamental rights. On the extensive obligations for ISPs to collect data see De Hert, González Fuster and Knoops, 'Fighting cybercrime in the two Europes' (n 70) 532.

investigate crimes in cyberspace. Settling the territorial jurisdiction is not only important for determining the lawfulness of investigative measures or nationally imposed cooperation duties, but also for the application of domestic constitutional or regional human rights protection. International norms could play a role in setting the boundaries and encouraging cooperation.

The following case study discusses the reach of domestic jurisdiction in the investigation of cybercrime. This case shows that little or no reference to international law is made. In consequence, very different criteria are applied to determine the jurisdiction of investigative authorities in cyberspace and limited attention is provided to the protection of fundamental (procedural) rights. Moreover, instead of relying on international cooperation to obtain data from ISPs, judges interpret their jurisdiction extensively in order to assert a direct competence to order ISPs to transfer data.

The Belgian case against Yahoo! concerns the jurisdiction of domestic authorities to force service providers to cooperate, even though they are not physically present on the territory.[80] On the basis of the Belgian Code of Criminal Procedure the public prosecutor may request a network provider to cooperate with the authorities and provide for the identification of the individuals behind an ICT application. Refusal to cooperate is punishable under Belgian law by a fine of a maximum of €10,000. The Belgian prosecutor requested Yahoo! to identify two individuals who had used a Yahoo! email account to commit fraudulent activities in Belgium. Both individuals concerned resided in the Netherlands and had operated from the Dutch territory. The victim of the cybercrime, however, was a Belgian national residing in Belgium.

The Belgian prosecutor sent an email to the Yahoo! headquarters in the United States requesting it to provide data identifying the persons behind the email addresses. Yahoo! refused to sanction the request. The company argued that the request was not binding on Yahoo!, given that it was not present on Belgian territory and therefore could not be required to comply with a Belgian investigative measure. Yahoo! did not have Belgian headquarters or any other commercial entity in Belgium at the time of the request. The company contended that if the Belgian prosecutor required the data, he should rely on the cooperation mechanisms with the US authorities, as entrenched in the Belgian–US MLAT[81] or on other international cooperation mechanisms. Yahoo! added that simply providing the data to the Belgian authorities might trigger its criminal responsibility under US law, given that it might be conceived as a serious breach of privacy if the

80 On these cases see P. De Hert and M. Kopcheva, 'International mutual legal assistance in criminal law made redundant: a comment on the Belgian *Yahoo!* case' (2011) 27 *Computer Law & Security Review* 291; J. Vandendriessche, 'Effect of virtual presence in Belgium and the duty to cooperate in criminal investigations: some prudence may be required when confronted with a request from a Belgian public prosecutor' (2011) 8 *Digital Evidence & Electronic Signature Law Review* 194.

81 Mutual Legal Assistance Treaty between the United States of America and Belgium. These MLATs allow for the exchange of information and evidence in crime and related matters. At the time of the request, the Convention on Cybercrime (n 14) had not yet entered into force.

company provided the data of individuals on the basis of an illegitimate order from a foreign authority that might be contrary to US law.

The Belgian prosecutor sued Yahoo! before the Belgian courts, holding that the refusal implied a breach of the cooperation duty for telecommunication companies entrenched in the Belgian Code on Criminal Procedure. Yahoo! reacted by holding in the first place that it was not under a duty to cooperate with the prosecutor, given that it was a foreign ISP and not present on Belgian territory. As such, Belgian law – including investigative orders – could not be enforced against Yahoo!. If the prosecutor requested the data, he should have made use of the MLAT between the US and Belgium.

Secondly, the ISP claimed that, even if it was under such obligation, Belgian courts would have no jurisdiction to adjudicate a potential breach, as Yahoo! had sent the refusal from its US headquarters and, hence, the offence had taken place in the US and not on Belgian territory. On the basis of the territoriality principle in criminal law, Belgian courts lacked jurisdiction to adjudicate the case.

The Ghent Court of Appeal and thereafter the Court of Cassation[82] of Brussels decided in favour of Yahoo!.[83] In particular, the Brussels Court of Appeal argued that the competence of the public prosecutor to issue orders to ISPs to cooperate is limited to the territorial boundaries of Belgium. The fact that the ISP can be reached by email does not render the ISP physically or virtually present in Belgium. The Court of Appeal accepted that the fact that the order was sent to the US must imply that the ISP was not present on Belgian territory and, hence, Belgian law did not apply.

The Court of Cassation dismissed the latter reasoning, holding that the simple fact that an order is sent from Belgium to an ISP with an address abroad does not imply that the order to cooperate is invalid.[84] Thus, the Court of Cassation supported the contention that the cooperation obligation may also apply to ISPs who have no legal or physical offices in Belgium. However, the Court of Cassation did not determine whether the cooperation duty also effectively applied to Yahoo! in the case at hand, given that this Court does not enter into the decision on the facts but merely controls the legality of judgments. However, implicitly it appears

82 The first judgment of the Supreme Court is of less importance as it concerned the definition of an ISP under the legal cooperation obligation in the Criminal Code of Procedure. The Supreme Court held that the obligation applied not only to operators of electronic communication networks, but to everyone offering services that consist, partly or wholly, of transmitting signals via electronic communication networks. See Court of Cassation (18 January 2011) AR P.10.1347.N www.juridat.be (last accessed 7 August 2015).

83 Court of Appeal Ghent (30 June 2010) *T. Strafr.* 2011, no. 2, 132 and Court of Appeal Brussels (12 October 2011) *T. Strafr.* 2012, no. 6, 472. The judgment of Ghent is also electronically available at www.juridat.be (last accessed 7 August 2015).

84 Court of Cassation (4 September 2012) AR P.11.1906.N www.juridat.be. See on this case K De Schepper and F. Verbruggen, 'Ontsnappen space invaders aan onze pacmannen? De materiële en formele strafrechtsmacht van België bij strrafbare weigering van medewerking door elektronische dienstverleners' (2013) 3 *Tijdschrift voor Strafrecht* 143; O. Leroux, 'Arnaques, fraudes et escroqueries sur internet: moyens concrets d'investigation – Point sur l'affaire dite Yahoo! à la suite du second arrêt de la Cour de cassation' (2012) *Journal des Tribunaux* 6500.

that the Court of Cassation supports the theory that ISPs might be considered to be present on Belgian territory and hence under the cooperation duty, even though they are merely virtually present in Belgium, namely by means of offering telecommunication services to Belgian internet users.

Surprisingly, the Court of Cassation did not engage with the argumentation that international treaties on judicial cooperation apply, in particular the MLAT between Belgium and the United States. The Supreme Court completely disregarded the ECtHR case law mentioned by both Yahoo! as the public prosecutor or the international conventions referred to, in particular the Convention on Cybercrime.[85] Whilst the courts of appeal did engage with these arguments, the Supreme Court held that the dispute was solely a question of domestic law. This is striking for a Court that in 1971 had already decided that national law should comply with international law.[86] It appears that while the Court in principle applies a monist view to international law, in practice international law plays a limited role in deciding cybercrime cases.

The Court of Appeal of Antwerp decided the case following the reasoning of the public prosecutor.[87] The Court first argued that the cooperation duty applied to Yahoo!. It held that those telecommunication providers offering services in Belgium are considered territorially present in Belgium and, therefore, under the cooperation duty entrenched in the Code of Criminal Procedure. Given that Yahoo! provided telecommunication services to Belgian users, in particular email services, the ISP was present on Belgian territory and therefore had to comply with Belgian law.

Secondly, the Court held that the offence, namely the refusal to provide the data, was committed in Belgium. Under the cooperation obligation the ISPs are to provide the data to the public prosecutor, which are therefore deliverable and not collectable. As such, the refusal to cooperate and, hence, the offence did not take place in the headquarters of Yahoo! in the US, but instead at the place where the data are to be delivered, namely in Belgium. The Court of Appeal also disregarded the importance of the MLAT; neither did it refer to the Convention on Cybercrime or other supranational or international rules concerning cybercrime.[88]

85 See De Hert and Kopcheva, 'International mutual legal assistance in criminal law made redundant' (n 80) 291.

86 Court of Cassation (27 May 1971) Arr. Cass. 1971, 959; 'National courts of Member States' (1972) 9(2) *Common Market Law Review* 229. For more on the monist approach in Belgium see E. Kindt, E. Lievens, E. Kosta, T. Leys and P. De Hert, 'Constitutional rights and new technologies in Belgium' in R. Leenes, E. Knoops and P. De Hert (eds), *Constitutional Rights and New Technologies: A Comparative Study* (Information Technology & Law Series, vol 15 TMC Asser Press 2008) 13–14.

87 Court of Appeal of Antwerp (20 November 2013); (2014) 1 *T. Strafr.* 73, with case note; G. Schoorens, 'De Yahoo!-saga: verstrekking van elektronische identificatiegegevens' (2004) 1 *T. Strafr.* 75.

88 Currently, a similar case is pending against Skype before the first instance court of Mechelen. On the basis of the same provision the public prosecutor requested Skype to provide the data of an online conversation

Clearly. this approach renders the cooperation mechanisms set up by the MLAT between the US and Belgium – and implicitly the Convention on Cybercrime with its focus on cooperation – superfluous in cybercrime cases, as the vast majority of data stored abroad are now accessible to the Belgian authorities by means of the cooperation duty for ISPs offering services in Belgium.[89] Such an approach seriously undermines the protection of privacy and data protection under the domestic law of the state where the server storing the data is established. These rights thus appear to be the collateral damage of the efforts to render cybercrime investigations more effective.

2.5 Conclusion

The internet demands that judicial authorities reassess the balance between protecting (constitutional) procedural rights, the right to privacy and data protection on the one hand and effective crime prosecution on the other. Defining jurisdiction and, therefore, localising cybercrime appears to be a key issue. This includes developing an approach to ISPs who hold the key to telecommunication data. The current approach is untenable.

On one hand, judicial authorities have started to accept the central role of ISPs and the need to curb their powers in view of the protection of privacy and data protection. On the other hand, judicial authorities are extending the cooperation duties of ISPs in the field of cybercrime. The international rules developed to facilitate international cooperation to this effect play in practice a limited or non-existent role in actual cases. Apparently, these norms entrenched in the Convention on Cybercrime, treaties on mutual cooperation in criminal cases and bilateral MLATs are deemed too slow or ineffective to deal with cybercrime.[90] Instead, courts define their jurisdiction extensively in order to gain jurisdiction over the actions of ISPs. Given the global nature of cyberspace and the wide playing field of these ISPs, a more coordinated approach by states is required in order to find the correct balance.

89 P. De Hert and M. Kopcheva, 'International mutual legal assistance in criminal law made redundant' (2011) 27 *Computer Law & Security Review* 291–97.

90 See Urbas, 'Cybercrime, jurisdiction and extradition' (n 22) 13; Aldesco, 'Demise of anonymity' (n 35) 81, 90–91.

3 A human rights perspective on US constitutional protection of the internet

*Molly K. Land**

3.1 Introduction

This chapter examines the approaches used by the US Supreme Court and the lower US federal courts to contend with the challenges presented by new Internet technologies for the protection of constitutional rights. It argues that, although US federal courts have been effective in updating individual constitutional protections to meet the demands of new technologies, their efforts in this respect have been hampered by the lack of a comprehensive constitutional theory for understanding the effects of new technologies on individual rights.

Section 3.2 of this chapter is a relatively abbreviated overview of the ways in which federal courts have regulated the Internet's effect on rights protected under the US Constitution. Although the Supreme Court has issued few decisions dealing directly with the Internet, its cautious and case-by-case approach has ensured that constitutional doctrine has responded to harms without rendering the law too inflexible to deal with new problems as they arise. At the same time, this approach has meant that the law has lagged behind in responding to issues raised by new technologies. The lower federal courts have struggled to provide clarity, but this has itself led to doctrinal challenges, as flexible constitutional standards have become less flexible through lower-court interpretations that have been outpaced by technological developments.

Section 3.3 of the chapter considers the role of courts in regulating constitutional rights online in terms of both institutional competence and doctrinal coherence. First, it argues that judicial regulation of the Internet is a story of inter-branch power sharing. Regulation has been most effective, and most coherent, when Congress and the courts are engaged in dialogue with one another in ways that play to the strengths of each – specifically, when courts either provide general principles against which Congress can legislate or review legislation after the fact to evaluate its constitutionality.

* The author is grateful for the feedback from the participants in the conference organized in conjunction with this volume, 'Internet law, protection of fundamental rights and constitutional adjudication' at Bocconi University in Milan. Dorothy Diaz-Hennessey provided outstanding research assistance.

Second, the chapter contends that what is missing from US constitutional adjudication of rights in the context of the Internet is a more comprehensive and cohesive frame for thinking about the relationship between this particular technology and individual rights. The approach to protecting constitutional rights on the Internet under US law has been relatively piecemeal, with courts addressing each right in isolation and using different frames to understand the particular values each embodies and the harms they address. This approach, however, necessarily fails to account for values and harms not captured by any of the frames. Specifically, it neglects the extent to which access to the Internet itself is in many instances a critical precondition to the effective enjoyment of human rights today.

Moreover, discussions about constitutional rights on the Internet often lose sight of the specific experiences and concerns of individual rights holders. The result is a skewing of constitutional doctrine towards the interests of speakers and intermediaries at the expense of listeners and users. The chapter proposes the international human right to equality as a frame that better recognizes the significance of access to the Internet in promoting the realization of rights and orients the discussion on the needs and experiences of the user with respect to both speech and privacy online.

3.2 US courts and Internet governance

In the United States, laws affecting Internet governance are a collection of rules, regulations and decisions that are legislative, judicial, administrative or constitutional in origin and which span a broad variety of doctrinal areas. Within constitutional law, there are several US constitutional rights that have implications for the Internet; the three most relevant are the First Amendment, the Fourth Amendment, and the Fifth and Fourteenth Amendments to the US Constitution, all but one of which are contained in the US Bill of Rights.[1] The US Supreme Court has issued remarkably few decisions dealing with the Internet. As of 2012, for example, only 17 of its decisions mentioned the Internet in a substantive manner, and only seven related to Internet governance in any significant way.[2] Most of the federal law affecting individual rights is developed by the legislature or the lower federal courts. As a result, this chapter considers decisions of the federal appellate and district courts in addition to those of the Supreme Court.[3]

1 Other areas of constitutional law relevant to Internet governance that are beyond the scope of this chapter include the dormant Commerce Clause, Article III of the US Constitution and the Sixth Amendment. See James Grimmelmann, *Internet Law: Cases and Problems* (4th edn, Semaphore Press 2014) 88, 104.

2 The Honorable M. Margaret McKeown, 'The internet and the constitution: a selective retrospective' (2014) 9 *Washington Journal of Law, Technology & Arts* 135, 152. The limited number of decisions by the Supreme Court is explained in part by the fact that its review is discretionary, and it hears only a small fraction of the cases that are presented to it each year. 'Supreme Court of the United States frequently asked Questions' http://www.supremecourt.gov/faq.aspx#faqgi9 (last accessed 8 August 2015).

3 Although state courts also have the ability and competence to review constitutional claims, much

3.2.1 First Amendment

The First Amendment to the US Constitution[4] protects expressive activity both online and offline. Courts have adopted a fairly broad understanding of what counts as expressive activity in the online context. Among other things, courts have found that 'likes' on Facebook,[5] video games[6] and source code[7] constitute constitutionally protected speech. There is less agreement about whether the control exercised by Internet content and service providers as they manage traffic on their networks and respond to user requests for information constitutes protected speech, but at least one court has held that Google's page ranks are constitutionally protected speech.[8]

Cases addressing the intersection of the Internet and the First Amendment have most frequently focused on the extent to which online speech may be limited to achieve valid public policy goals and to protect the rights of others. The government can prohibit some categories of expressive content because the content is unprotected under the First Amendment, owing to its intrinsically harmful nature.[9] Expression that is protected by the First Amendment can still be regulated, but the government will be required to justify the regulation. The burden on the government to justify regulation will depend on a variety of factors, including whether the restriction at issue is content-based or content-neutral and the nature of the speech regulated.[10] The possession of child pornography, for example, can lead to criminal sanctions because the government has a constitutionally compelling interest to protect children exploited in the production of child pornography.[11] Pornography not involving children may be regulated, but

of the constitutional doctrinal development of law in the context of the Internet has been in the federal courts.

4 'Congress shall make no law respecting an establishment of religion, or prohibiting the free exercise thereof; or abridging the freedom of speech, or of the press; or the right of the people peaceably to assemble, and to petition the government for a redress of grievances' US Const. amend. I.

5 *Bland v Roberts* 730 F3d 368, 386 (4th Cir 2013).

6 *Brown v Entertainment Merchants Assn* 131 S Ct 2729, 2733 (2011).

7 *Bernstein v US Dept of Justice* 176 F3d 1132 (9th Cir 1999), *withdrawn and reh'g en banc granted*, 192 F3d 1308 (9th Cir 1999). For a discussion of First Amendment jurisprudence and algorithms see Stuart Minor Benjamin, 'Algorithms and speech' (2013) 161 *University of Pennsylvania Law Review* 1445.

8 *Search King Inc v Google Tech Inc* 2003 WL 21464568, *6 (WD Okla 27 May 2003).

9 See e.g. *Miller v California* 413 US 15, 39 (1973); *Virginia v Black* 538 US 343, 359 (2003); *Freedman v America Online Inc* 412 F Supp 2d 174, 185–86 (D Conn 2005); *Cohen v California* 403 US 15, 20 (1971); *Brandenburg v Ohio* 395 US 444, 447 (1969).

10 *Cornelius v NAACP Legal Def & Educ Fund* 473 US 788, 797 (1985). The government's burden is highest for content-based regulation, when speech is being regulated because of its content. There are lower burdens for regulation that is content-neutral, regulation of commercial speech and regulation aimed at conduct rather than expression. *Simon & Schuster Inc v Members of the New York State Crime Victims Bd* 502 US 105, 116 (1991); *Turner Broadcasting System Inc v FCC* 520 US 180, 213 (1997).

11 *New York v Ferber* 458 US 747, 775 (1982).

not prohibited; it is lawful for adults to possess but may be regulated in order to limit access to these materials by minors.

Most of the cases involving the Internet that have reached the Supreme Court have addressed the constitutionality of legislative action designed to protect children from harmful online content. The first of these involved a challenge to the Communications Decency Act of 1996 (CDA), which was passed in response to growing concerns about online pornography and the desire to limit access to this content by minors. The Supreme Court held that, although the government has an important interest in protecting minors, the statute was overbroad because it would also burden a significant amount of speech that adults have the right to send and receive.[12]

Undeterred, Congress then passed the Child Online Protection Act of 1998 (COPA), which prohibited a more specific range of content. After several rounds of litigation, the Supreme Court upheld the lower court's injunction because the government had not established that less restrictive measures, such as the use of blocking and filtering software, were insufficient to accomplish its objectives.[13] The Supreme Court upheld the Children's Internet Protection Act (CIPA), a statute that required libraries to install pornography filters in order to receive federal funding, although without a decision of the Court.[14] The Court also upheld the Prosecutorial Remedies and Other Tools to end the Exploitation of Children Today (PROTECT) Act, which criminalized the possession and distribution of child pornography.[15]

In the lower courts, another line of cases has involved the question of the extent to which schools may constitutionally regulate the speech of students. Historically, schools have had significant leeway in regulating student speech while they are in school.[16] The Internet, however, blurs the distinction between speech that occurs inside and outside of schools. Faced with pressures to address a range of different kinds of threats, including cyberbullying and school shootings, school administrators have begun imposing more stringent regulations on online student speech that occurs off campus.[17] Although speech outside of school premises is entitled to full First Amendment protection, federal courts have begun allowing such regulation, as long as the speech causes disruptions within the school.[18]

12 *Reno v American Civil Liberties Union* 521 US 844, 874 (1997).

13 *Ashcroft v American Civil Liberties Union* 542 US 656, 673 (2004). Lower federal courts have also struck down state legislation as overbroad because less restrictive means were available. *Center for Democracy & Technology v Pappert* 337 F Supp 2d 606, 648 (ED Pa 2004).

14 *United States v American Library Assn* 539 US 194 (2003). The plurality opinion was written by Justice Rhenquist and joined by Justices O'Connor, Scalia and Thomas; Justices Kennedy and Breyer concurred in the judgment.

15 *United States v Williams* 553 US 285 (2007).

16 *Tinker v Des Moines Independent Community School District* 393 US 503 (1969).

17 McKeown (n 2) 158.

18 *Layshock v Hermitage School District* 650 F3d 205, 219 (3rd Cir 2013) (sanction not allowed because speech did not have disruptive effect on school); *Wynar v Douglas County School District* 728 F3d 1062, 1070 (9th Cir 2013) (sanction permitted because of effect of text messages about school shooting on school activities).

There is no federal legislation addressing online harassment such as cyberbullying, hate speech or revenge porn as such. The First Amendment applies to claims seeking recovery in tort for injuries sustained as a result of speech, including claims of defamation and intentional infliction of emotional distress, and a plaintiff's ability to recover will depend on whether he or she is a public or private figure and whether the speech can reasonably be interpreted as fact or addresses a matter of public concern.[19] Because of their nature, however, some kinds of expressive content do not receive First Amendment protection, including threats of violence and speech integral to criminal conduct.[20]

Thus, to the extent that online expression constitutes a true threat or is integral to criminal conduct such as stalking, the state may regulate it, and there are typically a variety of criminal and civil laws that provide victims of such acts with remedies. Even where the law does provide relief, however, victims may not be able to pursue remedies because Section 230 of the CDA shields Internet content and service providers from liability for the speech that they publish or transmit.[21] Some states are currently exploring legislative solutions in this area, but any such legislation would face an uphill battle because the regulated speech would likely be entitled to the highest level of protection.[22]

One of the most recent testing grounds regarding the limitations of First Amendment protection for harmful speech was *United States v Elonis*, a case in which the Supreme Court addressed whether the defendant's social media postings regarding his estranged wife constituted 'true threats' outside the scope of the First Amendment.[23] The questions before the Supreme Court related to whether, for a statement to constitute a true threat, there must be proof that a defendant subjectively intended to threaten, or whether proof that a reasonable person would interpret the statement as a threat is sufficient.[24]

The district court had applied the reasonable person standard, and the Third Circuit affirmed. The Third Circuit, noting that the prohibition on true threats is designed to protect individuals from the fear of violence, not merely violence itself, upheld the lower court's use of an objective standard for evaluating a threat.[25] The Supreme Court, consistent with its typically cautious approach in

19 *Milkovich v Lorain Journal Co* 497 US 1, 14–21 (1990); *Snyder v Phelps* 131 S Ct 1207, 1216 (2011).

20 *Chaplinsky v NH* 315 US 568, 573 (1942); *Watts v United States* 394 US 705, 707 (1969); *Virginia* (n 9).

21 Communications Decency Act 1996, s 230 (codified at 47 USC § 230(c)(1)).

22 Nancy S. Kim, 'Web site proprietorship and online harassment' (2009) 3 *Utah Law Review* 993, 1008–1012.

23 *Elonis v United States* Petition for writ of certiorari (2014), 2014 WL 4101234, *I.

24 The Ninth Circuit, Tenth Circuit and several state supreme courts require evidence of subjective intent. The other federal circuit courts and state courts of last resort use an objective standard. Kristina M. Williams and others, 'Facebook "Rapper" urges High Court to adopt subjective test for online threats' (2014) 32 *Westlaw Journal Computer & Internet* 11, *2. The Tenth Circuit joined the Ninth Circuit in late 2014. *United States v Heineman* 767 F3d 970, 975 (10th Cir 2014); *United States v Wheeler* 776 F3d 736, 740 (10th Cir 2015).

25 *United States v Elonis* 730 F3d 321, 327–32 (2013).

areas involving new technologies, overturned the conviction on statutory rather than constitutional grounds, holding that the criminal law requires more consideration of the defendant's mental state but declining to say what the appropriate mental state might be.[26]

Government surveillance and data collection practices online have also been challenged as a violation of the right to anonymous speech. The First Amendment protects the right to anonymous speech and association,[27] at least to the extent the expression constitutes 'political, religious, or literary speech'.[28] A lawsuit brought in the Southern District of New York claimed that the use of national security letters, which allow the government to obtain information from Internet service providers by certifying that the information is relevant to a terrorism investigation, violated the right to anonymous speech and association.[29] Although the Second Circuit invalidated portions of the statute prohibiting disclosure of national security letters, it did not address the effect on anonymous speech because the national security letter at issue in that case had been withdrawn.[30]

Federal courts have also addressed the question of whether regulation of the Internet elsewhere might impermissibly burden the First Amendment in the United States. In the well-known case of *La Ligue v Yahoo!*, for example, the Ninth Circuit Court of Appeals heard a challenge to a French court order requiring Yahoo! to block the access of French users of its service to Nazi memorabilia.[31] Yahoo! sought an injunction on the ground that enforcing the order in the United States would violate the First Amendment. The Ninth Circuit found that the case was not ripe for decision, given that Yahoo had already substantially complied with the French court decision, and because the possibility that Yahoo! would be forced to restrict the access of US users was too speculative.[32] As the ability of Internet service providers to localize content increases, pressures from concern about the extraterritorial application of national law have decreased considerably.

Both Congress and the federal courts have been more aggressive in policing speech that infringes on intellectual property rights. Although the goals of

26 *Elonis v United States* 135 SCt 2001, 2012–13 (2015).

27 *McIntyre v Ohio Elections Commission* 514 US 334 (1995); *Watchtower Bible & Tract Society of New York Inc v Village of Stratton* 536 US 150 (2002); *NAACP v State of Alabama ex rel Patterson* 357 US 449 (1958).

28 Susan W. Brenner, 'Constitutional rights and new technologies in the United States' in Ronald E. Leenes and others (eds), *Constitutional Rights and New Technologies: A Comparative Study* (TMC Asser Press 2008) 248; Sharon K. Sandeen, 'In for a calf is not always in for a cow: an analysis of the constitutional right of anonymity as applied to anonymous e-commerce' (2002) 29 *Hastings Constitutional Law Quarterly* 527, 551–69.

29 *Doe v Ashcroft* 334 F Supp 2d 471, 506 (SDNY 2006), vacated by *Doe v Gonzales* 449 F3d 415, 419 (2d Cir 2006).

30 *John Doe Inc v Mukasey* 549 F3d 861, 865–70 (2d Cir 2008) (describing litigation). State courts have found that anti-spam laws did not infringe the right to anonymous speech because they regulated false or misleading speech. *State v Heckel* 122 Wash App 60 (Wash Ct App 2004).

31 *Yahoo! Inc v La Ligue Contre le Racisme et l'Antisemitisme* 433 F3d 1199 (9th Cir 2006).

32 ibid 1221.

intellectual property and freedom of expression are not incompatible, since the goals of both are to promote expression,[33] the temporary monopolies created in the form of copyright and trademark rights can create tension with the First Amendment. By and large, however, courts and commentators have assumed that the copyright regime itself, through features such as the idea–expression dichotomy and the doctrine of fair use, ensures the protection of First Amendment rights.[34] As a result, courts have tended not to engage in external balancing of expression and intellectual property, assuming instead that the internal features of the intellectual property regime suffice to protect expressive interests. Legal and technological developments may be upsetting this balance. New and more aggressive approaches to enforcement today include technological protection measures, aggressive use of civil litigation and intermediary liability.[35]

3.2.2 Fourth Amendment

Although the US Constitution has no provision directly protecting privacy, courts have found privacy rights in the Fourth Amendment protection against unreasonable searches and seizures, the Fifth Amendment protection against compelled self-incrimination, First Amendment protections of speech and association and the Fifth and Fourteenth Amendment guarantees of due process.[36]

The Fourth Amendment[37] regulates law enforcement and imposes reasonable restrictions on the conduct of the police. When the Fourth Amendment applies, law enforcement officers are required to obtain a warrant in order to conduct a search, unless an exception applies. Courts can issue a warrant after making a showing of probable cause, which requires 'a fair probability that contraband or evidence of a crime will be found in a particular place'.[38] The Fourth Amendment only applies to individuals physically present in the United States and US citizens residing abroad and does not govern extra-territorial surveillance of the communications of non-citizens.[39] Surveillance of foreign communications is governed by the separate and less rigorous regime of the Foreign Intelligence Surveillance Act (FISA).[40]

33 *Eldred v Ashcroft* 537 US 186, 219 (2003).

34 ibid; Joseph P. Bauer, 'Copyright and the First Amendment: comrades, combatants, or uneasy allies?' (2010) 67(3) *Washington & Lee Law Review* 846, 848.

35 Henry H. Perritt, Jr, 'The internet at 20: evolution of a constitution for cyberspace' (2012) 20 *William & Mary Bill of Rights Journal* 1115, 1170–72; see generally Cory Doctorow, *Information Doesn't Want to Be Free: Laws for the Internet Age* (McSweeny's 2014); Department of Commerce Internet Task Force, *Copyright Policy, Creativity, and Innovation in the Digital Economy* (2013).

36 Brenner (n 28) 230.

37 'The right of the people to be secure in their persons, houses, papers, and effects, against unreasonable searches and seizures, shall not be violated, and no warrants shall issue, but upon probable cause, supported by oath or affirmation, and particularly describing the place to be searched, and the persons or things to be seized' US Const. amend. IV.

38 *Illinois v Gates* 462 US 213, 238 (1983).

39 *United States v Verdugo-Urquidez* 494 US 259, 264 (1990); Brenner (n 28) 246–47.

40 Foreign Intelligence Surveillance Act of 1978 (codified at 50 USC § 1801 ff 2010).

The challenge for federal courts addressing the application of the Fourth Amendment to new technologies such as the Internet rests with the relatively rigid interpretations of 'public' and 'private' adopted by later courts interpreting an early US Supreme Court case on the scope of Fourth Amendment protections. Contemporary Fourth Amendment doctrine owes its origins to the Supreme Court decision in *Katz v United States*, which tied Fourth Amendment protections to an individual's actual and reasonable expectation of privacy.[41] According to the Court in *Katz*, 'the Fourth Amendment protects people, not places'.[42] As a result, anything that an individual 'seeks to preserve as private' is constitutionally protected, whilst that which he or she 'knowingly exposes to the public' is not.[43]

The standard articulated in *Katz* and further developed by Justice Harlan's concurring opinion is a sensible one that in many ways would be well suited for regulating privacy even in a digital age. The Fourth Amendment protects those activities that a reasonable individual would expect to be private, even as those expectations change over time. In overruling *Olmstead*, in which the court had held that wiretapping did not implicate the Fourth Amendment because it involved no physical intrusion into the home,[44] the *Katz* court rejected overly categorical approaches to the Fourth Amendment and adopted instead a more flexible and evolving standard.

Nonetheless, the 'spatial conception of privacy' that has for so long permeated interpretations of the Fourth Amendment[45] continues to hold sway. A later Supreme Court decision applying *Katz* attempted to provide additional clarity and predictability to Fourth Amendment doctrine by drawing more bright line rules regarding what has been exposed to the public and thus loses the protection of the Fourth Amendment. Specifically, under the third-party doctrine, information disclosed to a third party loses constitutional protection. Thus, in *Smith v Maryland*, the Supreme Court held that, although one might have a reasonable expectation of privacy in the contents of a phone call, there was no such expectation with regard to the number dialed since, in order to place the call, the caller is required to disclose the number to the phone company.[46]

The third-party doctrine is particularly troubling for cases involving the Internet since all of the information transmitted over the Internet, both content and non-content information, is at various points transmitted to a third party.[47] Although the Supreme Court has yet to weigh in on this matter, most courts addressing the

41 *Katz v United States* 389 US 347, 361 (1967) (Harlan J dissenting).

42 ibid 351.

43 ibid.

44 *Olmstead v United States* 277 US 438, 465 (1928).

45 Brenner (n 28) 231.

46 *Smith v Maryland* 442 US 735, 742 (1979). For the same reason, bank records have been held outside the scope of the Fourth Amendment. *United States v Miller* 425 US 435, 440 (1975).

47 Daniel J. Solove, 'Fourth Amendment codification and Professor Kerr's misguided call for judicial deference' (2005) 74 *Fordham Law Review* 747, 753 (calling the third-party doctrine 'one of the most serious threats to privacy in the digital age'); see also Brenner (n 28) 238; Matthew Tokson, 'Automation and the Fourth Amendment' (2011) 96 *Iowa Law Review* 581, 585.

applicability of the Fourth Amendment to the Internet have followed the logic of *Smith* and drawn a clear distinction between content and non-content data. Courts have consistently held that, under the third-party doctrine, the Fourth Amendment does not protect IP addresses,[48] the quantity of data transmitted,[49] email addressing information[50] and subscriber information.[51] With respect to *content* data that has been disclosed to a third party such as unencrypted email, however, decisions have been more mixed. Earlier decisions indicated that emails that had already reached their intended recipient were not constitutionally protected.[52] More recent cases in federal courts have either indicated a willingness to protect email contents or have avoided the question.

The Supreme Court has heard one case involving a challenge to a warrantless search of email, but it avoided the question by deciding the matter on alternate grounds. In *City of Ontario v Quon*, the Court heard a police officer's challenge to the City of Ontario's search of his text messages but avoided reaching the question of the level of protection to be afforded content transmitted online.[53] The Ninth Circuit had rejected broad application of the third-party doctrine and found that the employee had a reasonable expectation of privacy in his text messages, even though they could be accessed by the Internet service provider.[54] The Supreme Court assumed without deciding that Quon had a reasonable expectation of privacy in his text messages and that the City's review of those messages was a search,[55] holding that the City's search was nonetheless reasonable because it 'was motivated by a legitimate work-related purpose, and because it was not excessive in scope'.[56]

Of the two federal circuit courts that have addressed the issue of email, one held that email contents were protected by the Fourth Amendment and the other explicitly avoided reaching a decision on the merits of that question. Citing the 'fundamental similarities between email and traditional forms of communication', the Sixth Circuit upheld the lower court's finding that the defendant had a reasonable expectation of privacy in his emails, explicitly noting that a third party's ability to access the content of the email did not necessarily deprive the email of protection.[57]

48 *United States v Forrester* 512 F3d 500, 510 (9th Cir 2008).

49 ibid.

50 *United States v Warshak* 631 F3d 266, 288 (6th Cir 2010).

51 *United States v Kennedy* 81 F Supp 2d 1103, 1110 (D Kan 2000); *United States v Perrine* 518 F3d 1196, 1204 (10th Cir 2008).

52 *United States v Lifshitz* 369 F3d 173, 190 (2d Cir 2004); *Guest v Lies* 255 F3d 325, 333 (6th Cir 2001).

53 *City of Ontario v Quon* 560 US 746 (2010).

54 *Quon v Arch Wireless Operating Co Inc* 529 F3d 892, 904–906 (9th Cir 2008), reversed and remanded by *Quon*, (n 53) 760.

55 *Quon* (n 53) 760.

56 ibid 764.

57 *United States v Warshak* 631 F3d 266, 285–86 (6th Cir 2010). The court declined, however, to exclude the evidence as a remedy for the violation because the officer had relied in good faith on the Stored Communications Act. ibid 292.

The Eleventh Circuit has been more cautious, holding initially that the Fourth Amendment did not protect the defendant's emails stored on the server of an Internet service provider.[58] After the Supreme Court's decision in *Quon*, the Eleventh Circuit vacated its prior decision and issued a new one disposing of the case on narrower grounds.[59] Citing the Supreme Court's reluctance to address this issue in *Quon* and the Court's caution to lower courts about establishing broad privacy rights in such a rapidly changing area, the Eleventh Circuit rested its decision instead on the plaintiff's failure to show a violation of a clearly established constitutional right, a showing necessary to overcome the presumption of qualified immunity.[60]

In part, the lack of cases addressing the constitutional protection to be afforded to email is a result of the fact that most searches of content and non-content data are carried out pursuant to statutory law, including the Stored Communications Act, passed as part of the Electronic Communications Privacy Act.[61] The Stored Communications Act provides greater protection than the Fourth Amendment in some ways, and less protection in others. It provides greater protection because it requires law enforcement to obtain a subpoena for non-content data, which courts have found not protected by the Fourth Amendment.[62] It likely provides less protection than the Fourth Amendment in most other cases, however, because it limits full warrant protection to unsent emails saved on a user's computer and unopened emails stored for fewer than 180 days.[63]

First, while the statute requires a warrant for electronic communications stored on a user's computer, communications stored on a third-party system such as Gmail prior to sending can be obtained with a subpoena. Second, once sent, an email again has protection but only until it has been opened or has been stored unopened on a third-party system for more than 180 days, at which point only a subpoena is needed.[64] The constitutionality of this statutory scheme depends on whether the Fourth Amendment extends to the content of emails stored on third-party servers, an issue that has not been resolved by the courts.[65]

58 *Rehberg v Paulk* 598 F3d 1268, 1281–82 (11th Cir 2010), vacated by *Rehberg v Paulk* 611 F3d 828, 847 (11th Cir 2010).

59 *Rehberg* (n 58).

60 ibid 846. The court noted that while individuals have clearly established rights in the content of their telephone conversations, their rights in their email are not clearly established at this time and thus Rehberg did not overcome the agents' qualified immunity. ibid 846–47.

61 Electronic Communications Privacy Act of 1986; see also Orin S. Kerr, 'Applying the Fourth Amendment to the internet: a general approach' (2010) 62 *Stanford Law Review* 1005, 1025; Brenner (n 28) 236.

62 Brenner (n 28) 238.

63 Kerr (n 61) 1025.

64 ibid; Tokson (n 47) 594. A subpoena can be obtained with only a showing of 'specific and articulable facts showing that there are reasonable grounds to believe that the contents of a wire or electronic communication . . . are relevant and material to an ongoing criminal investigation'. Stored Communications Act of 1986 (codified at 18 USC § 2703(d)).

65 Finding a reasonable expectation of privacy in email content in the *Warshak* case, the Sixth Circuit held that to the extent that the SCA purports to permit the government to obtain emails without

The Supreme Court has moved the doctrine forward with respect to cell phones, which are increasingly the primary way in which many individuals access the Internet. In *Riley v California*, the Supreme Court addressed the scope of the exception to the warrant requirement that allows an officer to search an individual without a warrant if the search was incidental to a lawful arrest.[66] The Court declined to extend the exception to digital content on a smart phone because the interests usually fulfilled by such a search (to ensure officer safety and prevent evidence destruction) are not presented by digital data and such a search involves a greater intrusion into privacy than a physical search.[67]

Thus, absent a warrant or exception to the warrant requirement, a law-enforcement officer cannot engage in a search of a suspect's cell phone. Although it does not directly deal with the Internet, the Court's decision in *Riley* represents an important development for Internet governance because of the Court's updating of the Fourth Amendment to address new privacy challenges presented by technological developments.[68] The decision provides a persuasive account of the ways in which new technologies raise new privacy issues and offers a blueprint for lower courts seeking to update existing case law to account for these challenges.

Finally, cases addressing the application of the Fourth Amendment to other new surveillance technologies may also have implications for the Internet. These decisions have tended to track the public/private divide that has characterized court reasoning in the Internet cases. In *Knotts*, the Supreme Court upheld the use of an electronic tracking device to follow a subject's movements because the information obtained had been voluntarily disclosed to the public.[69] In *Kyllo*, the Court held that the use of a thermal imaging device to sense heat signatures within a house was governed by the Fourth Amendment because the suspect's behavior would not have been visible without the technology absent a physical intrusion, and because the technology was 'not in general public use'.[70] More recently, in *Jones v United States*, the Supreme Court avoided the question of whether use of a global positioning device to track a suspect's movement violated the Fourth Amendment by finding that the installation itself constituted a trespass.[71]

a warrant, the SCA is unconstitutional. *Warshak* (n 50) 288; see also *United States v Graham* 846 F Supp 2d 384 (D Md 2012). (Fourth Amendment challenge to cell site location data).

66 *Riley v California* 134 S Ct 2473 (2014).

67 ibid 2485.

68 In response to the government's argument that data on a cell phone is 'materially indistinguishable' from comparable physical items, the Court responded: 'That is like saying a ride on horseback is materially indistinguishable from a flight to the moon': ibid; see also Mason Clutter, 'Symposium: the court starts to catch up with technology' (26 June 2014) SCOTUSblog http://www.scotusblog.com/2014/06/symposium-the-court-starts-to-catch-up-with-technology/ (last accessed 9 August 2015).

69 *United States v Knotts* 460 US 276, 282 (1983); see also *United States v Karo* 468 US 705, 712 (1984) (installation of beeper did not violate Fourth Amendment interest).

70 *Kyllo v United States* 533 US 27, 34 (2001).

71 *United States v Jones* 132 S Ct 945, 949 (2012).

3.2.3 Fifth and Fourteenth Amendments

The Fifth and Fourteenth Amendments to the US Constitution require the federal and state governments to provide individuals with due process before depriving them of life, liberty or property.[72] Among other things, this obligation of due process prevents states from exercising jurisdiction over a defendant unless he or she has such minimum contacts with the forum that the exercise of jurisdiction comports with 'traditional notions of fair play and substantial justice'.[73]

In the early years of Internet commerce, courts struggled to determine how best to apply standard principles of personal jurisdiction in the online environment. Many of these cases involved disputes over domain names – claims that domain names inappropriately incorporated the trademark of another.[74] One of the earliest tests for personal jurisdiction based on Internet activity was the *Zippo* test, which roughly classified Internet websites based on their level of interactivity.[75] Although helpful in orienting courts on some of the features of the Internet environment relevant to personal jurisdiction, the test has been critiqued as overly formulistic and too focused on the technology as opposed to the behavior the technology enables.[76] Other courts have relied on the 'effects' test drawn from cases addressing personal jurisdiction in the context of intentional torts, which finds personal jurisdiction appropriate if the defendant 'expressly aimed' his or her conduct at the state in question.[77] If the *Zippo* test has been seen as unduly narrow, the effects test has been critiqued primarily as being overbroad because it risks establishing jurisdiction wherever a website is viewed.[78]

In recent years, many courts have returned to traditional approaches to personal jurisdiction to Internet conduct, focusing on whether the defendant's

72 The Fifth Amendment provides: 'No person . . . shall be . . . deprived of life, liberty, or property, without due process of law . . .'. US Const. amend. V. The Fourth Amendment provides: '. . . [N] or shall any state deprive any person of life, liberty, or property, without due process of law'. US Const. amend. XIV, sec. 1. The Fifth Amendment also prohibits compelled self-incrimination. Although this constitutional protection is of limited relevance to Internet communications since online content is not compelled, it does affect whether an individual could be compelled to produce an encryption key via compelled testimony. Brenner (n 28) 255–56.

73 *International Shoe Inc v Washington* 326 US 310, 316 (1945).

74 Damon C. Andrews and John M. Newman, 'Personal jurisdiction and choice of law in the cloud' (2013) 73 *Maryland Law Review* 313, 354–60.

75 *Zippo Mfg Co v Zippo Dot Com Inc* 952 F Supp 1119, 1124–25 (WD Pa 1997); *ALS Scan Inc v Digital Serv Consultants Inc* 293 F3d 707, 714 (4th Cir 2002); *Cybersell Inc v Cybersell Inc* 130 F3d 414, 419 (9th Cir 1997).

76 See Joel R. Reidenberg, 'Technology and internet jurisdiction' (2005) 153 *University of Pennsylvania Law Review* 1951; Kevin F. King, 'Personal jurisdiction, internet commerce, and privacy: the pervasive legal consequences of modern geolocational technologies' (2011) 21 *The Albany Law Journal of Science & Technology* 61, 64; TiTi Nguyen, 'A survey of personal jurisdiction based on internet activity: a return to tradition' (2004) 19 *Berkeley Technology Law Journal* 519, 539–42. Courts have been similarly critical. *Best Van Lines Inc v Walker* 490 F3d 239, 252 (2d Cir 2007); *Boschetto v Hansing* 539 F3d 1011, 1016 (9th Cir 2008).

77 *Calder v Jones* 465 US 783, 789 (1984).

78 Andrews and Newman (n 74) 359; McKeown (n 2) 146.

actions were sufficiently purposeful towards the forum to establish minimum contacts such that the exercise of jurisdiction would be consistent with traditional notions of fair play and substantial justice.[79] Some employ a version of the *Zippo* test that merges the original categorical approach with the flexible due process standards of *International Shoe*, finding jurisdiction proper when a defendant has intentionally engaged in business with or directed their content towards someone in the state through the Internet.[80] Nonetheless, the effects test also retains considerable vitality, especially in the context of intentional torts online.[81]

New technological developments in Internet technology may complicate personal jurisdiction doctrine even further. The availability of geo-locational technologies that can be used to tailor online content to the needs of particular jurisdictions may make it more difficult for defendants to avoid being subject to jurisdiction wherever their websites are viewed. Some commentators have argued, for example, that a defendant's failure to employ geo-locational technologies to limit her contact with a forum is relevant to whether she has purposefully availed herself of the forum such that she may be subject to personal jurisdiction there.[82] Others have proposed a more contextual analysis that considers costs, the burden on expressive content and the relevance of geography to the conduct in question.[83] Future disputes are also likely to focus on the applicability of traditional approaches to personal jurisdiction to cloud computing.[84]

3.3 Equality and internet governance

Viewed as a whole, the varied approaches taken by US federal courts in dealing with the uncertainties of new technologies seem to have worked well in some areas, but not in others. For example, federal courts have countered overreach by Congress in the area of content regulation through the application of robust free-speech protections. Privacy protection, however, has been hampered by the third-party doctrine. In part, this may be a story of institutional competence. Regulation has been most effective, and most coherent, when Congress and the courts have been engaged in a dialogue with one another in ways that have drawn on their respective institutional strengths – that is, with the courts articulating principles of general applicability and Congress providing forward-looking precision.

However, even in the area of free speech, judicial protection of constitutional rights on the Internet has lacked the kind of comprehensive framework that will be needed to deal with future challenges in this area. This chapter argues that the human right to equality could be a helpful framework for understanding the ways in which new technologies present challenges to the protection of individual

79 Perritt (n 35) 1136–37.

80 *ALS Scan* (n 75); *Toys 'R' Us Inc v Step Two SA* 318 F3d 446, 452 (3d Cir 2003).

81 *Mavrix Photo Inc v Brand Technologies Inc* 647 F3d 1218, 1231 (9th Cir 2011).

82 Reidenburg (n 76) 1962.

83 King (n 76) 89.

84 Andrews and Newman (n 74).

rights. The frame of equality could reorient courts on the effect of online conduct on individual users, as well as the importance of access to the Internet.

3.3.1 Institutional competence

Assessing the role of the courts in regulating constitutional rights online inevitably raises the question of whether courts or Congress are better suited to respond to the challenges and opportunities presented by new technologies. Orin Kerr, for example, counsels against an 'aggressive judicial role' in the interpretation of Fourth Amendment law to new technology, at least when such technology is in flux.[85] He maintains that Congress should provide the primary rules for law enforcement in the context of new technologies because it is more nimble and better informed, able to develop precise rules that can anticipate technological developments in ways that backward-looking adjudication cannot, and better poised to revise those rules as technology evolves.[86] According to Kerr, judicially crafted rules do not provide clarity when the relevant factual context changes rapidly, both because such rules are highly fact dependent and because technology may have evolved considerably by the time an issue reaches a court.[87] Others add that constitutional courts, in particular, may be reluctant to change quickly given the importance of ensuring the law remains consistent and stable,[88] while legislatures are better at developing novel solutions and innovating quickly.[89]

Other scholars have emphasized the institutional advantages courts enjoy in addressing the challenges of new technologies. Daniel Solove, for example, maintains that courts have a better chance at getting the technology right precisely because they view cases ex post, once the factual record has been well developed.[90] Solove argues that the statutory rules Congress has created are neither clearer nor more comprehensive than the judicial development of Fourth Amendment law.[91] Congress is as reluctant as courts to update rules, and they are not necessarily better informed.[92] Other commentators have cautioned against judicial deference because of the strong role courts play as guardians of individual rights and in protecting those rights from the tyranny of the majority.[93]

As Solove and Kerr acknowledge, however, Internet regulation is not an

85 Orin S. Kerr, 'The Fourth Amendment and new technologies: constitutional myths and the case for caution' (2004) 102 *Michigan Law Review* 801, 805.

86 ibid 807.

87 ibid 862, 868.

88 Thomas Fetzer and Christopher S. Yoo, 'New technologies and constitutional law, public law and legal theory' Research Paper No. 13–30, 17. There may also be greater costs associated with courts getting it wrong with respect to new technologies because it is harder to overturn constitutional interpretations than to amend statutes. Tokson (n 47) 595–96.

89 Tokson (n 47) 643.

90 Solove (n 47) 768.

91 ibid 766 (characterizing the statutory framework as 'an uneven fabric of protections that is riddled with holes and that has weak protections in numerous places').

92 ibid 770, 772.

93 Fetzer and Yoo (n 88) 18.

'either/or' situation but rather one in which both Congress and the courts play important roles.[94] Thus, the relevant question is not whether Congress or courts should regulate but rather how to structure the interaction between the two branches. Inter-branch regulatory efforts appear to have been more successful when courts either provide general principles that constitute a backdrop for later congressional regulation, or respond to and review prior congressional action. For example, decisions articulating robust constitutional principles such as *Berger* and *Katz* provided a backdrop against which Congress was able to regulate to provide further clarity and specificity.[95]

Similarly, in the context of the First Amendment, the Court responded to congressional legislation regulating indecent content online by reiterating general principles and requiring Congress to return to the drawing board, which it did several times. Congress is then able to legislate both in response to decisions by the Court establishing robust frameworks for legislative action[96] and to fill in gaps left by court decisions not to extend rights.[97] By providing general frameworks that can guide legislative action and reviewing such action to ensure its constitutionality, courts foster greater inter-branch dialogue and thereby promote more effective regulatory outcomes.

Courts have been less successful, in contrast, when they respond to the challenges of new technologies by providing legislative-like rules – precise, ex ante rules oriented towards guiding prospective conduct. Although such an approach may offer much needed clarity, it can also undermine rather than enable legislative regulation. For example, although Congress responded to gaps left by the third-party doctrine by passing legislation restoring privacy protection for financial, credit, educational, cable television and video rental records otherwise vulnerable to disclosure,[98] such a piecemeal approach inherently addresses only the symptoms of a more fundamental problem. Instead of providing general guidance regarding how Congress should identify private conduct, the courts effectively eliminated a broad swathe of conduct from the ambit of the Fourth Amendment and left Congress to fill the gaps in a limited fashion that does not ultimately address the underlying problem the third-party doctrine poses for the transmission of knowledge and information in the digital age.

Recent developments in the area of net neutrality regulation provide a useful example for how this dialogue between courts and other branches of government can promote better decision-making. In January 2014, the DC Circuit struck down the Federal Communications Commission's (FCC) Open Internet Order.[99] This order required broadband service providers to be transparent about their network management practices and terms of their broadband services, and

94 Solove (n 47) 773; Kerr (n 85) 849–56.

95 Solove (n 47) 776 ('The Court laid down the basic principles and then let Congress work out the specifics').

96 Kerr (n 85) 849–50.

97 ibid 855–56; Solove (n 47) 757–58.

98 Solove (n 47) 757–58.

99 *Verizon v Federal Communications Commission* 740 F3d 623, 659 (DC Cir 2014).

prohibited them from blocking or engaging in unreasonable discrimination with respect to lawful Internet content. The court vacated all but the transparency provisions of the order as outside the authority of the FCC.[100]

The FCC's response to the decision was to open a new rule-making proceeding and invite public comment on a proposed set of net neutrality rules, including on the issue of whether the FCC should revise its position on how it classified broadband providers.[101] The decision that emerged from that process, which classified broadband providers as common carriers,[102] thus benefited from extensive public comment and engagement with industry. The DC Circuit's approach – which was not to rewrite the regulation but instead to require the FCC to return to the drawing board to get it right – promoted significant deliberation and input, including by the public, on an order with important implications for individual rights online.

3.3.2 Equality online

A second factor contributing to inconsistencies in constitutional jurisprudence regarding the impact of new Internet technologies on individual rights has been the absence of a comprehensive and coherent frame that more systematically accounts for both the subordinating and empowering effects of new technology. A frame can be understood as a way of understanding a problem and justifying choices with respect to outcomes.[103] Frames may be influenced by, among other things, the legal origins of a particular area of law, the choice of metaphors a court uses to understand the issue and the values it relies on to choose between alternative interpretations. In each of the areas of constitutional regulation of the Internet, different frames govern.

In the context of the First Amendment, the frame has typically been one of limited governmental interference enabling a 'marketplace of ideas' in which the appropriate response to harmful speech is 'more speech'.[104] For the Fourth Amendment, it has been at times property, at other times secrecy, and sometimes both.[105] For due process challenges, the touchstone for regulation has typically

100 ibid 655.

101 Jon Sallet, 'The process of governance: the FCC and the open internet order' (2 March 2015) http://www.fcc.gov/blog/process-governance-fcc-open-internet-order (last accessed 9 August 2015) (noting that the FCC received nearly four million comments during the open Internet rule-making process).

102 *In the Matter of Protecting and Promoting the Open Internet* FCC 15–24 (26 February 2015) para 331.

103 Molly Land, 'Human rights frames in IP contests' in Rochelle C. Dreyfuss and César Rodríguez Garavito (eds), *Balancing Wealth and Health: Global Law and the Battle over Intellectual Property and Access to Medicines in Latin America* (Oxford University Press 2014) 276, 280.

104 Cedric Merlin Powell, 'The mythological marketplace of ideas: RAV, Mitchell, and beyond' (1995) 12 *Harvard Blackletter Law Journal* 1, 1–2.

105 Kerr (n 85) 809–27 (discussing the way in which Fourth Amendment doctrine incorporates property concepts through the doctrine of reasonableness and the way in which this has persisted even post-*Katz*).

been the idea of fairness.[106] Frames may lose their relevance when the fundamental factual assumptions upon which they are built are called into question by technological developments. The continued influence of property law concepts, as Kerr notes, makes it difficult to contend with the impact of new technologies through the Fourth Amendment doctrine because of the way in which new technologies 'destabilize the relationship between property and privacy'.[107]

Similarly, Solove argues that the 'secrecy paradigm' of the Fourth Amendment becomes less helpful when basic assumptions about what is 'secret' change.[108] 'Secrecy' takes on a new meaning when we routinely send private correspondence to third parties without restricting their ability to access that content or install cameras that record our conduct on public sidewalks. In addition, considerations of fairness in measuring both the extent to which a defendant can anticipate harm in a particular jurisdiction and the burden he or she experiences in having to litigate in the forum can be altered radically when the relevant activity occurs in cyberspace.[109]

This chapter proposes the international human right to equality as a potential frame for thinking about how to regulate the Internet in ways that protect a fuller range of individual rights and interests online. One of the challenges of protecting constitutional rights under US law is the fragmentation of this protection among various frames. Having multiple different frames for each area of constitutional adjudication makes it difficult to account for harms that fall outside each frame, as well as the impact that decisions made in one frame can have in others.

Although the legal impact of international human rights law is limited in US courts,[110] the international human right to equality might nonetheless be a helpful frame with which scholars, advocates and, perhaps, eventually also courts could understand and evaluate the benefits and harms to rights of developments associated with new technologies, including those that do not necessarily fall within an established frame. The human right to equality can be helpful in two critical ways. First, this frame better recognizes the significance of access to the Internet in promoting the realization of rights, a harm that otherwise falls outside of current approaches under US constitutional law. Second, the frame of equality would serve to focus the discussion on the needs and experiences of the user with respect to both speech and privacy online, experiences which are often obscured by an emphasis on speakers and intermediaries.

106 Earl M. Maltz, 'Visions of fairness: the relationship between jurisdiction and choice of law' (1988) 30 *Arizona Law Review* 751, 764.

107 Kerr (n 85) 827.

108 Solove (n 47) 751.

109 Ryan J. Hunt and others, 'Achieving personal jurisdiction using internet contacts: the need to establish a unified standard' (2008) 18 *Southern Law Journal* 139, 146–51; Martin H. Redish, 'Of new wine and old bottles: personal jurisdiction, the internet, and nature of constitutional evolution' (1998) 38 *Jurimetrics* 575, 604.

110 See generally Richard B. Lillich, 'International human rights law in U.S. courts' (1993) 2 *Journal of Transnational Law & Policy* 1, 19; see also Ernest A. Young, 'Universal jurisdiction, the Alien Tort Statute, and transnational public-law litigation after *Kiobel*' (2015) 64 *Duke Law Journal* 1023, 1057–64.

First, the use of an equality frame may be helpful simply in orienting courts on the importance of the ability to access the Internet on a basis of equality in allowing individuals to fulfill other citizenship rights. Because US anti-discrimination law emphasizes the protection of individuals from intentional discrimination,[111] it does not provide a constitutional basis for responding to harms associated with lack of access to the Internet. International human rights law, in contrast, encompasses both the right to be free from discrimination and an affirmative entitlement to equality,[112] and it prohibits not only intentional discrimination but also actions that have the effect of imposing disproportionate burdens.[113] In addition, the human right to equality is not limited to addressing status-based harms but extends a guarantee of equality to all individuals regardless of group membership.[114]

Because it is more robust than US anti-discrimination law, international human rights law provides a basis for recognizing the role that access to the Internet increasingly plays in allowing individuals to realize a range of other rights. Today, access to the Internet is essential not only for the rights to education and to participate in culture, but also for the right to work and for economic self-sufficiency—it is an essential tool for entrepreneurs and farmers, as well as for anyone seeking employment, government services or public benefits. Given the vast quantity of knowledge and culture that is mediated through the Internet, access to this particular technology warrants special attention under human rights law. Moreover, even if there is no right to the Internet as such, international human rights law certainly protects at the very least the means of communication both as an aspect of the human right to free expression and as a critical precondition for other rights.[115]

For US courts, the international human rights to equality and non-discrimination may also offer a rationale for interpreting federal statutes in ways that promote access rather than exclusion. The *Charming Betsy* canon of construction counsels US courts to interpret federal statutes in ways that are not inconsistent with the United States' treaty obligations.[116] The International Covenant on

111 Although US statutory and constitutional employment law prohibits both intentional discrimination (disparate treatment) and practices that have disproportionate burdens on minority groups (disparate impact), it is more difficult to succeed on a claim of disparate impact. *Ricci v DeStefano* 557 US 557 578–79 (2009) (discussing steps for pursuing a disparate impact claim).

112 International Covenant on Civil and Political Rights, opened for signature 19 December 1966, 999 UNTS 171 (entered into force 23 March 1976); International Covenant on Economic, Social and Cultural Rights, opened for signature 16 December 1966, 993 UNTS 3 (entered into force 3 January 1976).

113 Gillian MacNaughton, 'Untangling equality and non-discrimination to promote the right to health care for all' (2009) 11(2) *Health and Human Rights Journal* 47, 55.

114 ibid 51; Stephanie Farrior, 'Introduction' in Stephanie Farrior (ed.), *Equality and Non-Discrimination Under International Law* (Ashgate Publishing 2015) 1, 2.

115 Molly Land, 'Toward an international law of the internet' (2013) 54 *Harvard International Law Journal* 393, 394.

116 *Murray v Schooner Charming Betsy* (1804) 6 US (2 Cranch) 64; see David Cole, 'The idea of humanity: human rights and immigrants' rights' (2006) 37 *Columbia Human Rights Law Review*

Civil and Political Rights (ICCPR), which the United States ratified in 1992,[117] requires states to respect and to ensure that individuals have both freedom of access and freedom of choice with respect to the means of communication.[118] Using the *Charming Betsy* canon, US courts could rely on the ICCPR to interpret the Americans with Disabilities Act (ADA) to better ensure the ability of individuals with disabilities to access information online. Although the ADA prohibits discrimination against disabled individuals in any 'place of public accommodation',[119] some courts have found that cyberspace is neither itself a 'place of public accommodation' under the ADA nor a place with a nexus to a place of public accommodation sufficient to trigger application of the ADA.[120] As a result, retailers with Internet websites are not required to make these sites accessible for individuals with disabilities. An equality framework would not only orient courts on the impact that lack of access can have on the ability of individuals to realize their rights, but also provide a legal basis for interpreting statutes in ways that promote greater access for marginalized groups.

Second, a focus on equality could also reorient discussions about freedom of expression to better account for the needs and experiences of individual users. This is particularly important in the context of online speech. Currently, far from treating online and offline speech in an equivalent manner, US law provides individuals with less protection from harmful speech online. In the offline environment, publishers are responsible under common-law principles for the distribution of tortious material, even if written by others.[121] The responsibility of publishers does not impose limits on speech itself, but it does limit how widely such speech can be circulated, thus minimizing its harm. With respect to the Internet, however, Section 230 of the CDA protects online content distributors from responsibility for the speech they distribute, providing that they shall not be considered to be the publisher or speaker of the content they distribute, as long as they are not involved in the creation of the content itself.[122]

Although US law treats online speech more protectively than offline speech, tortious speech online can actually be more harmful than its offline equivalent. As Danielle Citron has noted, key features of the online environment make

627, 645–53. The canon is typically used to interpret statutes; its application to constitutional interpretation is contested. Roger P. Alford, 'Foreign relations as a matter of interpretation: the use and abuse of Charming Betsy' (2006) 67 *Ohio State Law Journal* 1339, 1342–43.

117 Status of Ratifications of the International Covenant on Civil and Political Rights, UN Treaty Collection https://treaties.un.org/pages/viewdetails.aspx?chapter=4&src=treaty&mtdsg_no=iv-4&lang=en (last accessed 9 August 2015).

118 Land (n 115) 418–26.

119 42 USC § 12182(a).

120 *Access Now v Southwest Airlines* 227 F Supp 2d 1312, 1321 (SD Fla 2002). Other courts have reached the opposite conclusion. *National Fed'n Blind v Target Corp* 452 F Supp 2d 946, 955 (ND Cal 2006).

121 *Jones v Dirty World Entertainment Recordings LLC* 755 F3d 398, 407 (2014).

122 47 USC § 230; *Jones v Dirty World Entertainment Recordings LLC* (n 121). When the harmful content violates intellectual property policies, in contrast, US law provides intermediaries with safe harbor from liability only if they remove the content, once properly notified. 17 USC § 512.

destructive speech more likely.[123] Moreover, the consequences of tortious speech are exacerbated in the online context because speech is far more easily shared online[124] and also extraordinarily persistent; once shared, it may be nearly impossible to identify and remove all instances. Further, the harms of online harassment are considerable, forcing its victims – often women and people of color – to retreat from online engagement, which in many instances may be their chosen livelihood.[125] Rather than a forum for engagement and dialogue, cyberspace can become, for those who are targeted, a 'place where existing gender inequalities are amplified and entrenched'.[126]

Focusing on the human right to equality would counsel approaches to online speech that adequately attend to the unique features, and impact, of harmful speech online. This is not to say that we need different rules for Internet speech. Indeed, if anything, it may mean revisiting whether we should treat online speech more protectively than offline speech. Nor would it require reduction in the robust protections that freedom of expression enjoys under US law. It may, however, counsel greater attention to the experience of victims of harmful speech in the online context.

For example, in considering the definition of 'true threat' in the *Elonis* case, the Supreme Court was asked to choose between a subjective or objective standard for determining whether a statement is a threat. A subjective standard would focus on the perspective of the speaker, while an objective standard would focus on the perspective of a listener. Given the prevalence and harm associated with online threats, especially for women and people of color, an equality framework would counsel the adoption of a standard that included the perspectives of those who experience the speech, at the very least as part of the context in which the speech occurs.[127] The Supreme Court declined to answer the question fully, holding only that some consideration of the defendant's mental state was required.[128]

Viewing online speech issues through the lens of equality would not require

123 Danielle Keats Citron, *Hate Crimes in Cyberspace* (Harvard University Press 2014) 57–66.

124 ibid 66.

125 Mary Anne Franks, 'Unwilling avatars: idealism and discrimination in cyberspace' (2011) 20 *Columbia Journal of Gender & Law* 224, 229.

126 ibid 228.

127 The recklessness standard articulated by Justice Kagan during oral argument in *Elonis* may be a way to accommodate both perspectives. Oral argument, *Elonis v United States* No. 13-983, Supreme Court of the United States (1 December 2014) 8. The court did not address the adequacy of such a standard because the issue had not been briefed or argued below. *Elonis* (n 26) 2012.

128 *Elonis* (n 26) 2012–2013. Justice Roberts, a justice likely to champion a standard protective of First Amendment values, emphasized the importance of context in several examples during oral argument in *Elonis*, including examples of teenagers making statements in a chat room and citing Eminem lyrics. Amy Howe, 'Court difficult to read on Facebook threats: in plain English' (1 December 2014) SCOTUSblog http://www.scotusblog.com/2014/12/court-difficult-to-read-on-facebook-threats-in-plain-english/ (last accessed 9 August 2015); Oral argument, *Elonis v United States* (n 127) 10, 32, 47.

elimination of the safe harbor intermediaries currently enjoy with respect to the speech they transmit and display. Intermediary liability itself raises a host of problems for the protection of human rights. Most significantly, imposing liability on intermediaries for the content they display would represent a significant move towards privatization of speech regulation in the online environment, together with the lack of transparency and accountability that privatization entails. Such a move would also have significant chilling effects, particularly given that smaller intermediaries may have neither the resources nor the incentives needed to police content carefully. At the same time, while broad intermediary liability would not be a net positive for human rights, there may be ways to tailor intermediary liability to address some of the worst kinds of abuses. Citron argues, for example, that there may be ways for Congress to revise Section 230 to withdraw protections from bad actors who make encouraging harmful speech into a business model.[129]

An orientation on individual users may also help courts understand and better grapple with the challenges posed by new legal questions, such as whether search engines have First Amendment rights in the search results they generate. Currently, most of the debate has focused on the rights of the Internet content providers; a human rights approach, however, would counsel emphasis on the rights of users.[130] Finding that Internet content providers have First Amendment rights in search results and other display of content would have rights-promoting effects, since it would make it more difficult for governments to regulate Internet content providers. At the same time, however, such a decision would also make it more difficult for the government to regulate content providers in ways that are needed in order to ensure the protection of human rights. In the context of net neutrality, where First Amendment arguments have also been raised,[131] a perspective focused on users would likely embrace the value of government regulation in promoting access on a basis of equality and preventing unreasonable and distorting effects of discrimination.

A reorientation on users through the frame of equality may also counsel consideration of doctrinal shifts in some areas of Fourth Amendment jurisprudence and, in particular, the third-party doctrine. For example, the human right to equality encompasses a dignitary element that may require sufficient privacy for the full development of an individual's personality. The bright line rule of the third-party doctrine neglects the extent to which disclosure of non-content data

129 Citron (n123) 177.

130 See James Grimmelmann, 'Speech engines' (2014) 98 *Minnesota Law Review* 868, 893–907 (suggesting an 'advisor' theory focused on the interests of users as an approach distinct from the current editor and conduit theories regarding search-engine speech).

131 One of the arguments asserted by Verizon in its challenge to the FCC's first net neutrality order was that the order violated its constitutional rights because Verizon exercised editorial discretion over the content in its network. Brief for Appellant, *Verizon v FCC* 740 F3d 623 (DC Cir 2014) (No. 11-1355) 43; Meredith Shell, Note, 'Network neutrality and broadband service providers' First Amendment right to free speech' (2014) 66 *Federal Communications Law Journal* 303, 308–09.

can nonetheless have significant dignitary harms by revealing information about the nature and extent of our communications. Moreover, from the perspective of the user, the doctrine also has disproportionate effects on the privacy of communications online when compared to equivalent communications in the offline context, which is in tension with the obligations of Article 19 of the ICCPR.[132]

A human rights approach would also view the lower protection provided to foreign users with greater scrutiny[133] and is increasingly moving toward recognition of an obligation to respect the privacy of extraterritorial users.[134] Further, a human rights approach oriented on users would also counsel greater attention to the activities of non-state actors and their impact on the protection of individual rights, rather than focusing simply on the harms associated with governmental intrusion into individual rights.[135]

3.4 Conclusion

Although US federal courts have been effective in updating the individual constitutional protections to meet the demands of new technologies, their efforts in this respect have been hampered by the lack of a comprehensive theory for understanding the structural effects that new technologies have on individual rights. After providing an overview of some of the ways in which federal courts have regulated the Internet's effect on rights protected under the US Constitution, the chapter addresses arguments both about institutional competence and framing. It argues that effective protection of constitutional rights has been advanced best when courts and Congress engage in inter-branch dialogue, with courts either checking Congress's activity after the fact or establishing ex ante general principles against which Congress can legislate.

The chapter also argues that what is missing from constitutional adjudication of rights in the context of the Internet is a comprehensive understanding of

132 Land (n 115) 422–26 (Article 19 prohibits discrimination with respect to the mode of transmitting information and expression).

133 Although human rights law does not necessarily prohibit governments from treating individuals in disparate ways based on citizenship, it likely requires that such distinctions be justified and further a legitimate purpose and prohibits distinctions motivated by prejudice. Matthew Craven, 'Non-discrimination and equality' in Stephanie Farrior (ed.), *Equality and Non-Discrimination Under International Law* (Ashgate Publishing 2015) 105, 174.

134 Marko Milanovic, 'Human rights treaties and foreign surveillance: privacy in the digital age' (2015) 56 *Harvard International Law Journal* 81, 101–11; Peter Margulies, 'The NSA in Global perspective: surveillance, human rights, and international counterterrorism' (2014) 82 *Fordham Law Review* 2137, 2142–52; Anupam Chander and Molly Land, 'Introductory note to the General Assembly's resolution on the right to privacy in the digital age' (2014) 53 *International Law Materials* 727, 727.

135 The Fourth Amendment, as with much of US constitutional law, requires state action, which means that privacy violations by private actors are not cognizable as constitutional harms. McKeown (n 2) 162. Human rights law, in contrast, imposes obligations on the state to control the activities of private actors and prevent them from harming rights. Land (n 115) 444.

the impact of new technologies on individual rights. The chapter proposes the international human right to equality as a frame that might be used in judicial review of legislative policy in this area. Such a frame offers not only a means for recognizing the importance of access across a variety of rights but also a new orientation on the perspective of Internet users in developing and updating doctrines addressing the protection of rights online.

4 Freedom of expression in the internet

Main trends of the case law of the European Court of Human Rights

Joan Barata Mir and Marco Bassini***

4.1 Introduction: an historical background

The European Convention on Human Rights (ECHR) is the flagship treaty of the Council of Europe as the legal instrument that guarantees a European system (from Portugal to Russia and Turkey) for the common establishment and protection of basic human rights.[1] Article 10 of the ECHR establishes the fundamental right to freedom of expression. Generally inspired by Article 19 of the International Covenant on Civil and Political Rights, the formulation contained in the ECHR establishes a common general protection which is essentially in line with the different constitutional traditions within Europe.

Freedom of expression is, above all, a fundamental right which is rooted in the very origins of constitutionalism and the modern state. Since then, it has been at the baseline and fundamental element of any constitution that seeks to proclaim itself as democratic.

Article XI of the French Declaration of the Rights of Man and of the Citizen of 1789 established at the time that: '*La libre communication des pensées et des opinions est un des droits les plus précieux de l'Homme: tout Citoyen peut donc parler, écrire, imprimer librement, sauf à répondre de l'abus de cette liberté dans les cas déterminés par la Loi.*' It is also worth remembering the wording of its famous Article XVI, which states very clearly that: '*toute Société dans laquelle la garantie des droits n'est pas assurée . . . n'a pas de Constitution*'.

* Joan Barata Mir is the author of sections 4.1, 4.1.3, 4.1.4, section 4.2 and section 4.4.

** Marco Bassini is the author of section 4.1.1, 4.1.2 and section 4.3.

1 Article 10 states that: 1. 'Everyone has the right to freedom of expression. This right shall include freedom to hold opinions and to receive and impart information and ideas without interference by public authority and regardless of frontiers. This article shall not prevent States from requiring the licensing of broadcasting, television or cinema enterprises.
2. The exercise of these freedoms, since it carries with it duties and responsibilities, may be subject to such formalities, conditions, restrictions or penalties as are prescribed by law and are necessary in a democratic society, in the interests of national security, territorial integrity or public safety, for the prevention of disorder or crime, for the protection of health or morals, for the protection of the reputation or rights of others, for preventing the disclosure of information received in confidence, or for maintaining the authority and impartiality of the judiciary.'

This first recognition embraces two great principles that form the legal basis upon which the aforementioned constitutional provisions have been built and developed in various environments. First, freedom of expression is an essential fundamental right, directly linked to the ability of citizens to live and participate in a modern society and, secondly, the exercise of these rights by citizens must be duly respected, guaranteed and protected by the state and relevant public institutions.

The text and the basic elements of the constitutional provisions on the protection of freedom of expression have not changed substantially over the last 200 years on both sides of the Atlantic. However, the communications environment (i.e. the public sphere) of the twenty-first century is radically different from that which existed 150, 100 or even 50 years ago.

Historically, freedom of expression was born as an individual right designed to protect the activities of a small educated political *bourgeois* elite, which formed the core of what can be described as the 'public opinion' of the moment. In this historical context communication – at least political communication – was essentially written and available to only a minority of the population. At the same time, the idea that the state should protect the exercise of freedom of expression was understood only in the sense of absence of interference. After this seminal moment, the increasing emergence and abundance of a diverse number and variety of media, beyond the press, has created a public space for discussion that surely is far from the conceptions that were in the minds of Enlightenment thinkers and politicians in this first legal and conceptual approach to freedom of expression.

Television and radio led, in this sense, to an environment of 'massification' of communication, in which a relatively small number of powerful message issuers had the privileged capacity of shaping the conditions of formation of public opinion. Therefore, the communication model of the second half of the twentieth century, rather than relying on the dialogue and exchange of views by the elites of each society to control and influence the exercise of political power, has basically consisted of the mass production and consumption of audiovisual content previously prepared by a series of powerful 'voices' located in a social and economic preeminent position – usually in coordination with traditional state powers.

Although this system still prevails in our current societies in the twenty-first century, digitisation, media convergence and the increasing use of the internet as a new distribution platform have established a new communication paradigm in which the idea of verticality is gradually disappearing. This new virtual and networked public space is characterised by horizontal communication nodes, which engage in the global exchange of content without the intervention of traditional media intermediaries. This being said, it is also worth noting that states have not given up attempting to intervene and to try to shape and regulate the forging of public imagery, as well as the presence of large private corporations that control key elements of our new virtual communication processes (search engines, large content aggregators, internet service providers, holders of intellectual property rights, etc.).

Article 10 of the ECHR has in any event kept its original wording, drafted at the beginning of the second half of the twentieth century when conventional radio and television were just starting to gain some space within the public sphere in relation to the still dominant print media. However, its interpretation and application has had to adapt to the changes in the consumption of media and its impact on the political, social and cultural system.

4.1.1 The relevant parameter and the 'abuse clause'

Having said that the scope of application of the principle enshrined in Article 10 is very comprehensive while referring to media, it has been the triple-test encapsulated in paragraph 2 that has been the driving factor, and which has enabled the Court of Strasbourg to fine tune the protection of freedom of expression in its case-by-case scrutiny. While, in fact, this fundamental right is universally provided, those states with constitutional relevance still have room for 'manoeuvre' when it comes to defining the restrictions to which freedom of speech may be subject.

It was through setting this triple-test clause that the Strasbourg Court and the system of the Convention could produce the effect of fostering the level of freedom of speech and media freedom, most notably, as noted by Voorhoof,[2] in those countries which have joined the Council of Europe more recently after the fall of the Berlin Wall.

Being called to review domestic cases involving alleged restrictions on freedom of speech, the European Court of Human Rights (ECtHR) has assumed a supervisory role in this respect, in accordance with the view of the Convention as an additional layer of control over protection of human rights in Europe.[3] Such a supervisory role is even more important in light of the peculiar regard that modern constitutions pay to free speech as an essential precondition for democracy and the actual enjoyment of other fundamental rights, most notably of the political ones.

The enforcement of the triple-test, aimed at assessing whether the challenged interference was justified by 'social pressing needs', has therefore a key role in modelling the protection of freedom of speech in Europe. However, this does not prevent the signatories to the ECHR, through the case law developed by the ECtHR, to exercise their margin of appreciation even when it comes to regulating the scope of application of freedom of expression.

The triple-test relies on the second paragraph of Article 10, providing that the freedom in question may be subject to formalities, conditions, restrictions and penalties. These limitations may apply provided that they are 'prescribed by

2 See Dirk Voorhoof, 'Freedom of expression under the European human rights system' in Yves Haeck, Héctor Olàsolo, John Varvaele and Leo Zwaak (eds), *Inter-American and European Human Rights Journal* (Intersentia 2009) 3, 5.

3 Oreste Pollicino and Marco Bassini, 'Free speech, defamation and the limits to freedom of expression in the EU: a comparative analysis' in Andrej Savin and Jan Trzaskowski (eds), *Research Handbook on EU Internet Law* (Edward Elgar 2014) 508, 526.

law' and are 'necessary in a democratic society' to pursue legitimate aims, that is: 'in the interests of national security, territorial integrity or public safety, for the prevention of disorder or crime, for the protection of health or morals, for the protection of the reputation or rights of others, for preventing the disclosure of information received in confidence, or for maintaining the authority and impartiality of the judiciary'.

The Convention thus places a set of interests ('legitimate aims') at the same level as freedom of expression and so allows the latter to be limited for the sake of the former. This provision reflects the non-absolute protection afforded by the Convention and, generally speaking, in the European legal orders, to free speech. It goes without saying, however, that the balance required by the Convention must be respectful of the criteria laid down by Article 10.2. Whilst establishing that any restrictions on freedom of expression must have legal grounds (i.e. to be provided by law) reflects a distinguishing feature of the legal orders incorporating the principle of the rule of law (and guarantees legal certainty[4]), the requirement that restrictions are 'necessary in a democratic society' results, first of all, in a proportionality test.

Thus, when scrutinising whether the challenged restrictions were proportionate, the Court of Strasbourg has focused on two specific aspects, namely the nature and the intensity of the limitations. On one hand, then, the ECtHR has concentrated on the nature of the interference (whether prior restraints or penalties imposed ex post); on the other hand, however, the Court has taken into account the 'severity' of the restriction (e.g. the penalties imposed on the applicants).

As noted by Professor Barendt, although the scope of the possible limitations to freedom of expression looks fairly extensive, these 'exceptions must be narrowly construed'[5] and do not overcome the general 'presumption in favour of freedom of expression'.[6]

When exploring the degree of protection afforded by the case law developed by the ECtHR to freedom of expression, however, one cannot help considering also the impact in this regard of the abuse clause established by Article 17 of the ECHR.[7]

This provision, in fact, prohibits any acts aimed at the destruction of the rights and freedoms of third parties, even though formally these activities constitute an exercise of the rights and freedoms enshrined in the Convention.[8] This set of rights

4 Eric Barendt, *Freedom of Speech* (Oxford University Press 2007) 65.

5 ibid.

6 ibid.

7 Article 17 reads as follows: 'Nothing in this Convention may be interpreted as implying for any State, group or person any right to engage in any activity or perform any act aimed at the destruction of any of the rights and freedoms set forth herein or at their limitation to a greater extent than is provided for in the Convention.'

8 As pointed out by Mark Villiger, 'Article 17 ECHR and freedom of speech in Strasbourg practice' in Josep Casadevall, Egbert Myjer, Michael O'Boyle and Anna Austin (eds), *Freedom of Expression: Essays in Honour of Nicolas Bratza* (Wolf Legal Publishers 2012) 321, 322, the preparatory materials which led to the drafting of the Convention reveal that art 17 was intended to prevent any totalitarian tendencies from taking place in Europe.

and freedoms, in other words, cannot be exercised contrary to the ECHR itself. This clause finds its roots in the aftermath of the Second World War, when the Convention was drafted; against this background, the main purpose of the abuse clause was to preserve the functioning of democratic institutions. To a certain degree, Article 17 reflects a view of the European legal order as a militant democracy, but one that nevertheless has not managed to prevail in the legal system of the Council of Europe, which instead incorporates a model of tolerant democracy.

Despite this general provision applying to all the rights and freedoms set forth by the Convention, most of the cases where this clause has been enforced deal with the protection of freedom of expression. Most notably, it is with respect to cases of hate speech that the Court of Strasbourg has declined to review whether national authorities had actually infringed the Convention.

Established with the purpose of preventing the spreading of political parties and movements that had been banned throughout Europe, the clause has served many times to exclude protection under the ECHR for expressions inciting the most serious forms of racial hatred and violence. These decisions bring to light the strict connection between the normative tools provided by the ECHR and the protection of democracy from any threats that could stem from the exercise of the same rights and freedoms established by the Convention.

The Court of Strasbourg (and formerly the Commission) has referred to Article 17 using different approaches. It should be pointed out that in most of the cases the Court has applied Article 17 in combination with Article 10.2 ECHR, in order to support the view that the inference at issue met the requirement of 'necessary in a democratic society'.[9] As a source of moral suasion, then, the abuse clause has entered, even indirectly, in the balance to be drawn by the ECtHR between freedom of speech and other legitimate aims.

In other cases, the Court has enforced Article 17 directly, by excluding that the expressions at stake could enjoy the protection afforded by Article 10. As noted by Cannie and Voohroof,[10] this has resulted in the so-called 'guillotine effect'. The most significant judgments, in particular, have concerned Holocaust denial. Also, when approaching these cases the Court of Strasbourg has taken different paths: on one hand, enforcing Article 17 together with Article 10.2,[11] on the other, by giving direct application to Article 17.[12]

As pointed out,[13] the 'nonchalant' attitude of the Court of Strasbourg towards Article 17 has probably departed from the reasons that were originally behind the drafting of the abuse clause. The wide use made by the Court of this clause may

9 ibid 325.

10 Hannes Cannie and Dirk Voorhoof, 'The abuse clause and freedom of expression in the European Human Rights Convention' (2011) 29 *Netherlands Quarterly of Human Rights* 54, 58.

11 See *Lehideux v Isorni* Application no. 24662/94 (ECtHR, 1998); *Witzsch v Germany* Application No. 41448/98 (ECtHR, 2009).

12 See *Garaudy v France* Application no. 12184/86 (ECtHR, 2003).

13 See Cannie and Voorhoof (n 10) 62–63, who state that: 'the Court has explicitly associated the fight against anti-Semitism and racism as such with the fundamental values protected by the Convention'.

trigger consequences in respect of the view of the European legal order as 'tolerant' (as opposed to 'militant') democracy that is embodied in the Convention. Thus, a tool that was born with the purpose of protecting the democratic system in the aftermath of the experience of totalitarian regimes is likely to determine, where it is not properly handled by the Court, undesirable effects which could impact on the efficiency of the supervisory role that the Court is tasked with when it comes to fundamental rights, including freedom of expression.

These remarks are even more precious in light of the recent developments that, by the use of the internet, have connected people from various jurisdictions when exercising their freedom of speech.

4.1.2 Against the First Amendment: a European model of protection of freedom of speech

Although the ECHR and, most notably, Article 10 constitutes the most prominent source of the protection of freedom of expression in Europe, one should also consider the influence of at least two very crucial factors. First, in order to broaden the perspective on the European position, the entry into force of the Charter of Fundamental Rights of the European Union as primary law of the European Union has made the provisions protecting freedom of expression binding at the level of EU law. This resulted in making any acts adopted by the EU institutions, mainly dealing with economic issues, bound to respect the quasi-constitutional parameter mandating protection of free speech. Even though the dialogue between the ECtHR and the Court of Justice of the European Union has allowed the latter to avail itself, at least in the reasoning, of the well-established case law of the former, the incorporation of the Charter has nevertheless marked a significant advancement in this respect.

On the other hand, the more the world has become global, the more protecting freedom of expression has urged the adoption of a worldwide approach. In this respect, the rise of the internet in particular has resulted in various legal issues calling into question the degree of protection of free speech. Several cases have brought to light the problem of reconciling the quasi-absolute concept encapsulated in the First Amendment to the US Constitution[14] and the more limited protection afforded under the ECHR. This point is at the heart of several cases where different views and models of protection were potentially conflicting, exacerbating jurisdictional (prescriptive and adjudicative) issues.[15] The *Yahoo! v Licra* saga can definitely be considered as a leading example in this respect.[16]

In this case Yahoo!, a US-based internet service provider, was ordered by a

14 See further Barendt (n. 4) 48.

15 See Oreste Pollicino and Marco Bassini, 'The law of the internet: between globalisation and localisation' in Miguel Poiares Maduro, Kaarlo Tuori and Suvi Sankari (eds), *Transnational Law: Rethinking European Law and Legal Thinking* (Cambridge University Press 2014) 346; see also Uta Khol, *Jurisdiction and the Internet* (Cambridge University Press 2007).

16 See amongst others Tribunal de Grande Instance de Paris (22 May 2000); *Yahoo! Inc v LICRA and UEJF* 433 F3d 1199 United States Court of Appeals (9th Cir 2006).

French court to block a website for the sale of Nazi memorabilia (considered as a criminal offence under the French Penal Code). The internet service provider refused to comply with the order, claiming that the French court had no jurisdiction and that, in any cases, blocking a website constituted an interference with the freedom of speech protected by the First Amendment to the US Constitution. Finally, it was for a US court to hold that French jurisdiction was proper and the court was legitimate when imposing such a restriction. Here, the possible risk of a clash between different views rooted in the European and US positions is at its highest.

It is worth considering another important factor. Drawing attention to the European position, it is well known that the European Union, at least in its origins, was intended to create an economic community only. However, in more recent times the European Union has acquired a new supranational dimension as a 'non-economic' community, even though its road towards a constitutional identity is still very long.[17] In addition, the incorporation of the Charter of Fundamental Rights of the European Union into EU primary law[18] resulted in ranking freedom of expression (under Article 11) amongst the fundamental rights formally protected by the European Union. As a consequence, the Court of Justice of the European Union started to deliver remarkable decisions when interpreting EU law, by acting as a quasi-constitutional court and opening the doors to significant advancements in the wake of a process of emancipation from the original economic nature of the European Union.

That said, it is true that many differences characterise the rule-making process of the Strasbourg and Luxembourg courts. The main point to be emphasised lies with the fact that the European Court of Human Rights acts as a judge of fundamental rights, whilst the Court of Justice is tasked, most notably with (but not limited to) the assessment of conformity with EU law. This aspect, however, has not prevented the Court of Luxemburg from delivering decisions that, despite their prima facie focus, bring with them significant implications for the protection of freedom of speech. This has occurred especially in recent times by reason of the development of the internet and, more generally, new technologies.

These advancements have urged the Court to find new solutions to balance fundamental rights. Therefore, the Court of Justice has rendered an overwhelming judgment in the *Google Spain* case, offering crucial implications as far as the protection of freedom of expression is concerned. However, this perspective can be reversed: how would have the Court of Luxemburg considered the *Delfi* case,[19] when it was up to the Court of Strasbourg to review whether a violation of Article 10 of the ECHR had in fact occurred? [20]

17 See also Peter Roth, 'Freedom of expression and EU law' in Casadevall, Myjer, O'Boyle and Austin *Freedom of Expression: Essays in Honour of Nicolas Bratza* (n 8).

18 See Niilo Jääskinen, 'The place of the EU Charter within the tradition of fundamental and human rights' in Sonia Morando-Foadi and Lucy Vickers, *Fundamental Rights in the EU: A Matter for Two Courts* (Hart Publishing 2015) 11.

19 *Delfi v Estonia* Application no. 6465/09 (ECtHR 2013); Grand Chamber (ECtHR, 2015).

20 See Case C–131/12 Google Spain SL and Google Inc v Agencia Española de Protección de Datos

It would therefore be misleading to claim that an exhaustive analysis of the European view concerning the ECHR can be carried out without considering this peculiar intertwining of the European legal orders. Since the perspective of human rights protection rests no longer exclusively in the hands of the Strasbourg Court, the Court of Justice of the European Union should properly be considered as a new play-maker in this regard. As this role has emerged only recently (as a reaction to the renewed EU legal framework), the relevant decisions most notably deal with cases involving protection of freedom of expression in the digital world. Therefore, a question arising from this background may be whether, depending upon the respective legal order, the switch to the digital environment has led to extending or narrowing the degree of protection of free speech.[21]

4.1.3 *The importance of the connection between freedom of expression and the democratic principle*

The first fundamental question to be highlighted in relation to the protection of freedom of expression by Article 10 of the ECHR is its direct connection with the democratic principle. The jurisprudence of the European Court of Human Rights (ECtHR) has particularly emphasised the crucial role that the free flow of ideas and information plays in the construction and development of a fully democratic society. Probably the most illustrative decision in this regard is *Handyside v United Kingdom*,[22] in which the Court established a jurisprudence which has been maintained in many judgments even to this day. According to this decision (at para. 49), freedom of expression is in any democratic society 'one of the basic conditions for its progress and for the development of every man'.

This phrase sums up the double dimension that freedom of expression has in European legal systems. On the one hand, through freedom of expression individuals can express, share and compare their thoughts, opinions and ideas, as well as have access to and disseminate relevant information. On the other hand, protection of freedom of expression affects in more 'objective' terms the democratic quality of the overall political, institutional, cultural or economic system, therefore transcending a purely subjective perspective. Only in a society in which there is a plurality of voices that participate in an accessible and dynamic public sphere is there room for the development and improvement of democracy.

(AEPD) and Mario Costeja González CJEU (13 May 2014). See also Joined Cases C–293/12 and C–593/12 *Digital Rights Ireland and Others* CJEU (8 April 2014). For a comment see Oreste Pollicino and Marco Bassini, 'The Luxembourg sense of the internet: towards a right to digital privacy?' in Giuliana Ziccardi Capaldo (ed.), *The Global Community: Yearbook of International Law and Jurisprudence 2014, Vol. 1* (Oxford University Press 2014).

21 Oreste Pollicino, 'European judicial dialogue and protection of fundamental rights in the new digital environment: an attempt at emancipation and reconciliation: the case of freedom of Speech' in Morando-Foadi and Vickers, *Fundamental Rights in the EU: A Matter for Two Courts* (n 18) 93. See also Oreste Pollicino, 'Internet nella giurisprudenza delle corti europee: prove di dialogo?' in Michele Nisticò and Paolo Passaglia (eds), *Internet e Costituzione* (Giappichelli 2013) 374.

22 *Handyside v United Kingdom* Application no. 5493/72 (1976) 1 EHRR 737 (ECtHR, 1976).

Freedom to express all kinds of ideas or opinions has been protected since the establishment of the so-called liberal state and regarding any form or type of communication – existing at that time or still to be invented. Constitutional and legal protection of freedom of expression can be explained by the power and influence that words – and, indeed, images, signs or symbols – have within societies. Speech can be an instrument of political criticism, questioning of values and social principles and which therefore can cause major embarrassment or even shock. Opinions and information can arouse strong feelings of rejection. In particular, those who hold public power may feel that their activities and legitimacy are put into question because of the public expression of a sharp critique. This can, of course, lead to the 'temptation' to establish and implement mechanisms to limit and even suppress certain voices or messages.

It is for this reason that the Court in *Handyside* emphasised the fact that freedom of expression not only covers 'information or ideas that are favourably received or regarded as inoffensive or as a matter of indifference, but also to those that offend, shock or disturb the state or any section of the population. Such are the demands of that pluralism, tolerance and broadmindedness without which there is no democratic society' (para 49). This triad of verbs (to) 'shock, disturb and offend' has been repeatedly cited by the Court, and has been marking the analysis parameters of which such restrictions have been subject to review.

It is also important to note that this level of reasoning of the Court is directly connected to one of the limits that all restrictions on freedom of expression should meet – according to Article 10(2) ECHR – which is the existence of a compelling social need in a democratic society. Thus, Article 10 of the ECHR will protect any expressive act that contributes to the strengthening and developing of the entire democratic system, putting aside its potential negative or disruptive effects for a given part of the society or even erosion of the legitimacy of certain powers or institutions. In other words, the Court does not hold a 'militant' concept of democracy.[23]

However, the ECtHR has developed a very clear body of case law that does declare a violation of Article 10 of the ECHR in those cases in which the expressions used may lead to a feeling of rejection and antagonism, for example if the language points at certain communities (for example, Islamic communities) as 'the enemy' or 'occupants' of a European territory that should be 're-conquered'.[24]

23 Moreover, the Court has held that in the case of opinions and information referring to the activity of public representatives, the level of permissibility should be the highest one, protecting even those attacks that may be considered outrageous, provocative and extravagant. In the important judgment in *Lingens v Austria* Application no. 9815/82 (1986) 8 EHRR 407, (ECtHR, 1986), the Court held that 'the limits of acceptable criticism are accordingly wider as regards a politician than as regards such as individual private' (para 42). In this sense, a political figure 'inevitably and knowingly lays himself open to close scrutiny of his every word and deed by both journalists and the public at large, and he must consequently display a greater degree of tolerance'.

24 *Soulas and Others v France* Application no. 15948/03 (ECtHR, 2008). In *Leroy v France* Application no. 36109/03 (ECtHR, 2008) the Court analysed a cartoon providing a satirical depiction of the 9/11 attacks on New York as a way to show, in the words of its author, the decline of American imperialism. In this case, the Court considered that the cartoon glorified the violent

At the same time, the ECtHR has stated with particular emphasis that the wording of such provisions protects 'speakers' from restrictive state interference yet, at the same time, imposes some positive obligations in order to safeguard media freedom and create the conditions for a real and effective exercise of such rights.[25] In this same sense, the ECtHR and, more broadly, the Council of Europe as a regional institution, have been declaring the importance of the adoption of national public policies aimed at creating and guaranteeing a plural media system in order to promote the existence of the widest range of information sources and independent viewpoints.[26]

4.1.4 The privatisation of freedom of expression in the digital world

The growing social importance of the internet is forcing a profound reconsideration of the industrial model of broadcast mass media, as well as the terms in which it conditions the process formation of public opinion.

More particularly, it is interesting to outline the progressive introduction of a communications model based on so-called 'peer production'. As stated by the internet scholar Yochai Benkler,[27] this idea describes a process of production of information or culture by a potentially large number of individuals whose actions are not subject to influence or coordination, either by capital or by dynamics of the market of communication corporations. The radical distinction between senders and receivers, especially marked during the second half of the twentieth century, has started to crumble, as well as the still-existing dominance of commercial media discourses compared with those who might be regarded as non-commercial. Thus, despite the continuing influence and power of traditional broadcast media, many modalities of communication of this post-industrial age will no longer be subject to centralised manufacturing, ultimately developing unprecedented mechanisms of democratic civic discourse.

In a very similar sense, communications scholar Manuel Castells[28] uses the term 'mass self-communication' to define communication systems or networks organised strictly horizontally, established by myriad individual subjects, and of multimodal nature, covering areas such as photo-sharing, joint creation of online encyclopedias, the circulation of music and movies, the deployment of networks of political activists and also the creation and dissemination of audiovisual

destruction of certain models of society and diminished the dignity of the victims, creating a feasible risk of public disorder, so that this kind of expressive conduct could not possibly fall under the scope of art 10 of the ECHR as well. (It must also be underlined that the cartoon was published in the Basque Country, where at that moment the terrorist group ETA was still active.)

25 *Özgur Gündem v Turkey* Application no. 23144/93 (ECtHR, 2000).

26 See the different Recommendations and other documents approved by the Council of Europe in this field: http://www.coe.int/t/dghl/standardsetting/media/Themes/Div_en.asp (last accessed 11 August 2015).

27 Yochai Benkler, *The Wealth of Networks: How Social Production Transforms Markets and Freedom* (Yale University Press 2006).

28 Manuel Castells, *Communication Power* (Oxford University Press 2009).

content. Such networks are in contrast to those that organise conventional radio and television, in which communication flows strictly from the top down.

It seems, therefore, that we are entering an era of decentralisation of communications and culture in which new opportunities for any individual to receive content, and to speak as well, are emerging. At the same time, old powerful actors are losing their oligopoly over information control and distribution. However, these changes do not seem to bring us to an ideal situation in which a general clause of freedom of expression would be sufficient as a legal framework in order to guarantee the complete absence of any danger of censorship or, more broadly, the exercise and abuse of certain domination powers. The key issue, however, will be the fact that this danger of domination or censorship will now mostly come from private corporations instead of state powers.

The new internet landscape would seem to provide citizens with powerful new tools that can in some way alleviate the need for direct public intervention to protect or preserve freedom of expression. However, as some authors have pointed out, the internet also brings with it new difficulties that can emerge, in particular in areas including searching, exercising choice and trust, and gaining access under fair and affordable conditions.[29]

In this sense, specific matters such as fairness of contractual conditions, the guarantee of fair and non-discriminatory use of competing and interoperable applications and devices, and the access to reliable, fair and non-biased sources of information or search instruments are related to very important regulatory challenges (for example, net neutrality) that are now in the midst of important public policy debates. In this context, it is not clear whether a reasonable degree of autonomy and literacy from every individual consumer, together with the general protection brought by consumer and competition law[30] will be sufficient to guarantee not only a free content market, but also the protection of many relevant public values in the relation between citizens and companies, including free access to a wide range of information sources, the right to accurate information and protection of minors.

For example, looking at the most popular formats and offers of internet on-demand content, it is evident that in almost all of them the power of individual consumers/citizens is not as wide as common perceptions of this issue might suggest. Device manufacturers, content aggregators and managed networks of ISPs are the most common intermediaries who grant consumers access to content. In these cases, the range of choice and, for example, the conditions under which a specific search will be managed depend on the criteria and the decisions previously taken by media/telecom/device companies. Thus, despite a superficial vision of a free, open on-demand audiovisual market with unlimited access to material of a consumer's choice, the reality is that the most relevant systems for

29 Natali Helberger, 'From eyeball to creator – toying with audience empowerment in the Audiovisual Media Services Directive' (2008) 19(6) *Entertainment Law Review* 128.

30 That is to say, rules that are applied to every economic sector, in order to protect market competition and a fair treatment of consumers.

the provision of these kinds of services are managed according to the interests of just a few powerful gatekeepers.

As has been pointed out, the distortions that could result from this dominant position not only would seriously impair the rights and expectations of individual consumers but may also erode the principles of pluralism, free access and diversity that apply to citizens, both as individuals and as a part of the public opinion, that participate in the public sphere in modern democracies. What is at stake, once again, is not only the capacity of each individual to choose among different services within a competitive market but, more importantly, the real access for citizens to an offer of content that is fair, with a diverse range of different and plural voices, non-harmful and varied enough to guarantee an open public sphere and the protection of rights, principles and values that are beyond the specific interests of its participants.

On the other hand, it is also necessary to take a look at these matters from a different perspective. Individuals are not only consumers of on-demand or internet content, but for the first time they have the possibility of becoming content producers or 'audiovisual voices'. This second perspective raises many different regulatory problems, particularly on a realistic view, which would accept that most of the user-generated content is not placed in private individual websites but in popular and profitable distribution platforms, managed by big media and internet companies.

It is clear that in such cases, the owner of the platform becomes in some way the 'regulator' (and may even become the 'censor') of the content that will finally be made available to the general public. Its privileged position as a reliable and well-known provider of user-generated content plays a key role. Should this regulatory power (and possible political power as well)[31] remain in private hands without public regulatory – and of course, democratic – supervision, according to the principles that we have been mentioning here? Is it reasonable to move, in a very few decades, from the terrain of statutory regulation to the land of essentially private-based control of content that is distributed through electronic networks, portals and search engines?

4.2 Landmark decisions of the Court: access to the internet and blocking of websites: the *Yildirim v Turkey* case

One of the most important decisions of the Court related to internet freedom and its reach and impact goes beyond the country concerned. The case refers to an order issued by a domestic criminal court ordering a website accused of insulting the memory of Ataturk to be blocked. At the request of the Telecommunications and Information Technology Directorate (the regulator) and for the apparent

31 Think, for example, of the content criteria that apply to YouTube videos, which the company established and enforces itself. These rules affect and limit in different ways the exercise of freedom of expression and information and are applied following a 'private' procedure and no administrative and judicial control: http://www.youtube.com/t/terms (last accessed 11 August 2015).

reason that it was the only means of blocking the offending website, the Court varied its decision and extended it to all access to Google sites according to the provisions of the national law. The regulator implemented such order and therefore all the content posted on Google sites became unavailable from Turkey, this including of course their own managers. In this case, the applicant before the ECtHR is a Turkish academic completely unrelated to the website originally blocked who found out that his site had become inaccessible.

As is well known, one of the important elements of the ECtHR's scrutiny on whether a restriction of freedom of expression complies with Article 10 of the Convention consists of the analysis of the necessity of such measure in a democratic society. This analysis implies to some extent the application of a proportionality test in order to avoid those restrictions whose aims are legitimate but at the same time would provoke an excessive and unnecessary restriction to protected speech.

This kind of approach can also be found in the jurisprudence of the US Supreme Court, for example in *Reno v American Civil Liberties Union*, where some provisions of the Communications Decency Act were struck down owing to the fact that they actually prevented not only minors but adults as well from having access to 'indecent content' – a very good example of it a restriction of freedom. However, in this instance the ECtHR does not need to use such a test first, on the basis that the restriction imposed by Turkish authorities is already problematic vis-à-vis the requirement that it must have been prescribed by law, although proportionality is also indirectly considered in the reasoning.

Along these lines, the Court concluded that the Turkish law regulating the internet 'did not lay down any obligations for the domestic Courts to examine whether the wholesale blocking of Google Sites was necessary', in line with the provisions of the Convention. In other words, the European Court stressed that when potentially expansive restrictions are provided or at least can be imposed according to the terms of the law, it has to ensure tight control over the scope of bans and effective judicial review to prevent any abuse of power.

To summarise, *Yildirim v Turkey*[32] represents a very interesting jurisprudential innovation to the extent that it applies traditional and very consolidated criteria in terms of assessing the legitimacy of certain restrictions to freedom of expression in the online world, establishing for the first time the detailed conditions and restrictions that would apply to any attempt to restrict access to specific internet content.

4.2.1 Struggling with a new notion of editorial responsibility: the Delfi case

Delfi v Estonia[33] is clearly a very important decision, and one which particularly touches upon the controversial and still unresolved matter of intermediaries' liability in the internet.

32 *Yildirim v Turkey* Application no. 3111/10 (ECtHR, 2012).
33 Note 19.

Delfi.ee is a popular internet news portal in Estonia, where readers can post their comments online. In 2006 comments were uploaded automatically, without being subject to either editing or moderation. On certain dates, Delfi published some reports describing inappropriate conduct of a transportation company. Immediately afterwards, readers posted a large number of offensive comments directed towards one of the members (L) of the board of the company. Despite the fact that the comments were removed after L's lawyers filed a notify-and-take-down procedure, the Supreme Court decided in 2009 that L should be awarded €320 in non-pecuniary damages. In particular, the Court held that Delfi was to be considered as the publisher of the comments and that it could not avoid responsibility by publishing a disclaimer excluding liability for the content of the comments.

The ECtHR considered that there was no violation of Article 10 of the ECHR in this case. The Court based its assessment on four principal considerations. First, in light of the context of Article 10, Delfi could have anticipated the higher-than-average-risk of receiving negative comments, and that they could reach the level of insult or hate speech. Secondly, as Delfi was in a position to predict the nature of possible comments, it would have been able to take technical or manual measures, but it failed to do so. Thirdly, it was Delfi's choice to allow comments from non-registered users and that, by doing so, it must be considered to have assumed a certain responsibility for them. Finally, the moderate sanction of €320 imposed by the civil courts was seen as a fully justified and proportionate sanction.

The decision can be seen as problematic, for several reasons. First, it applies traditional media liability and editorial criteria in order to resolve a case concerning comments that were, for the most part, freely uploaded by readers. Therefore, it does not seem particularly convincing to compare such technological platform to – for example – the letters that are selected and published in a printed newspaper. Secondly, the Court ignored the liability exemptions that should be applied to content intermediaries vis-à-vis the content they host, store or transmit. These exemptions are clearly established by EU directives on electronic commerce or the Digital Millennium Copyright Act in the US. Finally, a decision of such a nature does in fact place enormous power in the hands of internet publishers, at least in terms of private censorship.

4.2.2 *A few interesting cases regarding the application of traditional criteria of the Court to the digital world*

There is no doubt that the ECtHR has played an important role in the protection of freedom of expression in the online world. In the case law specifically related to this area of communication the Court upholds and applies its consolidated criteria that form the backbone of the protection of freedom of expression and, at the same time, as we have started to see, tries to find the best way to adapt them to the specific trends of the digital environment. Sometimes the specific methodology and reasoning behind such adaptation leads to very interesting conclusions and results.

In the *Perrin v United Kingdom* case,[34] the Court insisted on the idea that despite the importance of freedom of expression within a democratic society and the particular relevance of the internet as a platform which facilitates the free flow of ideas, some restrictions remain legitimate and proportionate in order properly to protect rights and values enshrined in paragraph 2 of Article 10 of the ECHR. Moreover, in particular, the Court validated a criminal conviction of 30 months' imprisonment for the online publication – accessible to anyone – of scenes of coprophilia, coprophagia and homosexual fellation. Although it is true that the website in question was rarely accessible by accident and had to be sought out by the user, the Court gave more weight to the fact that it was a preview website without any age-check and therefore freely available to anyone surfing the internet, including minors.

Consequently, the criminal conviction was seen as proportionate considering the value being protected – the rights of young persons – and the fact that the applicant could have easily put in place a few measures in order to avoid direct accessibility to such raw images. The importance of properly protecting minors on the internet is also particularly emphasised in the more recent case of *Aleksey Ovchinnikov v Russian Federation*[35] regarding the identification by the press of a child involved in a sexual abuse event. However, it is worth noting that on this occasion the national decision being examined by the ECtHR was a civil judgment in the course of a defamation case.

It has already been noted that in the *Delfi* case the Court had to face the changes in the way editorial responsibility is being transformed in the digital era. As we have seen, the final stance of the judges lies somewhere in between traditional criteria and a new and adapted doctrine. There are also other cases where the Court has established very important criteria regarding the application of traditional media law institutions to the online media.

One of the earliest interesting cases along these lines was the decision in *Editorial Board of Pravoye Delo and Shtekel v Ukraine*.[36] In this case the Court analysed a decision in a defamation case against a newspaper and its editor-in-chief for publishing a report on political corruption based on a letter downloaded from the internet. The Court considered that the absence of a specific national legal regime regarding the use by journalists of information coming from internet sources makes any restriction imposed by authorities a violation of Article 10 of the ECHR. Moreover, according to the judges the absence of provisions 'allowing journalists to use information obtained from the internet without fear of incurring serious sanctions seriously hinders the exercise of the vital function of the press as a public watchdog' (para 64).

This is an interesting decision in so much as it limits the possibilities of introducing legal restrictions to investigative journalism to those cases in which these restrictions are clearly established by law, together with the necessary safeguards

34 *Perrin v United Kingdom* Application no. 5446/03 (ECtHR, 2005).

35 *Aleksey Ovchinnikov v Russian Federation Application* no. 24061/04 (ECtHR, 2010).

36 *Editorial Board of Pravoye Delo and Shtekel v Ukraine* Application no. 33014/05 (ECtHR, 2011).

in order to avoid any sort of 'chilling effect' or self-censorship. However, this view of the Court should not be interpreted in the sense that internet speech always requires new and specific regulations. In order words, this decision of the Court should be interpreted in the sense that only when existing legal provisions do not fit new realities – and of course when and only when there is a necessity according to the parameters of Article 10.2 ECHR – specific provisions and safeguards are to be introduced by states.

In *Times Newspapers Ltd v United Kingdom (nos. 1 & 2)*,[37] the Court assessed the requirement by a national court to add a notice to the online version of a series of articles previously published in the print version of *The Times*, announcing that they were subject to libel litigation. According to Strasbourg Court's judges, this requirement does not represent a disproportionate restriction on freedom of expression because the notice referred to specific content published by *The Times* in different formats and – particularly regarding the online version – the fact that such content was not affected at all – i.e. not removed or restricted in any way – this decision cannot be seen as excessive.

Consistently with this decision, in *Węgrzynowski and Smolczewski v Poland*,[38] the Court noted that: 'it is not the role of judicial authorities to engage in rewriting history by ordering the removal from the public domain of all traces of publications which have in the past been found, by final judicial decisions, to amount to unjustified attacks on individual reputation' (para 65). Therefore, the Court considered sufficient the remedy consisting of making available on the newspaper's website full information about the judicial decisions concerning an article which was declared to violate the applicant's rights and reputation.

This last doctrine of the Court probably contrasts with the terms in which, at the level of the European Union, the Court of Justice recognises and gives legal status to the so-called right to be forgotten.[39] Although the EU in itself is – still – not a signatory to the ECHR and, therefore, the influence of Strasbourg case law and the Convention is indirect, the ruling should be understood as part of the ongoing dialogue of jurisdictions between the EU legal system and the human rights scheme of the Council of Europe. In this framework, the vague references made by the European Court of Justice to the right to information as a legal element to be taken into account in the context of the application of the right to be forgotten seem not to properly consider, at least in an explicit way, the

37 *Times Newspapers Ltd v United Kingdom* Application nos. 3002/03 and 23676/03 (ECtHR, 2009).

38 *Węgrzynowski and Smolczewski v Poland* Application no. 33846/07 (ECtHR, 2013).

39 Case C-131/12 *Google Spain SL* (n 19). The decision was adopted following a request by a national Spanish court for a preliminary ruling regarding the claim of a citizen (the now famous Mario Costeja) asking Google to suppress search results related to the forced sale of his properties, which was ordered by a judge in a bankruptcy case that took place more than 20 years ago. The search results referred to the official notice published by the newspaper *La Vanguardia* in compliance with a court order. The links to this notice started to appear in prominent positions in search results related to the name 'Mario Costeja' when the print edition of *La Vanguardia* was fully digitalised several years later.

vast implications of the former within a democratic society according to the very consolidated case law of the ECtHR.[40]

Last but not least, it is also worth referring to an important decision regarding the possible violation of Article 8 of the ECHR by media and journalists in the online world. In *Mosley v United Kingdom*[41] the Court clearly refused to accept that Article 8 requires a legally binding prenotification requirement of intended publications, which refers to an individual's private life. On this issue, the Court acknowledged the impact that the dissemination of certain information, images or videos on the internet may have, as well as the difficulty of removing such content, even when it is declared illegal by a court. However, 'the limited scope under Article 10 for restrictions on the freedom of the press to publish material which contributes to debate on matters of general public interest' together with 'the chilling effect to which a pre-notification requirement risks giving rise' and 'the significant doubts as to the effectiveness of any pre-notification requirement and to the wide margin of appreciation in this area' led the Court to dismiss this requirement (paras 130–32).

4.3 The attitude of the Court towards freedom of expression in the digital age: an involution or evolution?

Having explored the leading cases where the ECtHR had to face the challenges posed by the internet, one of the most debated questions amongst scholars concerns whether the switch from the sphere of mere atoms to the digital world has led to an improvement of the protection of freedom of speech.[42] The rise of the internet has, in fact, brought with it a number of factors that reflect the way in which courts approach the issue of protection of the freedom of speech.

As the internet connects people from everywhere in the world, different standards of protection may be required. A US resident may claim, for instance, that his or her speech is covered by the First Amendment and therefore benefits from a high level of protection, whilst EU residents may feel that the same opinions and ideas – circulated via the internet – are harmful and outside the scope of constitutional protection. From a legal standpoint, this could result in problems of regulatory arbitrage, especially in light of the contrast between the consideration attached to free speech in the US and the lower degree of protection in Europe.

40 The ECJ describes such balance in the following terms: '. . . inasmuch as the removal of links from the list of results could, depending on the information at issue, have effects upon the legitimate interest of internet users potentially interested in having access to that information, in situations such as that at issue in the main proceedings a fair balance should be sought in particular between that interest and the data subject's fundamental rights under arts 7 and 8 of the Charter. Whilst it is true that the data subject's rights protected by those articles also override, as a general rule, the interest of internet users, that balance may however depend, in specific cases, on the nature of the information in question and its sensitivity for the data subject's private life and on the interest of the public in having that information, an interest which may vary, in particular, according to the role played by the data subject in public life' (para 81).

41 *Mosley v United Kingdom* Application no. 48009/08 (ECtHR, 2011).

42 See Pollicino and Bassini (n 3).

Several judgments (of which the *Yahoo! v Licra* case discussed above is one of the most prominent) have been delivered in cases where the appropriateness of a given domestic jurisdiction was disputed.

Such judicial clashes have also affected, at least indirectly, the reasoning of the European Courts, and of the Court of Strasbourg in particular, which became aware of the unprecedented power of the internet to spread ideas and opinions. The reaction of the ECtHR and, generally speaking, of the European Courts seems to be focused more on the threats that the development of the internet has raised, rather than on the opportunities derived from it. This approach has impacted on the reasoning and, accordingly, on the judgments handed down by the ECtHR concerning alleged violations of Article 10 of the ECHR by the EU Member States.

However, it should also be pointed out that the ECtHR has adapted the relevant principles developed in its case law without calling into question the appropriateness of applying the same to the internet. This has not prevented the ECtHR from taking into account the characteristics of this medium. This approach has frequently resulted in the suggestion that certain aspects of existing legislation should be adjusted, although the well-established methodology of the ECtHR has never been reversed when reviewing applications caused by alleged violations of Article 10.

The same trend, however, can also be observed with respect to the Court of Justice of the European Union, as noted by Oreste Pollicino.[43] Although taking different paths, in fact, the European Courts seem to have adopted a similar approach. Both the courts are thus far from considering the protection of freedom of expression on the internet as a matter to be addressed through the lenses of the same categories applying to the world of atoms.

These nuances emerge in the words used by the Court of Strasbourg in the case *Węgrzynowski and Smolczewski v Poland.* Here the ECtHR has quoted what it had already remarked in the *Editorial Board of Pravoye Delo* case, namely that: 'the internet is an information and communication tool particularly distinct from the printed media, especially as regards the capacity to store and transmit information . . . The risk of harm posed by content and communications on the internet to the exercise and enjoyment of human rights and freedoms, particularly the right to respect for private life, is certainly higher than that posed by the press.'[44]

By this argument, the ECtHR tried to support the provision of a different regulatory approach in respect of the phenomena taking place online: 'the electronic network, serving billions of users worldwide, is not and potentially will never be subject to the same regulations and control'.[45] It is therefore in light of this assumption that the ECtHR has carried out the balancing of interests at stake in the various applications complaining of interference with the freedom of speech on the internet. As Pollicino has pointed out, this led to breaking the

43 See Pollicino, 'Internet nella giurisprudenza delle corti europee' (n 21).
44 See para. 58.
45 ibid.

illusion of a 'promised land' that the internet was supposed to constitute for the exercise of the freedom of expression.[46]

The same view of the internet is mirrored by the important decision of the ECtHR in the *Delfi* case, recently upheld by the Grand Chamber. As clarified above, the Court found that there had been no violation of Article 10. The ECtHR has now taken into account whether the requirements set out in Article 10.2 had been actually fulfilled in the case. However, this decision is likely to pose unintended as well as undesirable consequences, albeit indirectly, for the protection of freedom of expression on the internet. In particular, although the reasoning of the Court was focused on the balance between the right to freedom of expression and the legitimate interest to the protection of reputation, the ruling significantly affects the legal regime of internet service providers.

Burdening intermediaries with obligations such as those required by the Estonian authorities in order not to incur liability is likely to undermine the protection of freedom of expression, as pointed out by Justices Sajò and Tsotsoria in their joint dissenting opinion:[47] 'active intermediaries and blog operators will have considerable incentives to discontinue offering a comments feature, and the fear of liability may lead to additional self-censorship by operators'.[48] Imposing obligations on internet service providers that are not even grounded in EU law, in the view of the dissenting judges, is likely to result in the introduction of a private self-censorship that in certain cases may also hinder forms of governmental pressure. In other words, claiming more responsibility from ISPs for content posted by third parties would result in putting in their hands the power to restrict the circulation of ideas, thought and opinion.

Also, the effects of the judgment handed down by the ECtHR are likely to conflict with EU law. As noted,[49] had the CJEU dealt with such a case, the judges of Luxembourg would most likely have found that no liability lies with internet service providers when it comes to defamatory comments posted in news footers by third parties. The CJEU, in fact, is more inclined to enforce the liability exemptions laid down by the E-Commerce Directive, provided that the conditions set out regarding safe harbours are met. On the contrary, the reasoning of the Court of Strasbourg pays no regard to the legislation in force in the European Union (i.e. in the national laws of the Member States), but only involves the scrutiny on the requirements set out in Article 10.2 to limit the protection of freedom of speech.

It is worth noting that the recent decision of the Grand Chamber makes express reference to the legal framework in force in the European Union and mentions the leading decisions taken by the Court of Justice in interpreting the E-Commerce Directive. Most notably, the attention paid by the dissenting

46 See Pollicino, 'Internet nella giurisprudenza delle corti europee' (n 21).

47 Joint dissenting opinion of Sajò and Tsotsoria JJ (16 June 2015) *Delfi v Estonia* Application no. 64569/09.

48 ibid para 1.

49 Pollicino and Bassini (n 3).

opinion to the consequences that the judgment may raise in the perspective of EU law is remarkable. In the view of Justice Sajò and Justice Tsotsoria, in fact, by confirming that an order such as that imposed on the applicant does not violate Article 10 of the ECHR the Court goes against the well-established *acquis* as far as the role of internet providers is concerned with respect to freedom of expression.

One of the most critical points of the judgment lies with the choice not to challenge the Estonian Supreme Court's assumption that the news portal operated by Delfi was to be treated as a publisher. According to the dissenting judges, equating an active intermediary to a publisher is likely to lead to critical consequences if these categories have to be applied to publications on the internet.

The ECtHR, in the words of Justices Sajò and Tsotsoria, is formally acknowledging the need to draw a difference between the rules governing traditional media and those applying to internet operators, although in fact it approaches these phenomena in the same way. The rationale behind the consideration paid to these distinct subjects is that the grounds of the activity of both a publisher and an active intermediary is an economic interest. However, this reason does not sound sufficient to hold that the responsibilities and duties of publishers and intermediaries are the same. Both the dissenting judges are far from considering that an active provider will never incur liability in connection with third parties' content.

Even though an intermediary is also capable of exercising certain control over content, some factors differentiate the regime applying to publishers: whilst the publisher has knowledge of the content to be published in advance, an intermediary has no means to exercise such control. When it comes to an 'active' intermediary this holds only partially true, as it is well established (although not entirely clear) that such operators exercise more control than 'passive' intermediaries over content. In this respect, the position taken by the dissenting opinion reflects the state of the art with respect to the liability of internet service providers in the case law of the Court of Justice of the European Union and some domestic courts.[50] Although 'active' intermediaries can exercise some control over third parties' content, this does not mean that they have the same power as publishers (i.e. content providers) in this respect.

The second key point of the dissenting opinion, accordingly, concerns the liability regime applied to Delfi by the Estonian Supreme Court. The choice to apply a regime of 'strict liability' has not been disputed by the Grand Chamber. The opinion observes that the applicant has been ordered to pay damages on the basis of the provisions of the Civil Code, even though the Court had confirmed that the liability exemptions set out in the Information Society Services Act (which implemented the E-Commerce Directive in Estonia) were applicable.

50 See Joined Cases C-236/08 to 238/08 *Google France SARL and Google Inc* CJEU (23 March 2010); Case C-324/09 *L'Oréal and Others* CJEU (12 July 2011). See also Patrick Von Eecke, 'Online service providers and liability: a plea for a balanced approach' (2011) 48 *Common Market Law Review* 1455.

These remarks reveal the relevant EU law provisions 'in action' in the eyes of the European Court of Human Rights, which more properly acts as a court of fundamental rights. Despite the website apparently being operated as a publisher, the defamatory comments that led to Delfi's liability vis-à-vis the individuals concerned were 'user-generated-content'.[51] Justices Sajò and Tsotsoria disagreed with the ECtHR, finding that activity consisting of storage has a 'commercial nature' and therefore falls outside the scope of application of the E-Commerce Directive. In this respect, the qualification of Delfi as a publisher (i.e. as a content provider) prevented the Court from regarding the defamatory comments as 'user-generated' and then to consider the regime of service providers as applicable to Delfi.[52]

To a certain degree, this part of the decision, which Justices Sajò and Tsotsoria correctly criticise, seems to mirror the trend, ever more common amongst several EU Member States' courts, to consider 'active' intermediaries 'more' responsible than purely passive and neutral ones. The Court of Justice of the European Union has clarified that internet service providers should not benefit from the liability exemptions set out in the E-Commerce Directive. However, some domestic courts have frequently denied that the liability exemptions were applicable to 'active' intermediaries by reason of a 'something plus' (*quid iuris*) element, compared to the internet service providers, which nevertheless have no clear grounds at all.[53]

The judgment of the Grand Chamber thus validates – even though only indirectly – the approach taken by various domestic courts that have drawn a difference between purely passive providers and active providers, most notably when it comes to hosting services, in order to exclude the latter from the benefit of exemptions liability.

That said, by adopting an interpretation that equates publishers (i.e. content providers) and active intermediaries, the ECHR seems to confirm the general trend towards limiting the protection of freedom of expression when it comes to the internet. As pointed out,[54] this view is shared by the Court of Justice of the European Union, which seems to have reacted in a similar way to the rise of the perils and evils of the internet. This also confirms that the protection of fundamental rights, and most notably of freedom of expression requires public authorities to take into account the role played by these new actors and the peculiar characteristics of the same. Looking at the dissenting opinion, the idea emerges that although content and service providers have very different natures, the regime applicable to a publisher is not affected by the changes brought by the internet, whilst intermediaries are bringing to light unprecedented problems.

51 This uncertainty also reflects on another crucial aspect of the 'provided by law' requirement pursuant to art 10(2) of the ECHR in the case law of the Court of Strasbourg, i.e. the 'foreseeability' of the law, which constitutes an interference with freedom of expression.

52 Sajò and Tsotsoria JJ, dissenting opinion (n 46) para. 17.

53 See in more detail Oreste Pollicino and Ernesto Apa, *Modeling the Liability of Internet Services Providers: Google vs. Vivi Down. A Constitutional Perspective* (Egea 2013).

54 See further Pollicino (n 3).

Conversely, the approach by the ECtHR has been more protective of freedom of expression with respect to the enforcement of the right to be forgotten, even 'under the appearance of the right to reputation'. The Court of Justice of the European Union, as noted elsewhere,[55] has delivered a decision which pays very limited regard to the constitutional breadth of the freedom of information (as well as the freedom to conduct business). Rather, the stand-out part of the judgment goes to the right to data protection that prevails not only in the findings of the Court but in the entire reasoning followed by the Luxembourg judges.

On the other hand, the ECtHR in the case of *Węgrzynowski and Smolczewski v Poland* has found that the removal of a web page is not justified for the sake of the right to data protection and right to reputation. As discussed above, the view of the ECtHR was that making available in an online newspaper the text of the judgment declaring the defamatory nature of a challenged Article was a proper remedy to reconcile freedom of expression and protection of individual reputation. The reasons behind this decision mainly deal with the peculiar judicial technique of the Court of Strasbourg, which unlike the Court of Justice is tasked only with assessing whether a violation of the fundamental rights enshrined in the Convention has occurred.

Clearly, the dialogue between courts ranks amongst the factors to be taken into account when exploring trends and tendencies of the European Courts towards freedom of expression. The case law of the ECtHR has always been influential with respect to several decisions of the Court of Justice of the European Union involving the balance between economic freedoms and fundamental rights. Neither has the coming into force of the Charter of Fundamental Rights of the European Union prevented the Court of Luxembourg from taking at least inspiration from the case law of the ECtHR. However, this influence has most likely led the Court of Justice to follow the same approach as the Strasbourg Court's judges when it comes to considering the phenomenal rise of the internet. Thus, the new medium has been felt predominantly as a threat for certain competing rights, rather than as an opportunity extensively to exercise freedom of expression.

4.4 Conclusions

The ECtHR has established a relevant body of case law on freedom of expression on the internet. This case law should be read and understood within the framework of the almost four-decade-old case law of the Court regarding Article 10 of the ECHR. In other words, the judges from Strasbourg do not appear to see the digital or online world as something completely different or separated from our material environment. Article 10 of the ECHR therefore fits naturally in protecting expressive activities which are disseminated in the bit stream.

55 See Oreste Pollicino and Marco Bassini, 'Reconciling the right to be forgotten and freedom of information in the digital age: past and future of personal data protection in the EU' (2014) 2 *Diritto pubblico comparato ed europeo* 640.

Of course, as we have already noted, in some cases specific rules and principles will be required in order to cope with specific and unprecedented problems that may arise online. In this area the Court has stimulated national institutions to adapt legal systems, whilst respecting freedom as the general principle and restrictions as the exception. In other cases old and well known notions – editorial responsibility, protection of minors, hate speech etc – have been rethought and adapted to the characteristics of the internet. This adaptation is sometimes problematic and has raised doubts about the way in which the Court sees the internet, the way in which the idea of editorial responsibility is considered in the *Delfi* case being probably the best example.

The ECtHR case law must also be understood within the context of a wide and complex legal and institutional system within the Council of Europe for the protection of freedom of expression, both online and offline. This organisation has several bodies and institutions in charge of both establishing specific standards for the interpretation and application of Article 10 of the ECHR to the internet and responding to possible violations of the rights protected in such provision. The Court is indeed the most 'formal' and decisive institution within the Council of Europe to protect citizens' rights to freedom of expression on the internet, but at the same time institutions such as the Commissioner for Human Rights, the Committee of Ministers or the Parliamentary Assembly – to mention only the most important ones – can swiftly supervise and publicise violations and other problematic practices undertaken by EU Member States.

5 The Court of Justice of the European Union and the illusion of balancing in internet-related disputes

*Filippo Fontanelli**

5.1 Introduction

Society evolves over time and law must cope with (and apply to) an ever-changing *substratum*. This has always been the case and the application of EU law to internet-related matters is no exception. The practice of legal interpretation and application in this field is complicated by the engagement of fundamental rights (FRs), which also lend themselves to evolutive construction,[1] if only because of their formulation through principles, which requires actualisation in particular cases.[2]

FR-adjudication concerning the use of novel technologies occurs in an epistemic scene which changes continuously. Namely, its coordinates inevitably shift along two different axes. On the one hand, technological advancement causes social practices to reconfigure and adopt new formats; on the other hand, the flexible application of general principles to specific circumstances cannot be assessed statically or a priori. The process of normative refinement required to regulate these activities can take place at the legislative level and/or through legal interpretation and application, including through the activity of judicial bodies.

The nature of technological advancement makes it impossible to rely on a backward-looking analysis of established general practice (see e.g. the identification of customs in international law) to build appropriate analogies for the regulation of future events and circumstances. Refinement must instead take the form

* The author is indebted to Paolo Cavaliere, Giuseppe Franco Ferrari, Theodore Konstadinides, Tobias Lock, Oreste Pollicino, Graziella Romeo and the participants in the Bocconi workshop of 17–18 October 2014 for useful comments.

1 Kanstantsin Dzehtsiarou, 'European consensus and the evolutive interpretation of the European Convention on Human Rights' (2011) 12 *German Law Journal* 1730, 1732; Christos L. Rozakis, 'The European judge as comparatist' (2005) 80 *Tulane Law Review* 257, 260 (referring to the rudimentary nature of the provisions of the ECHR).

2 This simplification draws from the famous notion of principles in Ronald Dworkin's *Taking Rights Seriously* (Harvard University Press 1978) 35, where he notes that rules determine the outcome of a dispute and, if they do not, they have been disregarded. Instead, '[p]rinciples do not work that way; they incline a decision one way, though not conclusively, and they survive intact when they do not prevail'.

of reformative law-making (or judicial standard-setting), rather than codification or consolidation of state practice, if it intends to be effective.

Whereas law cannot anticipate technological innovations, it should react to them as promptly as possible. As Advocate General Cruz Villalón noted: 'there are currently many legal categories the conception and scope of which require a reconsideration where they affect social and commercial relationships occurring on the internet'.[3]

This chapter advances a bold proposition, which can be roughly reduced to a warning against received thinking. Namely, I posit that the proportionality test – as we know it – is an inadequate heuristic device to grasp and regulate the influence of the internet on fundamental rights.[4] Consequently, judgments that turn on a determination of proportionality are ultimately ill-founded or simply seek artificial legitimacy for conclusions based on another policy trade-off.[5] My tentative conclusion is that constitutional (that is, FR-based) adjudication in the hands of the CJEU is increasingly impracticable and the regulation of internet-based activities that have FR-implications is better left to legislators. This conclusion is reminiscent of Balkin's own regarding the realisation (limited to the issue of free speech) that case law could hardly moderate the digital new world: technical and regulatory decisions replace constitutional elaboration through judicial precedents.

> Protecting free speech values in the digital age will be less and less a problem of constitutional law – although these protections will remain important – and more and more a problem of technology and administrative regulation.[6]

The assumption that the CJEU performs constitutional adjudication requires clarification. *Substantively*, the CJEU reviews the validity of EU secondary legislation with respect to the treaties and international law. Fundamental rights provisions are among the norms of primary law, respect of which determines the validity of secondary legislation. In the present analysis, questions of interpretation or validity of EU law acts[7] or national law implementing EU

3 Joined Cases C–509/09 *eDate Advertising GmbH* and C–161/10 *Olivier Martinez and Robert Martinez v MGN Limited* [2011] ECR I–10269, Opinion, para. 31.

4 On the risks of basing moral and legal judgments on generic heuristic short-cuts see Cass R. Sunstein, 'Moral heuristics' (2005) 28(4) *Behavioral and Brain Sciences* 531–41.

5 Criticism of the use of proportionality in FR-adjudication is not a novelty in the literature. See Stavros Tsakyrakis, 'Proportionality: an assault on human rights?' (2009) 7(3) *International Journal of Constitutional Law* 468–93; Matthias Klatt and Moritz Meister, 'Proportionality: a benefit to human rights? Remarks on the I·CON controversy' (2012) 10(3) *International Journal of Constitutional Law* 687–708.

6 Jack M. Balkin, 'The future of free expression in a digital age' (2008) 36 *Pepperdine Law Review* 427, 441. Balkin discusses the continuing relevance of the Constitution's First Amendment on free speech, arguing somewhat similarly to the gist of this chapter that the technological revolution amounts to: 'a transition of enormous irony. At the very moment that our economic and social lives are increasingly dominated by information technology and information flows, the First Amendment seems increasingly irrelevant to the key free speech battles of the future. Or, more precisely, the judge-made doctrines that I teach in my First Amendment classes seem increasingly irrelevant'.

7 Submitted to the Court under art 263 or art 267 TFEU.

law turn on the compliance of these measures with fundamental rights standards: this kind of judicial review is, in the substance, typical of constitutional adjudication.

Besides the substantive affinity, the CJEU has a *formal* mandate to engage in constitutional adjudication. Namely, the Court arbitrates the vertical division of powers between Member States and the Union, another common aspect of constitutional adjudication at the national level.[8] In particular, the review of secondary legislation for compliance with treaty law ultimately speaks to the compliance with the principle of conferral. Formally, respect of treaty law is a safeguard against undue encroachment of Member States' competences.

This chapter introduces a distinction between internet-native rules and other rules that might be applicable in internet-related cases (section 5.2). The purpose of this distinction is to focus on the constitutional component of the Court's case law, which is more clearly visible when it considers the compatibility of internet-native rules with fundamental rights. Section 5.3 uses the *Google Spain* case[9] as an illustration of the shortcomings of proportionality in this field. The analysis develops in section 5.4, which discusses other judgments to support the idea that the Court is less engaged in actual proportionality than in a pragmatic moderation of conflicting interests. The core argument of this work, synthesised in the conclusive section, is that the Court should let go of the proportionality formula and expose the policy-oriented thrust of its decisions in the field of internet-related matters.

5.2 Internet-native norms and adaptation of non-internet norms

FR-adjudication inevitably entails the interpretation and application of principles. Regulation of conduct relating to the use of the internet, conversely, can be very thorough and comprise detailed rules. In fact, the EU has legislated copiously in the field.[10] The process of refinement of the nexus between the EU legal order and internet activities has resulted in an increased specialisation of the applicable rules of EU law. New legal disciplines have emerged governing the impact that technologies have on several human activities (production, distribution and consumption of information, access to intellectual products, entertainment, marketing strategies, management of personal data and use of intangible networks to support the activity of public entities). In other words, the EU relies on a wide basis of *internet-native* regulation.

The subject-matter of this chapter is the constitutional case law of the CJEU in the digital *milieu*. The cases are selected to gauge the process of evolutive refinement described above, whereby adjudication promotes the realignment of

8 Michel Rosenfeld, 'Comparing constitutional review by the European Court of Justice and the US Supreme Court' (2006) 4(4) *International Journal of Constitutional Law* 618, 623.

9 See Case C–131/12 Google Spain SL and Google Inc v Agencia Española de Protección de Datos (AEPD) and Mario Costeja González CJEU (13 May 2014).

10 For instance see Directive 95/46; Directive 2000/31; Regulation 45/2001; Directive 2002/22; Directive 2002/58 (replacing Directive 97/66); Directive 2006/24.

applicable norms and social reality. All the disputes considered fall somewhere within a casuistic range relating to the EU applicable norms (the application of EU law is a prerequisite for the jurisdiction of the CJEU). At one end, the Court is called to interpret or apply internet-native rules, and the refinement relates to their compliance with fundamental rights.

At the other end, the Court must apply rules that are not internet-specific to an internet-related situation; in these cases, the evolutionary refinement regards the optimisation of existing rules to new practices, and ensuring compliance with fundamental rights is not the only constitutional exercise of the Court. Quite simply, the 'updated' application of the rule of conduct must also respect fundamental rights. This is a routine check that the Court must perform on all EU rules.[11]

Two examples might help to illustrate this distinction, which is not clear-cut but might be helpful to appreciate the work of the Court.

5.2.1 *Type 1: consistent interpretation of internet-native rule to fundamental rights*

Article 15 of Directive 2000/31 (on e-Commerce)[12] provides that: 'Member States shall not impose a general obligation on providers . . . to monitor the information which they transmit or store, nor a general obligation actively to seek facts or circumstances indicating illegal activity.'

The application of this internet-specific rule might raise issues of compatibility with fundamental rights. For instance, certain stakeholders might question the compatibility of this rule with their right to protection of property, insofar as this provision spares internet service providers from a duty of monitoring and preventing (a) the exchange of materials protected by IP-rights (see *L'Oréal*,[13] *Scarlet*,[14] *SABAM*,[15] *Bonnier*[16]); (b) access to pictures taken and distributed illegally (see *Max Mosley v Google*, French[17] and German[18] orders); and (c) the

11 The FR compliance of all acts of the EU, including normative sources, is mandated by art 51 of the EU Charter of Fundamental Rights. Domestic measures implementing EU law are similarly subject to the Charter. See generally Filippo Fontanelli, 'National measures and the application of the EU Charter of Fundamental Rights: Does curia.eu know iura.eu?' (2014) 14(2) *Human Rights Law Review* 231–65.

12 Directive 2000/31/EC of the European Parliament and of the Council of 8 June 2000 on certain legal aspects of information society services, in particular electronic commerce, in the Internal Market, Official Journal L178 (17.7.2000) 1–16.

13 Case C–324/09 *L'Oréal and Others* [2011] ECR II–6011.

14 Case C–70/10 *Scarlet Extended* [2011] ECR I–11959.

15 Case C–360/10 *SABAM* (not yet reported), judgment of 16 February 2012.

16 Case C–461/10 *Bonnier Audio and Others* (not yet reported), judgment of 19 April 2012.

17 TGI Paris, 17e ch. (6 November 2013) RG 11/07970, *Max Mosley c. Google Inc et Google France* http://droitdu.net/2013/11/tgi-paris-17e-ch-6-novembre-2013-rg-1107970-max-mosley-c-google-france-et-google-inc/ (last accessed 12 August 2015).

18 Landgericht Hamburg (24 January 2014) Case 324 O 264/11 http://tlmd.in/u/1456 (last accessed 12 August 2015).

exchange of tickets for which resale is prohibited (see UK SC's judgment in *Rugby Football Union v Viagogo*[19]).

5.2.2 *Type 2: update of non-internet specific rule*

Article 5(3) of Regulation No. 44/2001[20] provides that: '[a] person domiciled in a Member State may, in another Member State, be sued: . . . in matters relating to tort, delict or quasi-delict, in the courts for the place where the harmful event occurred or may occur'.

In this case, the interpretation of this general principle of territorial connection might prove critical when the alleged wrongdoing and its effects (the 'harmful event') take place over the internet. In cases relating to defamation through the web, indeed, it is not obvious whether 'the place' where the event occur or might occur can be *any* state where the incriminated webpage is merely accessible. Usually, this interpretation would mean that the defendant can be sued in any state of the world, as long as an internet connection exists in that state.

As is clear from this example, the fundamental right aspect of the issue is somewhat incidental to the main ones (i.e. whether a simple possibility to access the defamatory material online qualifies as 'harmful event', and whether the location of the internet user identifies where the 'harmful event' occurs for the purpose of establishing jurisdiction). In this case, fundamental rights guarantees must inform the determination of the court, but only insofar as it must ensure that the interpretation of Article 5(3) of Regulation No. 44/2001 does not restrict disproportionately the plaintiff's right to privacy and the ensuing right to seek vindication thereof in court.[21]

Why is this distinction relevant? It perhaps allows discerning in the cases relating to internet the parts of the Court's reasoning, which use fundamental rights argumentation as a decisive thrust towards the finding, as opposed to a simple standard of legality applied by way of routine. In other words, to simplify, Type 1 cases will have a clearer constitutional imprint, on average, because the reasoning is free from false positives. The evolutive component in Type 2 cases could be more concerned with the updating of pre-internet rules than with the FR-component of the review. In this sense, Type 1 cases are noise-free.

Make no mistake: reasoning of the latter category is of vital importance and tests the ability of the Court to mould the interpretation of EU law to modern needs. However, when the former kind of reasoning is deployed, the adaptive exercise (what I referred to earlier as 'refinement') regards precisely (and exclusively) the fundamental rights standards. To simplify brutally, argumentation of the first category (dealing with internet-native rules) calls upon the Court to

19 *The Rugby Football Union v Consolidated Information Services Ltd* [2012] UKSC 55 (21 November 2012) http://www.bailii.org/uk/cases/UKSC/2012/55.html (last accessed 12 August 2015).

20 Council Regulation (EC) No. 44/2001 of 22 December 2000 on jurisdiction and the recognition and enforcement of judgments in civil and commercial matters, Official Journal L012 (16.01.2001).

21 This was one of the issue in the Joined Cases *eDate* and *Martinez* (n 3).

interpret fundamental rights as a 'living instrument'. It forces the Court to devise the particularisation of human rights principles for new factual predicaments and legal regulations, for which often no precedent can be applied, by analogy.[22]

Type 1 reasoning is therefore more directly 'constitutional', in the limited (and heavily qualified) sense explained. Its deployment is clearly visible when the application of internet-native rules is at stake, for the reasons mentioned. However, it can be traced also when Type 2 rules apply. Simply, there can be hybrid case where the updating of non-internet-native rules occurs *alongside*, or *through*, FR-based arguments appealing to the balancing discretion of the court. If the Type 1/2 distinction is relatively clear, we can interpret any case without worrying too much about whether each specific instance is a pure example of either category. Most cases, in fact, are not pure specimens. However, tracing the constitutional undercurrent of each is easier if we are able to isolate it from the concurring elements of the court's reasoning.

Let me explain why I claim that precedents are of little help for FR-based adjudication in internet matters. After all, there exists an established practice of human rights adjudication, both at the Court and in other jurisdictions from which the Court can draw inspiration. The chapters of this collection compose a comprehensive picture that gives an idea of how convenient it can be for each court and tribunal to borrow segments of reasoning and take advantage of the authoritativeness of another court's ruling to reinforce its own pronouncements. However, internet-related activities hardly fit into the traditional models of fundamental right conflicts: we need new bottles for the new wine.

To put it otherwise, application of FR principles to digital activities is less a question of subsumption of new facts under existing standards than it is a question of balancing policies.[23] The best way to illustrate the unsettling novelty of internet-based activity is through selected cases. I do my best to justify my claim that certain aspects of these cases can be generalised and, accordingly, the comments on those cases apply to the whole field.

The precursor in this gallery is the *Lindqvist* case.[24] A volunteer catechist uploaded the personal information about some colleagues on a webpage, without securing their consent. She had built the website as an assignment of a web-designing course. From the factual background of the main proceedings, one can appreciate the good faith of Mrs Lindqvist (who promptly removed the information as soon as she realised somebody was unhappy). However, criminal prosecution was launched, and Mrs Lindqvist had to endure it: this is a watershed case, a case that symbolises the loss of innocence – or legal impunity – of the internet.

22 Thomas M. Scanlon, 'Adjusting rights and balancing values' (2004) 74 *Fordham Law Review* 1477.

23 For a distinction between subsumption and balancing, and an attempt to describe the latter process as a neutral process (like the former) see Robert Alexy, 'On balancing and subsumption: a structural comparison' (2003) 16(4) *Ratio Juris* 433–49.

24 C–101/01 *Lindqvist* [2003] ECR I–12971. For comment see Ludovic Coudray, 'Case C–101/01, Bodil Lindqvist' (2004) 41(5) *Common Market Law Review* 1361–76.

Amongst the relevant issues, the Court had to consider whether the mere fact that the incriminated webpage was accessible anywhere in the world meant that Mrs Lindqvist had transferred the personal information she had processed to a third country. Transfer of personal data to third countries is only allowed, under Directive 95/46,[25] subject to certain conditions. The reasoning of the Court is critical and exemplary:

> Given . . . the state of development of the internet at the time Directive 95/46 was drawn up . . . one cannot presume that the Community legislature intended the expression transfer [of data] to a third country' to cover the loading, by an individual . . . of data onto an internet page, even if those data are thereby made accessible to persons in third countries with the technical means to access them.

If Article 25 of Directive 95/46 were interpreted to mean that there is transfer [of data] to a third country every time that personal data are loaded onto an internet page, that transfer would necessarily be a transfer to all the third countries where there are the technical means needed to access the internet. The special regime provided for by Chapter IV of the directive would thus necessarily become a regime of general application, as regards operations on the internet. Thus, if the Commission found, pursuant to Article 25(4) of Directive 95/46, that even one third country did not ensure adequate protection, the Member States would be obliged to prevent any personal data being placed on the internet.

This is on its face a schoolbook example of a Type 2 question: update of a non-internet rule to a world-*cum*-internet situation. However, it reveals the Court's readiness to alter the balance of established principles, even if ever so slightly. The rationale of the applied rule is to prevent personal data from being diffused where insufficient guarantees exist for their protection. If the rationale is valid, indeed, the internet amplifies this concern indefinitely; this much is unquestionable. The protection of the affected parties would indeed require Member States 'to prevent any personal data being placed on the internet'. Why should they not?

The Court discarded this conclusion as absurd, implicitly relying on a reapportioning of the responsibilities based on a new analysis of expected costs, that is, a covert utilitarian assessment. Anybody uploading any personal data online would be likely to incur liability; *therefore* this liability is lifted, even if it was effectively designed to protect a fundamental right. Invoking arguments relating to the original intention of the legislator (that could not foresee the functioning of the internet) and a sloppy reasoning *ex absurdo* (every uploader would be liable) the Court produced a Type 1 determination in disguise, where strict proportionality (see below) determined the outcome.

Specifically, it altered the established balance between the right to privacy

25 Directive 95/46/EC of the European Parliament and of the Council of 24 October 1995 on the protection of individuals with regard to the processing of personal data and on the free movement of such data, Official Journal L281 (23/11/1995) 31–50; see in particular art 25.

and the right to impart information, acknowledging that the current social and technological situation has eroded irreversibly part of the former in favour of the latter. In a sense, this judgment has inadvertently signalled the demotion of privacy protection to a policy objective (down from a fundamental right). I will explain the nature and the implications of this shift below.

5.3 Proportionality between fundamental rights in digital matters: unworkable *formulae*

A constant of constitutional adjudication in Europe is the use of the proportionality test to balance competing values.[26] Proportionality, or the process that the test entails, is a defining element of constitutionalism globally.[27] The test of proportionality is normally used to assess the justification of restrictions to fundamental rights caused by private or, more commonly, public measures.[28] A proportion must exist between the interference to a given right and the benefit that that interference brings to another right or public interest. Proportionality has become a general principle of EU law[29] and has informed the case law of the ECtHR,[30] under the moniker of necessity.

Roughly, the proportionality test in use at the CJEU traces the one developed by the German Federal Constitutional Court (the BvfG)[31] and theorised as a prototype by Robert Alexy.[32] It is a three-step test informed by the principle of Pareto optimisation;[33] each step ensures that the measure under scrutiny is efficient, that is, there cannot be any unnecessary waste of rights' protection. The measure must be suitable to achieve the goal it is designed for (step 1) and must be, amongst those equally suitable and reasonably available, the least encroaching on the right restricted (step 2). The third step, usually called proportionality *stricto sensu*, requires an actual weighing between the two values at stake, when it is clear that one of the two must suffer some cost.[34]

26 A history of the principle is provided in Eric Engle, 'The general principle of proportionality and Aristotle' in Liesbeth Huppes-Cluysenaer and Nuno M. M. S. Coelho (eds), *Aristotle and the Philosophy of Law: Theory, Practice and Justice* (Springer 2013) 265–76.

27 Alec Stone Sweet and Jud Mathews, 'Proportionality balancing and global constitutionalism' (2008) 47 *Columbia Journal of Transnational Law* 72; Mads Andenas and Stefan Zleptnig, 'Proportionality and balancing in WTO law: a comparative perspective' 2007 20(1) *Cambridge Review of International Affairs* 71–92.

28 Julian Rivers, 'Proportionality and variable intensity of review' (2006) 65(1) *Cambridge Law Journal* 174–207.

29 Tor-Inge Harbo, 'The function of the proportionality principle in EU law' (2010) 16 *European Law Journal* 158.

30 Yutaka Arai-Takahashi, *The Margin of Appreciation Doctrine and the Principle of Proportionality in the Jurisprudence of the ECHR* (Intersentia 2002).

31 The seminal case is *Lüth*, BVerfGE 7, 198.

32 Robert Alexy, 'Constitutional rights, balancing, and rationality' (2003) 16(2) *Ratio Juris* 131–40.

33 Aurelien Portuese, 'Principle of proportionality as principle of economic efficiency' (2013) 19(5) *European Law Journal* 612–35.

34 That is, when there is no measure available that is Pareto superior to the *status quo* with respect to all values involved.

The purpose, again, is to preserve efficiency: the measure will be considered disproportionately restrictive of a right if its contribution to the competing value is inferior to the restriction caused, in terms of intensity. The test, on closer inspection, invites a comparison between states of the world (rather than values as such): one in which the interference operates and one where it does not. More on this below.

This 'Disproportionality Rule'[35] is defined by the BvfG as follows:

> An interference with a constitutional right is disproportionate if it is not justified by the fact that the omission of this interference would give rise to an interference with another principle (or with the same principle with respect to other persons or in other respects), provided that this latter interference is at least as intensive as the first one.[36]

The proportionality test has for decades been the tool of choice for the CJEU to deliver judgments in 'hard cases' without forfeiting its legitimacy. Proportionality's high level of proceduralisation and its operation, reminiscent of a mathematical formula, facilitate the Court's ungrateful task to second-guess Member States' preferences and EU law's compliance with FRs. This section discusses the use of proportionality and FR-adjudication in selected CJEU judgments.

The case of *Google Spain*, like *Lindqvist*, is a hybrid of Types 1 and 2. Unlike in *Lindqvist*, however, the Type 1 component (the evolutionary interpretation of fundamental rights) is not disguised. The facts are notorious but warrant a synthetic account. Mr Costeja González, a martyr of the digital age if ever there was one, Googled his name on one fateful day in 2009. He noticed that the first results were links to the digitalised copy of a local newspaper, which had published in 1998 the notice of a public auction on real estate properties, including his own, seized to recover social security debts. He therefore requested Google to remove these links from the results of a search under his name, alleging that the exposure of the facts implied in that notice breached his right to privacy. More specifically, he invoked a right to have certain past events not reported in publicly available documents in the absence of an overriding public interest.[37]

First, we can observe the Type 2 component of the ruling. The Court was called to answer a gateway question, namely whether Google qualified as a controller of personal data under Directive 95/46. Google claimed that it did not, because its activity merely consisted in content-blind indexing of all words uploaded online. This indexing allows Google to populate search results for the users of its search engine.

35 Alexy, 'Constitutional rights' (n 32) 139.

36 ibid, from the *Titanic* judgment, BVerfGE vol. 86, 1.

37 Two insightful commentaries are Eleni Frantziou, 'Further developments in the right to be forgotten: the European Court of Justice's Judgment in Case C–131/12 *Google Spain SL, Google Inc v Agencia Espanola de Proteccion de Datos*' (2014) 14(4) *Human Rights Law Review* 761; John W. Kropf, '*Google Spain SL v Agencia Española de Protección de Datos (AEPD)*: Case C–131/12' (2014) 108(3) *American Journal of International Law* 502–509.

To understand how delicate this finding was, think of a real-life situation. A webpage that simply contained all whole numbers from 3200000000 to 9999999999 was inundated by urgent requests (ranging from courteous inquiries to threats of criminal prosecution) by internet users. These people had reached the page by searching the web using their own mobile numbers as keyword, or by searching online the identity of an unknown caller and finding the corresponding number on that page.[38] They asked, alternatively, that their number be taken down from the page, or that the identity of the anonymous caller be revealed by the website's manager. Implicitly (and mistakenly), these people assumed that the webmaster had the duties that are typically imposed on all subjects processing personal information, such as telephone numbers (although the requests to reveal the owner of a given number even exceeded what can be demanded from a data processor, presumably).

Was there any processing involved, of the kind that would make the webmasters 'controllers' or 'processors' under EU data protection law? Of course not, the correspondence between the numbers listed and the users' mobile numbers was a meaningless coincidence. In *Google Spain*, Google argued that its activity was comparable to that of the subjects responsible for the webpage listing whole numbers sequentially: an automated processing with no meaningful editorial intervention. Here, the Court was satisfied that Google, by indexing online data, had performed a deliberate commercial activity for which responsibility can arise. In other words, Google is a controller under the directive.[39]

The Type 1 part of the judgment, however, is the one that openly employed a constitutional reasoning. The Court laid the ground for its determination by acknowledging that the outcome, although seemingly framed as a question of principle, depended on the context. Quite simply, information loaded online is too readily available, to anyone. Availability of truthful information published lawfully has become a problem – this is not something that had ever raised particular concerns in a pre-internet era.[40] Now, instead, regulation to manage the

38 See http://www.matteoweb.it/scripts/elenco-numeri/ (last accessed 12 August 2015). For a caustic comment on the absurdity of the requests in the comments see http://www.kronic.it/artGet.aspx?cID=37775 (last accessed 12 August 2015). Various references to the numbers listed as 'prime numbers' seem inaccurate, as this is a progressive table of all whole natural numbers. In all honesty, it is plausible to suspect that the web-master knew that the list of numbers could confuse many users into concern, and therefore serve as phenomenal click-bait.

39 *Google Spain* (n 9) paras 32–34.

40 ibid para. 80: 'It must be pointed out at the outset that . . . processing of personal data, such as that at issue in the main proceedings, carried out by the operator of a search engine is liable to affect significantly the fundamental rights to privacy and to the protection of personal data when the search by means of that engine is carried out on the basis of an individual's name, since that processing enables any internet user to obtain through the list of results a structured overview of the information relating to that individual that can be found on the internet – information which potentially concerns a vast number of aspects of his private life and which, without the search engine, could not have been interconnected or could have been only with great difficulty – and thereby to establish a more or less detailed profile of him. Furthermore, the effect of the interference with those rights of the data subject is heightened on account of the important role played by

negative externalities of this information overload is required. This is partly the result of just how good online search engines are: information is only as public as search engines make it available.

The Court concluded that the search provider is a controller engaging in the processing of personal data. As a consequence, state regulatory agencies can order the removal of the search results relating to the use of one's name as a keyword, when they are seized with a request to review Google's refusal to do so.[41] This order can be granted when the results shown obtained with a search engine entail an excessive interference in the data subject's private life, without a concurring (and overriding) justification. Because time soothes some of the justifications available based on public interest, this finding was saluted as establishing a 'right to be forgotten'. The resulting instruction of the Court, which read into the applicable rules of the directive a specific duty (on the part of the controller) and right (of the data subject), stems from an overt use of proportionality.

The passage where the reasoning of the CJEU reveals the use of proportionality *stricto sensu* calls for closer analysis:

> As the data subject may, in the light of his fundamental rights under Articles 7 and 8 of the Charter, request that the information in question no longer be made available to the general public by its inclusion in such a list of results, it should be held . . . that those rights override, as a rule, not only the economic interest of the operator of the search engine but also the interest of the general public in finding that information upon a search relating to the data subject's name. However, that would not be the case if it appeared, for particular reasons, such as the role played by the data subject in public life, that the interference with his fundamental rights is justified by the preponderant interest of the general public in having, on account of inclusion in the list of results, access to the information in question.[42]

This excerpt evokes and contrasts at least four discrete principles/values: (1) the data subject's 'right to oblivion' (in turn an elaboration of her rights to private life and data protection under Articles 7 and 8 of the Charter, subsumed under the 'compelling reasons' under Article 14(a) of the directive); (2) the operator's economic interest, protected by Articles 15–17 of the Charter; (3) the public's right to impart and obtain information, protected by Article 11 of the Charter; and (4) unspecified 'particular reasons' that could tip the balance in favour of the general public's interest at the expense of the data subject's own interests.

Balancing four rights is a devilish task even if we assume, for the sake of ease, that a given measure *x* can only either respect or breach each of them (that is, we disregard the degree of contribution to the achievement of each right and the

the internet and search engines in modern society, which render the information contained in such a list of results ubiquitous.'

41 ibid para. 99.

42 ibid para. 97.

intensity of the breach thereof[43]). A mere head-count does not work: the Court itself confirms that the data subject's right prevails over two competing interests (of the public and of the economic operator). If we added the analysis of the intensity of the measure's marginal impact on the enjoyment of each right,[44] we would be able perhaps to determine it statically.[45]

For instance, we could agree that the solution envisaged by the Court protected the rights of Mr Costeja González and of those like him from a *substantial* harm, restricting *slightly* the interests of the public to know about their past, as well as the newspaper's right to inform the public about it through online diffusion. It also imposed a *significantly burdensome* restriction on the right to exercise a business enterprise onto Google and other search engines. How do these magnitudes relate to each other?

It is not clear whether the Court attempted to factor into the equation the degree of restriction of all values involved. In fact, certain wording suggests that instead privacy *by default* prevails over freedom of information and of conducting business:

> [the rights under] Articles 7 and 8 of the Charter . . . override, *as a rule*, not only the economic interest of the operator of the search engine but also the interest of the general public in having access to that information upon a search relating to the data subject's name.[46]

It cannot be excluded that the Court performed an accurate balancing test but, since this does not emerge from the ruling, we have to re-create it and compare the results of the actual decision with the hypothetical exercise. Can the 'Disproportionality Rule' clarify the calculus?

Under this rule, the solution envisaged by the Court is proportionate insofar as its absence would determine a graver breach of rights than the restriction it causes (a negative overall utility balance with respect to r1, r2 . . . to rn).[47] In other words, we should ascertain whether establishing Google's obligation to enforce the 'right to oblivion' is *less* restrictive of the rights under Articles 11, 15, 16 and 17 of the Charter than rejecting it would be of the rights under Articles 7 and 8. Each vari-

43 On the problem of commensurability between values and between interferences to values see Niels Petersen, 'How to compare the length of lines to the weight of stones: balancing and the resolution of value conflicts in constitutional law' (2013) 14 *German Law Journal* 1387. For a discussion of how to represent commensurate values without using numerical indications see Giovanni Sartor, 'Logic of proportionality: reasoning with non-numerical magnitudes' (2013) 14 *German Law Journal* 1419, 1429 ff.

44 See Aharon Barak, 'Proportionality and principled balancing' (2010) 4 *Law and Ethics of Human Rights* 1, 8.

45 That is, we could try to analyse its collective 'realisation-impact' across the relevant values. See Sartor (n 43) 1436: '[t]he realisation-impact of an action α on a value v is the difference between the realisation-quantities of v resulting from α and [the status quo]'.

46 *Google Spain* (n 9) para. 99. Emphasis added.

47 Sartor (n 43) 1391: '[W]e do not compare the weight of the stone to the length of the line. Instead, we analyze whether we add proportionally more length to the line than we shed weight of the stone.'

able in the calculation is adjusted for the intensity of the restriction and, presumably, for the number of people actually or potentially affected. In short, although certainly it is possible to justify the outcome of the Court along these lines, the outcome is not falsifiable because too many variables hinge on a discretionary approximation. An outcome opposite to the one indicated by the Court, indeed, would be plausible, in light of the magnitude of the burden imposed on Google and the number of people whose access to the relevant information is restricted. Unsurprisingly, the reasoning of the Court is very cavalier in treating the steps of the proportionality analysis, and in specifying the relative strength of its variables.[48]

The proportionality test, in this field, is not a heuristic device to reach the right decision. Indeed, the outcome of this contrived proportionality calculus is not falsifiable, but only opinable or contestable. Instead of selecting the outcome of the decision, the balancing provides a malleable template that shapes only its supporting reasoning. In other words, at least in the particular circumstances of this dispute, one can understand Habermas's critique to the notion of proportionality: '[in the proportionality test Values must be brought in to a transitive order with other values from case to case. Because there are no rational standards for this, weighing takes place either arbitrarily or unreflectively, according to customary standards and hierarchies.'[49] I will return to this wider critique below, in relation to other digital disputes. For the moment, I want to stress how the factual matrix of the Google case is, *ab initio*, hard to frame as a stand-off between established fundamental rights.

What bothered Mr Costeja, in whose honour the Streisand-effect[50] should be renamed, was not so much the existence of that piece of news, published lawfully and buried at page 23 of an old magazine but, rather, the real problem was that his 'Google-identity' or 'Google-footprint' was unflattering; consequently, he requested that Google obey, to an extent, his instructions on which aspects of his web-relevant *persona* should pop out first through a name search. The 'right to be forgotten' tag is misleading, and so is the reference to the removal of the results from the results: what really mattered is that the troublesome results came at the top of the list. Had the infamous links been listed at page 23 of the Google research results, Mr Costeja would simply not have cared, exactly as he presumably did not care in 2009 about the 1998 print publication of the very same tainting news. In short, Mr Costeja objected to the enormous scavenging powers of Google algorithms, and the sorting of the results.

Is there a nascent fundamental right to the fairness, accuracy or representativeness of our digital *persona*? If so, how can this right trump Google's interest to carry out its distinctive line of business, through a lawful collection of lawfully published content? Clearly, Google's business performance has unintended

48 Frantziou (n 37) 8: 'while Articles 7 and 8 of the Charter suggest the creation of some obligations for EU institutions and Member States, they do not specify what the role of private actors such as Google should be in the enforcement of the relevant standards, or what limitations to these rights are acceptable and how they ought to be balanced against other, equally fundamental, rights'.

49 Jürgen Habermas, *Between Facts and Norms* (The MIT Press 1996) 259 ff.

50 http://en.wikipedia.org/wiki/Streisand_effect (last accessed 12 August 2015).

consequences on somebody's life, which are perceived as unfair even if they derive from lawful facts and acts. Is Google's mind-blowingly efficient archiving and sorting activity the kind of dangerous conduct that, although legal per se, imposes a surplus of responsibility on the subject? Is one's online personality so vulnerable that it also deserves protection against certain lawful acts?[51]

In the folds of the Court's reasoning lay the idea that, in a context of obsolescence of public authorities, Google must operate as a quasi-public authority.[52] Therefore, it has non-reciprocal and non-contractual obligations towards its stakeholders (both the users and the persons affected by its activity). This notion is not the result of a balancing operation but of a regulatory choice, however reasonable and legitimate.

I am not claiming that the judgment is wrong on the merits: the interference with one's private life is evident, and the bigger question was probably whether the Court should have endorsed this 'shooting the messenger' technique, rather than focusing on the application of the data protection duties of the newspaper. The crucial point is how much novelty the Court has nonchalantly reined in through legislator-like discretion, simply flashing the proportionality test at the beholders. The Court combined the right to private life and the right to a lawful use of personal data (neither of which was breached by the publication) to enforce an *unprecedented* right, in *unprecedented* circumstances and implicating an *unprecedented* role for Google, establishing in the process its *unprecedented* duty to arbiter individual applications of data removal.

In other words, I find no manifest error in the static assessment of the values at stake and of the relative restrictions entailed by the *status quo*. What is unsatisfactory, perhaps, is the lack of reasoning regarding the proportionality of the indicated solution (Google's duty to remove the personal data in certain circumstances). Proportionality *stricto sensu* only operates – as seen above – through the comparison between the aggregate right-implementation of the *status quo* and an alternative measure. The Court found a disproportion in the *status quo* and provided a solution. The better option would have been to show that the solution brings about a more favourable view of right-implementation. The Court has failed to show this necessary element of proportionality: the putative advantage of changing the *status quo*.

5.4 Low-intensity actions with momentous reach: protecting collateral victims of internet measures

Proportionality operates not between values but between marginal variations of value-realisation entailed by alternative states of the world (induced or mandated

51 This is one step further from the AG's remark that: 'the universal scope of the information contributes to the harm being potentially more acute than that suffered, for example, by means of a conventional medium'; see *eDate* (n 3) para. 48).

52 Johan Eriksson and Giampiero Giacomello, 'Who controls the internet? Beyond the obstinacy or obsolescence of the state' (2009) 11 *International Studies Review* 205–30.

by identified normative measures). However, as argued in the previous section, internet-based activities do not lend themselves to the intuitive generalisations that allow reviewers to attach quantitative judgments to the realisation of rights and compare them in a *pre*-measure and *post*-measure comparison.

This difficulty was prefigured in *Lindqvist* (where the low-intensity threat to privacy was multiplied by the accessibility of online content, causing a formal disproportion that required a policy-oriented ruling). A less risky assessment was necessary in *Schecke*.[53] The applicants claimed that the publication online of their companies' names amongst the recipients of EU funding (within the Common Agricultural Policy) was unnecessarily restrictive of the company's privacy. The values involved were the public's interest in knowing the exact allocation of EU funds, the Union's duty of transparency and the recipients' interest in privacy. On that occasion, however, the problem was solved through simple Pareto optimisation. The *status quo* entailing the diffusion of unnecessary information, it was sufficient to reduce or qualify the range of data published to increase the implementation of the right to privacy without decreasing the enjoyment of the concurring values.

When Pareto optimisation cannot occur, however, internet cases reveal their non-manageability through balancing. A case on point is *L'Oréal v eBay*, which mixes the Type 1 and Type 2 reasoning in one judgment. The case apparently revolved around a purely Type 2 issue, and apparently regarded fundamental rights only tangentially. Nonetheless, the involvement of several stakeholders and several fundamental rights makes it an ideal case to discuss the elusiveness of digital litigation to balancing parsing.

L'Oréal sued eBay for unlawful use of its trademark. In fact, eBay buys from the likes of Google the search engine optimisation (SEO) service necessary to make its links appear first on web search engines' results. eBay's links relate to items that are on sale on the website, many of which are branded items. Therefore, the relative trademarks are amongst the words that eBay selects and pays SEO for. Sometimes, private parties sell counterfeit goods through eBay. eBay cannot be liable for that directly (the only way to avoid the practice would be to set up a preventive filtering system, which goes against Article 15 of the 2000/31 Directive, see above). However, L'Oréal argued that eBay, by actively buying SEO services for the search word 'l'oréal' was using its brand and was essentially exploiting or at least abetting (also) the sale of counterfeit products – an indirect breach of trademarks rights.

The Type 2 question, in short, was whether the use of the brand L'Oréal by eBay qualified as 'use' under the relevant EU norms on trademarks.[54] If so, the use of the brand could be objected by the trademark-holder, if unlawful. Whether in 1989 the EU legislator could possibly conceive of the purchase of SEO through keywords that can correspond to brands is beyond the point: the rationale being the IP-holder's power to prevent third parties from using its IP-rights

53 Joined Cases C–92/09 and C–93/09 *Volker und Markus Schecke and Eifert* [2010] ECR I–11063.

54 Specifically, art 5(1)(a) of Directive 89/104 and art 9(1)(a) of Regulation No. 40/94.

without consent, the refinement required to apply pre-internet rules could occur without much conceptual trouble.

The Type 1 component of the dispute, however, was less straightforward, and did not emerge in the judgment. It did, however, in the Opinion of the Advocate General, who reminded the parties at the outset that eBay listings are covered by freedom of expression and information, under Article 11 of the Charter.[55] AG Jääskinen conceded that freedom of expression cannot normally justify a breach of property rights, including trademarks. However, the protection of a trade mark proprietor's rights in the context of electronic commerce may not take forms that *would infringe the rights of innocent users* of an electronic marketplace or leave the alleged infringer without due possibilities of opposition and defence.[56]

In other words, it would be generally unfair to set up a system of shorthand remedies for the benefit of IP holders, if sellers of genuine goods were adversely affected unnecessarily. This remark reveals the endemic problem of regulation of all internet-related conduct: any standard potentially applies to millions of users. It is impossible to identify a priori innocent bystanders and fraudulent users, and fine-tune regulation to exclude false positives. The slippery slope is around the corner every time regulation of internet behaviour is based on a seemingly neutral balancing of values, because the sheer scale of massive behaviour online makes it impossible to strike a balance that is acceptable to all people involved whose fundamental rights must be considered.

In short, any regulation of the activity 'using internet' is inevitably over-inclusive with respect to the regulatory goal pursued. It is as if obtaining a driving licence or avoiding drinking were required conduct for all those 'breathing', because all those who drive are certainly 'breathers'. Unfortunately, there seems to be no better way to circumscribe internet regulation *ratione personae* or *ratione materiae*. As a result, balancing is normally and demonstrably impossible to achieve. This is so since internet-regulating measures have such a massive inefficiency-creating externality (i.e. they create useless restrictions for users whose action is compatible with the goal pursued by the regulation) that it is impossible to prove their proportionality. That is, it is often impossible to demonstrate that internet regulations arbitrating between competing rights secure, if applied, an overall positive balance of rights enjoyment compared with the *status quo*.

To its credit, the findings of the Court are rarely the direct result of a proportionality test, and more often reflect a policy choice, often dictated by the concern of avoiding false positives and minimising the number of stakeholders whose interest is sacrificed in the trade-off. The Court in *Lindqvist* spared billions of web-users from the regime applicable to those who transfer personal information to third countries. In *Google Spain*, the Court operated a policy choice: when the individual's concern is plausible, Google's duty to act upon it is the more convenient option, as opposed to sacrificing her fundamental right,

55 Joined Cases C–92/09 and C–93/09 *Volker und Markus Schecke and Eifert* (n 53) Opinion, para. 49.

56 ibid para. 158. Emphasis added.

or asking the news outlet to retract a lawful exercise of the freedom to impart information. However, note how this idea of (utilitarian) convenience is candidly spelled out in the preamble of Directive 2001/29[57] on copyright protection in the information society:

> In the digital environment . . . the services of intermediaries may increasingly be used by third parties for infringing activities. In many cases such intermediaries *are best placed to bring such infringing activities to an end.* Therefore, without prejudice to any other sanctions and remedies available, rightholders should have the possibility of applying for an injunction against an intermediary who carries a third party's infringement of a protected work or other subject-matter in a network. . . . The conditions and modalities relating to such injunctions should be left to the national law of the Member States.[58]

There is a clear utilitarian foundation to the rightholders' right to seek court injunctions ordering intermediaries to remove the breach. The corresponding intermediaries' duty does not stem from their legal responsibility or the optimal balance between their rights and duties, but from their being 'best placed' to counter illegality. The intermediaries have quasi-public responsibilities reflecting their quasi-public authority: it is difficult not to draw a parallel with the outcome of the *Google* case, as constructed in the previous section.

In *L'Oréal v eBay* the rights of the legion of users selling their property on eBay could not be curtailed by preventive restrictions. eBay was held liable for infringement of IP rights only if it was 'aware' of it, for instance when it cooperated with the user on the preparation of the listings. Likewise, IP holders in the *SABAM* dispute[59] could not enforce their rights at the expense of internet users who do not engage in illegal practices, nor could the provider shoulder the task of filtering the traffic pre-emptively to avoid breaches. In another case (*UPC Telekabel*[60]), the intermediary was not eBay, and the alleged infringement of IP rights was not camouflaged amongst millions of innocent personal advertisements. The intermediate was an internet provider, which had been ordered by a national court to block the users' access to a website granting access to pirated movies. In this dispute, the very possibility of a blanket shutdown was less of a concern for the Court: the website was clearly up to no good, hence there was no risk of false positives being unfairly affected by the injunction. The balancing with the hypothetical countervailing rights was briefly accounted for as follows:

57 Directive 2001/29/EC of the European Parliament and of the Council of 22 May 2001 on the harmonisation of certain aspects of copyright and related rights in the information society OJ L167 (22.6.2001) 10–19.

58 ibid recital 59.

59 Case C-360/10 *SABAM*, judgment of 16 February 2012.

60 Case C-314/12 *UPC Telekabel*, judgment of 27 March 2014.

> [i]n order to prevent the fundamental rights recognised by EU law from precluding the adoption of an injunction such as that at issue in the main proceedings, the national procedural rules must provide a possibility for internet users to assert their rights before the court once the implementing measures taken by the internet service provider are known.[61]

Even in a case like *Schecke*, where the outcome is based on a proper proportionality analysis (to the point that the Court assessed the necessity of the measure challenged, and suggested a less restrictive alternative),[62] the underlying problem was more mundane. Because any information on the internet receives disproportionate exposure, anything uploaded beyond the strictly necessary breaches somebody's rights significantly, even when the additional disclosure is per se not particularly harmful.

The fragmentation of *practical* responsibility for the downstream consequence of online conduct is difficult to decipher with certainty (consider the recent Snapchat issue, involving third party services[63]). The vast disproportion that can occur (in size, timespan, reach, effects, harmfulness) between conduct and events makes it impossible to apportion *legal* responsibility according to a principled analysis such as that underpinning proportionality balancing. The northern star of the Court seems to be the minimisation of costs, which is not the same as maximisation of rights. Responsibility is regularly attributed to those who suffer the least from bearing it. Slippery slopes are regularly shunned, a pragmatic result that betrays the Court's preference for sustainability over principles. There seems to be a twist, however, which confirms the impossibility to refer to a unique method of balancing: millions of internet users are allowed to sell goods (*L'Oréal*) and exchange files (*SABAM*) freely, even if this relatively unregulated practice occasionally encroaches on the rights of private individuals. When what is at stake is a public interest, instead, the focus shifts and defusing the internet's multiplying effect of disorderly conduct becomes the priority:

> It must be acknowledged that a prohibition measure covering any offer of games of chance via the internet may, in principle, be regarded as suitable for pursuing the legitimate objectives of preventing incitement to squander money on gambling, combating addiction to the latter and protecting young persons, even though the offer of such games remains authorised through more traditional channels.[64]

61 ibid para. 57.

62 ibid paras 79–82.

63 See 'The snappening: how were Snapchat user's images hacked and should we all be worried?' *The Independent* (14 October 2014) http://www.independent.co.uk/life-style/gadgets-and-tech/the-snappening-how-were-snapchat-users-images-hacked-and-should-we-all-be-worried-9794296.html (last accessed 12 August 2015).

64 Case C–46/08 *Carmen Media Group* [2010] ECR I–8149, para. 105.

An exception to this very pragmatic approach is the case of *Digital Rights v Ireland*,[65] in which the Court annulled the Data Retention Directive,[66] in a flamboyant exercise of proportionality testing. However, the Court maybe tried a bit too hard to sell this decision as an obvious application of balancing. Consider the following statement, relating to the minimum period for which telecommunications operators must retain the data:

> That period is set at between a minimum of 6 months and a maximum of 24 months, but it is not stated that the determination of the period of retention must be based on objective criteria in order to ensure that it is limited to what is strictly necessary.[67]

This remark purports to prove too much: why should an EU directive specify that its application must comply with the principle of proportionality, or respect for fundamental rights? Is proportionality not a general principle of EU law that applies, by default, to the interpretation, implementation and application of EU measures? Is respect for fundamental rights not already a binding principle on state acts? If the directive leaves a huge margin to state implementation, would not Article 51 of the Charter suffice to prevent the risk that implementing measures breach fundamental rights? These are rhetorical questions. Certainly, the potential breach entailed by defective implementing state action cannot be attributed to the directive, but to the Member States. FR-based review should hit the implementing measures, not the implemented act, unless the latter mandates a breach of human rights, *quod non* in the specific case.

In truth, it is plausible to concede that the directive was probably badly drafted, and that a tighter wording with respect to the FR-implications could have helped Member States to implement it in the appropriate way, and achieve more coherence from state to state. Ultimately, the inefficient (i.e. disproportionate) measures were the national implementing acts. The Court, perhaps knowing that the directive would necessarily need an overhaul in any event, applied the proportionality directly to it, in a display of righteousness that conveyed the notion that the EU is under a rule of FR law and the Court is ready to enforce it.

As for the proportionality test itself, this case was relatively simple, with essentially two interests in tension: the privacy of the data subjects and the public security.[68] The duty of telecommunication providers to retain personal information

65 Joined Cases C-293/12 and C-594/12 *Digital Rights Ireland and Seitlinger and Others*, judgment of 8 April 2014.

66 Directive 2006/24/EC of the European Parliament and of the Council of 15 March 2006 on the retention of data generated or processed in connection with the provision of publicly available electronic communications services or of public communications networks and amending Directive 2002/58/EC.

67 Joined Cases C-293/12 and C-594/12 *Digital Rights Ireland and Seitlinger and Others* (n 65) para. 64.

68 That the directive's goal was certified as being the protection of public order and security is another point of possible contention. The directive, indeed, was adopted under the first pillar as a measure

was in fact a mere exception to the former for the benefit of the latter, not an autonomous element for the balancing. In essence, the dispute hinged on the regulatory limits of the extension. Using the privacy-restrictive scenario allowed (if not required) by the directive as the *status quo* baseline, the Court performed an approximate proportionality analysis.

The Court opened the analysis using several degree-qualifying terms, which seemed to set the scene for an intensity assessment. Protection of personal data plays an '*important* role' and the directive causes a '*serious*' interference, hence the Court's judicial review thereon 'should be *strict*';[69] moreover, the fight against organised crime and terrorism is 'of the *utmost importance*'.[70] The suitability of data retention – in general – for the purposes of fighting crime went uncontested,[71] but the necessity of its limitation under the directive – in particular – was very much contestable. The Court went as far as to remind the reader that 'derogations and limitations in relation to the protection of personal data must apply only insofar as is strictly necessary'.[72] This statement should probably serve as a reminder of just how important the necessity step is, lest we admit that limitations of certain rights other than data protection can be *non-strictly* necessary.

The Court then introduced a spurious element at the outset of the necessity test: the obligation for the EU legislator to provide in its acts minimum safeguards against the risk of abuse of fundamental rights.[73] This unheard of legislative duty is borrowed 'by analogy' from the case law of the ECtHR regarding domestic statutes, whose vagueness could unduly empower executive authorities to decide the scope of FR limitation.[74] However, this parallel oddly overlooks the nature of directives as sources of law which, by definition, are not directly applicable in the member states. The positive duty that the ECtHR bestows on national legislators cannot be attributed inattentively to the EU legislator drafting directives by analogy. Because directives *require* national implementing legislation, there is no need to concoct an analogy. Reasonably, the required safeguards must be included precisely in the national statutes implementing the directives, at the hand of national authorities.

The call for clauses of minimum protection is also problematic because it injects an inherent vice in the proportionality reasoning. See how Alexy describes similar instructions:

providing for the harmonisation of national rules, aimed at the removal of obstacles to the realisation of a common market of services. This economic goal, the only official one, was somewhat side-lined in the Court's analysis in favour of the second-level purpose (the 'material objective') of facilitating the fight against crime; see Data Retention Directive (n 66) para. 41.

69 Joined Cases C–293/12 and C–594/12 *Digital Rights Ireland and Seitlinger and Others* (n 65) para. 48, emphases added.

70 ibid para. 51, emphasis added.

71 ibid para. 49.

72 ibid para. 52, quoting Case C–473/12 *IPI* (not yet reported, 7 November 2013) para. 39.

73 ibid para. 54.

74 See, for instance, *Rotaru v Romania* Application no. 28341/95, Judgment (Merits and Just Satisfaction), Grand Chamber (4 May 2000) paras 57–59.

> A guarantee of a minimum, if not determined by balancing, would, indeed, not be the same as optimization. It would, however, not only be different from optimization but also different from proportionality. It would not be an alternative interpretation of proportionality. Rather, it would be an alternative incompatible with proportionality. One who recommends the substitution of a guarantee of a minimum for the principle of proportionality in the narrower sense is recommending the abolishment of this principle.[75]

Even allowing that this requirement be compatible with proportionality, the notion that the directive should have included minimum safeguards (something it most certainly did not) skewed irremediably the necessity analysis towards a finding of breach. The Court limited itself to note that the directive applied to a wide and largely undifferentiated range of communications, means of communications and users.[76] Moreover, the directive did not set a specific requirement that persons whose data ought to be retained are suspected of a crime,[77] any objective criteria to calibrate the state's access to the data retained[78] or any guidelines on how to restrict domestically the period of retention, down from the over-inclusive range provided in the directive.[79]

The Court hence concluded peremptorily that the directive caused an interference with FRs, and the interference was not 'precisely circumscribed by provisions to ensure that it is actually limited to what is strictly necessary'.[80] Failure to meet the necessity requirement entailed a failure to respect the proportionality principle and, ultimately, led to the annulment of the act.

In this case, it is difficult to take the proportionality reasoning seriously, for the reasons stated above. This judgment features, in my view, in the Court's trend of using proportionality-based arguments to produce policy-based decisions. Technically, the enhanced necessity analysis, including the duty to provide normative safeguards, made for an atypical proportionality test that cannot be traced back to the classic model. There is an easy way to appreciate how the Court used the proportionality narrative in an unorthodox manner. Even if the measure failed the necessity test, the Court did not even try to identify alternative measures, which were reasonably available and equally effective to fight crime. In other words, the Court condemned the *status quo* without proving with any precision that another possible counterfactual situation could secure a better overall balance of FR protection.

This was held implicitly when the Court noted the over-inclusiveness of the directive. However, it is fair to suppose that narrowing down the scope of the retention to an optimal level was a difficult task, hence it could not be assumed

75 Robert Alexy, 'Constitutional rights and proportionality' (2014) 22 *Revus* 51, 59.

76 See Joined Cases C-293/12 and C-594/12 *Digital Rights Ireland and Seitlinger and Others* (n 65) para 56.

77 ibid paras 56–59.

78 ibid paras 60–62.

79 ibid paras 63–64.

80 ibid para. 65.

that simply because the directive balance appeared unfortunate a better solution was readily available: perhaps it was not. Possibly, requiring that retention only occur when the conduct of the persons involved is suspicious might hinder significantly the effectiveness of the investigation. Likewise, the indication that the time-range for the period of retention is excessive should have come with a cost–benefit analysis of alternative ranges, or additional criteria to narrow the range down domestically. In short, there is no hint of real comparison in the Court's reasoning, which reveals that the Court itself (forget this author) did not take proportionality seriously either.[81]

5.5 Conclusions

In conclusion, the Court is couching its decisions in a familiar jargon, namely, that used in the balancing of fundamental rights. This is an understandable approach, but the recurrent use of proportionality does not evince a *fil rouge* of the case law. Sometimes, proportionality fails to account for the outcome of the single decisions. Balancing as such would make sense only if one hoped to find a point of equilibrium, the end of a zero-sum game, where any other alternative would be wrong (because unbalanced). This aspiration is futile in the field of internet activities, where various recurring features advise against using balancing as a heuristic tool. Specifically, balancing often occurs between three or more groups of stakeholders and three or more different rights:[82] lawful conduct can result in harmful effects that are difficult to gauge and that, just by virtue of the online-multiplier, could be incalculable; sweeping regulation is likely adversely to affect innocent subjects; rarely will all rights be preserved through balancing (to achieve Pareto optimisation).

The challenge for the Court, in these conditions, is to let go of the comfortable terminology on proportionality and allocate liability using a pragmatic policy-oriented approach, as it has done with some regularity so far, although covertly.

81 Incidentally, AG Jääskinen had at least tried harder to apply proportionality. For instance, he argued that time measured 'in years' is inherently disproportionate because it pertains to the 'memory' of the 'historical time' of the users, rather than their 'present life' (better measured in months). See para. 146 of the Opinion. Whereas he conceded that the distinction is bound to prove unhelpful in certain cases (when criminal plans 'are prepared well in advance', see para.149), he at least tried to argue that a counterfactual measure yields a better FR outcome than the *status quo*.

82 See Case C–314/12 *UPC Telekabel* (n 60) para. 47: 'it must be observed that an injunction such as that at issue in the main proceedings, taken on the basis of Article 8(3) of Directive 2001/29, makes it necessary to strike a balance, primarily, between (i) copyrights and related rights, which are intellectual property and are therefore protected under Article 17(2) of the Charter, (ii) the freedom to conduct a business, which economic agents such as internet service providers enjoy under Article 16 of the Charter, and (iii) the freedom of information of internet users, whose protection is ensured by Article 11 of the Charter'. See also Rebecca Wong and Joseph Savirimuthu, 'All or nothing: this is the question – The application of Article 3(2) Data Protection Directive 95/46/EC to the internet' (2007) 25 *John Marshall Journal of Computer & Information Law* 241, 260 ('Identity management and privacy considerations now compete with market expectations of choice, availability, and efficiency').

Ultimately, however, the refinement of legal categories cannot be entrusted to the Court alone: the incoming regulatory reform of the field is bound to provide more guidance (and more precise rules, of course) to judges and EU citizens alike. I am aware of the risks of abandoning the FR discourse and relying on policy-oriented adjudication. Torre rightly noted that if 'fundamental rights are seen as policies, they will however lose their point, which is controlling and limiting State action'.[83]

However, limiting the exercise of public authority is hardly the most pressing problem of the regulation of internet-related conduct, for the simple reason that public authority is comparatively weaker in this field. What needs urgent management are the interplay between private rights and private interests, and the public policy inputs necessary to arbitrate or moderate this relationship. The *Google Spain* and *L'Oréal* cases are, in this sense, illustrative of how the difficulty does not lie in the nature of public interference into private conduct, but in the sustainability of a reciprocal arrangement between human activities with numerous externalities.

Ultimately, I am proposing to let go of the 'mathematical' proportionality championed by Alexy, which has provided the Court for too long with a comfort zone where anything goes, in terms of legal argumentation. If the motivation of the Court's decisions is policy-oriented, there is no plausible benefit in their disguise as proportionality *calculi*. *Google Spain* is a pragmatic apportionment of duties, and so is *L'Oréal v eBay*. *UPC* spurs from a matter-of-fact consideration: the website's conduct is prima facie illegal. *Digital Rights Ireland* is really a revise-and-resubmit note to the EU legislator. This list could go on, and most certainly future cases will join it: internet disputes are bound to fit uncomfortably in the proportionality straitjacket. Better: the proportionality test is bound to fit too loosely or too tightly on internet-based realities. *Ad hoc* adjustments are routinely necessary, to the point that it is not clear anymore why we should stick to a test that systematically needs *à la carte* stretching.

Habermas famously criticised proportionality balancing for undermining the claim to correctness of adjudication of principles. Proportionality-based reasoning, in short, would not reflect the legal categories of right and wrong, but the policy categories of adequateness and opportunity, thus depriving FRs of their status of legal principles.[84] Alexy's rebuttal is convincing, in general: proportionality *is better than nothing*. The three-step test, in fact, envisages 'abundant criteria to label a proposition as correct or incorrect':[85] it provides an articulate template for judicial reasoning in cases where free-style reasoning could be conceived as unprincipled. In his words,

83 Massimo La Torre, 'Nine critiques to Alexy's Theory of fundamental rights' in Agustín J. Menéndez and Erik O. Eriksen (eds), *Arguing Fundamental Rights* (Springer 2006) 53–68, 61.

84 Habermas, *Between Facts and Norms* (n 49) 256–59.

85 Matthias Klatt and Moritz Meister, *The Constitutional Structure of Proportionality* (OUP 2012) 69.

> [proportionality is] an argument form of rational legal discourse. As such, it is indispensable in order to introduce 'order into legal thought'. It makes clear which points are decisive and how these points are related to one another.[86]

This is undisputable. What makes this remark less compelling in the cases studied here is the set of idiosyncrasies of human affairs in the digital arena, underlined above. Because optimisation is not a realistic task, proportionality cannot operate its 'ordering' effect and becomes a hollow formula. If the assessments of necessity and strict proportionality are based on fuzzy and truncated reasoning (intensity of infringements is not measured; alternative measures are not explored and compared with the *status quo*; the interests of various groups are contrasted 'impressionistically' and not analytically; the reasoning shifts uncontrollably and inadvertently from the interests of the parties to the dispute and the interest of society at large, etc.), it is not better than nothing; it is *worse.*

Habermas's warning ring true, in these cases. Whereas I do not object to the Court's engagement in policy-based balancing (what else?), I take issue with its masquerading as neutral-looking proportionality. If free-style judicial reasoning is the best that we can expect (if the legislator stalls, that is), let reasoning be free indeed and not constrained by formulaic incrustations.

86 Alexy, 'Constitutional rights and proportionality' (n 74) 64. Footnotes omitted.

6 Protection of fundamental rights and the internet

A comparison between Italian and French systems of constitutional adjudication

Paolo Passaglia *

6.1 Introduction

The Italian Constitutional Court and the French Constitutional Council fulfil a crucial role in their respective legal orders and embody, therefore, veritable milestones in the protection of fundamental rights and the implementation of the rule of law. This much is uncontested and, in the light of the evolution of constitutional adjudication in both countries, is not contestable.

Such a premise could easily suggest that cyber law has become a crucial field for Italian and French constitutional case law, simultaneously with the growth of the internet's influence over almost every area of law. Such a conclusion does not appear to be unquestionable. Or rather, it must be investigated further. Indeed, the number of judgments concerning the internet in both bodies of case law is not impressive (although a clear difference must be drawn between Italy and France); therefore, in order to establish the real connection between internet law and constitutional adjudication, different factors must be taken into account. This is the main aim of this chapter, which will deal, first, with the system of constitutional adjudication in general (section 6.2), and then with the constitutional case law concerning the internet (section 6.3). The conclusion (section 6.4) explains what emerges from the analysis of the case laws under review, having regard to the structure of the systems of constitutional adjudication, without neglecting the sources of internet law.

6.2 General comments on the Italian and French systems of constitutional adjudication (with specific reference to the protection of fundamental rights)

6.2.1 The establishment of the two systems of constitutional adjudication

After the Second World War, the Italian legal and political reconstruction began with a popular referendum, the outcome of which favoured a republican system, and with the consequent election of a Constituent Assembly, which drafted the

* The author wishes to thank Sarah Pasetto for her comments and suggestions.

new Constitution and adopted it at the end of 1947. Italian constitutionalism thus entered a brand new phase, marked by the establishment of a human rights-oriented system, and in which a new wave of case law inspired by natural law imposed limits on the government and even on the legislature, which were now bound by a constitution conceived as the supreme law of the land. In this connection, two features of the new Charter must be highlighted.

On the one hand, for the first time, a genuine bill of rights was adopted to protect human rights from all kinds of infringement, committed by any type of authority: the only way to avoid the obligations enshrined in the Constitution was supposedly through the adoption of constitutional amendments, for which it was necessary to follow a complex procedure that was practically guaranteed either to generate parliamentary opposition or to grant the people the chance to block any illiberal initiatives on part of the majority. Unfortunately, another method of avoidance would be discovered very soon: delaying the implementation of constitutional provisions. The use and abuse of this 'instrument' (a form of 'majority filibustering')[1] paralysed the concrete protection of many constitutional rights, especially social rights and rights to equality, for a very long time, so that several constitutional provisions were implemented only in the 1970s.

On the other hand, for the first time, a mechanism for constitutional review was established to provide the system with an effective means of reacting against infringements of the supreme law. This aim was pursued by Articles 134–137 of the Constitution, which contained the provisions on the Constitutional Court. Oddly enough, but perhaps not surprisingly, these articles too were subjected to majority filibustering, since the court began its functions only in 1956, that is over eight years after the Constitution's entry into force. However, constitutional review preceded the Constitutional Court thanks to clause 2 of the VII Transitional and Final Provisions of the Constitution, which allowed ordinary courts to decide the controversies that would ordinarily have been referred to the Constitutional Court.[2]

The Italian Constitutional Court was thus conceived and established as the paramount protector of human rights vis-à-vis any branch of government, and in particular political bodies and institutions.

The French Constitutional Council does not share the same origin. As a matter of fact, when the Constitution of the 5th Republic was drafted, the main aim was

1 See Piero Calamandrei, *L'ostruzionismo di maggioranza* (Il ponte 1953) 129, 274 and 433.

2 See Pasquale Costanzo, 'Disposizioni transitorie e finali I-XVIII: Leggi costituzionali e di revisione costituzionale (1948–1993) – commentario della Costituzione' in Giuseppe Branca and Alessandro Pizzorusso (eds), *Disp. trans. VII* (Zanichelli-Il Foro italiano 1995) 143; Marco Bignami, *Costituzione flessibile, Costituzione rigida e controllo di costituzionalità in Italia (1848–1956)* (Giuffrè 1997); Andrea Simoncini, 'L'avvio della Corte costituzionale e gli strumenti per la definizione del suo ruolo: un problema storico aperto' (2004) *Giurisprudenza costituzionale* 3065; Ugo De Siervo, 'L'istituzione della Corte costituzionale: dall'Assemblea costituente ai primi anni di attività della Corte' in Paolo Carnevale and Carlo Colapietro (eds), *La giustizia costituzionale fra memoria e prospettive: a cinquant'anni dalla pubblicazione della prima sentenza della Corte costituzionale* (Giappichelli 2008) 55.

to do away with Parliament's supremacy and establish a more efficient government, based on a strong executive branch and the limitation of Parliament's powers. General de Gaulle's real challenge, therefore, was to strengthen the decision-making process to secure the correct operation of a democratic system that was already established (unlike in Italy, when the Republican Constitution was drafted) and was considered (whether the assumption was right or wrong is irrelevant here) to be rather effective in terms of protecting rights. It is noteworthy, in this regard, that the 1958 Constitution focused on the structure of government, almost neglecting any reference to the protection of human rights.[3]

Furthermore, the French constitutional tradition had been very much influenced by Rousseau's theory of the law as the expression of the general will, and thus of popular sovereignty.[4] Before 1958, the idea that laws (to be more precise, the acts adopted by the Parliament as the body representing the people) could not be subject to judicial review was rooted in French legal culture since the Revolution, along with a fear of a 'government of judges', namely of those officials that were supposed to be 'the mouth that pronounces the words of the law'.[5]

Given such a background, one could hardly assert that the establishment of the Constitutional Council by the 1958 Constitution was the result of adoption, on the part of France, of foreign models of constitutional adjudication. Indeed, the role that was designated for the new institution was very different from that of (other) constitutional courts: the Constitutional Council was meant to be the 'gun pointed at the Parliament',[6] to prevent any possible recovery of those powers that the drafters of the Constitution had wanted to remove from it.

Rather than protecting individual rights against political bodies, the main task of the council was therefore to arbitrate legal disputes between Parliament and government so as to safeguard the new balance that was designed by the Constitution. The council was indeed the guardian of the Constitution, like foreign constitutional courts, but the contents of the 1958 Constitution, which essentially focused on the interaction between branches of government, made the council a highly peculiar body from a comparative point of view.

6.2.2 *The original competences of the Italian Constitutional Court and of the French Constitutional Council*

The original conceptions of the Constitutional Court and the Constitutional Council has had a profound impact on the competences endowed on the two bodies.

3 For an analysis of the Constitution-making process and the purposes of the main actors see Didier Maus, Louis Favoreu and Jean-Luc Parodi (eds), *L'écriture de la Constitution de 1958* (Economica – Presses universitaires d'Aix-Marseille 1992).

4 See Jean-Jacques Rousseau, *Du contrat social ou Principes du droit politique* (1762) Liv. II, ch VI.

5 This definition was introduced by the Baron de Montesquieu in his *De l'Esprit des Lois* (1748) Liv. XI, ch VI.

6 See François Luchaire, *Le Conseil constitutionnel: Tome I – Organisation et Attributions* (Economica 1997) 36.

6.2.2.1 The Italian system

As far as the Italian court is concerned, since the beginning, its most important task has been to rule on disputes 'regarding the constitutional validity of legislative acts and instruments having the same force of the laws adopted by the State and the Regions'.

For this review of legislation, both abstract and concrete forms were established. Abstract review addresses either claims from the national government against a regional legislative act or claims lodged by a region against a national legislative act. Complaints must be filed within 60 days of the publication of the challenged act(s). In these cases, the court decides – in principle – without referring at all to the concrete implementation of legislative provisions, even though the submission of a complaint does not paralyse the implementation of the provisions questioned, such that the latter may have already produced effects by the time that the court reviews them.[7] Indeed, the constitutional proceedings are designed to resolve disputes on the limits of the central state's and regions' respective powers; therefore, the court either protects the autonomy of the regions from encroachment by the central government, or protects the state's legislative power against misuse of power by regional legislatures.[8]

In Italy, contrary to what Kelsenian orthodoxy would suggest,[9] constitutional review can also be concrete. The Constituent Assembly rejected the idea of giving individuals the power to appeal to the court directly: the protection of individual rights – and, more generally, the constitutionality of legislative acts – must be invoked through the activity of ordinary courts, which are empowered to refer a question to the Constitutional Court when there are doubts as to the constitutionality of a legislative provision that applies in proceedings before them. Thus, the Constitutional Court reviews provisions' constitutionality on the basis of the case in which the issue arose, such that the concrete implementation of the provision is one of the elements that should be germane to the court's judgment.[10]

7 It is noteworthy that this statement is true for complaints brought pursuant to the entry into force of the 2001 constitutional reform. Previously, the review of provisions already in force was conceivable only for national primary legislation, since regional legislation was to be challenged before it was promulgated by the regional president, such that the law-making process was suspended and the Act could enter into force only after the court had decided upon its consistency with the Constitution. On this subject see Carlo Padula, *L'asimmetria nel giudizio in via principale. La posizione dello Stato e delle Regioni davanti alla Corte costituzionale* (Cedam 2006); in French, see Massimo Luciani and Paolo Passaglia, *Autonomie régionale et locale et Constitutions – Rapport italien* (2006) *Annuaire international de justice constitutionnelle* 229.

8 However, the national government can censure any kind of breach of the Constitution; thus, its appeal is not necessarily related to the aim of protecting the state's legislative power.

9 See Kelsen's criticism of the Austrian constitutional reform of 1929 that introduced the instrument of judicial reference to the Constitutional Court: Hans Kelsen, 'Judicial review of legislation: a comparative study of the Austrian and the American Constitutions' (1942) 4 *The Journal of Politics* 183.

10 Owing to the sheer number of contributions, it is impossible to compile a complete bibliography

The power to strike down legislation is clear evidence that the Kelsenian conception of constitutional courts as 'negative legislators', which do not make law but only strike down legislation that is inconsistent with a higher law, was adopted.[11]

The principle of the unity of constitutional justice, and the corollaries that ensue from it, is limited to primary legislation. The Constitutional Court is empowered to review all legislative acts, both national and regional, and governmental decrees that have the same force as parliamentary legislation either by virtue of a delegation of power from the Parliament to the executive (Article 76 of the Constitution) or because an emergency has arisen that requires immediately effective provisions (Article 77 of the Constitution). When it comes to subordinate legislation, however, the Constitutional Court does not exercise any competence: the consistency of this category of measures with (the Constitution and) primary legislation is ascertained by ordinary courts; the latter have the power to refuse to apply inconsistent measures, whilst administrative courts may also strike them down, and thus achieve general effects for their declarations.

Apart from legislative review, the Italian court was not endowed with many 'accessory' competences: for instance, the court – unlike many other European constitutional courts – does not have any say as far as elections are concerned. As a matter of fact, there are only four competences other than the review of legislation.

The court decides on constitutional controversies arising between the regions

on the judicial reference procedure. *Ex plurimis* see, however, Giuseppe Abbamonte, *Il processo costituzionale italiano. Il sindacato incidentale* (Jovene 1957); Franco Modugno, 'Riflessioni interlocutorie sull'autonomia del giudizio costituzionale' (1966) *Rassegna di diritto pubblico* 221; Adriana Gardino Carli, *Giudici e Corte costituzionale. Gli elementi diffusi del nostro sistema di giustizia costituzionale* (Giuffrè 1988); Corte costituzionale, *Giudice* a quo *e promovimento del processo costituzionale* (Giuffrè 1990); Antonino Spadaro, *Limiti del giudizio costituzionale in via incidentale e ruolo dei giudici* (Edizioni Scientifiche Italiane 1990); Silvia Bagni, *La questione incidentale nel controllo di costituzionalità. I sistemi italiano e spagnolo a confronto nel quadro dei modelli elaborati dalla dottrina* (Clueb 2007); Lorenzo Delli Priscoli and Paolo Giovanni Demarchi, *L'eccezione di incostituzionalità: profili processuali* (Zanichelli 2008); Nicola Pignatelli, *Le 'interazioni' tra processo amministrativo e processo costituzionale in via incidentale* (Giappichelli 2008).

11 As a matter of fact, however, currently such a definition can be confirmed only with some difficulty, if anything because the court has granted itself the power not only to strike down provisions, but also individual words or expressions in the text of a provision. In this case, by erasing part of the text but not the provision itself, the court changes the provision's contents. The idea of the court as 'negative legislator' is even more remote in cases when the court declares a legislative provision to be unconstitutional for what it *fails* to contain, and thus adds a part to its contents to make the provision consistent with the Constitution. With regard to these so-called 'manipulative judgments' see Gaetano Silvestri, 'Le sentenze normative della Corte costituzionale' (1981) 1 *Giurisprudenza costituzionale* 1684; Leopoldo Elia, 'Le sentenze additive e la più recente giurisprudenza della Corte costituzionale' in *Scritti su La giustizia costituzionale in onore di Vezio Crisafulli* (Cedam 1985) 299; Giustino D'Orazio, 'Le sentenze costituzionali additive tra esaltazione e contestazione' (1992) *Rivista trimestrale di diritto pubblico* 61; Roberto Pinardi, *L'*horror vacui *nel giudizio sulle leggi* (Giuffrè 2007).

and the state with regard to measures, provisions and conducts that do not fall within the scope of the abstract review of legislation, and thus any sort of action or enactment (adopted by any branch, including the judiciary) which is not primary legislation. This competence amounts to the completion of the abstract review, since it shares with the latter the same parties (regions and state) and the same grievances: the region that alleges an encroachment upon its constitutional autonomy challenges the state (represented by the president of the Council of Ministers) or another region; likewise, the national government challenges the authority of a region (represented by its president) on the grounds that its action or enactment exceeds the limits of regional powers or interferes with the powers of the state.

The court is also called upon to arbitrate 'conflicts of attribution' arising 'between the powers of the State', when the bodies capable of represent their branch claim that the powers assigned to them by the Constitution have been encroached upon by another branch of government. In all likelihood, this is the court's most 'political' competence, since conflicts may arise, for example, between a judicial body and a chamber of Parliament (regarding e.g. the immunity guaranteed to members of Parliament by the Constitution) or between a minister and a chamber of Parliament that has passed a vote of no confidence against him.

The Constitutional Court is also called upon to verify whether a referendum – requested by at least 500,000 voters or five regional legislatures – can take place, pursuant to Article 75, for the total or partial repeal of a national legislative act or an instrument having the same force. In particular, the court must verify whether the request for the referendum exceeds the limits identified by the Constitution and constitutional case law. Thus, for example, the court does not admit requests for referenda in which a single question incorporates several distinct items to be repealed, so as to guarantee the free choice of voters with respect to each component of the referendum; requests for referenda are also blocked when they seek to repeal laws the contents of which derive directly from constitutional provisions (since these contents represent the only way that the provisions can be implemented), or which cannot be amended without revising the Constitution itself; nor can a referendum take place if its aim is not simply to repeal, but rather to introduce new legal provisions by rewriting a legislative text; finally, a referendum is also blocked when it could give rise to international responsibility on part of the state, meaning that no referendum can take place to repeal laws required by international or European Union obligations.

Finally, the court is the judge in criminal proceedings against the head of state for high treason or attacks upon the Constitution. Until 1989, the court was also the judge for criminal proceedings against members of the government for crimes committed in the exercise of their duties. In the course of its history, the court has acted as a criminal judge only once, in the 1978–1979 *Lockheed* corruption trial, in which two former ministers were charged. For ministers, Constitutional Law No. 1/1989 transferred the court's jurisdiction to the ordinary criminal courts, subject to special procedures.

6.2.2.2 The French system

The 1958 Constitution endowed the French Constitutional Council with several competences, related not only to constitutional review but also to other kinds of functions.

Legislative provisions were subject to the council's scrutiny only *ex ante*, that is before the presidential promulgation.[12] Parliament's ordinary laws could be challenged before the Council by the president of the Republic, the prime minister, the president of the National Assembly (the lower chamber) and the president of the Senate. The council's review of the Parliament's organic laws[13] was mandatory, as well as of that concerning Parliament's internal regulations. These reviews aimed to prevent the Parliament from regaining, through its rules or legislative acts, powers and functions that the Constitution transferred to other branches, in particular to the government.

Other competences had the same purpose, namely those related to the delimitation of the areas that legislative power can regulate (Article 34 of the Constitution): whenever a bill or an amendment provided for regulation concerning areas which did not fall within the competence of Parliament, the government was able to challenge it before the Constitutional Council (Article 41 of the Constitution). The government also had the power to challenge, for the same reasons, a legislative provision already in force, to obtain its 'downgrading' by the Constitutional Council to the level of governmental enactments.

The council was also endowed with the power to oversee the regularity of the election of the president of the Republic (who has been elected by the people since 1965) and of referenda. In both cases, the council also proclaims the results. Furthermore, it is the judge of parliamentary elections and it rules on the eligibility of members of Parliament and any incompatibilities between their individual pursuits and their public role.

The Constitutional Council was given an advisory power in the case of the implementation of Article 16 of the Constitution, according to which

> Where the institutions of the Republic, the independence of the Nation, the integrity of its territory or the fulfillment of its international commitments are under serious and immediate threat, and where the proper functioning of the constitutional public authorities is interrupted, the President of the Republic shall take measures required by these circumstances, after formally consulting the Prime Minister, the Presidents of the Houses of Parliament and the Constitutional Council.

12 Indeed, the theory according to which legislation is the expression of the general will prevented the Constitutional Council from *a posteriori* review, since legislative acts, once in force, were conceived of as the expressions of rationality.

13 Organic laws are legislative acts subordinated only to the Constitution and prevailing over ordinary laws.

On the whole, the competences of the council turned it into an entity very different from a protector of individual rights,[14] consistently with the aim pursued by the drafters of the Constitution, which was not to reorganise the way in which rights were to be guaranteed, but to establish a (very) 'rationalized parliamentarism', in the words of Mirkine Guetzevitch.[15]

6.2.3 *The evolution of the Italian and French systems of constitutional adjudication*

The different origins of the Italian and the French systems naturally affected their respective evolutions. In Italy, the constitutional and legislative framework of the system has remained very much the same throughout the decades, apart from some reforms of relatively low impact. On the contrary, in France, dramatic reforms were passed to adapt the Constitutional Council to the new needs of the legal system, so as eventually to turn it into a body endowed with powers comparable to those that characterise a real constitutional court.

6.2.3.1 *The Italian experience*

Despite a rather stable legislative and constitutional framework, the role and activity of the Italian Constitutional Court have changed significantly over the years.

In particular, as far as the protection of rights is concerned, a major change occurred especially at the end of the twentieth century, in connection with European integration.[16] On the one hand, over the years the European Court

14 An analysis in English of the birth (and evolution) of the French Constitutional Council is available in A. Stone, *The Birth of Judicial Politics in France: The Constitutional Council in Comparative Perspective* (Oxford University Press 1992).

15 See Boris Mirkine-Guetzevitch, *Les constitutions de l'Europe nouvelle* (Librairie Delagrave 1928) 12.

16 With regard to the subject see, *ex plurimis*, Paolo Falzea, Antonino Spadaro and Luigi Ventura (eds), *La Corte costituzionale e le Corti d'Europa* (Giappichelli 2003); Antonio D'Atena and Paolo Grossi (eds), *Tutela dei diritti fondamentali e costituzionalismo multilivello* (Giuffrè 2004); Paola Bilancia and Eugenio De Marco (eds), *La tutela multilivello dei diritti* (Giuffrè 2004); Nicolò Zanon (ed), *Le Corti dell'integrazione europea e la Corte costituzionale italiana* (Edizioni Scientifiche Italiane 2006); Vincenzo Sciarabba, *Tra Fonti e Corti: Diritti e principi fondamentali in Europa: profili costituzionali e comparati degli sviluppi sovranazionali* (Cedam 2008); Pietro Perlingieri, *Leale collaborazione tra Corte costituzionale e Corti europee* (Esi 2008); Daniele Butturini, *La tutela dei diritti fondamentali nell'ordinamento costituzionale italiano ed europeo* (Esi 2009); Tommaso Giovannetti, *L'Europa dei giudici: La funzione giurisdizionale nell'integrazione comunitaria* (Giappichelli 2009); Giuseppe Martinico, *L'integrazione silente. La funzione interpretativa della Corte di giustizia e il diritto costituzionale europeo* (Jovene 2009); Giuseppe de Vergottini, *Oltre il dialogo tra le Corti. Giudici, diritto straniero, comparazione* (il Mulino 2010); Giancarlo Rolla (ed), *Il sistema europeo di protezione dei diritti fondamentali e i rapporti tra le giurisdizioni* (Giuffrè 2010). In English see Giuseppe Martinico and Oreste Pollicino, *The Interaction Between Europe's Legal Systems: Judicial Dialogue and the Creation of Supranational Law* (Edward Elgar 2012). In French see Massimo Luciani, Paolo Passaglia, Alessandro Pizzorusso

of Human Rights had developed a body of case law concerning fundamental rights that created the conditions for it to compete with the Constitutional Court. Nevertheless, the possibility of invoking the adjudication of the Strasbourg Court requires all internal remedies to be exhausted first: because of this limitation, the Constitutional Court can easily intervene before the European Court, so that problems can arise, at most, in relation to the influence of European case law over constitutional case law. In other words, the Constitutional Court can be influenced by the Strasbourg Court only insofar as the interpretation of constitutional provisions is concerned. Thus, the competition between the two courts relates to the kind of protection granted to a fundamental right and the settlement of conflicts between opposing rights, but does not imply an actual alternative between the protection granted at the national level and that granted by the Strasbourg Court.

Instead, the real 'rival' of the Constitutional Court appears to be the Court of Justice of the European Union, which has been taking full advantage of the expansion of the Union's competences, especially of the enforcement of the European Charter of Fundamental Rights. The latter allows the Court of Justice to develop a body of case law on rights that has the potential to become a genuine alternative to that issued by the Constitutional Court, for the simple reason that the preliminary ruling mechanism is very similar to the internal system for referring cases to the Constitutional Court: indeed, judges can often choose between the two, to determine which (the constitutional or the European one) is more convenient to pursue. The dialogue between national courts and the Court of Justice has greatly intensified, so that the Constitutional Court no longer enjoys a 'monopoly' in interacting with ordinary courts. In other words, the protection of rights is ensured at both national and European levels.

The Constitutional Court's role as a protector of rights has also been changing, in relation to the type of interaction established with ordinary courts. One of the reasons that led to the establishment of the Constitutional Court was that ordinary courts were not considered sufficiently responsive to the new constitutional values. Since the entry into force of the Constitution, the situation has changed significantly: the Constitution has been recognised as the foundation of the legal system; constitutional provisions have proven to be effective in shaping a new civil society; and legal education has considered constitutional law to be a key field of study. All of these factors have resulted in judges adopting a different approach to the Constitution: they have increasingly chosen to apply it directly, considering it as a law endowed with direct effect, and not only as a political document that requires legislative implementation.

One of the most powerful demonstrations of the cooperation established between the Constitutional Court and ordinary courts over the years concerns legislative interpretation. The time when conflicts between the Constitutional Court and the Supreme Court of Cassation as to which of the two authorities

and Roberto Romboli, 'Justice constitutionnelle, justice ordinaire, justice supranationale: à qui revient la protection des droits fondamentaux en Europe? – Rapport italien' (2004) *Annuaire international de justice constitutionnelle* 251.

had the final say over legislative interpretation is long gone. In the 1960s, those conflicts had led to the so-called 'war between the Courts', which eventually ended with the courts mutually recognising their respective responsibilities. Today, the Constitutional Court is acknowledged as the supreme interpreter of the Constitution, and the Court of Cassation as the supreme interpreter of legislation.[17]

Since then, the Constitutional Court defers to the Court of Cassation's interpretation of laws, claiming the power to strike down legislation or, at most, proposing its own interpretation of primary legislation only when there is no consolidated interpretation. This is the 'living law' doctrine, an expression that may recall Roscoe Pound's distinction between 'the law in books' and 'the law in action',[18] the latter being – in the Italian adaptation – the law as it 'lives', that is the law resulting from the way in which a text (the legal provision) is interpreted. By accepting this doctrine, the Constitutional Court bound itself to accepting the consolidated interpretation of a provision; thus, the court cannot override an interpretation that is generally adopted by ordinary courts.

The Constitutional Court itself became the forerunner of a new role for ordinary courts in the context of constitutional review by encouraging a new approach to legislative provisions, based on the expansion of judicial means of interpretation. In Judgment No. 356/1996 of 22 October 1996, the court expressed the new approach with words that would later be repeated continuously:

> In principle, legislative acts are not declared unconstitutional because it is possible to interpret them so as to render them unconstitutional (and there are courts willing to apply such an interpretation), but because it is impossible to interpret them so as to render them constitutional.

This led to constitutional case law that required ordinary courts to refrain from submitting a reference to the Constitutional Court until they had examined – and excluded – the possibility of interpreting the provision at issue so as to render it constitutional.[19] A third condition for the submission of a judicial reference to the Constitutional Court was thus introduced by means of case law: in addition to *rilevanza* and *non manifesta infondatezza*, established, respectively, by Article 1 of Constitutional Law No. 1 of 1948 and Article 23 of Ordinary Law No. 87

17 On this subject see Giuseppe Campanelli, *Incontri e scontri tra Corte suprema e Corte costituzionale in Italia e in Spagna* (Giappichelli 2005) 217.

18 Roscoe Pound, 'Law in books and law in action' (1910) 44 *American Law Review* 12.

19 On this subject see Giusi Sorrenti, *L'interpretazione conforme a Costituzione* (Giuffrè 2006); Pasquale Femia (ed.), *Interpretazione a fini applicativi e legittimità costituzionale* (Edizioni Scientifiche Italiane 2006); Roberto Romboli, 'Qualcosa di nuovo . . . anzi d'antico: la contesa sull'interpretazione conforme alla legge' in Carnevale and Colapietro (n 2) 89; Marilisa D'Amico and Barbara Randazzo (eds), *Interpretazione conforme e tecniche argomentative* (Giappichelli 2009); Corte costituzionale, *Corte costituzionale, giudici comuni e interpretazioni adeguatrici* (Giuffrè 2010); Elisabetta Lamarque, *Corte costituzionale e giudici nell'Italia repubblicana* (Laterza 2012).

of 1953, ordinary courts must now first examine the possibility of making the legislative provision conform to the Constitution by means of interpretation.[20]

Indeed, it is a well-established doctrine that the Constitutional Court will not decide on the merits of a case unless the referring court has documented the need for the reference owing to the ineffectiveness of interpretation alone. In the 1990s, the Constitutional Court delivered at least 471 judgments each year (except for 1996, when it delivered 'only' 437 judgments); after 2002, the number of judgments never exceeded 482 (in 2005). In 2012, there were 316 judgments, in 2013 the number was 326 and in 2014 only 286, the lowest number since 1982. Admittedly, a change is taking place.

Considering that conflicts between the central state and regions have increased, and thus the number of judgments leading to abstract review of legislation has been rising, and considering too that the number of conflicts either between the state and regions or between supreme bodies of the state arising from administrative or judicial acts has little impact, it cannot be doubted that the significant reduction of the judgments issued is the consequence of the dramatic fall in judicial references.

This fall can be easily explained by the concurrence of supranational courts and, above all, by the new approach to legislative interpretation.

The problem does not lie in the numbers, but rather in the type of cases that are submitted to the Constitutional Court. On the one hand, the court must often deal with minor issues, in which the constitutional matter remains in the background; thus, the number of judicial references could, and probably should, decrease even further. On the other hand, by giving ordinary courts the power to apply legislation through interpretation, the Constitutional Court accepted the risk that it would not be called upon to decide pivotal constitutional matters, since the condition for avoiding a reference to the Constitutional Court is (simply) to argue that the legislation in question *can* be interpreted consistently with the Constitution. In recent years, for instance, high-profile debates on constitutional matters such as euthanasia and living wills, or the definition of asylum-seekers, to mention only a few, did not lead to a judgment by the Constitutional Court, because the Court of Cassation had the power to end them. One could certainly ask whether it is acceptable that the Constitutional Court, the supreme interpreter of the Constitution, did not take part in the debate on such matters.

To conclude on this point, it is fair to say that the Italian system of constitutional adjudication has experienced huge changes in the last few years, most notably concerning the end of the monopoly of the Constitutional Court as the interpreter of the Constitution and, therefore, as the cornerstone in the protection of individual rights. Currently, the Constitutional Court is *one* of

20 The question should arise on the compatibility of the new condition and the *non manifesta infondatezza*, since when the Constitutional Court requires ordinary courts to state that it is impossible to give the provision a constitutional interpretation, it can be hardly maintained that the condition for submitting a question for constitutional review is a mere lack of certainty as to the provision's consistency with the Constitution.

the protectors, together with the European Courts and the ordinary courts – a complex system, therefore, in which many actors share responsibilities, but also one in which some actors risk being incapable of effective participation. The Constitutional Court may sometimes be one of the latter.

6.2.3.2 The French experience

The evolution of the Fifth Republic greatly affected the role of the Constitutional Council, which was established to protect the government against the Parliament and that eventually became the protector of fundamental rights. Such a major change was the result of multiple factors.

First, the French political system experienced a dramatic change in the aftermath of the entry into force of the 1958 Constitution. The drafters of the Constitution were constantly concerned about the attitude displayed by the Parliament, since recent history had shown its overwhelming predominance compared with the other branches, in particular the executive one. This concern led to the adoption of a constitution that was very efficient in pursuing the aim of limiting Parliament's action. Or rather, the Constitution was so efficient that the Parliament became a relatively weak institution, at least compared with the president of the Republic and the government. In this context, the need for a 'gun pointed' at the Parliament appeared increasingly useless: therefore, the role of the Constitutional Council was to supervise an institution which often acted as a lapdog of the executive branch and that, when it tried to oppose the president of the Republic, did not prove to have enough power to prevail, or even significantly influence policies and decision-making processes. In other words, the Constitutional Council, initially conceived as a gun pointed at a dangerous neighbour, was turning into the warden of an inmate, assuming that Parliament's action was restricted to a severely delimited area.

During the 1960s, the Constitutional Council was thus in a very uncomfortable position: on the one hand, its main mission appeared increasingly outdated; on the other hand, its competences could hardly offer opportunities for new roles. To this end, the main problem resided in the authorities empowered to submit appeals to the council, since all of these were part of the majority, and thus had no interest in enabling it to review legislation or policies: owing to the changes introduced by the 1958 Constitution, legal standing was not conferred on stakeholders. The council thus risked a protracted, forced, inactivity: as a matter of fact, the number of judgments delivered in the 1960s was far from remarkable; above all, the cases brought before the council were almost all of very low constitutional status.

Amongst the authorities entitled to submit claims, only the president of the Senate was not directly linked to the governmental majority (the Senate does not vote for confidence) and, thus, despite its right-wing political affiliation, it was in a relatively independent position towards the right-wing government, especially after General de Gaulle's resignation as president of the Republic in 1969. Therefore, it is no coincidence that the turning point of the Constitutional

Council's history originated from a claim of the president of the Senate, the only authority that could submit a case of high interest.

In 1971, a statute reforming some aspects of freedom of association was criticised by the opposition and a large part of public opinion because of its restrictive effects. Once adopted by Parliament (and prior to presidential promulgation), the president of the Senate submitted the text to the council, although the missions of the latter could hardly give it the power to review infringements of individual rights. Notwithstanding such a major obstacle, the council, in Judgment No. 71-44 DC of 16 July 1971, seized the opportunity and declared the statute unconstitutional. In doing so, the council interpreted the Constitution so as to broaden the standards of judgment: first, it recognised the legal force of the preamble of the 1958 Constitution; consequently, it extended this recognition to the acts and documents to which the preamble referred, namely the 1789 Declaration of the Rights of the Man and of the Citizen and the preamble of the Constitution of the Fourth Republic (1946). Through the latter preamble, two sets of principles gained constitutional status: the political, economic and social principles enumerated in the preamble and defined as 'especially necessary to our times' and the 'fundamental principles recognized in the statutes of the Republic', which were not enumerated, and were thus to be identified by the interpreters, scanning through the legislation of the previous Republics, in particular the long-standing Third Republic (1875–1940).[21]

Thanks to the new construction of this 'block of constitutionality' (*bloc de constitutionnalité*),[22] the Constitutional Council arrogated the power to review legislation not only in light of the organisation of powers established by the 1958 Constitution, but also of the rights that had been recognised over the course of time, and in particular the liberty rights typical of classical liberalism (1789 Declaration), the group rights recognised in the late nineteenth century (fundamental principles recognised by the statutes of the Republic) and the claim rights typical of the welfare state (principles defined as 'especially necessary to our times').[23]

In 1971, the Constitutional Council thus became a potential protector of individual rights. However, the main problem was still the number and the type of subjects endowed with the power to appeal before it. The president of the Senate had played a key role thus far and could be a significant actor also in the future, but could not be the only authority to submit questions to the council: after all, its independence was relative, since it often shared the views of the governmental majority.

21 I discussed the importance of Judgment No. 71-44 DC in Paolo Passaglia, *La Costituzione dinamica. Quinta Repubblica e tradizione costituzionale francese* (Giappichelli 2008) 247. In that contribution, further bibliographical references are also available.

22 The expression was introduced by Louis Favoreu, *Le principe de constitutionnalité. Essai de définition d'après la jurisprudence du Conseil constitutionnel* (Cujas 1975) 33. Formerly, Claude Emeri and Jean Louis Seurin, 'Vie et droit parlementaire' (1970) *Revue du droit public et de la science politique* 678, had spoken of a 'block of the constitutionality' (*bloc de la constitutionnalité*).

23 In 2005, the French Constitution will be enhanced with the 2004 Charter of the Environment, which ensures the protection of the so-called third-generation rights.

The Constitutional Council would have probably undergone only minor changes to its position if a crucial constitutional reform had not been adopted in 1974.[24] To balance the power of the majority and to strengthen the opposition's position, the president of the Republic Valéry Giscard d'Estaing supported a reform seeking to give the opposition the power to submit challenges to legislative acts to the Constitutional Council, on the same conditions as those established for other authorities, after Parliament's adoption and prior to presidential promulgation. The power to challenge legislation was then conferred on 60 members of the National Assembly and 60 senators.

Since the entry into force of this reform, the number of claims brought before the Constitutional Council has dramatically increased; nearly all of these were submitted on the opposition's initiative: having lost the political struggle in Parliament, the opposition was given the chance to continue the fight in legal terms, with the further benefit of being able to claim a key role in the protection of fundamental rights. As a matter of fact, thanks to the constitutional reform, the Constitutional Council has gradually become an effective protector of rights, increasingly similar to other 'real' constitutional courts based on the European model of constitutional adjudication.

The path towards an accomplished system of constitutional adjudication could not be completed until Article 6 of the 1789 Declaration was conceived as a barrier against review of legislation in force: the definition of legislation as the expression of the general will, that Article 6 borrowed from Jean-Jacques Rousseau, made it impossible for anyone to question and review acts that were expressions of both sovereignty and rationality (the general will having both of these attributes). The role of the Constitutional Council was, in fact, limited to the legislative process (since proceedings before it could be defined as a phase of the decision-making process), without any regard to legislative provisions as applied in practice. Such a limitation clearly distinguished the council vis-à-vis the other national constitutional courts in Europe and, above all, prevented it from ensuring a complete protection of the Constitution (and thereby of individual rights) with regard to legislation, as carried out in the everyday life of the legal order.

Another constitutional reform was required to strengthen the protection of the Constitution with an *ex post* review. Attempts to introduce the method of judicial reference to the Constitutional Council were made in 1990 and in 1993 but, after a long and controversial debate, the Parliament rejected the constitutional reform bill, thus preserving one of the key features of the French constitutional tradition.

In fact, during the 1990s and even more so at the beginning of the twenty-first century, one could easily observe that there was little remaining to preserve. Indeed, ordinary courts were endowed with the power to review legislation.

24 See Association française de Droit constitutionnel – Gerjc (Institut Louis Favoreu), *30 ans de saisine parlementaire du Conseil constitutionnel* (Economica – Presses Universitaires d'Aix-Marseille 2006).

The review concerned legislation already in force, due to be applied in judicial proceedings. This competence, however, did not result in the adoption of the American model of judicial review, because the standard of judgment adopted by ordinary courts was neither the Constitution nor the block of constitutionality: courts were allowed to review the 'conventionality' of French law (primary legislation included), that is its consistency with European Union law and with international conventions, among which the European Convention on Human Rights.[25]

The review for conventionality was fostered by the Constitutional Council and its refusal, since 1975, to review the constitutionality of statutes inconsistent with international law, notwithstanding the theoretical possibility, once such an inconsistency has been proven, to invoke the indirect violation of Article 55 of the Constitution, according to which '[t]reaties or agreements duly ratified or approved shall, upon publication, prevail over Acts of Parliament, subject, with respect to each agreement or treaty, to its application by the other party'. The paradox is that, over the years, the huge development of the review for conventionality became an issue, because it increasingly based the protection of rights on international sources rather than on the French Constitution. As a further result, the Constitutional Council, being the guardian of the Constitution, risked playing only a secondary role in the protection of rights, to the benefit of the European Court of Human Rights and probably, in the near future, of the European Court of Justice.

To prevent the risk of outsourcing the protection of rights, reforms were necessary. In particular, the Constitution had to be restored as the cornerstone of the system, and to do so its guardian had to be empowered with adequate competences. The answer was precisely the introduction of a judicial reference procedure, thanks to which legislative provisions could also be reviewed when they were already in force and the protection of rights could be, first and foremost, the result of judgments on consistency with the Constitution, rather than with international human rights instruments. It is therefore no coincidence that the introduction of a judicial reference procedure was one of the most important provisions of the general reform of the Constitution adopted in 2008:

> If, during proceedings in progress before a court of law, it is claimed that a legislative provision infringes the rights and freedoms guaranteed by the Constitution, the matter may be referred by the Council of State or by the Court of Cassation to the Constitutional Council which shall rule within a determined period. (Article 61(1), para. 1 of the Constitution as revised)

The conditions for the application of the new procedure were to be determined by means of an organic law. The act carrying out the constitutional reform made the main aim of the reform itself explicit, by establishing a *question prioritaire de constitutionnalité* (QPC), namely a 'prior preliminary ruling on the issue

25 See Olivier Dutheillet de Lamothe, *Contrôle de constitutionnalité et contrôle de conventionnalité* (Dalloz 2007) 315.

of constitutionality': the adjective 'prior' refers, indeed, to the ordinary courts' obligation to raise a question of unconstitutionality *before* engaging in any review for compatibility with supranational law.

In March 2010, with the entry into force of the organic law and the concrete application of this judicial reference procedure, the French legal order eventually gained a system of constitutional adjudication in which the Constitutional Council was able to protect fundamental rights in ways that were comparable to those of its foreign counterparts, amongst which was, of course, the Italian Constitutional Court, since the Italian judicial reference procedure was one of the models that inspired the French legislator.[26]

6.3 The constitutional case law concerning internet law

6.3.1 The protection of individual rights within the context of internet

Both the Italian Constitutional Court and the French Constitutional Council (the latter at least since 2010) are endowed with competences that allow them – at least in theory – to perform an efficient protection of individual rights. Therefore, both appear to be in a good position to protect rights relevant to the internet context. An analysis of the relevant constitutional case law will now be performed, to confirm this hypothesis or to refute it.

6.3.2 The Italian experience

There is no doubt that the Italian Constitutional Court has been, since its inception, a crucial actor in protecting fundamental rights. Several rights that are recognised today were identified by the court through its interpretation of the Constitution; some rights were not even explicitly mentioned in the Constitution and were thus recognised precisely on the basis of a judgment, in which the court deducted the existence of the right from a constitutional provision or from a constitutional principle. Moreover, the status of many rights, as well as their effects and their limits, have been clarified by judgments of the court.

Nonetheless, the Constitutional Court does not appear to engage in such a key role when it comes to internet law, in relation to the protection of individual rights. As a matter of fact, an analysis of the relevant constitutional case law shows

26 With reference to the *question prioritaire de constitutionnalité* see Guy Carcassonne and Olivier Duhamel, *QPC. La question prioritaire de constitutionnalité* (Dalloz 2011); Mathieu Disant, *Droit de la question prioritaire de constitutionnalité. Cadre juridique, pratiques jurisprudentielles* (Lamy 2011); Xavier Magnon, *QPC – La Question Prioritaire de Constitutionnalité. Pratique et contentieux* (Litec 2011); Jean-Baptiste Perrier (ed.), *La question prioritaire de constitutionnalité* (PUAM 2011); Xavier Philippe and Marthe Fatin-Rouge Stefanini (eds), *Question prioritaire de constitutionnalité. Premiers bilans* (PUAM 2011); Jacques-Henri Stahl and Christine Maugüé, *La question prioritaire de constitutionnalité* (Dalloz 2011); Dominique Rousseau (ed.), *La question prioritaire de constitutionnalité* (Lextenso 2012); Émmanuel Dupic and Luc Briand, *La question prioritaire de constitutionnalité, une révolution des droits fondamentaux* (PUF 2013).

an unexpected scarcity of internet law issues coming before the court. Apart from judgments in which the internet is simply invoked, and thus no specific consideration is expressed by the court, there are only 13 judgments that can be cited, the oldest dating back to 2004 and the most recent in 2013. The number may not be irrelevant per se; the problem is, however, that the contents of only a few of these judgments have any significance.

Moreover, and above all, most of the judgments are related to disputes on the limits of the central state's and regions' respective powers, and thus the main concern of the court does not lie so much in the protection of rights within the internet context, but rather in the distribution of (legislative) powers among territorial entities. In other words, the Constitutional Court has not been given a real opportunity to deal with the most important issues concerning internet law. Notwithstanding this difficulty, the court has undoubtedly striven to sketch out its doctrine on certain aspects of the subject.[27]

6.3.2.1 The struggle against the digital divide as a major duty of the Republic

The most important and the most renowned of these efforts is certainly embodied in Judgment No. 307 of 21 October 2004, the oldest of the 13 judgments mentioned above. The region of Emilia-Romagna contested national legislative provisions which established special funds to help young or low-income people to purchase personal computers: these provisions were challenged as infringements of the region's autonomy, from both the legislative and the financial-administrative point of view.

The Constitutional Court rejected the region's arguments. The court observed that the case concerned

> The mere provision of financial aids by the State, granted automatically to people who were identified by their age or income, and [they] were aimed at the purchase of personal computers enabled to connection to the Internet, obviously in order to foster the dissemination of a culture of information technology.

Such a provision could not be considered as an infringement of regional legislative power, since the establishment of special funds was not associated with 'any substantive regulation' linked to specific regional competences. The provision, indeed, 'pursue[d] an objective of general interest, such as the development of culture, in particular though the use of computers': the pursuit of this purpose is a task entrusted to all the entities which form the Republic,[28] and therefore does

27 I addressed the subject in part, in a comparative perspective, in Paolo Passaglia, 'Diritto di accesso ad internet e giustizia costituzionale. Una (preliminare) indagine comparata' in Marina Pietrangelo (ed), *Il diritto di accesso ad Internet* (Edizioni Scientifiche Italiane 2011) 59.

28 The Court made specific reference to art 9 of the Constitution, according to which '[t]he Republic shall promote the development of culture and scientific and technical research' (para. 1).

not fall within the application of the ordinary criteria of the division of legislative powers between the state and the regions.[29]

The legal reasoning of the court does not go further, but the reader can infer from the court's words the crucial commitment that is assigned to the Republic as a whole in favour of computer literacy and, consequently, in favour of the removal of (financial) barriers that hinder the dissemination of culture of information technology (at least among young people): the struggle against this kind of digital divide is so important that it must take precedence over the compliance with provisions concerning the division of legislative powers between territorial entities.

The struggle for computer literacy (i.e. against the digital divide relating to one's knowledge of information technology) is therefore conceived as part of the struggle against inequality, a struggle which characterises (or rather, should characterise) the Italian model of a welfare state from its very origins, according to the solemn commitment to so-called 'substantial equality' expressed by Article 3, paragraph 2 of the Constitution:

> It is the duty of the Republic to remove those obstacles of an economic and social nature which in fact limit the freedom and equality of citizens, impede the full development of the human person and the effective participation of all workers in the political, economic and social organization of the country.[30]

29 Commentaries on the judgment were written by Alessandro Pace, 'I progetti "PC ai giovani" e "PC alle famiglie": esercizio di potestà legislativa esclusiva statale o violazione della potestà regionale residuale?' (2004) *Giurisprudenza costituzionale* 3214 and, more recently, by Federico Gustavo Pizzetti, 'Il progetto "PC ai giovani" nel quadro della promozione dell'eguaglianza digitale da parte dello Stato e delle Regioni' (2008) Federalismi.it. The judgment is considered to be the most important statement of the Constitutional Court related to internet access, a notion that has been debated at length by Italian legal scholars: see Pasquale Costanzo, 'L'accesso ad internet in cerca d'autore' (2005) 3 *Diritto dell'Internet* 247; Fiammetta Borgia, 'Riflessioni sull'accesso a internet come diritto umano' (2010) 3 *Le Comunità internazionali* 395; Pietrangelo (n 27); Marco Betzu, 'Interpretazione e sovra-interpretazione dei diritti costituzionali nel cyberspazio' (2012) 4 *Rivista AIC*; Pasquale Costanzo, 'Miti e realtà dell'accesso ad internet (una prospettiva costituzionalistica)' (2012) Consulta OnLine; Lorenzo Cuocolo, 'La qualificazione giuridica dell'accesso a internet, tra retoriche globali e dimensione sociale' (2012) *Politica del diritto* 263; Palmina Tanzarella, 'Accesso a internet: verso un nuovo diritto sociale?' in Elisa Cavasino, Giovanni Scala and Giuseppe Verde (eds), *I diritti sociali dal riconoscimento alla garanzia: Il ruolo della giurisprudenza* (Editoriale Scientifica 2013) 517; Corrado Caruso, 'L'individuo nella rete: i diritti della persona al tempo di internet' (2013) Forum di Quaderni costituzionali; Giovanna De Minico, 'Uguaglianza e accesso ad internet' (2013) Forum di Quaderni costituzionali; Tommaso Edoardo Frosini, 'L'accesso a internet come diritto fondamentale' in Oreste Pollicino, Elisa Bertolini and Valerio Lubello (eds), *Internet: regole e tutela dei diritti fondamentali* (Aracne 2013) 65; Lorenzo Nannipieri, 'Costituzione e nuove tecnologie: profili costituzionali dell'accesso ad internet', speech held at the Second seminar of the 'Gruppo di Pisa', University of 'Roma Tre' (20 September 2013); Marina Pietrangelo, 'Oltre l'accesso ad internet, tra tutele formali ed interventi sostanziali: a proposito dell'attuazione del diritto di accesso ad internet' in Michele Nisticò and Paolo Passaglia (eds), *Internet e Costituzione* (Giappichelli 2014) 169.

30 The issues concerning the digital divide(s) have caught the attention of Italian scholars over the last

The core of the *ratio decidendi* of Judgment No. 307 of 2004 would probably have been confirmed by the court in Judgment No. 151 of 12 April 2005. In this case, the region of Emilia-Romagna contested several legislative provisions adopted by the national Parliament that established funds to grant aid to individuals who purchased or hired technological devices, which included those enabling a broadband internet connection. With specific regard to some of these grants, including that concerning the internet, the court did not issue a judgment on the merits, because of an inappropriate exposition of the reasons that founded the question of constitutionality in the region's claim.

As far as other grants (namely, those relating to the dissemination of TV decoders) were concerned, however, the court adopted a similar approach to that expressed in Judgment No. 307 of 2004, although in this case it did not refer to a duty of the Republic as such, as it had done in the internet case: the purpose of the contested provisions was, obviously, 'to foster the dissemination of digital television broadcasting as an instrument for implementing the principle of pluralism of information', which plays a key role as a 'prerequisite for the implementation of the founding principles of a democratic State'; as a result, 'the contested provisions certainly concern[ed] a plurality of subjects and interests (safeguarding of competition, technological development, protection of pluralism in information), belonging to the exclusive or concurrent legislative competence of the State'.

The definition of the dissemination of internet connection as a duty of the Republic and, above all, of the state, which is the highest level of government and, thus, exercises the most important competences within the Republic, was implicitly confirmed in other judgments.

In this regard, the judgments concerning national policies seeking to establish and strengthen the electronic communications network are worthy of mention. In Judgment No. 336 of 27 July 2005, the Constitutional Court dealt with the national implementation of the European Directives of 7 March 2002, Nos. 2002/19/EC (Access Directive), 2002/20/EC (Authorisation Directive), 2002/21/EC (Framework Directive) and 2002/22/EC (Universal Service Directive). The provisions that were contested by the regions of Tuscany and Marches concerned, in particular, the framework for electronic communications

15 years. See e.g. Valeria Bianchini and Alfonso Desiderio, *Atlante del divario digitale* (I quaderni speciali di Limes 2001) 42; Tommaso Pucci, 'Il diritto all'accesso nella società dell'informazione e della conoscenza: Il digital divide' (2002) *Informatica e diritto* 119; Giuseppe Anzera and Francesca Comunello (eds), *Mondi digitali. Riflessioni e analisi sul Digital Divide* (Guerini Associati 2005); Marina Da Bormida and Daria Domenici, 'Software libero, copyleft e digital divide' (2006) 2 *Dir. autore e nuove tecnologie* 143; Laura Sartori, *Il divario digitale: internet e le nuove disuguaglianze sociali* (il Mulino 2006); Eugenio De Marco (ed.), *Accesso alla rete e uguaglianza digitale* (Giuffrè 2008); Sara Bentivegna, *Disuguaglianze digitali. Le nuove forme di esclusione nella società dell'informazione* (Laterza 2009); Francesco Amoretti and Enrico Gargiulo, 'Dall'appartenenza materiale all'appartenenza virtuale? La cittadinanza elettronica fra processi di costituzionalizzazione della rete e dinamiche di esclusione' (2010) *Politica del diritto* 353; Lorenzo Nannipieri, 'La dimensione costituizonale del digital divide: in particolare, gli ostacoli cognitivi alla proiezione dell'individuo nello spazio virtuale' in Nisticò and Passaglia (n 29) 189.

infrastructure and procedures established to install facilities. All the questions of constitutionality were rejected by the court because the leading role of the state, which was questioned by both regions, was justified by the plurality of competences that are conferred exclusively on the national authorities, namely the competences of 'civil order', 'coordination of statistical information and information on data of state, regional and local administration', 'safeguarding of competition', as well as 'protection of the environment'.

The same approach was adopted in Judgment No. 163 of 27 June 2012. The region of Liguria contested the provision according to which, on one hand, the Ministry of Economic Development, with the participation of companies and bodies owning electronic communication facilities, prepared a strategic plan for the establishment and implementation of broadband and ultra-broadband telecommunication facilities and, on the other hand, the Minister for Economic Development, in cooperation with the Minister of Economy and Finances, adopted provisions to carry out said plan.

The Constitutional Court affirmed, in principle, the competence of the central state in both establishing the strategic plan and carrying it out. Nevertheless, the contested provision was found to be unconstitutional insofar as it did not provide for any participation of the regions in the preparation and adoption of the strategic plan and the carrying out of regulations: since the subject was related to regional competences, the constitutional principle of loyal cooperation required allowing the regions to have their say upon the strategy and the policy concerning electronic communications.

6.3.2.2 The electronic publication of legal and administrative provisions as an appropriate substitute for publication in paper journals

The use of the internet to disseminate knowledge of legislation and administrative activity cannot be an issue as far as electronic publication is only one of the methods that are used; on the contrary, when electronic publication is used as a substitute of the traditional form, the existence of digital divides could endanger the basis of the principle according to which 'no one should be unaware of the law' (*nul n'est censé ignorer la loi*), with its corollary that implies that the law must be public if it is to be respected.[31]

More recently, some disputes on the limits of the central state's and regions' respective powers have concerned provisions relating to the electronic publication of legal and administrative provisions. Unfortunately, to date, the Constitutional Court has never seized the opportunity to rule upon electronic publication as opposed to traditional publication. In Judgment No. 227 of 22 July 2011, the court declared unconstitutional a legislative act of the region of Friuli-Venezia Giulia that provided for a regulation of public information concerning projects and studies of environmental impact; one of the means of information

31 On this subject see also Bruno Brancati, 'La conoscibilità del diritto online' in Nisticò and Passaglia (n 29) 221.

was considered to be publication on the website of the region. The reason for the unconstitutionality, however, was not related to electronic publication: the regional provision failed to be consistent with the standards determined on a nationwide basis to ensure environmental information.

Judgment No. 178 of 4 July 2013 appears to be slightly more interesting, since the Constitutional Court declared unconstitutional a legislative provision of the region of Liguria insofar as it was inconsistent with the national standards concerning the contents of the results of preliminary screenings for eventual environmental impact assessments, that should be available on the website of the region. In this case, the court implicitly considered electronic publication as an appropriate way to ensure public information; nevertheless, the judgment does not allow the observer to infer more than a general and summary approval, on the part of the court, of the use of electronic publication, at least in certain specific areas such as environmental law.

The last judgment to be mentioned is Judgment No. 219 of 19 July 2013, in which a national legislative provision was found unconstitutional. By means of an enabling act, the Parliament gave the government the power to regulate the electronic publication of budgets and financial statements of regions and local authorities. In the government's legislative decree, the government forced regions to draft, at the end of every five-year legislature, a very detailed report of the legislative and administrative activities carried out by the region; the reports were to be published on the website of the region. Such a report, and obviously also its electronic publication, was declared unconstitutional by the court because the governmental provision was inconsistent with the limits imposed by the Parliament; furthermore, it infringed the regional competence of self-organisation.

6.3.2.3 The internet as a means to implement citizens' contacts with public administrations

One of the most interesting decisions of the Constitutional Court relating to internet law was Judgment No. 365 of 22 December 2010. A Milan court of first instance submitted to the Constitutional Court a question of constitutionality concerning the provision according to which individuals challenging administrative sanctions who resided outside the territory of the municipality in which judicial proceedings were to take place, could not receive judicial notification through the post or even through electronic communication. The contested provision thus obliged the opponent to appoint an *ad litem* representative in the municipal territory, failing which notification would be fulfilled through a simple filing at the court registry.

The Constitutional Court declared the provision unconstitutional, since it did not allow other forms of notification that were admitted instead in other types of proceedings. The *rationale* of the decision was that both technological development and the increasing spread of new forms of communication made the contested provision unreasonably discriminatory, compared with provisions concerning other proceedings, which claimed the existence of easier ways to communicate in judicial processes to foster access to courts for private citizens.

Although the court did not explain its doctrine further, it is clear that it seized the opportunity to evoke new forms of contact between private citizens and the government, contacts that could greatly benefit from electronic forms of communication.[32]

6.3.2.4 Digitalisation and reduction of public expenditure

In recent years, the internet has been applauded as a way to reduce public expenditure, thanks to cuts relating to paper and postal costs, as well as a deeper and more efficient means of control on how public resources are spent. In several cases, regions brought claims before the Constitutional Court to challenge the constitutionality of national legislative provisions imposing the use of the internet by regions and local authorities.

In Judgment No. 133 of 14 May 2008, the court dismissed the claim of the region of Lombardy concerning national provisions which granted financial aid, on the one hand, for projects aiming to foster the 'information society' and the identification of its priorities and, on the other hand, for local authorities' projects of digitalisation of administrative activities. The Constitutional Court did not consider these provisions as breaching regional competences, since they complied with the need to guarantee common languages, procedures and standards for computer systems of the entire public administration, thus creating the conditions for computer communication between national, regional and local administrations.

A month later, in Judgment No. 190 of 6 June 2008, the Constitutional Court rejected the question submitted by the Province of Bolzano against the obligation for regional and local administrative authorities to transmit, every year, information concerning their activity to the National Department of Civil Service, which then disseminated it on its website. The court observed that this obligation pursued the objective of ensuring compliance with the standards of the Stability and Growth Pact of the European Union: indeed, the information transmitted enabled the National Department to gain adequate knowledge of public expenditure at regional and local levels, and is therefore one of the conditions for an efficient rationalisation and restraint of expenditure.

Expenditure restraint was also the main aim of the legislative provision that was declared unconstitutional in Judgment No. 297 of 20 November 2009. The state obliged regions to adopt several measures that had the effect of cutting the costs of their activities. Amongst these measures, there was the use of email instead of traditional letters, and of Voice over Internet Protocol (VoIP) instead of traditional telephone communications. The Constitutional Court agreed with the

32 On the implementation of citizens' contacts with the public administration thanks to the internet see Alessandra Valastro, 'Internet e strumenti partecipativi nel rapporto fra privati e amministrazioni' in Nisticò and Passaglia (n 29) 245.

claimant, the region of Veneto, in stating that the contested provisions, because of their specificity, did not express a fundamental principle of coordination of public finance (that would have been possible for the state to establish): they did not determine a limit upon general expenditure, but rather, they affected specific expenditures, thus introducing specific constraints on individual items.

In relation to the case at issue, the court did not censure the cutting of costs in itself, but only the breach of regional competences in deciding the best way for any region to reduce its expenditure. In other words, the use of the internet had nothing to do with the declaration of unconstitutionality.

6.3.2.5 The internet and the frontiers of the freedom of press

There is no doubt that the internet has profoundly changed the way in which freedom of the press can be exercised. The possibility for anyone to communicate to a vast audience was one of the key arguments brought by the attorney of a senator whose declarations were considered libellous against the president of the Republic, to support his claim, before the Constitutional Court, to grant immunity to members of Parliament who exercised their political activity in a new form, more open towards the external audience – thanks to 'new forms of communication technology (websites, blogs, Twitter, Facebook)' – and less rooted within the internal activity of the chambers.

In Judgment No. 313 of 17 December 2013, the court rejected this argument, observing that the notion of the 'functional link' between parliamentary activities and external declarations of the member of Parliament, that is the standard for granting immunity, would be excessively vague if it were extended to all activities through which the member of Parliament reaches out to citizens, and thus the extension of the immunity for free speech would be inconsistent with the limits that emerge from the Constitution.

The case of members of Parliament is, of course, quite peculiar. In a more general perspective, it is fair to say that the limitations introduced for the traditional press have been extended to the electronic press and publishing. Nevertheless, there are some notable exceptions; amongst these is the provision according to which the civil liability of the owner and of the publisher of a newspaper does not apply to the owner and the publisher of a website that hosts an online newspaper.

This differential regulation was considered by a court of first instance of Alessandria to be a discrimination against victims of crimes of libel committed through the electronic press. The Constitutional Court, in Order No. 337 of 16 December 2011, excluded that it was endowed with the power to decide upon the merits of the case: as a matter of fact, a possible declaration of unconstitutionality would not be of any interest to the plaintiffs, since the *ex post facto* law's prohibition would prevent the retroactive application of the criminal provision extended to online newspapers. As a result, there was no basis for the ordinary court to invoke a declaration of unconstitutionality of a provision that it would not be able to apply anyway in the proceedings before it.

The strict observance of procedural rules prevented the Constitutional Court from delivering a vital decision for the regulation of internet publishing. It is possible that this decision could have been so important that readers may find that the court failed to take advantage of a very good opportunity to have its say on a key issue of internet law. Perhaps the same reader, when skimming through the court's main judgments on internet law, could also gain the impression that the court has never yet really seized the chance to become a significant actor in governing the internet in Italy.

6.3.3 The French experience

Unlike the limited number of cases that characterise the Italian experience, to date the French Constitutional Council has developed an extensive body of case law concerning the internet. Amongst the judgments delivered, only a few can be considered to be leading cases; nevertheless, the number of interesting statements that can be detected in the council's judgments is far from insignificant, largely because of the wide range of issues that the council has been asked to address.

The French constitutional case law on internet law is actually one of the most cited in comparative studies worldwide, especially with regard to a judgment of 2009 in which the Constitutional Council defined internet access in legal terms. This judgment can be considered as merely the tip of the iceberg, since many other specific aspects of the internet have been analysed in the French system.

6.3.3.1 The right to internet access

Internet access is still very controversial in many legal orders, including in Italy, for instance.[33] The issue essentially lies in the fact that it is difficult to determine whether internet access can be defined as a right and, if this definition is accepted, the question that remains is what kind of right can the access be: is access to the internet a fundamental right or an 'ordinary' one? Is it a right protected by the Constitution or by legislation? Is it a liberty right or a claim right? Several constitutional courts and homologous institutions have expressed their views. The French Constitutional Council was one of the first, and its statement on the issue is one of the clearest.

In Judgment No. 2009-580 DC of 10 June 2009, members of the opposition of the National Assembly submitted a legislative provision to the Constitutional Council contending that: 'by giving an administrative authority, albeit an independent one, the power to impose penalties in the form of withholding access to the Internet, Parliament . . . infringed the fundamental right of freedom of expression and communication, and secondly, introduced patently disproportionate penalties'.

The Council referred to Article 11 of the Declaration of the Rights of Man and the Citizen of 1789, according to which: 'The free communication of ideas

33 Note 29.

and opinions is one of the most precious rights of man. Every citizen may thus speak, write and publish freely, except when such freedom is misused in cases determined by Law'. From this provision, the council inferred that:

> In the current state of the means of communication and given the generalized development of public online communication services and the importance of the latter for participation in democracy and the expression of ideas and opinions, this right implies the freedom to access such services.

The Constitutional Council has therefore considered internet access as a right protected by the 1789 Declaration, which is part of the 'block of constitutionality' defined above. Protection by a constitutional text does not mean that access to the internet can be defined as a *fundamental* right: owing to the official commentary written by the Secretary of the Council,[34] the point is indisputable, since it is clearly expressed that: 'affirming the freedom to access the Internet does not mean to recognise, to anyone, a general and absolute right to be connected'.[35]

Despite the claimants' more radical request of recognition of a fundamental right, the Constitutional Council thus chose a cautious position,[36] which, in any case, still allowed it to declare the unconstitutionality of a provision that endowed an administrative authority with the power to withhold access to the internet as a penalty for individuals who, subscribing to internet access for online public communication services, did not comply with the duty to ensure that said access was not used for reproducing, showing, making available or communicating to the public works or property protected by copyright or a related right without the authorisation of the copyright holders. Precisely because of the significance accorded to the internet and to the right to access it, the Constitutional Council decided in favour of the unconstitutionality of the challenged provisions. In the Council's terms,

> The powers to impose penalties created by the challenged provisions vest[ed] the Committee for the Protection of Copyright, which [was and] is not a court of law, with the power to restrict or deny access to the Internet by access holders and to those people whom the latter allow to access the Internet. The powers vested in this administrative authority [were] not limited to a specific category of persons but extend[ed] to the entire population. The powers of this Committee [might] thus lead to restricting the right of

34 *Commentaire de la décision n° 2009-580 DC – 10 juin 2009 (Loi relative à la diffusion et à la protection de la création sur internet)* 27 Les Cahiers du Conseil constitutionnel http://www.conseil-constitutionnel.fr/conseil-constitutionnel/root/bank/download/2009580DCccc_580dc.pdf (last accessed 14 August 2015).

35 ibid 7.

36 Oddly enough, the Council's judgment was explicitly mentioned by the Constitutional Division of the Supreme Court of Justice of Costa Rica in Judgment No. 12790 of 30 July 2010, and thus became the basis of its legal reasoning which led to the recognition of internet access as a fundamental right in that country.

> any person to exercise his or her right to express himself and communicate freely, in particular from his own home. In these conditions, in view of the freedom guaranteed by Article 11 of the Declaration of 1789, Parliament was not allowed, irrespective of the guarantees accompanying the imposition of penalties, to vest an administrative authority with such powers for the purpose of protecting holders of copyright and related rights.[37]

Although access to the internet was not defined as a fundamental right, the council made it clear that its significance requires special protection; as a result, a conflict between internet access and copyright should not be resolved by prioritising the latter.

The rationale of Judgment No. 2009-580 DC was also applied in Judgment No. 2009-590 DC of 22 October 2009, in which the Constitutional Council decided on the constitutionality of the statute amending the one partially struck down in Judgment No. 580 DC.[38] The council affirmed the consistency with the Constitution of the provision allowing the members of the Committee for the Protection of Copyright, together with its duly authorised and sworn agents before the judicial authority, to ascertain conduct and acts that were likely to constitute offences punishable by the supplementary penalty of the suspension of access to a public online communication service.

37 The council's judgment was one of the most deeply analysed by legal scholars in France (see Jean-Michel Bruguière, *Loi 'sur la protection de la création sur internet': mais à quoi joue le Conseil constitutionnel?* (Recueil Dalloz 2009) 1770; Florence Chaltiel, 'La loi Hadopi devant le Conseil constitutionnel' (2009) 125 *Les petites affiches* 7; Jacques Francillon, 'Téléchargement illégal: heur et malheur de la loi création et internet: la loi HADOPI censurée par le Conseil constitutionnel' (2009) *Revue de science criminelle et de droit pénal comparé* 609; Allan Gautron, 'La "réponse graduée" (à nouveau) épinglée par le Conseil constitutionnel: Ou la délicate adéquation des moyens aux fins' (2009) 51 *Revue Lamy Droit de l'Immatériel* 63; Laure Marino, 'Le droit d'accès à internet, nouveau droit fondamental' (2009) 33 *Recueil Dalloz* 2045; Dominique Rousseau, 'Hado-pirate la Constitution: le Conseil sanctionne!' (2009) 51 *Revue Lamy Droit de l'Immatériel* 103; Michel Verpeaux, 'La liberté de communication avant tout. La censure de la loi Hadopi 1 par le Conseil constitutionnel' (2009) 39 *Semaine juridique. Édition générale* 46; William Benessiano, 'L'inconstitutionnalité, sanction de l'identification d'un pouvoir de répression pénale dévalué' (2010) *Revue française de droit constitutionnel* 168, and also abroad (for instance, with regard to the Italian scholarship see Giulio Votano, 'Internet fra diritto d'autore e libertà di comunicazione: il modello francese' (2009) *Diritto dell'informazione e dell'informatica* 533; Bruno Carotti, 'L'accesso alla rete e la tutela dei diritti fondamentali' (2010) *Giornale di diritto amministrativo* 643; Nicola Lucchi, 'La legge "Création et internet": le censure del Conseil constitutionnel' (2010) *Quaderni costituzionali* 375, as well as Paolo Passaglia, 'L'accesso ad internet è un diritto (il Conseil constitutionnel francese dichiara l'incostituzionalità di parte della c.d. "legge anti file-sharing")' (2009) 4 *Il Foro italiano* 473.

38 See Iliana Boubekeur, 'De la "loi HADOPI" à la "loi HADOPI 2": analyse de la décision du Conseil constitutionnel 2009-580 DC et de ses conséquences' (2009) 51 *Revue Lamy Droit de l'Immatériel* 107; Emmanuel Derieux, 'Validation par le Conseil constitutionnel de l'essentiel des dispositions de la loi "Hadopi 2"' (2009) 54 *Revue Lamy Droit de l'Immatériel* 6; Michel Verpeaux, 'Loi Hadopi 2, contrôle à double détente: À propos de la décision du Conseil constitutionnel du 22 octobre 2009' (2009) 46 *Semaine juridique. Édition générale* 15.

Since no constitutional rule or principle precludes an administrative authority from participating in the enforcement of the penalty of withholding or suspension of access to the internet, the protection of individual rights was thus guaranteed by the clear distinction between the power to investigate and the power to convict, which was further emphasised by the council's clarifications: the relevant judicial authorities would be able to decide on a case-by-case basis, as they are required to do, whether further investigations or inquiries were necessary or whether the evidence obtained by the civil servants and agents vested with police powers was sufficient to prove the guilt of the accused and, as the case might be, make it possible to determine the applicable penalty.

Withholding or suspending internet access is therefore not to be conceived in itself as an unlawful penalty, unless it is so defined by a court. Therefore, the legislator is free to introduce penalties resulting in the withholding or suspension of access to the internet, as long as it complies with constitutional constraints related to the necessity and proportionality of penalties.

In the same Judgment No. 2009-590 DC, the Constitutional Council affirmed this principle when it judged the natures of the penalties provided for by the challenged legislation. In this respect, it first stated that the introduction of a supplementary penalty designed to punish offences of copyright infringement, committed by the use of a public online communication service and consisting in suspending access to such a service for a maximum period of one year, together with a prohibition on entering into another contract for the same services with any other provider, did not fail to comply with the principle of the necessity of punishments.

Even the obligation imposed on the subscriber to pay the subscription fee, notwithstanding the penalty of suspension of internet access, in the absence of any termination of the contract, was considered to be neither a penalty nor a measure of a punitive nature, since it was based on the fact that the breach of contract was attributable to the subscriber.

A one-month maximum suspension of internet access can also be imposed in the event of gross negligence, on the holder of a right of access to a public online communication service to whom the Committee for the Protection of Copyright previously sent a recommendation requiring the implementation of security tools for its internet access. In the council's view, the legislator, exercising its discretion, did not introduce a presumption of guilt in breach of the presumption of innocence, nor did it create a patently disproportionate penalty.

On the basis of the above considerations, regardless of the limitations that can be imposed on the holder of the right, it is fair to conclude that the constitutional rank of the right to access the internet is, in any case, currently unquestionable. Unfortunately, the cases brought before the Constitutional Council did not give it the chance to specify whether the access is simply a liberty right (as expressed in the judgment) or is also a claim right. As a matter of fact, French constitutional case law does not provide details on this point, although the close link between the internet and the right to communicate freely could suggest that, where and when necessary, the government should be proactive in creating the conditions to ensure access, technical or personal difficulties notwithstanding. Nevertheless, it cannot be denied that this statement is a personal interpretation, rather than a conclusion authorised by the council's judgments.

6.3.3.2 The right to identity on the internet

In Judgment No. 2012-652 DC of 22 March 2012, the Constitutional Council dealt with a legislative provision establishing a new function for the national identity card, that: 'If requested by its holder, [it might] also contain data, stored separately, enabling him/her to identify him/herself on electronic communication networks and to affix his/her electronic signature.' Upon each use, the holder was to decide which identification data was to be transmitted electronically.

The council observed that:

> Under the current state of the means of communication and having regard to the general development of online communication services for the public as well as the importance of these services in economic and social life, the general conditions under which the national identity card issued by the State [might] enable a person to identify him/herself on electronic communication networks and to affix his/her electronic signature, in particular for civil and commercial purposes,

fell within the domain that the Constitution reserves to legislative authority:

> on one hand it permit[ted] the national identity card to include 'electronic functions', enabling its holder to identify him/herself on electronic communication networks and to affix his/her electronic signature, whilst on the other hand it guarantee[d] the optional nature of these functions.

Nevertheless, the challenged provision did not specify 'the nature of the "data" through which these functions [might] be implemented nor the guarantees ensuring the integrity and confidentiality of these data'; moreover, it did not define 'in any greater detail the conditions under which agents implementing these functions [were] to be authenticated, especially when they [were] minors or [were] subject to legal protection'.[39]

Obliging the Parliament to regulate electronic communications in detail through the identity card, the Constitutional Council drew attention to the significance of the subject and, above all, to its sensitivity: since the internet is a new dimension of social relationships, the individual must be protected as much

39 On this judgment see Vincent Tchen, 'L'informatisation des documents d'identité numérisés' (2012) 5 *Droit administratif* 24; Marlène Trezeguet, 'Cadre légal de la carte d'identité biométrique mais inconstitutionnalité du fichier central commun et de la puce "signature électronique"' (2012) 83 *Revue Lamy Droit de l'Immatériel* 47.

as possible against any infringement. In the French (and European continental) cultural tradition, this type of protection requires legislative intervention. Such an important subject cannot be left to the regulation of government, but rather mandates the intervention of Parliament, because the provisions must not be the expression of a political majority, but must be adopted by the body representing the people as a whole.

6.3.3.3 The right to privacy and the internet

The right to privacy has been invoked in several cases before the Constitutional Council, having regard to different areas of regulation in which infringements could take place.

In one of the earliest decisions concerning internet law, Judgment No. 2004-496 DC of 10 June 2004, the Constitutional Council dealt with communication on the internet through emails. The claimants, members of Parliament, challenged the definition of emails as ‘any textual, voice, sound, or image message, sent by a public net of communication, stocked in a net server or in the recipient’s terminal until the recipient recovers it’. Being a technical definition, the Constitutional Council found that it neither affected privacy nor was too general and indeterminate. Therefore, the Parliament was not required to provide further details in defining email and, in any case, if a problem of infringement of the right to privacy (protected by Article 2 of the 1789 Declaration) occurred, ordinary courts would be able to review it.

The right to privacy was also invoked to challenge the legislative provision which established that copyright management companies were allowed to retain data concerning offences, convictions and security measures. The Constitutional Council, in Judgment No. 2004-499 DC of 29 July 2004, did not declare this provision to be inconsistent with the Constitution, on one hand because its goals were to fight new piracy practices on the internet and to protect intellectual and cultural property rights and, on the other hand, because the data retention activity required the prior authorisation of the National Commission for information technology and freedoms, and could result in a nominative in formation only pursuant to judicial orders. Taking this regulation into account, the Constitutional Council concluded that the provision reasonably combined the protection of the right to privacy and the pursuit of other goals.[40]

A ‘patently unbalanced’ combination between the protection of copyright and the right to privacy was also challenged in the above-mentioned Judgment No. 2009-580 DC. The claimants argued that the powers conferred upon a private agent such as the Committee for the protection of copyright, empowered with

40 The judgment is commented upon by Jean Frayssinet, ‘L’accouplement du droit de la protection des données personnelles avec le droit d’auteur: la naissance d’un avorton, l’article 9-4 de la loi modifiée relative à l’informatique, aux fichiers et aux libertés’ (2004) 216 *Légipresse* 119; Jean-Éric Schoettl, ‘La refonte de la loi sur l’informatique, les fichiers et les libertés devant le Conseil constitutionnel’ (2004) 160 *Les petites affiches* 8.

the collection of personal data pertaining to offences, convictions and security measures of subscribers suspected of sharing files of protected works, were not accompanied by sufficient guarantees.

The Constitutional Council observed that the Committee for the protection of copyright acted upon referrals by sworn agents appointed by professional defence organisations, by companies in charge of collecting and apportioning copyright fees and by the National Cinematographic Centre. Nevertheless, this condition was not sufficient to make the challenged regulation consistent with the Constitution. Indeed, unlike the provisions challenged in Judgment No. 2004-499 DC, the contested provisions made it possible for data collected in that way to be nominative even in the proceedings before the Committee for the protection of copyright, and even in the absence of any judicial orders to authorise it. As a result, the authorisation granted to private agents to collect data that made it possible indirectly to identify people having a right to access to online public communication services resulted in the situation in which these same private agents could process data of a personal nature in connection with offences.

In the council's view, such an authorisation could constitute a disproportionate infringement of the right to privacy if it was not limited to the purpose of enabling copyright holders to institute legal proceedings on the same basis as any individual or legal entity who had suffered an offence. In any case, subsequently to the declaration of unconstitutionality of the provision endowing an administrative authority with the power to withhold access to the internet as a penalty (see section 6.3.3.1 above), the sole role of the Committee for the protection of copyright should have consisted in measures adopted preliminarily with respect to judicial proceedings: in other words, its intervention was justified only in relation to copyright infringements committed via the internet, and only insofar as it was useful, in the interests of good administration of justice, to the aim of limiting the number of offences brought before the courts of law.

Hence, to avoid a possible infringement of the right to privacy, when requested to authorise processing of nominative-type data, the National Commission for information technology and freedoms had to ensure that the manner in which such processing was carried out was strictly limited to the purpose to be achieved. The declaration of unconstitutionality, thus, restored a regulation that was rather similar to that which was declared to be consistent with the Constitution in Judgment No. 2004-499 DC, which still appears to be the leading case concerning the proper balance between the right to privacy and copyright protection.

6.3.3.4 Freedom of communication on the internet

The Constitutional Council has faced some interesting issues pertaining to the changes brought by the internet to the exercise of the freedom of communication. In the above-mentioned Judgment No. 2004-496 DC, the council dealt with provisions concerning unlawful information published on a website.

One of the challenged provisions of the Act on 'confidence in the digital economy' concerned the time in which the period allowed for replying began, compared with the limitation period for press offences: whilst, for the written press, the limitation period was three months starting from the date of publication, the provision at issue stated that for online press the starting date was postponed until the time when the unlawful information was withdrawn.

The Constitutional Council declared the regulation unconstitutional: although differences in the conditions of implementation applying to written and online communications might justify different arrangements, the council concluded that the Parliament had violated the principle of equality by introducing excessive differences in civil and criminal proceedings during the periods, depending solely upon the medium used.

In the same judgment, No. 2004-496 DC, a question of constitutionality was brought against the legislative provision implementing Article 14(1) of Directive 2000/31/EC of the European Parliament and of the Council of 8 June 2000, according to which:

> Where an information society service is provided that consists of the storage of information provided by a recipient of the service, Member States shall ensure that the service provider is not liable for the information stored at the request of a recipient of the service, on condition that: (a) the provider does not have actual knowledge of illegal activity or information and, as regards claims for damages, is not aware of facts or circumstances from which the illegal activity or information is apparent; or (b) the provider, upon obtaining such knowledge or awareness, acts expeditiously to remove or to disable access to the information.

The national provision was challenged because, in the claimants' view, it was not sufficiently detailed to avoid infringements of the freedom of communication and of the rights of defence and to a fair trial. The Constitutional Council dismissed the claim, considering that the national provision was a close implementation of the European one; moreover, the provision's consistency with the Constitution was granted when a 'host' did not incur civil or criminal liability simply by failing to withdraw information denounced as unlawful by a third party, but only when the unlawful nature of the information complained was manifest, or when the removal was ordered by a court.[41]

41 Judgment No. 2004-496 DC appears to be one of the most debated among legal scholars, both in France and abroad. See e.g. Philippe Blanchetier, 'Point de départ du délai de prescription des délits de presse sur internet: l'occasion manquée' (2004) 29 *Semaine juridique* 1335; Florence Chaltiel, 'Nouvelles variations sur la constitutionnalisation de l'Europe: à propos de la décision du Conseil constitutionnel sur l'économie numérique' (2004) *Revue du marché commun* 450; Emmanuel Derieux, 'Instabilité et incertitudes législatives dans le domaine des communications au public par voie électronique' (2004) 230 *Les petites affiches* 3; Henri Oberdorff, 'Le Conseil constitutionnel et l'ordre juridique communautaire: coopération et contrôle (à propos de la décision du Conseil constitutionnel no. 2004-496 du 10 juin 2004 relative à la loi pour la confiance dans l'économie numérique)' (2004) *Revue du droit public* 869; Jean-Éric Schoettl, 'Le nouveau régime juridique de la communication en ligne devant le Conseil constitutionnel' (2004) 122 *Les petites affiches* 10; Jean-Claude Zarka, 'La décision no. 2004-496 DC du 10 juin 2004 du

The liability for offences committed on the internet was again at issue in Judgment No. 2011-164 QPC of 16 September 2011. The contested provisions specified people who could incur criminal liability for offences committed through a public online means of communication. The editor of the publication or, depending on the circumstances, the co-editor of the publication, could be prosecuted only if the unlawful message was subject to review before it was communicated online to the public. Under certain circumstances, if the offence was committed by virtue of the contents of a message addressed by an internet user to a public online communication service, the criminal liability of the editor or the co-editor of the publication would be engaged only if he was aware of the message before it was posted online or if he promptly took action to withdraw this message as soon as he had become aware of it. Alternatively, if neither the editor of the publication nor the author were prosecuted, the 'producer' of the online website should be prosecuted as the principal author.

On the basis of the Court of Cassation's interpretation in its judgment of 16 February 2010, the person who took the initiative to create a public online communication service to exchange opinions regarding issues that were determined in advance might be prosecuted in his capacity as producer, and this person could not invoke the defence that the messages posted online were not subject to prior control, or that the author of the messages could not be identified.

The applicant contested the provisions because their effect was to create a presumption of guilt of the producer of a public online communication service; moreover, they were argued to be inconsistent with the principle of equality in criminal law, because they treated the editor of the publication and the internet producer differently, without any justification.

Having regard to the nature of the internet, which, 'under the current state of rules and techniques, allows the author of a message broadcasted over the Internet to remain anonymous', the Constitutional Council overturned the Court of Cassation's interpretation. In its view, the provisions were consistent with the Constitution only if they were not interpreted as establishing criminal liability for the producer or the host of a public online communication website that makes messages posted by internet users available to the public, by virtue of the mere content of a message of which he was unaware before it was posted online.

The Constitutional Council thus confirmed the strict regulation concerning the producer's liability but, at the same time, excluded the constitutionality of an irrebuttable presumption of criminal liability deriving from the mere online

Conseil constitutionnel relative à la loi pour la confiance dans l'économie numérique' (2004) 29 *Semaine juridique* (JCP) 1332; Jacqueline Dutheil de la Rochère, 'Conseil constitutionnel (French Constitutional Court), Decision no 2004-496 du 10 juin 2004, Loi pour la confiance dans l'économie numérique (e-commerce)' (2005) *Common Market Law Review* 859; Jan Herman Reestman, 'Conseil constitutionnel on the status of (secondary) Community law in the French internal order: decision of 10 June 2004, 2004-496 DC' (2005) *European Constitutional Law Review* 302.

availability of messages: the effects of such an exclusion on online forums without a preventive moderation are easily imagined.[42]

The protection of freedom of communication was the main issue also in Judgment No. 2013-345 QPC of 27 September 2013. The workers' union that originated the judicial reference contested the legislative provision that recognised the unions' right to communicate with workers using either a special website of the company's intranet or the company's internal mailing list. The use of these communication tools was, however, submitted for the company's approval, to avoid any risk of hampering the performance of the company's computer network, the fulfilment of workers' duties and the protection of workers' free choice to accept or refuse a message. Such approval was considered to be an unlawful obstacle to the unions' freedom of expression and communication.

The Constitutional Council dismissed the claim because the terms of unions' communications by electronic means must be adapted to each company and, in particular, to the organisation of work and the state of development of its communications.

The aim of the contested provision was therefore proportionately to balance the protection of both employers' rights and workers' rights concerning the unions' communications and efficiency of work within the factory. The limitations on the unions' freedom of communication were, in fact, not disproportionate.[43]

6.3.3.5 Economic freedom and the internet

Several cases decided by the Constitutional Council concern various aspects of economic freedom on the web. Amongst the most interesting is Judgment No. 2010-45 QPC of 6 October 2010, related to the regulation of the assignment of domain names.

The claimant in this prior preliminary ruling on the issue of constitutionality contended that legislative provisions conferred on the administrative authority and the bodies appointed by it an excessive discretion in defining the principles governing the assignment of domain names, and omitted to lay down even a minimal framework for and limits to their action: by doing so, Parliament had failed to fully exercise its functions. Indeed, legislation merely provided that the assignment, by administrative authorities, of a domain name was carried out 'in the general interest, under publicized non-discriminatory rules designed to ensure compliance with intellectual property rights'. For other detailed provisions, the legislation referred to a governmental decree.

42 With regard to the council's opinion and its effects see Céline Castets-Renard, 'QPC sur la responsabilité pénale des "producteurs" d'un site en ligne: un éclaircissement dans le maquis de la responsabilité du web 2.0?' (2011) 76 Revue Lamy Droit de l'Immatériel 48; Emmanuel Derieux, 'Responsabilité du " producteur" d'un site en ligne' (2011) 76 *Revue Lamy Droit de l'Immatériel* 44; Emmanuel Dreyer, 'Réserve sur la responsabilité pénale du producteur en ligne' (2011) 46 *La Semaine juridique. Édition générale* 2238.

43 On this judgment see Philippe Icard, 'Communication par voie électronique: question de constitutionnalité' (2013) 48 *La Semaine juridique. Social* 37.

The Constitutional Council observed that:

> In view of the current state of the means of communication and the generalized development of online public communication services, and the substantial part played by such services in economic and social life, in particularly for those whose business is carried out on online, supervision, both with regard to private individuals and commercial companies, of the choice and use of Internet domain names affects intellectual property rights, freedom of communication and freedom of enterprise.

Although Parliament had protected intellectual property rights, it has entirely delegated the power to supervise the conditions in which domain names are assigned, refused or withdrawn. No other statutory provision offered guarantees ensuring the absence of any infringement of rights and freedoms. Parliament had thus failed to exercise its functions; as a result, the contested legislative provisions were declared unconstitutional.[44]

Notwithstanding the interest raised by this judgment, the subject area in which the French constitutional case law has developed most is probably the protection of copyright on the internet. Section 6.3.3.1 above analyses judgments on the balance between these rights and internet access; in section 6.3.3.6 below, the issue concerning the blocking of websites because of copyright infringements will be discussed. Further questions were addressed to the Constitutional Council and deserve some remarks.

In Judgment No. 2009-580 DC, amongst other issues, members of the National Assembly challenged the provision that established that a decree had to be adopted to specify the conditions in which the High Authority for the diffusion of works and protection of copyright on the internet could award a label making it possible 'to clearly identify the lawful nature' of offers of online communication services. The claimants contested, in particular, the discretionary power to determine the offers that, in the High Authority's opinion, were lawful.

The council replied that 'the awarding of labels attesting to the "lawful nature" of offers of online public communication services is designed solely to facilitate identification, by the public, of offers of services respecting intellectual property rights', and were thus 'to facilitate the use of security devices intended to ensure the monitoring of access to the Internet'. Moreover, leaving it to a decree to set the conditions for awarding such a label was simply meant to determine the manner in which applications for the award were to be received

44 See Emmanuelle Borner-Kaydel, 'Le nom de domaine: quand le droit économique rencontre les droits fondamentaux' (2011) *Revue française de droit constitutionnel* 292; François Gilbert, 'Le législateur doit encadrer les conditions dans lesquelles les noms de domaine sont attribués, renouvelés, refusés ou retirés' (2010) 351 *Gazette du palais* 35; Cédric Manara, '"Tout citoyen peut parler, écrire, imprimer librement", ainsi qu'enregistre et utiliser les noms de domaine!' (2010) 35 *Recueil Dalloz* 2285; Frédéric Sardain, 'Séisme pour le régime juridique des noms de domaine français' (2011) 1 *Communication commerce électronique* 11.

and examined: therefore, the provisions did not confer any arbitrary power on the High Authority.

In Judgment No. 2009-590 DC, the Constitutional Council affirmed the principle that the infringement of copyright with use of the internet can be subject to a specific regulation. However, the claimants contested the legislative provision that introduced specific proceedings for infringement of copyright committed with the use of a public online communication service, which made it possible for the offence to be tried by a single judge or under the summary procedure of a criminal order. They argued that this 'regression of procedural guarantees' was unconstitutional because it breached the principle of equality, in comparison with proceedings for other infringements of copyrights.

The Constitutional Council observed that Parliament is free to provide for different rules of procedure depending on the facts of a case, the situations and the people involved, unless such differences are based on unjustified distinctions, and that everyone enjoys the same guarantees, in particular with reference to respect for the rights of the defence, which imply that proceedings should be just and fair.

With regard to the particularities of the offence of infringement of copyright committed with the use of a public online communication service, when providing that these offences be tried by the *Tribunal correctionnel* sitting with a single judge or prosecuted under a summary procedure, Parliament intended to take into account the extent of the infringement of copyright committed via communication services, and thus the rules of procedure introduced by the challenged provisions did not create any difference between persons committing similar acts.

Nevertheless, the provision was declared unconstitutional, because Parliament had failed to exercise its powers fully. In fact, this provision did not determine the manner in which such a claim might be brought. It did not specify the effects of any opposition by the injured party and did not guarantee the right of the accused to limit his opposition to only civil or only criminal effects. The significance of the choice in terms of response to infringements of copyright requires legislative provisions to arrange a suitable framework of guarantees.[45]

Compliance with procedural guarantees established by the legislator was also the core principle in Judgment No. 2006-540 DC of 27 July 2006. The Constitutional Council held unconstitutional a provision changing the legal status of certain criminal conduct, which would cease to be indictable offences or felonies, and would become summary offences or misdemeanours. That conduct was: 'unauthorized reproduction for personal purposes of a work, a performance, a phonogram, a video recording, or a software protected by copyright or a related right' when the latter had been 'made available to the public through a peer-to-peer software exchange'; 'communication to the public for non-commercial

45 As far as this part of Judgment No. 2009-590 DC is concerned see William Benassiano, 'Décision no 2009-590 DC du 22 octobre 2009: la sanction de l'incompétence négative' (2010) *Revue française de droit constitutionnel* 390; Florence Chaltiel, 'La loi Hadopi II de nouveau censurée' (n 37) 7.

purposes' of such subject-matter 'by way of an online service of communication to the public when such communication [wa]s an automatic and secondary consequence of their reproduction' through peer-to-peer software exchange.

The legislative provision was challenged because it introduced an unjustified difference in treatment between people who reproduced or communicated subject-matter protected by copyright or related rights, depending on whether they used peer-to-peer software or other forms of electronic communication. The Constitutional Council agreed on the point that: 'the particularities of peer-to-peer exchange networks are not such as to justify the difference in treatment which the challenged provision introduce[d]'.

In the same Judgment No. 2006-540 DC, the Constitutional Council applied its doctrine concerning the need for criminal provisions to be clear regarding the conduct of making available to the public or of communicating to the public software which was patently not designed to be available to the public without authorisation.

In particular, the council declared unconstitutional the exonerating clauses according to which no criminal liability could be assessed, on one hand, for editors of software designed for 'work in collaboration' and, on the other, in the case of exchanging of files or subject-matter that was not subject to the payment of copyright. Both clauses were considered neither to assist delimitation of the scope of the offence nor to give an exhaustive enumeration of conduct that was necessarily excluded. Moreover, they did not ensure any protection under criminal law of the moral rights of authors who had waived the economic benefits of copyright. They therefore infringed the principle of the legality of offences and punishments and the principle of equality.[46]

In Judgment No. 2013-370 QPC of 28 February 2014, the council was called upon to balance intellectual property rights with the safeguard of bibliographic heritage. The contested provisions were intended to make available in digital form 'unavailable books' published in France before 1 January 2001 and that had not yet become part of the public domain.

To this end, a public database of 'unavailable books' was created and implemented by the National Library of France; a royalties collecting and distributing society approved by the Minister of Culture exercised the right to authorise the reproduction and representation in digital form of any book in this database for over six months and ensured the distribution of amounts received as a result of this operation among the beneficiaries. Libraries open to the public were freely allowed to reproduce and digitally distribute 'unavailable books' to their subscribers.

The author and publisher of an 'unavailable book' could object to the collecting society's authorisation and had the right to reproduce the book in print, thus blocking the authorisation.

46 On Judgment No. 2006-540 DC see Jean-Éric Schoettl, 'La propriété intellectuelle est-elle constitutionnellement soluble dans l'univers numérique? (1ère partie)' (2006) 161 *Les petites affiches* 4, and (2006) 162–63 *Les petites affiches* 3.

According to the Constitutional Council, this regulation pursued an objective of general interest without affecting authors' rights. Indeed, the contested provisions applied only to works that were no longer subject to commercial distribution by an editor and the collecting society's authorisation to reproduction was subject to the absence of opposition by the author or publisher, within six months of the book's entry in the public database. After this period, the publisher maintained a priority right to the reproduction and display of the book in digital form.

It followed from these provisions that, on the one hand, the law that applied to the collecting society did not infringe the author's and editor's rights of property; on the other hand, the interference with the copyright and intellectual property rights was not disproportionate, considering the objective pursued.

6.3.3.6 The blocking of websites

Offences committed through the internet can result in blocking access to the website on which offences are committed. The conditions and the effects of the block vary considerably, depending on the kind of offences that are committed through the website. French constitutional case law provides a good example of the different degrees of the response to cyber-offences. In this regard, two judgments can be mentioned, one concerning copyright infringements and the other on online child pornography: the different seriousness of the offences justifies responses that are carried out either by administrative authorities or by courts directly.

In the above-mentioned Judgment No. 2009-580 DC, the Constitutional Council found consistent with the Constitution the legislative provision according to which, in case of infringement of copyright or a related right due to the contents of an online public communication service, the *Tribunal de grande instance* may order – at the request of holders of copyright or other qualified subjects – any measures preventing or halting such an infringement.

The members of the National Assembly argued that blocking websites might deprive many internet users of the right to receive information and ideas. The council dismissed the appeal in this regard but not, however, without highlighting that the Tribunal de grande instance was able to decide after having heard all parties, and that it was up to the courts called upon to hear such petitions to order only those measures that were strictly necessary to preserve the rights involved.

The council's legal reasoning changed significantly in Judgment No. 2011-625 DC of 10 March 2011, in which the Council elaborated its doctrine on the fight against online child pornography. According to the challenged legislation, when seeking to fight against the distribution of pornographic pictures or representations of minors, the administrative authority had the power to notify the breach of criminal law provisions, and the recipients of the notification were required promptly to block access to the website.

The creation of a blocking device for electronic addresses providing access to certain websites was criticised by the claimants as an inappropriate or counter-productive measure, and as having an excessive cost with regard to the objective pursued of combating the distribution of child pornography. Moreover, it was criticised for the absence of any judicial authorisation, which resulted in a disproportionate violation of the freedom of communication.

In the council's view, by establishing a device that made it possible to block access to public online communications services that distributed pornographic images of children, the legislator did not commit any manifest error of assessment. Furthermore, by providing that any additional costs resulting from the obligations imposed on operators could be compensated, as the case might be, it did not violate the constitutional requirement of the proper use of public funds.

The Constitutional Council also observed that the contested provisions only granted the administrative authority the power to limit access to public online communications services in order to protect internet users if, and insofar as, these services distributed child pornography. The decision of the administrative authority could be challenged in court at any time and by any interested party.[47]

As a result, these provisions ensured that the objective of safeguarding public security was suitably balanced with the freedom of communication. The seriousness of offences thus justified the blocking of the website by an administrative authority, unlike the courts' intervention that was required in case of copyright infringements.

6.3.3.7 The internet and public participation in decision-making process

The internet can be an effective means to favour public participation in decision-making processes. In several cases, the Constitutional Council has assessed this assumption, especially with regard to environmental matters. In fact, the Charter of the Environment of 2004, which entered into force in 2005, recognises, at Article 7, the right of anyone 'to have access to information relating to the environment held by public authorities and to participate in the elaboration of public decisions having an impact on the environment'; the legislator, when implementing this Article, often referred to the internet.

Some of these implementation provisions were submitted to the council's review. In some cases, administrative measures, plans and regulations were to be published, and the legislator allowed the public authority to choose between paper publication and electronic publication. The Constitutional Council never found that this alternative could breach the Constitution, thus implicitly confirming the equivalence of the two kinds of publication (Judgments Nos. 2011-18/184 QPC of 14 October 2011; 2012-262 QPC of 13 July 2012; 2012-282 QPC of 23 November 2012).

47 On this judgment see Philippe Bonfils, 'La LOPPSI 2 et le droit pénal des mineurs' (2011) 17 *Recueil Dalloz* 1162; David Ginocchi, 'Le contrôle de la LOPPSI par le Conseil constitutionnel' (2011) *Actualité Juridique – Droit Administratif* 1097; Annabelle Pena-Gaïa, 'Commentaire de la décision no 2011-625 DC du 10 mars 2011' (2011) *Revue française de droit constitutionnel* 803.

Recently, the Council has gone further, extending this standard of judgment to provisions in which electronic publication was supposed to be the 'ordinary' form of publication (Judgment No. 2014-395 QPC of 7 May 2014). In the most recent case, electronic publication was even conceived as the only form of publication: the council did not object on this point, even if that may have been due to the possibility to provide a consultation in hard-copy form at prefectures and under-prefectures, when such form was expressly requested (Judgment No. 2014-396 QPC of 23 May 2014).

The fact that the Constitutional Council has never questioned the increasingly extensive use of electronic publication is a clear demonstration that it sees the internet as an additional resource for participation, rather than a danger for equality, having regard to contingent digital divides.

This does not mean that the internet is, in itself, a solution: after all, in all the judgments mentioned, the council declared the challenged legislation unconstitutional, since it provided for the publication of acts but did not also guarantee an adequate implementation of the principle of public participation in the decision-making process; in other words, the absence of detailed regulation on this point resulted in Parliament's failure fully to exercise its functions.

If environmental matters are those most concerned by public participation through the internet, other areas are also affected. Notwithstanding differences in the various areas, the Constitutional Council has adopted a rather more uniform approach: two recent judgments can demonstrate the assumption.

In Judgment No. 2013-678 DC of 14 November 2013, the council did not object to provisions of the organic law of New Caledonia, according to which emails could be used by the president of the territorial legislative assembly to disseminate working documents amongst the members of the assembly. Nor did it question the provision concerning the electronic publication, on the *Official Journal* of New Caledonia, of administrative acts and regulations.

In Judgment No. 2013-681 DC of 5 December 2013, the organic law implementing Article 11 of the Constitution, concerning referenda, was at issue. The provisions concerning the procedures whereby voters could provide support for a bill required that this support be collected in electronic form. The council considered this condition to be consistent with the Constitution, probably taking into account the fact that the legislator had ensured that the digital divide would not hinder participation. Indeed, it was mandatory to establish access points to the internet in the most populated town of each district. Furthermore, any voter could ask an agent of the municipality to register his support electronically.[48]

6.3.3.8 *The internet and elections*

The internet has had a deep impact on elections, having regard to both electoral campaigns and voting processes. This impact has had significant consequences

48 On this judgment see Christophe Tukov, 'Une touche finale apportée par le Conseil constitutionnel à un tableau en "trompe-l'oeil"' (2013) 52 *La Semaine juridique. Édition générale* 2366.

in the context of electoral disputes. The Constitutional Council expressly recognised as much in Statement No. 201-26 ELEC of 11 July 2013, in which it noted that the use of the internet is likely to raise new issues. Nevertheless,

> although the use of Internet raises new issues, they seem to find a solution within the application of general rules governing the elections and do not seem to require adaptation of legislation to take into specific account these new communication technologies and the uses that can be made of them.[49]

For instance – in the council's words – 'the use of Internet mailing lists' can be considered as 'equal to the use of postal mailing lists'. Thus, the council must take into account 'the irregularities that may result from the transmission of Internet documents'. Similarly, it admits 'that candidates' websites may exceed the limit of the election controversy'. However, in order to take these new media into account, the council 'must have evidence submitted by the claimant relating to the extent of the distribution, or to the importance of the site's audience'.

Complaints about 'a candidate's "blog" and links to this blog on the official sites of the County Council or the National Assembly' can also be raised. The Constitutional Council, 'adopting a pragmatic approach', considers that such links cannot be regarded, 'in the absence of any element promoting the candidate', as a breach of the Election Code. The same goes, for instance, 'for the publication of a letter from the candidate to the president of an association on the website of the association'.

From a more general perspective, the internet can have both positive and negative impacts on elections. On the one hand, the internet can substantially help transparency in the electoral process; nonetheless, on the other hand, the increased communication flow can easily result in unlawful interferences that jeopardise the real freedom of voters.

Negative impacts can derive, first of all, from contamination of the electoral campaign and the candidates' arguments. There are several examples in French constitutional case law of this risk. To mention but a few of these, Judgment No. 97-2230 AN of 6 February 1998 is noteworthy; in that case, the council declared that information available on a website created by a private person involving the conduct of a candidate did not alter the electoral outcome in the circumstances of the case and, particularly, in view of the very limited website traffic.

Judgment No. 2012-4599 AN of 4 October 2012 also deserves mention: a long anonymous email with a critical presentation of the political career of a candidate and insinuations casting doubt upon his honesty and his family, along with a request to forward it widely, did not lead to the annulment of the elections, because, even if the message was likely to discredit the applicant in the minds of voters, its dissemination was not proved and, moreover, given the difference of

49 The function of the Constitutional Council in electoral processes is analysed by Jean-Pierre Camby, *Le Conseil constitutionnel, juge électoral* (Dalloz 2013).

votes between the claimant and the winning candidate, any dissemination that may have taken place was not likely to have affected the electoral outcome.

A similar judgment was delivered with regard to a candidate whose identity was stolen by a website that disseminated discrediting information: in the absence of any data related to the website's audience, and taking into account the final difference in the numbers of votes obtained by the candidates, the Constitutional Council confirmed the validity of the elections (Judgment No. 2012-4630 AN of 7 December 2012).

The council, in Judgment No. 2012-4627 AN of 15 February 2013, also confirmed the validity of elections in which the website of the Ministry of Foreign Affairs, in the pages concerning the elections, indicated an incorrect political affiliation for one of the candidates: indeed, the mistake did not affect the electoral outcome, since it was brought to the attention of voters 36 hours after the opening of electronic voting; in any event, the margin of votes between the elected candidate and the claimant was too great to contest the elections' general outcome.

A peculiar risk for voters' freedom can be the result of an early disclosure of the elections' outcome. In Judgment No. 2007-3975 AN of 29 November 2007, the council dismissed a claim based on the disclosure of the electoral outcome, which was available on the internet one hour before the closing of the polling stations. The claimant did not prove that the contested facts were true; but even if they were, the difference of votes between the candidates did not allow the council to infer that the early disclosure could have affected the final results.

As a matter of principle, however, the issue could not be ignored. Indeed, in Statement No. 2007-142 PDR of 7 June 2007, the Constitutional Council expressed the wish for Parliament to take action against the influence upon voters in presidential elections that could derive from the dissemination of electoral results and exit polls on foreign websites available to French voters.

Finally, a negative impact on voters can be the result of deficiencies in the electronic voting system. The issue was brought before the council in Judgment No. 2012-4597/4626 AN of 15 February 2013, but the council rejected the claim because the assumed malfunctioning of the system was not proved, both with regard to the lack of security and to the faulty mechanism for vote counting.

With reference to positive impact, the Constitutional Council has observed that the internet can be a very effective means of ensuring transparency for both candidates and voters, for example if the list of official supporters of a candidate for the presidency of the Republic is published (Statement Nos. 2002-129 PDR of 7 November 2002; 2005-22 ELEC of 7 July 2005). The use of the internet can also help electoral bodies and agents to enhance efficiency: since the end of the 1990s, the council has expressed the wish that the internet be used to provide complete information concerning the role of prefectures and municipalities in the electoral process (Statement No. 98-15 ELEC of 4 June 1998).

In Judgment No. 2013-673 DC of 18 July 2013, members of the Senate submitted to the council the legislation regulating the information provided to voters for the election of the Assembly of French nationals living abroad. The claimants argued that the information was given to voters by electronic transmission or, in the alternative, by mail, no later than 50 days before the polling date. In their view, failing to provide ballot papers, and providing simple circulars sent to voters only by electronic transmission, the legislation in question breached the voters' right to information. In addition, the provision was also considered as infringing the equal treatment of voters, having regard to those who did not have access to the internet.

Omitting to make any considerations concerning the digital divide, the council replied that the Parliament pursued the aim of ensuring adequate information for every voter, taking into account the specificity of the elections at issue, and especially the geographical distance and the risks inherent in postal delivery. Indeed:

> In the current state of communication and given the generalized development of public communication services online, as well as the growing importance of these services for the exercise of democracy, the legislature could, without violating any constitutional requirement, provide that the information be communicated to voters electronically.

In other words, the internet had to be considered as a resource for democracy, even though the existence of digital divides could have some negative impact, in factual terms. In the judgment, the council did not deal with this issue, but it is fair to say that, on the one hand, it should have done so and, on the other hand, it may very well be called upon to clarify its doctrine on this point in the near future. After all, the French constitutional case law related to internet law, which is undoubtedly numerically rich in cases, lacks significant statements on this subject, regardless of the key role that it plays in connecting the regulation of the internet to constitutional requirements.

6.4 Final remarks

The analysis of the Italian and the French systems of constitutional adjudication and the review of their respective constitutional case laws concerning the internet has led to some results that are apparently far from insignificant for the purposes of investigating the relationship between internet law and constitutional adjudication in centralised systems, with specific regard to those systems that lack direct access for individuals.

Oddly enough, at first glance, it could be concluded that it is impossible to establish a direct connection between the features of the systems of constitutional adjudication and the trend of constitutional case law concerning the internet. As a matter of fact, the conclusion drawn in section 6.2 above was that the evolution of the two systems can be described as an important development of their similarities, despite the distance of the respective starting points of the Italian Constitutional Court and the French Constitutional Council. On the contrary, what emerged in section 6.3 was the different pace of the two constitutional case laws.

Nevertheless, the conclusion that is suggested by the juxtaposition of the two sections appears simplistic, rather than rational. Indeed, it is based solely on the general trends, and thus neglects any closer examination concerning, with regard to systems of constitutional adjudication, the real extent of similarities and consequences of differences and, when it comes to case law, the definition of the differences between the Italian and the French experiences.

To advance a different conclusion, and therefore to assert that some connections between systems of constitutional adjudication and cases on internet law can be proved, an outline of possible explanations for the differences between Italian and French constitutional case law can be sketched.

In general terms, the differences are both quantitative and qualitative: with regard to the first, it is indisputable that in France the number of cases concerning the internet is much higher than in Italy; with reference to the kind of issues brought before the Italian court or the French council, it is fair to say that only a small fraction of the subjects investigated in judgments is shared by the two bodies.

Arguments exist to support linking both points of view with the structure of the systems of constitutional adjudication. With specific regard to the type of issues that the Italian court and the French council must deal with, many of the differences derive from the way in which cases and questions can be submitted to the guardian of the Constitution.

In Italy, most of the constitutional case law concerning the internet is related to conflicts of competences between the state and the regions; thus, many issues do not deal actually with individual rights, but rather with the distribution of legislative and financial powers between territorial authorities. It is therefore no coincidence that the court must generally settle disputes on provisions concerning public grants; however, the court has taken the opportunity to express its doctrine on rights-related issues in only a few cases.[50]

This type of issue goes beyond the French council's jurisdiction, since it does not settle disputes between territorial authorities; such an incompetence is, in turn, the result of the limited autonomy recognised to entities within the Republic.

The Italian court's advantage with regard to disputes between territorial authorities is balanced by the French council's jurisdiction on elections. As seen above, this kind of jurisdiction has given rise to several judgments in which the internet was mentioned and, sometimes, played a crucial role in the council's decision.

These remarks can at least partially justify the different issues that are brought before the Italian court and the French council. It is obvious, however, that the distance between France and Italy cannot be explained only with reference to these types of access to the council or the court.

The abstract review of legislation challenged by parliamentary oppositions is

50 The most important judgment in this regard is Judgment No. 307/2004, which is undoubtedly the leading case on internet law.

another way to bring questions before the French Constitutional Council, and is another greatly distinctive feature that contributes to explain the differences with the Italian system, especially with reference to the number of judgments delivered concerning internet law. Indeed, a large part of the judgments on the internet is subsequent to an abstract review, to the extent that the mere existence of this type of access to the Constitutional Council could explain the different pace of constitutional case law, at least in terms of the number of judgments.

These findings per se should be able to confirm the connection between the development of the constitutional case law concerning the internet and the structure of the systems of constitutional adjudication. Even this conclusion, however, seems slightly too simplistic: if the connection is unquestionable, this does not mean that the constitutional case law depends on the structure of the system of constitutional adjudication. In other words, the structure of the system of constitutional adjudication is certainly one of the factors that influences the pace of constitutional case law, but this cannot automatically lead to the conclusion that it is the only factor, nor that it is the main factor.

In centralised systems of constitutional adjudication, the jurisdiction of constitutional courts depends not only on the way in which cases are submitted but also, and in particular, on the acts and the enactments that courts can review. In systems where no direct access for individuals is provided, the courts' jurisdiction is generally limited to a review of primary legislation or, at most, of executive regulations, since questions concerning other enactments or actions can be brought before the courts only in relatively exceptional circumstances.

This feature of systems of constitutional adjudication is likely to influence the case law concerning the internet very strongly; indeed, both the Italian and the French case laws demonstrate that cases relating to the internet are submitted to the court or to the council by questions of constitutionality that target legislative provisions, with the sole exception of those on electoral proceedings in France.

Such a 'bottleneck' affects the entire system of protection of rights, since any protection claimed needs legislation to be challenged before the court (or the council), without which the claimant would hardly be able to have the merits of his or her case decided.[51] The protection of rights within the context of the internet is, of course, subject to these general conditions, to the extent that this bottleneck is probably the most important feature of the Italian and French systems of constitutional adjudication to influence the case law on the internet, because it gives space to a huge influence by the system of the sources of law and, in particular, of the type of sources that regulate the internet within the legal order.

51 This peculiar feature of centralised systems of constitutional adjudication without direct access for individuals casts a shadow on F. Rubio Llorente's distinction between norms-oriented jurisdictions and rights-oriented jurisdictions (see Francisco Rubio Llorente, 'Tendencias actuales de la jurisdicción constitucional en Europa' in Francisco Rubio Llorente and Javier Jiménez Campo, *Estudios sobre la jurisdicción constitucional* (McGraw-Hill 1998) 155. Although the universal trend is towards the second type of jurisdiction, the systems analysed in this chapter cannot neglect the first dimension, since the existence of norms (and thus their review) is a mandatory condition for any form of protection of individual rights.

As a result, apart from the few cases in which no question of constitutionality is necessary, because the proceedings deal with factual circumstances (such as the electoral processes judged by the French Constitutional Council), all of the constitutional case law on the internet is actually conditioned and oriented by the activity of legislatures: the de facto boundaries of the jurisdiction of the constitutional court or council are drawn by the legislators, and by their choices to regulate the internet or to leave the task to different authorities. Constitutional adjudication can play a significant role in reviewing internet law only if the legislator decides to exercise its powers or, at most, to delegate them to the executive branch, authorising it to adopt decrees having the force of primary legislation (such as those regulated by Articles 76 and 77 of the Italian Constitution); otherwise, the chance for constitutional courts or councils to have a say on the subject becomes increasingly theoretical.

In the light of the foregoing, a comparison between Italy and France having regard to the legislative framework governing the internet appears to be far from insignificant. Indeed, the French approach to the internet is characterised by a recognition of the importance of regulations adopted by different bodies and even of soft law;[52] however, the core principles must be defined by the legislator, so as to guarantee legal security and clarity through the legislative implementation of the unwritten principles that govern the protection of rights on the web.[53] This means, of course, that Parliament must also adopt provisions that limit 'digital rights', to protect other rights that are deemed to deserve priority.[54]

After all, it is no coincidence that some of the Constitutional Council's most important judgments have concerned pivotal acts for internet law, such as, for instance, the Act on Confidence in the Digital Economy (Judgment No. 2004-496 DC),[55] the Act Pertaining to Copyright and Related Rights in

52 In this regard see the Annual Study for 2013 by the French Council of State, precisely concerning the soft law: *Le droit souple* (Documentation française 2013) 91 http://www.ladocumentationfrancaise.fr/var/storage/rapports-publics/144000280/0000.pdf (last accessed 14 August 2015).

53 See the Annual Study for 2014 by the French Council of State concerning digital technology and fundamental rights: *Le numérique et les droits fondamentaux* (La Documentation française 2014) http://www.ladocumentationfrancaise.fr/var/storage/rapports-publics/144000541/0000.pdf (last accessed 14 August 2015), in which the Council of State, on one hand, acknowledges that '[h]eavy-handed intervention by the legislature tended to *prevent the negative aspects* of digital technology *risks hindering its positive potential* at the same time' (*Digital technology and fundamental rights and freedoms* (English summary) 8 http://www.conseil-etat.fr/content/download/33163/287555/version/1/file/Digital%20technology%20and%20fundamental%20rights%20and%20freedoms.pdf (last accessed 14 August 2015, emphasis in the original), but on the other expresses the wish for legislative interventions, for example with regard to certain rights 'such as the right to security . . . and intellectual property rights', for which 'digital technology appears to present more of a risk, which legislators need to tackle' (ibid 4).

54 A good example of this balance is the opposition between the protection of copyright and the recognition of the right to internet access. As discussed above (section 6.3.3.1), in Judgment No. 2009-580 DC, the Constitutional Council criticised and declared unconstitutional Parliament's choice to give priority to copyright, because of the importance of the internet in contemporary society.

55 See sections 6.3.3.3 and 6.3.3.4.

the Information Society (Judgment No. 2006-540 DC),[56] the Act Furthering the Diffusion and Protection of Creation on Internet, the so-called 'Hadopi 1 Law' (Judgment No. 2009-580 DC),[57] the Act Pertaining to the Protection under Criminal Law of Literary and Artistic Property on Internet, the so-called 'Hadopi 2 Law' (Judgment No. 2009-590 DC)[58] and the Act on Guidelines and Programming for Internal Security (Judgment No. 2011-625 DC).[59]

On the contrary, the Italian approach appears to be somewhat 'pessimistic' regarding the capability of the law (and in particular of hard law) to regulate the internet effectively,[60] so that the legislator does not even attempt to provide for a systematic framework in which both public interests and rights are protected pursuant to a ranking of priorities. The internet is therefore largely regulated by secondary legislation, which is adopted by the government or even authorities (the Authority for Communications Guarantees in particular),[61] not to mention the crucial role of sources of soft law.

On the basis of the structure of the Italian system of constitutional adjudication, the political choice for a low-profile regulation of the internet results in great difficulties for the Constitutional Court to receive cases and to decide questions.

The comparison between Italy and France concerning the review of legislation in force subsequent to judicial reference is the most effective demonstration of the significant effects of the difference in the legislative approaches to constitutional case law.

Constitutional review upon judicial reference is definitely the most important similarity between the Italian and the French systems, despite the many differences that characterise the proceedings in the two systems, and that generally result in easier access to the Italian court than to the French council. Many factors could be mentioned in this respect; two in particular appear to be crucial. First, whilst in Italy any court can submit a question of constitutionality to the Constitutional Court, in France courts must submit a question of constitutionality to the Court of Cassation or to the Council of State, which are the sole judicial authorities endowed with the power to bring cases before the council, and this two-phase procedure strongly limits the number of questions that reach the council.

Secondly, the effects of dismissing the cases are extremely different, since the judgment of the Italian court rejecting a question does not prevent any court from submitting the question again in the future; on the contrary, dismissal of a case from the French council has the effect of attesting the consistency of the

56 See section 6.3.3.5.

57 See sections 6.3.3.1, 6.3.3.3, 6.3.3.4, 6.3.3.5 and 6.3.3.6.

58 See sections 6.3.3.1 and 6.3.3.5.

59 See section 6.3.3.6.

60 For a recent study see Gian Luca Conti, 'La governance dell'internet: dalla Costituzione della rete alla Costituzione nella rete' in Nisticò and Passaglia (n 29) 77.

61 For instance, the blocking of websites to fight copyright infringement is regulated by an enactment of this authority (resolution no. 452/13/CONS of 25 July 2013), whereas in France, legislation has provided for a rather detailed framework on the subject (see section 6.3.3.6).

legislative provision under review with the Constitution, which makes it impossible, apart from exceptional cases owing to major changes over time, to submit a question involving provisions that have already been reviewed.

The number of judgments rendered by the Italian court and the French council upon judicial references indisputably show the difference in terms of access to court. In France, since the judicial reference was introduced in March 2010, there have been 363 judgments (until 30 September 2014), which decided 416 questions submitted over four and a half years, that is approximately 80 judgments deciding slightly over 92 questions every year; in Italy, despite the crisis of this competence,[62] in 2013, 145 judgments were delivered deciding 291 questions, and, of course, the numbers are much greater if one simply examines the last five years.

Although internet issues appeared before courts from well before 2010, and therefore the French judicial reference procedure began operating *in medias res*, and even if the most important acts concerning the internet were challenged before the council by parliamentary opposition, so that a large part of the most disputed aspects of the subject were already settled when the legislation was to be applied by the courts (and, therefore, the previous judgment of the Constitutional Council prevented judicial references), there is no doubt that the impact of this type of proceedings has been far more important than in Italy, in terms of both the number of judgments (nine to two) and of the interest of the issues discussed.[63]

This comparison shows the extent to which centralised systems of constitutional adjudication, in which direct access for individuals is not available, are influenced by external choices regarding the legislative framework of internet law. The ultimate question is, therefore, whether constitutional courts or councils can do anything other than accept the *status quo*, or whether they can somehow be 'masters of their fate'.

Of course, it is not up to courts to change the structure of the system of constitutional adjudication; nor can they replace Parliament in shaping the legislative framework of any subject matter. Therefore, it is impossible for courts or councils truly to be 'masters of their fate'. However, this does not mean that they are condemned to maintaining a passive attitude. As a matter of fact, it is unanimously acknowledged that courts can enlarge their jurisdiction by adopting 'activist doctrines': with specific regard to internet law, the main challenge for activism is

62 See section 6.2.3.1 above.

63 Indeed, Judgment No. 2010-45 QPC concerned the assignment of domain names, Judgment No. 2013-345 QPC was about communication of workers' unions via the internet. In Judgment No. 2013-370 QPC, the council had to balance intellectual property rights with safeguarding bibliographic heritage. Several judgments were related to electronic publication. Finally, Judgment No. 2011-164 QPC was related to criminal liability for offences committed on the internet. The Italian court dealt with a similar issue in Order No. 337 of 2011, whilst the only other judgment worthy of mention concerned the internet and the implementation of citizens' contacts with public administrations (Judgment No. 365 of 2010).

to ensure the existence of a legal framework in which access to a constitutional court may be facilitated.

Such activism is displayed by the French council, rather than by the Italian court. Indeed, in French constitutional case law, the *incompétence négative* doctrine has played a key role in compelling Parliament to exercise its powers,[64] insofar as the council has censored Parliament – by declaring the legislative provisions adopted unconstitutional – when it failed fully to exercise the functions that the Constitution has reserved to the legislator.[65] On the contrary, the Italian court has shown evident self-restraint in this respect, not only because it has never elaborated a doctrine similar to the *incompétence négative*, but also because it has generally been rather deferential towards the Parliament's choices with regard to legislative delegation and deregulation.[66]

To conclude, the scarcity of judgments on internet law that characterises the Italian experience is mostly related to the legal framework of the subject; however, the Constitutional Court does not appear to be in a good position to plead 'not guilty', essentially because of its deferential doctrines. Taking this into account, comparison with the French system appears to be helpful because, on the one hand, it reveals some of the inadequacies of the Italian system of constitutional adjudication and, on the other, it shows a possible way to overcome them, at least to some extent. It is to be hoped that, if Parliament will not change its attitude, the court will soon do so.

64 On the *incompétence négative* doctrine see Georges Schmitter, 'L'incompétence négative du législateur et des autorités administratives' (1989) *Annuaire international de justice constitutionnelle* 137; François Priet, 'L'incompétence négative du législateur' (1994) *Revue française de droit constitutionnel* 59; Florence Galletti, 'Existe-t-il une obligation de bien légiférer? Propos sur "l'incompétence négative du législateur" dans la jurisprudence du Conseil constitutionnel' (2004) *Revue française de droit constitutionnel* 387; Patricia Rrapi, '"L'incompétence négative" dans la QPC: de la double négation à la double incompréhension' (2012) 1 *Les Nouveaux Cahiers du Conseil constitutionnel* 163.

65 Some examples of application of this doctrine were provided above, in section 6.3.3.6 and 6.3.3.7.

66 See contributions to the book edited by the Constitutional Court, *La delega legislativa* (Giuffrè 2009) and to Marta Cartabia, Elisabetta Lamarque and Palmina Tanzarella (eds), *Gli atti normativi del Governo tra Corte costituzionale e giudici* (Giappichelli 2011).

7 Protection of fundamental rights and the internet

A comparative appraisal of German and Central European constitutional case law

András Jóri

7.1 'Internet law'

Although those countries with a centralised system of judicial review can be easily identified,[1] 'fundamental rights and the internet' is a topic that is not so easy to grasp. Courts, and constitutional courts are facing new questions posed by new technology all the time. Privacy protection as a legal concept emerged in the United States as a consequence of one of the most important technological advances of the late nineteenth century: the appearance of modern cameras, which could record the image of a person instantly and, thus, without her or his consent.[2] As we move closer in time, we can observe that some of the problems we are facing and are trying to solve today actually preceded the widescale use of the open network we call today the 'internet'.

These new issues would be better identified as the ones linked with the revolutionary advance of information technology, having started in the 1960s. Terminology has changed over the last decades: early authors and scholars of data protection law wrote about 'data banks',[3] a term forgotten today. Before the internet was known to mainstream users, books devoted to the legal aspects of information technology appeared under the title 'Computer Law';[4] later, with the appearance of computer networks, the new word cyberspace emerged and the term cyber law appeared.[5]

Most recently, actually or allegedly new challenges posed by data mining and data warehousing were widely discussed; and today 'big data',[6] 'cloud computing' and the 'internet of things' are the current buzzwords. Thus, the topic of this

1 However, in this chapter only some decisions of the German, the Czech, the Slovene and the Hungarian Constitutional Courts will be discussed.
2 See Samuel D. Warren and Louis D. Brandeis, 'The right to privacy: the implicit made explicit' in Ferdinand D. Schoeman (ed.), *Philosophical Dimensions of Privacy: An Anthology* (Cambridge University Press 1984) 75–103.
3 Even the German Constitutional Court used this term in its landmark *Census* Decision (BVerfG 65,1).
4 See e.g. David Bainbridge, *Computer Law* (FT Pitman Publishing 1996).
5 Jonathan Rosenoer, *CyberLaw: The Law of the Internet* (Springer 1997).
6 Viktor Mayer-Schönberger and Kenneth Cukier, *Big Data* (John Murray 2013).

chapter will be defined as the protection of fundamental rights and the challenges posed by these evolving new technologies. Note, however, that 'internet law' can also be defined in a more narrow sense, covering only the issues that are closely linked to the technology that serves the internet infrastructure, for example the operation of the domain name system, the trademark law challenges of the domain delegation process or legal issues relating to search engine optimisation.

Technology	Affected rights and main problems
Mainframe computers	First DP acts from 1970: Registration of databases
Stand-alone PCs, BBSs, internet	~ 1983–1997 DP: Right to 'informational self-determination' Freedom of expression (CDA–1996)
Internet of things Cloud computing Social networks 'Big data' Mobile apps	~ 1997–to date DP: Regulating technology 'Privacy by design'; data retention 'IT Grundrecht' Freedom of expression (and domain names) Electronic freedom of information (whistleblowing, leaking platforms)

The above figure shows how the principal changes in IT technology have posed new challenges in the previous decades. The figure is very much based on a generational description of European data protection legislation,[7] but some important developments from other fields are also added. Data protection law appeared in the age of mainframe computers (in the late 1960s and early 1970s); the first data protection laws then obliged data controllers to register with data protection authorities. The 1980s and early 1990s was the period of the stand-alone personal computer; in data protection law, the theory of informational self-determination[8] appeared, whilst the first cases regarding computer networks (e.g. regarding the applicability of copyright law) also appeared.

At first, these cases concerned not the internet as we now know it, but other, early models of computer networks, such as bulletin board systems (where individual users could connect to servers via phone lines, but these servers were not in direct connection with each other). In the second half of the 1990s, widescale use of the internet appeared, together with the first regulatory attempts, for example the Communications Decency Act 1996 in the US.

Since then, many things have changed and many have remained the same.

7 For such a generational description of data protection law see Viktor Mayer-Schönberger, *Generational Development of Data Protecton in Europe* in Philip E. Agre and Marc Rotenberg (eds), *Technology and Privacy: The New Landscape* (The MIT Press 1997) 219–41; see also András Jóri, *Adatvédelmi kézikönyv* (Osiris 2005) 24–66.

8 See the 1983 *Census* Decision Supra note 3.

Jurisdictional issues, issues regarding liability, problems linked to the hazards that increasing computation capacity can mean to privacy are still on the agenda, discussed under frequently changing buzzwords: 'Big data', the 'internet of things', and so on.

7.2 Systems of centralised judicial review with direct access to the Constitutional Court

The cases presented in this chapter are from Germany, Hungary, the Czech Republic and Slovenia. The system of judicial review in all of these countries is centralised (judicial review being carried out by constitutional courts); and the system of judicial review is open to the citizens directly, in most cases, through the instrument of constitutional complaints.

According to the Basic Law for the Federal Republic of Germany, the Federal Constitutional Court shall rule 'on constitutional complaints, which may be filed by any person alleging that one of his basic rights or one of his rights under [several articles of the Basic Law] has been infringed by public authority'.[9] The landmark decision of the German court regarding mandatory data retention, described below, was initiated through constitutional complaints, as well as the decision on online searches.

The judicial review system of Hungary between 1989 and 2011 has been based on a model where the review could be initiated without any interest by any party. According to the Constitution in force in this period: '[e]veryone has the right to initiate proceedings of the Constitutional Court in the cases specified by law'.[10] Judicial review of laws already in force could be initiated by 'anyone'.[11] This system was changed with the adoption of the new Constitution ('Basic Law') of the country, having come into force on 1 January 2012. The Basic Law – and the new Act on the Constitutional Court – sets out a system, where *ex post* 'abstract' constitutional review (previously open to all citizens) can be initiated only by a limited set of actors (the Government, one-fourth of the MPs, the president of the Curia, the Prosecutor General or the Commissioner for Fundamental Rights (Ombudsman)),[12] whereas other persons can use the channel of constitutional complaints.[13] A constitutional complaint can be submitted by a persons affected by a case, 'if, due to the application of a legal regulation contrary to the Basic Law in their judicial proceedings (a) their rights enshrined in the Fundamental Law were violated, and (b) the possibilities for legal remedy have already been exhausted or no possibility for legal remedy is available'.[14] The

9 Basic Law, art 93(1)4a.
10 Act No. XX of 1949 on the Constitution of the Republic of Hungary (as amended), art 32/A, para. (3).
11 Act No. XXXII of 1989 on the Constitutional Court, art 21(2).
12 Basic Law, art 24(2)(e).
13 The Court 'shall, on the basis of a constitutional complaint, review the conformity with the Fundamental Law of any judicial decision'; see Basic Law, art 24(2)(d).
14 Act No. CLI of 2011 on the Constitutional Court, art 26(1).

case presented in this chapter was initiated by the submission of a constitutional complaint.

In the Czech Republic, judicial review of statutes (that is, legislative acts of the Senate ratified by the Assembly of Deputies) can be initiated by a limited number of actors (the President, a group of at least 41 deputies or a group of at least 17 senators, a panel of the court in connection with deciding a constitutional complaint; the government, under set conditions) or by 'anyone who submits a constitutional complaint'.[15] Such complaint can be submitted by natural or legal persons if they 'allege that [their] fundamental rights and basic freedoms guaranteed in the constitutional order . . . have been infringed as a result of the final decision in a proceeding to which [they were parties] of a measure, or of some other encroachment by a public authority'.[16] In the case described below, a group of 51 deputies submitted a petition with the Court.

In Slovenia, the parties that can initiate a procedure by the Constitutional Court include the National Assembly, one-third of the deputies, the National Council, the Government, the ombudsman for human rights, the information commissioner, the Bank of Slovenia or the Court of Audit, the State Prosecutor General, representative bodies of local communities, representative associations of local communities and national representative trade unions for an individual activity or profession.[17] A petition can be lodged by persons demonstrating a legal interest as well.[18] In the case presented, the procedure was initiated by the information commissioner.

In addressing the new challenges, the constitutional courts of Germany, Slovenia, Hungary and the Czech Republic addressed the motions initiated by members of Parliament, data protection authorities, citizens or industry representatives; nevertheless, in all the cases presented, they had the opportunity to shape how fundamental rights are interpreted in the context of IT technologies in their jurisdiction and sometimes (as in the cases of the German Constitutional Court described below) globally.

7.3 Selected cases of constitutional courts within systems of centralised judicial review with direct access to the Constitutional Court

In this chapter we feature selected cases from the above-mentioned four countries; and some of the everlasting issues of the computer age, that has been addressed by the constitutional courts of these countries in the recent years.

15 Constitutional Court Act of 16 June 1993, art 64(2).
16 Constitutional Court Act of 16 June 1993, art 72(1)(a).
17 Constitutional Court Act (ZUstS), art 23a.
18 ibid.

7.3.1 Reinterpretation of a traditional rights in the light of the new IT environment: data retention

First of all, some cases on *data retention* are described, including the German, the Czech and the Slovenian cases. Data retention is a particularly important topic for data protection law today; it does not simply involve the issue of balancing between privacy and other interests, such as security. Assessing data retention laws from this perspective is not more than purely applying a traditional proportionality test. The reason why these cases are interesting is that they reveal a hidden change in the paradigm of data protection law, and show how the principles of traditional data protection law, as invented in the 1970s, have been challenged recently. One of those principles is the principle of purpose-bound processing: the rule, that no processing of personal data can take place without a previously set, legal and specified purpose. No data can be gathered without a concrete purpose: one which necessitates the obtaining and storage of that particular piece of information.

Data retention, however, is challenging this principle. In 2006, EU Directive 2006/24/EC, amending Directive 2002/58/EC (the E-Privacy Directive), prescribed a mandatory retention of traffic data relating to fixed and mobile telephony, internet access, email and telephony to EU Member States. These data, according to the European legislator, are necessary to identify the source, destination, date, time, duration, type, equipment and location of the communication; the period for the retention[19] was also set out by the directive as being 'not less than 6 months'.[20] The purpose of data retention is 'to ensure that the data are available for the purpose of the investigation, detection and prosecution of serious crime, as defined by each Member State in its national law'.[21]

As Member States started to implement the rules as prescribed by the Data Retention Directive, some constitutional courts addressed the issue of whether data retention is in line with established standards of constitutionality as regards the right to data protection. In 2014, the Court of Justice of the European Union declared that data retention was no longer compliant with the European Charter of Fundamental Rights;[22] in some countries, the national Constitutional Court addressed the issue only after the CJEU decision. A dialogue between courts has taken place starting in the German Federal Constitutional Court.

In its decision published in March 2010,[23] the German Court had to decide on the constitutionality of the provisions implementing the directive in German

19 Directive 2006/24/EC of the European Parliament and of the Council of 15 March 2006 on the retention of data generated or processed in connection with the provision of publicly available electronic communications services or of public communications networks and amending Directive 2002/58/EC. See art 5 of the directive.

20 ibid art 6.

21 ibid art 1(1).

22 Joined Cases C-293/12 and C-594/12 *Digital Rights Ireland and Seitlinger v Minister for Communications, Marine and Natural Resources* [2014] ECR I-238.

23 BVerfG, 1 BvR 256/08.

law. Some provisions were included in the Telecommunications Act; others were transposed in the Criminal Procedure Code. The German legislation set out direct and indirect uses of the stored data, direct use meaning the use of data covered by the data retention obligation to prosecute crimes or for intelligence purposes, whilst indirect use meant establishing a link between an already known IP address and a user. The complainants alleged that the right to telecom secrecy and informational self-determination was infringed, and the storage of all traffic data was a disproportionate limitation of these constitutional rights. According to them, stored data could therefore be used to create personality profiles, since these data reflected every aspect of the life of an individual.

The German Constitutional Court held that: 'storage of telecommunications traffic data for six months for strictly limited uses in the course of prosecution, and for intelligence service duties, as is provided is not in itself incompatible with Article 10 of the Basic Law'. According to the Court, it is a very important factor that these data are stored in a decentralised way, and data retention is a tool that can be used for averting specific dangers of 'the modern world'. It has been mentioned above that data retention is challenging the traditional principles of European data protection law. In this instance, the Court, although rather vaguely, admitted that personal data processing without a specific goal could be accepted in this 'modern world'.

Although this view is not necessarily disputed here, it is clear that this slow 'watering down' of the traditional principles of data protection are occurring without proper reflection by legal scholars or by legislators. The new draft data protection regulation, in essence, incorporates all the principles of the 1995 EU Data Protection Directive (including that of purpose-bound processing),[24] whilst at the same time excluding some of its principles.

According to the Court, whilst data retention might theoretically be a useful tool, it is, at the same time, a 'serious' limitation of the right to informational self-determination. The court continues to set up standards for the constitutionality of laws prescribing mandatory data retention. The first of such standards concerns data security, which is a rather vague requirement and also one of a technical nature. (Note that data protection authorities in Europe carried out a coordinated investigation on data security measures regarding the processing of data in context of data retention,[25] but few of them challenged the national laws prescribing data retention. This, according to the author, reflects another contemporary tendency of European data protection law, which we could call *technicisation*: instead of politically sensitive topics, national data protection acts are dealing more and more with technical issues; many of them are now acting more like data security authorities. Obviously, fighting battles for privacy with

24 According to art 5(b) of the draft General Data Protection Regulation, personal data shall be 'collected for specified, explicit and legitimate purposes and not further processed in a way incompatible with those purposes (purpose limitation)'.

25 Report 01/2010 of the second joint enforcement action, art 29 Working Party http://ec.europa.eu/justice/policies/privacy/docs/wpdocs/2010/wp172_en.pdf (last accessed 18 August 2015).

governments might prove risky; however, monitoring data security is a safe and peaceful area of operations.)

The second standard is about the use of data: there must be 'sufficiently evidenced concrete danger to the life, limb or freedom of a person, to the existence or the security of the Federal Government or of a *Land* (state) or to ward off a common danger'. Data transmissions must be transparent, and efficient sanctions need to be put in place. For indirect use as defined above, the court set out less stringent standards. According to the court, security measures were not determined in the German implementation of data retention; the data could be used for investigating all kinds of criminal offences and the legislation itself created a pool of data that could be used for many purposes in the future. The court held that the German regulation regarding data retention was unconstitutional.

But what is the solution instead of data retention? The German Government proposed the 'quick freeze'[26] instrument, which would allow storage of only those data relating to an individual user by the service provider, if a reasonable cause exists, and to transmit those data to law enforcement authorities with a judicial warrant. This solution was not accepted by the European Commission, which took Germany to the Court of Justice of the European Union (CJEU) in 2012,[27] requesting that fines be imposed on Germany because of non-implementation of the directive. After the decision by the CJEU in *Digital Rights Ireland*[28] the case was removed from the register.

Some EU Member States followed Germany's lead. In 2011, the Czech Constitutional Court declared unconstitutional the provisions implementing the Data Retention Directive.[29] Data protection is acknowledged at a constitutional level in the Czech Republic, and is interpreted by the Constitutional Court as a right to informational self-determination. Whilst, as the court noted, there was room for manoeuvre for the Czech legislator to implement the directive, the actual implementation was successfully challenged. The court held that the right to informational self-determination covers traffic data; it is notable that it built its definition of 'private life' on the practice of the European Court of Human Rights (ECtHR) (*Niemietz*,[30] *Malone*[31]), and referred to the German case frequently in its argumentation, but the court mentioned also the decisions of Romanian, Bulgarian and Cyprus courts.

As to the test applied, the Czech court used the usual proportionality test and found that whilst a constitutional goal can be established, the public authorities that can request data in the context of data retention are not well defined, and

26 http://www.dw.de/germany-calls-for-a-quick-freeze-data-compromise/a-15829029 (last accessd 18 August 2015).

27 http://europa.eu/rapid/press-release_IP-12-530_en.htm (last accessed 18 August 2015).

28 Note 22.

29 2011/03/22 - Pl. ÚS 24/10.

30 Niemietz v Germany Application no. 13710/88, Merits and Just Satisfaction A/251-B [1992] ECHR 80, (1993) 16 EHRR 97 ECtHR (16 December 1992).

31 *Malone v United Kingdom* Application no. 8691/79 (1984) 7 EHRR 14, [1984] ECHR 10, [1985] ECHR 5.

the data is overused for the investigation of 'common crimes'. As in the German court, the Czech judges criticised the lack of data security rules. It is also remarkable that in the *obiter dictum* part of the decision, the court mentions the quick freeze solution, also originating from Germany.

Data retention was also subject to scrutiny in Slovenia. However, Slovenian judges had the opportunity to decide on the case after the CJEU judgment in *Digital Rights Ireland*.[32] The decision, delivered in July 2014, was issued in a case initiated by the Information Commissioner of the country.[33] The court, whilst not requesting a preliminary ruling from the CJEU, waited for the decision in *Digital Rights Ireland*. It then issued its decision, according to which it held that data retention might be a valuable tool (so the necessity of the limitation of the rights can be established), but that the actual national implementation was unconstitutional.[34]

The main novelty of the cases described above is that some of these decisions implicitly acknowledged the fact that in the new environment of information technology the traditional data protection principle of purpose-bound processing is outdated, although there is still a reluctance to state this expressly. Whilst quick freeze, proposed in Germany, would be a solution that maintains this traditional principle amongst the new environment of mass processing of personal data, courts have instead chosen another track: they have accepted the concept of data retention, but (perhaps fearing the consequences) have held the actual implementing rules to be unconstitutional.

7.3.2 Creating a new right: the right to confidentiality and integrity of IT systems

Whilst data-retention judgments fit into the paradigm of data-protection law, new technologies have also led to the construction of a new constitutional right by the German court. In its landmark decision published in February 2008,[35] the German Constitutional Court declared unconstitutional some provisions of an act on online searches carried out via the internet, targeting computers used by persons allegedly involved in anti-constitutional activities. The court held that there is a constitutional right to the confidentiality and integrity of IT systems, and these systems can in fact be regarded as part of the private sphere of the individual, even if they are not in the person's home, but, to use the contemporary term, in the cloud. It is notable that this right was concretised from the general

32 Note 22.

33 For the motion of the IC see https://www.ip-rs.si/fileadmin/user_upload/Pdf/ocene_ustavnosti/ZEKom_-_Zahteva_za_oceno_ustavnosti__data_retention_.pdf (last accessed 18 August 2015).

34 For an analysis of this case see Samo Bardutzky, 'The timing of dialogue: Slovenian Constitutional Court and the Data Retention Directive' (2014) VerfBlog http://www.verfassungsblog.de/en/timing-dialogue-slovenian-constitutional-court-data-retention-directive (last accessed 18 August 2015).

35 BVerfG, 1, BvR 370/07.

right of personality set out in the Basic Law of Germany, in a way that resembles the 1983 *Census* decision on informational self-determination.[36]

It is interesting to analyse how the court distinguished this right from other rights that come into play, and how it made an argument that such right is necessary in the new IT environment. According to the court, secrecy of telecommunications (Article 10.1 of the Basic Law) covers only cases of 'source telecommunications surveillance', where data are on the sender's computer or under transmission, although this right cannot be relied upon when the data have already been received. Secondly, whilst inviolability of a person's home (Article 13.1 of the Basic Law) would cover surveillance 'inside' the dwelling, including computers operated there, it might be the case that the data are uploaded onto a computer network in the cloud, and therefore the inviolability of the home principle cannot be applied. Thirdly, there is a need to distinguish this new right from the right to data protection or, as interpreted by the Court, to informational self-determination. According to the Court, the right to informational self-determination traditionally deals with processing structured sets of personal data, but third-party access to IT systems can lead to the dissemination of large-scale and potentially sensitive information about an individual, even without further data processing operations.[37]

The Court found the provisions under challenge unconstitutional, and held that this kind of regulation of online searches can be permitted only if the existence of a concrete danger to a predominantly important legal interest can be established, whereupon a judicial warrant will be required.[38]

7.3.3 Old constitutional debates revisited: comments and freedom of expression

One of the earliest questions of internet law, and a favourite topic for discussion in the late 1990s, was how freedom of expression on the internet should be regulated, and whether this medium should be framed as something totally new or whether the existing models of press and media law should remain unchanged. A heated debate on the constitutionality of the 1996 Communications Decency Act, the US Supreme Court decision in *Reno v ACLU*, the regulatory attempts of European Member States (e.g. the 1997 Informations- und Kommunikationsdienste-gesetz in Germany) and the European Union (leading

36 Note 3.

37 Note that this argument could be rebutted, and the new right to confidentiality and integrity of IT systems might even be found superfluous by emphasising that not only structured file systems, but even individual pieces of personal data are covered by the right to informational self-determination. According to the author, this would be the case in Hungary, based on the interpretation of the right to informational self-determination by the constitutional court in that country.

38 Despite the remark in footnote 24, this decision by the German court had an impact in other countries of the region, i.e. it is quoted in the recommendation drafted by the author as the then data protection commissioner of Hungary covering online searches, requesting the government to extend the requirement of judicial warrant to these activities; see http://abi.atlatszo.hu/index.php?menu=aktualis/ajanlasok&dok=1813_T_2008-4 (last accessed 18 August 2015).

to Directive 2000/31/EC on electronic commerce) featured issues such as distinguishing between access providers, content providers and service providers, the limitation of liability of intermediaries, or the advantages and disadvantages of state intervention in a free marketplace of ideas created by the new technology.[39]

Remarkably, in 2014, constitutionality of content published on the internet is still an issue. In a recent case, the Hungarian Constitutional Court decided on the liability of content providers for third party comments.[40] The complainant was an association that had been held liable for third-party user comments appearing on its site by the Curia, the Supreme Ordinary Court of Hungary. According to the Constitutional Court, liability for third-party comments can be established because of an existing constitutional purpose (safeguarding personality rights), and because such regulation is also appropriate to achieve this goal (since without liability, no remedy can be provided for the offended persons).

As to proportionality, the court held that establishing the liability of those providers publishing third-party comments with prior moderation is undoubtedly proportional, and there should be no distinction between the liability of those providers using the system of prior moderation and those not using this method: 'liability depends upon the fact of the publication, not on the moderation'. The court also stated that, in the context of defending personality rights, establishing liability of press organs (and not authors) had been held constitutional in previous cases. Note, however, that the decision does not cover 'opinion pages' (examples of those given by the court included 'Facebook', 'Web 2.0' and 'blogosphere').

7.4 Concluding remarks

Protection of fundamental rights and the internet within systems of centralised judicial review with direct access to the Constitutional Court is an extremely wide topic; we have touched upon the issue of 'internet law' at the beginning; and, of course, even if the issues of fundamental rights in the internet were adequately catalogued, with constitutional courts having developed a vast body of case law in these areas, we would need to devote separate studies for the practice of each one. In this chapter I have tried to present cases: (1) where the paradigm remains the same; however, hidden changes reflect new developments regarding the interpretation of existing rights; (2) where a paradigm shift occurs (i.e. a new right emerges as a reaction to new a IT environment); and (3) where issues and conflicts posed by the internet are still framed by constitutional courts as identical to the ones that characterised them in a pre-internet age.

39 Cf. Lawrence Lessig, 'What things regulate speech: CDA 2.0 vs filtering' (1998) Publications of the Berkman Center for Internet & Society http://cyber.law.harvard.edu/works/lessig/what_things.pdf (last accessed 18 August 2015).

40 Case IV/5/2013 (27 May 2014).

8 Constitutional adjudication on internet issues in Poland

*Krystyna Kowalik-Bańczyk**

8.1 Introduction

Internet regulation in Poland is not treated in one single legal text. In the field of civil and commercial law, the majority of laws or amendments to pre-existing laws are implementing the EU legal framework. The biggest significance is attributed to the Law of 18 July 2002 on services provided electronically,[1] which implements Directive 2000/31 (the e-Commerce Directive).[2] On the other hand, the regulation of e-government or e-administration is mainly a local phenomenon and the main legal text remains a statute on informatisation of entities fulfilling public duties.[3] The doctrine underlines that the Polish regulation is dispersed within the national law, that it is partly incoherent and that there would be a strong need to introduce a basic, central statute that could unify the existing legislation.[4]

The aim of this chapter is to explain the scope of constitutional adjudication that occurred in matters linked with the use of the internet in the practice of the

* I am grateful to Graziella Romeo and Oreste Pollicino for their comments on an earlier draft of this chapter. All mistakes remain mine only.

1 Act of 18 July 2002 on the Provision of Services in Electronic Way (OJ 2002 no. 144, pos 1204). Cf. Jacek Gołaczyński and others, *Act on the Provision of Services in Electronic Way: Commentary (Ustawa o Świadczeniu Usług Drogą Elektroniczną. Komentarz)* (Wolters Kluwer 2009); Monika Namysłowska and Dominik Lubasz, *Act on the Provision of Services in Electronic Way and Act on Conditional Access: Commentary (Ustawa o Świadczeniu Usług Drogą Elektroniczną i Ustawa o Dostępie Warunkowym. Komentarz)* (Lexis Nexis 2011).

2 Directive 2000/31/EC of the European Parliament and the Council of 8 June 2000 on certain legal aspects of information services, in particular electronic commerce, in the Internal Market [2000] OJ L178/1; Directive 1999/93/EC of the European Parliament and of the Council of 13 December 1999 on a Community framework for electronic signatures [2000] OJ L13/12; Directive 2002/58/EC of the European Parliament and of the Council of 12 July 2002 concerning the processing of personal data and the protection of privacy in the electronic communications sector [2002] OJ L201/37; Directive 2001/29/EC of the European Parliament and of the Council of 22 May 2001 on the harmonisation of certain aspects of copyright and related rights in the information society [2001] OJ L167/10.

3 Act of 17 February 2005 on the Informatization of Entities Fulfilling Public Duties (OJ 2005 no. 64 pos 565).

4 Przemysław Polański *Internet Law (Prawo Internetu)* (CH Beck 2014) x.

According to Article 42 of the Constitutional Tribunal Act (1997), in both abstract and concrete constitutional review, there are three possible arguments for the non-conformity that the Polish Constitutional Tribunal can verify. First, the tribunal examines the material conformity of normative provisions of the Constitution, ratified international agreements or statutes. Secondly, it can control the fulfilment of procedural requirements binding at the adoption of the provisions in question. Thirdly, the Constitutional Tribunal can verify the powers (competences) of the organ that had issued the provisions being challenged. In all of the cases presented below only the first of those arguments is analysed – the material conformity with the Constitution of 1997 and, in some cases, in parallel, also with the provisions of the ECHR.[16]

8.3 Cases of constitutional adjudication on the internet issues in the jurisprudence of the Constitutional Tribunal

In the practice of the Polish Constitutional Tribunal there are, to the knowledge of this author, only four cases in which this court was directly faced with the questions of constitutionality of regulation on internet or use of electronic services implying the reference to internet. The only constitutional complaint in this field was unfortunately not examined as to the merits. It is to be regretted because it concerned a case resembling the facts of the judgment of the European Court of Human Rights (ECtHR) in *Delfi v Estonia*.[17]

8.3.1 Constitutional Complaint: (an unfulfilled) example of the Polish Delfi case

In Case SK 52/13, the Polish Constitutional Tribunal received a constitutional complaint from a former Polish politician Roman Giertych on the conformity of Article 14 of the law of 18 July 2002 on the provision of services by electronic means[18] with Articles 2 and 47 in connection with Article 31.3 of the Constitution and, in parallel, with Articles 8(1) and 8(2) of the European Convention on Human Rights. Article 14 is an implementation of provisions of Directive 2000/31, excluding the liability of intermediaries for contents placed on their servers.

The complainant instituted a constitutional complaint after having led a civil law proceeding for protection of his personal rights against an internet version of

decision of 8 November 2005 *Pachla v Poland* Application no. 8812/02; ECtHR decision of 7 September 2010; *Urban v Poland* Application no. 23614/08.

16 See generally Bogumił Szmulik, *Constitutional Complaint: Polish Model in Comparative Analysis (Skarga Konstytucyjna: Polski Model na Tle Porównawczym)* (Wydawnictwo Sejmowe 2006); Leszek Bosek and Mikołaj Wild, *Control of Constitutionality (Konstrola Konstytucyjności Prawa)* (CH Beck 2014).

17 ECtHR judgment of 10 October 2013 *Delfi v Estonia* Application no. 64569/09.

18 Act of 18 July 2002 on the Provision of Services in Electronic Way (n 1). This act constitutes an implementation of Directive 2000/31.

a newspaper called 'Fakt' (edited by Ringier Axer Springer Polska). The article about the complainant was published both on paper and in electronic form. In the electronic version of the article, there were several very offensive comments placed under the article. The complainant asked the newspaper to remove offensive comments concerning the complainant and also to apologise and to pay damages. The newspaper removed the comments upon notification.

The civil courts of two instances dismissed the claims for breach of personal goods and for damages and stated that the comments to the internet newspaper article are not covered by press law and thus the newspaper was exempted from any liability. The complaint was claiming that the accepted interpretation of Article 14 of the Law on the provision of services by electronic means was unconstitutional because it in fact allowed for infringements of a person's right to good name and reputation. Unfortunately the Polish Constitutional Tribunal did not consider this very interesting question because it turned out that the constitutional complaint was inadmissible as the questioned judicial decision was not final.

In the meantime, the Supreme Court[19] had accepted the cassation claim of the applicant and the decision of the Appellate Court was quashed and returned to the second instance. Because of this, in an order of 19 February 2014 the Constitutional Tribunal discontinued the legal proceedings.[20] It is to be expected that if the new judicial decision will not be favourable to the complainant, he will deposit the constitutional complaint again. The interesting aspect of this constitutional complaint consisted in a clear analogy of the facts to the *Delfi* case but, however, with a different practice of treating the comments placed under the articles than the ECtHR suggested in its first judgment.

The constitutional complaint was not examined because the Polish Supreme Court decided to quash the judgment of the Court of Second Instance, reflecting the pre-existing practice of Polish courts that relied on the interpretation of Directive 2000/31's exemptions from liability for internet service providers. It is certain that the Supreme Court must have been inspired by the *Delfi* case, as it directly cited this judgment.[21] Probably the Constitutional Tribunal would also have been inspired, considering the fact that the complainant referred to Article 8 of the ECHR. Thus, indirectly, the ECtHR is influencing the interpretation of national laws implementing the e-Commerce Directive and changing pre-existing stable legal practice.[22]

8.3.2 Abstract control of conformity

There are very few examples of constitutional adjudication on internet issues by way of abstract control of conformity. Those that exist indicate that the

19 Judgment of the Supreme Court of 10 January 2014, I CSK 128/13.

20 Order of 19 February 2014, SK 52/13.

21 Reasons of Judgment of the Supreme Court of 10 January 2014, I CSK 128/13 at 20–21.

22 Cf. the previous interpretation of questions of exclusion of liability: judgment of Supreme Court of 8 July 2011, IV CSK 665/10; judgment of Appellate Court of Lublin of 18 January 2011, 1ACa 544/10, Lex No. 736495.

Constitutional Tribunal is first of all applying the principle of technical neutrality to the constitutional protection (the constitutional protection should not be different depending of the method of communication used) and, secondly, trying to guarantee an equivalent level of protection for individuals using electronic means.

8.3.2.1 Question from Chief Administrative Court on technological neutrality

In a case constituting an answer to the question posed by the Chief Administrative Court,[23] the Polish Constitutional Tribunal was complying with Article 2[24] in connection with Article 32(1)[25] and Article 69[26] of the Constitution of the provision of law regulating professional and social rehabilitation and employment of persons with disabilities.[27] That provision limited the possibility of entities employing such persons to deposit information on the employment and the level of disabilities of such employees and motions on monthly financing from the National Fund to the electronic applications using the internet, even in cases where employers overcame serious difficulties to use those methods of communication (e.g. breakdown of computer system).

The Constitutional Tribunal found that the limitation of methods of communication in electronic form of communication only, with no viable other option in cases of system failure, was unconstitutional. It is an interesting reaction to the factual development of the way the administration communicates with some of its clients – the Polish Constitutional Tribunal excluded the possibility that the law allows only one way of communication, namely electronic communication. Other forms of communication must also be available and acceptable.

8.3.2.2 Professional secret of legal advisers in cases concerning money laundering

In a different context to that analysed above, the Polish Constitutional Tribunal has incidentally referred to the question of distinction of means of communication as a possible reason for a different level of constitutional protection. This was so in Case K 41/05,[28] where the National Council of Legal Advisers (*Radcy prawni*) was questioning the constitutionality of the law on prevention of the use of financial systems for the purposes of money laundering.[29] The amendment of

23 Order of 3 March2006, II GSK 395/05.

24 'The Republic of Poland shall be a democratic state ruled by law and implementing the principles of social justice.'

25 'All persons shall be equal before the law. All persons shall have the right to equal treatment by public authorities.'

26 'Public authorities shall provide, in accordance with statute, aid to disabled persons to ensure their subsistence, adaptation to work and social communication.'

27 Act of 27 August 1997 on the work and social rehabilitation and on employment of persons with disabilities (OJ 1998 no. 123 pos 776 with amendments).

28 Judgment of 2 July 2007, 72/7/A/2007.

29 Act of 16 November 2000 on the prevention to introduce into financial system of money from illegal or unreported sources and on the prevention of terrorist financing (OJ 2003 no. 153 pos 1505 with amendments)

this law was an implementation of Directive 2001/97,[30] together with Directive 91/308.[31]

The Polish Constitutional Tribunal did not find any infringement of the Constitution; it referred, however, *obiter dicta* to the question of protection of confidentiality of lawyer–client exchanges, depending on the means of communication used. It clearly stated that the obligations of legal advisers to keep professional secrecy is not dependent on the means of communication – whether the communication takes place in a direct or indirect way (via phone or internet). Such a division would be artificial and irrational, and it could lead to the introduction of different standards of protection of lawyer–client confidentiality.[32]

The only factual reason for such a distinction is that methods of indirect communication are more easily (or, indeed, at all) accessible or available for third parties and thus, even more emphatically, they require strong constitutional protection. This case occurred when the Belgian Constitutional Court referred its preliminary question on the validity of some provisions of Directive 2001/97 (Case C–305/05 *Ordre des barreaux francophones et germanophone and others*[33]), although the CJEU did not find that the directive would be in breach of the right to a fair trial or rights of the defence. This position of the CJEU was further reflected in the ECtHR case of *Michaud v France*.[34] The judgment of the Polish Constitutional Tribunal was in line with this assessment.

8.3.2.3 Data Retention Domino – the Polish version of Digital Rights Ireland

On 30 July 2014 the Polish Constitutional Tribunal sitting as a full bench[35] issued a ruling referring in the broadest manner to the questions linked with internet and constitutional protection. It was adjudicating on seven joint complaints from the Commissioner for Civil Rights Protection (Ombudsman) and Public Prosecutor General of the Republic of Poland as to the conformity with the Constitution[36] and to Article 8 of the ECHR of provisions of several normative acts allow-

30 Directive 2001/97/EC of the European Parliament and of the Council of 4 December 2001 amending Council Directive 91/308/EEC on prevention of the use of the financial system for the purpose of money laundering [2001] OJ L344/76.

31 Council Directive 91/308/EEC of 10 June 1991 on prevention of the use of the financial system for the purpose of money laundering [1991] OJ L166/77, since then repealed by Directive 2005/60/EC of 26 October 2005 of the European Parliament and of the Council on the prevention of the use of the financial system for the purpose of money laundering and terrorist financing [2005] OJ L309/15.

32 Para 5.1.

33 Case C–305/05 *Ordre des barreaux francophones et germanophone v Conseil des ministres* [2007] ECR I–5305, ECLI:EU:C:2007:383.

34 *Michaud v France*, Application No. 12323/11 (ECtHR, 6 December 2012).

35 According to art 25.1 letter e) of the Constitutional Tribunal Act of 1 August 1997 (Dz.U. Nr 102 poz. 643) http://trybunal.gov.pl/en/about-the-tribunal/legal-basis/the-constitutional-tribunal-act/ (last accessed 23 August 2015).

36 The Constitution of the Republic of Poland adopted by the National Assembly on 2 April 1997 http://trybunal.gov.pl/en/about-the-tribunal/legal-basis/the-constitution-of-the-republic-of-poland/ (last accessed 23 August 2015).

ing some public bodies to undertake operational control of data retained by telecom undertakings.[37] The seven motions were deposited during 2011 and 2012 and examined jointly. In 2014 the Constitutional Tribunal stayed the proceedings because it was awaiting the CJEU's judgment in the joined cases of *Digital Rights Ireland* and *Seitlinger*;[38] however, in the later judgment of the Constitutional Tribunal it did not analyse the implications of that judgment. It has thus joined a long and developed jurisprudential activity on different issues linked with the data retention in Europe.[39]

The possibility of collecting and analysing data concerned various forms of information gathering on individuals. It covered telecommunication data, content data, billings and data allowing for localisation of an individual. The judgment in Case S 23/11 did not question the very possibility of secret retention of such data and the obligations falling on the telecommunication enterprises to retain them. In this sense it was different from the CJEU *Digital Rights* case. The difference stemmed from the formulation of complaints. What was questioned was the insufficient level of procedural guarantees available to data subjects.[40]

However, the Constitutional Tribunal took this opportunity to comment broadly on the particularities on new technologies and their relationship with privacy protection, protection of correspondence and protection of one's informative autonomy. It commented on the nature of the internet and new technical means of acquisition of data, stating that these new forms of human activity are fully covered by constitutional protection and therefore there should be no distinction depending on the form of activity undertaken. It thus proclaimed a very strong principle of technical neutrality for constitutional protection of individual rights and freedoms.

The provisions of various provisions of Polish normative acts have been analysed as possibly infringing the following provisions of the Constitution, that is Article 2 of the Constitution (the principle of legal certainty), Article 47 (the protection of private life and family life) Article 49 (freedom and privacy of communication). Both Articles 47 and 49 were analysed in connection with Article 43(3) (the principle of proportionality and legality) or Article 8 of the ECHR

37 Judgment of Polish Constitutional Tribunal of 30 July 2014 in Case K 23/11. The reasons of the judgment were published on 6 October 2014. The oral reasons of the judgment are available at http://www.obserwatorkonstytucyjny.pl/video/okreslenie-katalogu-zbieranych-informacji-o-jednostce-za-pomoca-srodkow-technicznych-w-dzialaniach-operacyjnych-zasady-niszczenia-pozyskanych-danych/ (last accessed 23 August 2015) .

38 Joined Cases C–293/12 and C–594/12 *Digital Rights Ireland Ltd and Seitlinger and Others*, judgment of 8 April 2014.

39 Supreme Administrative Court of Bulgaria (11 December 2008, No. 13627); Romanian Constitutional Tribunal (8 October 2009, No. 1258); Bundesverfassungsgericht (2 March 2010, 1 BvR 256/08); Czech Constitutional Court (22 March 2011, Pl. ÚS 24/10); Slovenian Constitutional Court (3 July 2014); Austrian Constitutional Court (27 July 2014, G 47/2012, G 59/2012, G 62/2012, G 70/2012, G 71/2012).

40 In this sense, it criticised the quality of the regulation, in a way similar to the reasoning of Advocate General Villalón in his opinion of 12 December 2013 in Joined Cases C–293/12 and C–594/12 *Digital Rights Ireland Ltd and Seitlinger and Others* (n 37) paras 102, 125–29.

(the protection of privacy). The tribunal has stated that several provisions of law on operational secret control against individuals do not comply with the requirements of the Constitution. However, it has postponed their invalidation by 18 months, in order not to create a legal gap that, in the words of the tribunal, might be detrimental to the security of the Republic of Poland.[41]

Thus, the tribunal has acted in a much more prudent (or less radical) way than the CJEU did in its *Digital Rights Ireland* judgment, where the Data Retention Directive[42] had been invalidated in its totality. It has granted the Polish legislator several indications and directives as to the future shape of the regulation of data retention and secret surveillance of both Polish citizens and foreigners in the territory of Poland.

The protection of privacy and communication privacy covers the whole process of gaining, gathering, processing and retention of information, including any analysis or comparison of data. Therefore, any transfer of information on the content of communication taking place within telecommunication networks in the form of operational control stemming from an obligation of telecom enterprises is an interference with constitutional individual rights that should always be reasoned. Such operations include an obligation of retention of data on traffic of data and on localisation, access to such data, their verification or transfer to other organs.

According to the Constitutional Tribunal, in a democratic state an individual (indeed, any individual) should be able to participate in the public sphere in an anonymous way. In cases where individuals take advantage of their freedom, they should not be required to relinquish their anonymity, both towards the state or towards private entities. The protection of privacy in a democratic state thus gives a guarantee of anonymity if an individual chooses not to reveal his or her identity.

8.4 The development of technology and constitutional protection in the eyes of the Polish Constitutional Tribunal

In the case on data retention, the Polish Constitutional Tribunal underlined that this case arose as a result of the rapid development of new technologies involved in creating, collecting and retaining different data and metadata. This technological development extends the spheres of human activity and opens new and to date unknown possibilities of using constitutionally guaranteed freedoms and rights. The internet plays a particular role here – as it has become no longer merely a communication tool to be used for the transfer of information alone. Instead, it has become a multi-dimensional tool for the transfer of different data and one that allows an individual to function in multi-dimensional ways.

41 Similarly to the suggestion of AG Villalón in his opinion of 12 December 2013 in Joined Cases C-293/12 and C-594/12 *Digital Rights Ireland* (n 37) paras 154–58.

42 Directive 2006/24/EC of the European Parliament and of the Council of 15 March 2006 on the retention of data generated or processed in connection with the provision of publicly available electronic communications services or of public communications networks and amending Directive 2002/58/EC [2006] OJ L105/54.

In this context, the tribunal confirmed that the protection of constitutional rights and freedoms within the context of use of the internet and other electronic means of communication is by no means different from the protection of normal traditional communication. The data transferred on the internet cannot be perceived as functioning next to or on the margins of constitutionally protected forms of individual activity. There are no reasons for distinguishing the data transfer or communication via the internet from the constitutional rights and freedoms. The internet is a complex phenomenon and thus the activities of individuals by its use are to be protected in different ways, depending on the actual activity that is constitutionally protected.

Sending mail by electronic means is covered by the same privacy correspondence protection as the traditional sending of mail by post. Communication with one's lawyer via internet or other electronic means is covered by the rights of defence. The protection of professional secrets is the same, regardless of the means of communication used. Expressing one's opinion and spreading information using the internet and other electronic means is the same as for tradition media, as set out in Article 54 of the Polish Constitution. Freedom of the press is also fully protected when it is functioning in electronic form, according to Articles 14 and 54 of the Constitution. The constitutionally protected economic freedom also covers all forms of economic activity, either on the internet or in other methods of communication.

Thus, according to the Polish Constitutional Tribunal, the principle of technical neutrality of constitutional protection should be fully applied. It is underlined by the statement made by the Constitutional Tribunal that any legislative limitation of the technical means of surveillance might turn out to be more detrimental than beneficial for the protection of interests involved. The issue that is to be verified is mainly the procedural framework for using such means, rather than the technical means themselves.

8.4.1 Fight with crime as an exception to the protection of privacy

Apart from a broad protection of privacy and privacy communication, the state must have the possibility of preventing and fighting serious crime. The specificity of new technologies and the new dangers that they bring led the Polish Constitutional Tribunal to state that the public authorities such as the police or other state protection authorities should be able to prevent and discover crime or infringers or investigate dangers against legally protected goods. A democratic state cannot ignore dangers stemming from the use of new technologies; otherwise, the state would infringe its obligations to protect Poland's independence, the integrity of Polish territory and citizens' security (Article 5 of the Polish Constitution[43]).

The principle of efficient functioning of state authorities might also be

43 'The Republic of Poland shall safeguard the independence and integrity of its territory and ensure the freedoms and rights of persons and citizens, the security of the citizens, safeguard the national

breached (the principle stems from the preamble to the Constitution of 1997). It might also breach the binding international agreements concluded by the Republic of Poland. Obtaining information on the content, time and form of communications of individuals, together with the monitoring of their activities, is unavoidably in conflict with the right to privacy, privacy of correspondence, information autonomy and protection of domicile. The very provisions allowing some public authorities to invigilate breaches the constitutional status of a citizen (a status that, as mentioned above, is based on human dignity). The consciousness of invigilation might detract individuals from free use of the constitutionally guaranteed freedoms and rights.

Consequently, there is a fear of abuse of powers by the authorities leading these types of investigations. According to the Constitutional Tribunal, such fears are particularly strong in Polish society, where the authorities of previous communist regimes have for decades secretly investigated citizens, which is not in accordance with the tenets of the tribunal, nor serves the best interests of the state or its citizens.

If some state authorities are permitted to conduct secret inquiries, this will always be linked with the creation of data collections. Some data are accessed by such authorities when they are collected by private or public entities. The tribunal finds that the preventive retention of telecommunication data is particularly noxious. The knowledge of existence of such data collections is by itself proof of fundamental rights infringement. Thus, allowing for operational control of data requires that the legislator sets requirements that should protect an individual from such excesses of authority and undue interference with the rights of individuals to their privacy. It is not admissible to register the totality of one's private life.

The Constitutional Tribunal refers in this respect to the ECtHR's jurisprudence on secret surveillance and other forms of the gathering of data. In light of Article 8 of the ECHR, there is a need that any infringement of a person's privacy zone should have a clear legal basis. The legal basis should be of high quality and fully accessible to those concerned. Individuals should be able to preview under what conditions they can be surveyed, which of course does not require that they should know when exactly they would be surveyed. The law should clearly state under which circumstances and under what conditions an individual might be surveyed by state authorities in such a way. This has to be motivated by one of the reasons listed in Article 8(2) of the ECHR.

The Polish Constitutional Tribunal also analysed the CJEU case of *Digital Rights Ireland Ltd*,[44] as well as the 'European' jurisprudence of some national constitutional tribunals on the Data Retention Directive, including Germany, Austria, Bulgaria, Romania, the Czech Republic and Slovenia. All those tribunals have taken a very similar position, questioning either the directive itself or its

heritage and shall ensure the protection of the natural environment pursuant to the principles of sustainable development.'

44 Note 37.

implementation. The interference with one's privacy by the retention of personal data constitutes one of the deepest and most serious ways of infringement of privacy, when it is left unnoticed and unknown to the person concerned and is not an object of social control. Therefore, it is strictly necessary to create strong procedural guarantees, including ex ante approval of a body controlling the access to such data.

8.4.2 Indications for the legislator on how to regulate the issues of secret surveillance in new media

In its judgment on data retention, the Constitutional Tribunal retains its previous jurisprudential position as to the requirements towards legal regulations on secret interference in constitutional freedoms and rights through the means of operational control. The tribunal underlined that the Polish legislator has not fulfilled those requirements, despite a clear order of this tribunal (S 4/10[45]). For four years this signalling order has not been implemented. The new, previously unknown forms of secret acquisition of data through means of new technologies, extension of the scope of state organs that have powers to use operational control and to have access to data, together with an appearance of new practices of application of existing rules – all this has led the tribunal to recall the order S 4/10 and to give the legislator broader directions and indications as to the further development in this field. Thus, the Constitutional Tribunal found it necessary to give to the legislator clear indications:

1. The rules allowing public authorities for secret retention of data should take into account the fact that collecting, gathering and processing of information concern individuals and their privacy, therefore it must be led under an express and precise provision of law.
2. The state organs that are allowed to undertake such operational control have to be clearly named and listed.
3. The operations that such organs are allowed to undertake have to be clearly listed.
4. The law has to list the premises lying at the ground of undertaking operational control – they may refer to prevention, statement or fight with serious crimes, but those crimes have to be clearly listed.
5. The law has to indicate the categories of subjects against which such operations can be undertaken.
6. It is desirable that the law states the means of secret collection of information as well as the kinds of information that can be retained.
7. Such operational means of control should always be only a subsidiary source of obtaining information, when obtaining the information or proofs by

45 Order of 15 November 2010 in Case S 4/10, to the effect that a constitutional problem was also signalled in a TK judgment of 5 October 2010 in case P 79/08, ZU 2010/8A/88.

other means is not possible. However, sometimes it might turn out that such means are the only way of obtaining information.

8. The law should indicate the maximal period of time for operational control towards individuals, which cannot exceed the framework necessary in a democratic state of law.
9. It is necessary to clearly regulate in law the procedure of managing such operational means, including an obligation to receive a special approval from an organ that is independent of executive powers.
10. There is an obligation to create clear rules on how to proceed with materials (data) gathered during operational control, and in particular the rules on how to use such materials in criminal proceedings should be regulated.
11. The rules on destruction of data that turn out to be useless or not allowed should be clearly stated.
12. The security against access to the collected data by not allowed subjects or bodies should be guaranteed.
13. The procedure of informing the subject concerned on the secret surveillance and allowing this subject a *post facto* judicial control should be guaranteed.
14. It is allowed to differentiate the scope of protection upon the criteria if the subject controlled is a Polish citizen or a foreigner.

The Constitutional Tribunal has also clearly indicated the procedural standard that should be applied by the state organs if they intend to undertake secret surveillance. A margin of arbitrary decision for police and security forces should be as limited as possible. A sufficient level of procedural protection is guaranteed only if: (1) the chief of the organ concerned makes a motion for approval to use technical means of surveillance; (2) the approval is granted either by the prosecutor or by the district court; (3) in cases of approval granted by the prosecutor there is a possibility to appeal it to the court; (4) the motion should contain all the important information on the case and it should be reasoned. The requirements that the motion should fulfil should be stated by law (in a normative act); and (5) the approval should define the ways in which the operational control can be undertaken (for example, if the conversations can be registered, if filming of persons concerned is allowed, and so on). Only in this way can the organs undertaking the surveillance be said to be acting within limits set by law.

8.4.3 Professional secret and secret surveillance in new media

The Polish legislator has not, in the eyes of the Constitutional Tribunal, sufficiently regulated the problem of the possibility of controlling persons who, owing to their professions, are obliged to keep professional secrets (mainly lawyers). The tribunal has stated that the lack of procedure for the immediately destruction (by a group commission and with the confirmation of a protocol) of information covered by proof prohibitions, constitutes a breach of Poland's Constitution. People performing jobs that imply some element of public trust (such as advocates or journalists) should be covered by higher constitutional standards than 'lay persons'.

The example of legal aid is illustrative in this respect. Contacts between a lawyer and his or her client are based not only on some legal expertise of the part of the lawyer but also on the relationship of trust and a guarantee of discretion on the part of the lawyer. The information exchanged in such a relationship should be particularly protected, so that not only are the parties to it protected but so also is their communication and particularly its content. The legislator is obliged to guarantee a higher protection of such information, otherwise it would clash with both public and individual sense of trust towards the state. Rights of defence or media freedom cannot be fully exercised without real guarantees of such protection of information. Any instances of a clash between the protection of individual rights or freedoms (including privacy, rights of defence, freedom of belief, freedom of press etc) and conflicts with criminal infringements have to be considered on a case-by-case basis. If there is any danger for a broader group of the population, such protection of individual freedoms or rights must be set aside, but only in respect of procedural requirements and with the exclusion of any arbitrary behaviours of executive powers.

Such model procedural guarantees are set out in the Polish Code of Criminal Procedure (Article 180 § 2);[46] however, this type of solution should also be copied in all cases of secret surveillance of citizens. The standard of protection applied in criminal proceedings should always be used in cases of operational control of citizens. In order to achieve this, two elements are necessary. First, the preventive court must retain control of the selection of material used in the secret surveillance. Secondly, the mechanism of effective, immediate destruction (in front of a group commission with a confirmation on protocol) of any information obtained through such control, if this information is redundant or inadmissible because of the professional privilege protection.

8.4.4 Destruction of redundant or unnecessary information

The Constitutional Tribunal has stated that the lack of regulation on the basis of how and what circumstances the retained data should be destroyed is breaching the Constitution. But for the provisions of the law on fiscal control, other provisions analysed by the tribunal did not contain any information on the fate of information gathered under those provisions. The provisions should contain a procedural mechanism explaining how the data should be destroyed. This mechanism should be based on the preliminary and immediate assessment of data gathered as to their use for the proceedings in which they were gathered. All data that seem redundant should be destroyed immediately, as should all data protected from disclosure. This should prevent any undue use of information once collected, kept 'just in case' for any future claims. The breach of privacy would otherwise occur not only at the moment of collection of data on an individual,

46 Those provisions have been judged as fully constitutional in Case SK 64/03.

but also at each moment where such data are analysed or used in any further proceedings.

The legislator has clearly failed in its regulation of permitted operational control by not regulating the treatment of data after their retention. Such data, under the existing law, cannot be verified or destroyed if they are redundant for the aims of proceedings in which they were gathered. The tribunal admits that the data of foreigners, especially those supposed to be involved in crimes endangering the security of state (such as terrorism or organised crimes), can be retained by the Polish state under Article 51(2)[47] and Article 37(2)[48] of the Constitution. However, such regulation is clearly absent in the Polish legal system. Thus, the Polish legislator is obliged to amend this lacuna.

8.5 Conclusions

To conclude, in his book on various legal aspects of the internet Ziccardi states that: 'the serious problem of our times is not to create human rights, but to protect them'.[49] One cannot agree more with what the Polish Constitutional Tribunal has stated in its judgment on data retention, but the real problem is the implementation of the directions given in this judgment and their real application to the use of new technologies by the police and security forces.

In the judgments discussed above, there are two common features. First, it is clear that the principle of constitutional neutrality is understood, in a sense that all individual rights and freedoms should be protected regardless of the technical means used in order to infringe them. Secondly, the Polish Constitutional Tribunal is clearly seeking additional arguments 'outside' of the narrowly defined Polish Constitution. The tribunal refers to the CJEU, the ECtHR and other constitutional courts of the EU Member States in order to strengthen or explain its position. This phenomenon is of course not limited to the issues of internet regulation but it seems that such a judicial inspiration is particularly proper and even necessary in regard to this universal medium of communication. Only such development of European constitutional adjudication upon internet issues can lead to a coherent protection of individuals, despite the fact that the constitutional adjudication is by definition a national matter, in addition to one that is linked with a particular territory.

It would be optimistic to obtain this type of coherence. However, the jurisprudence presented, particularly the last of the cases on data retention, clearly shows that constitutional protection might in fact be weakened in the internet environment. Despite the strong words of the tribunal used in this data–retention case,

47 Public authorities shall not acquire, collect nor make accessible information on citizens other than that which is necessary in a democratic state ruled by law.

48 Article 37(1): Anyone, being under the authority of the Polish State, shall enjoy the freedoms and rights ensured by the Constitution. (2) Exemptions from this principle with respect to foreigners shall be specified by statute.

49 Giovanni Ziccardi, *Resistance, Liberation Technology and Human Rights in the Digital Age* (Springer 2013) 125.

the implicit message on the question of what prevails – the potential conflict with crime or the protection of privacy – is that individual freedoms have to take a step back before the collective interest: that of state security and crime prevention. One cannot but notice that, in reaching this decision, the Polish Constitutional Tribunal has taken a different path from that of the Court of Justice of the European Union in *Digital Rights Ireland*, where the protection of privacy prevailed over other protected values (such as the fight against crime[50]). This is a surprising turn, as in other judgments the Polish Constitutional Tribunal seems to have been strongly inspired by the jurisprudence of European courts, both the European Court of Human Rights and the Court of Justice of the EU.

The overall assessment of the Polish Constitutional Tribunal's adjudication on internet issues is that it has only recently directed itself towards the question of specificity of the internet as a sphere where constitutional rights might be broken. Despite the fact that, in both private law and public law, Polish legislation broadly regulates use of the internet, the jurisprudence does not reflect the scale of those provisions. Only a few cases before the Polish Constitutional Tribunal have concerned the constitutional problems linked with the internet itself and it was only in July 2014 when this court discussed the role of the Polish Constitution in cyberspace, stating – optimistically – that the same constitutional protection should be granted to both online and offline matters. It thus proclaimed the principle of constitutional neutrality towards the technique used as far as constitutional protection is concerned.

50 Agnieszka Grzelak, 'The frontier between the effective fight with crime and the right to privacy and personal data protection: commentary to the ECJ's judgment of 8 April 2014 in Joined Cases C–293/12 and C–594/12 *Digital Rights Ireland*' *(Granica między skuteczną walką z przestępczością a prawem do prywatności i ochrony danych osobowych – glosa do wyroku TS z 8.04.2014 r. w sprawach połączonych: C-293/12 i C-594/12* Digital Rights Ireland*)* (2014) 7 *Europejski Przegląd Sądowy* 45, 48.

9 The protection of expression in the UK

Old principles in a digital world

Jacob Rowbottom

9.1 Introduction

At the conference at which this chapter was first presented, the UK Constitution was categorised as a system with a 'weak form' of judicial review.[1] The categorisation as 'weak' was based on the type of remedy available to the UK courts in the event of a breach of a fundamental right. British judges cannot strike down legislation. However, under the Human Rights Act (HRA) 1998 the courts have significant powers to interpret legislation in a way that gives effect to fundamental rights.[2] When that is not possible, the courts can make a declaration that a piece of legislation is incompatible with a Convention right.[3]

In several relatively recent decisions, the courts have also emphasised that, aside from the HRA, fundamental rights are protected in the common law. In the UK Supreme Court's decision in *Kennedy*, Lord Mance noted that there is often no difference between the protection of freedom of expression under the common law and Article 10, and in some cases the common law may provide more expansive protection.[4] As a result, Lord Mance stated that the domestic common law should be 'the natural starting point' in disputes concerning rights before considering the Convention.[5] Whilst the scheme of rights protection is designed to work alongside the principle of legislative supremacy (providing Parliament with the ultimate power to restrict rights), the UK courts have numerous tools with which to protect fundamental rights.

Whether the system is deemed to be strong or weak may have more to do with the courts' use of these tools. The extent of rights protection will often depend

1 In this chapter I refer to the UK Constitution, as all the countries within the Union are subject to the European Convention on Human Rights (ECHR) and the Human Rights Act 1998. However, some discussion of the substantive controls regulating expression will refer to the law of England and Wales.

2 Human Rights Act 1998, s 3. See *Ghaidan v Godin-Mendoza* [2004] UKHL 30, [2004] 2 AC 557, in which Lord Nicholls at [32] noted that s 3 is 'apt to require a court to read in words which change the meaning of the enacted legislation, so as to make it Convention-compliant'.

3 Human Rights Act 1998, s 4.

4 *Kennedy v Charity Commission* [2014] UKSC 20, [2014] 2 WLR 808 at [46].

5 ibid.

on the interpretation of the content of the rights and the understanding of the court's role within the separation of powers. The discussion of the latter point has been dubbed the 'deference debate', which I do not propose to enter for the purposes of this chapter.[6]

On the content of the rights, the courts' interpretation is largely guided by the Article 10 jurisprudence developed in Strasbourg,[7] and in some cases the domestic court has departed from the Strasbourg jurisprudence both to give greater or more limited protection.[8] However, for the most part the UK courts and the European Court of Human Rights (ECtHR) share the same approach to freedom of expression, and both will be discussed together in this chapter.

The key features of the Article 10 jurisprudence were developed in the final decades of the twentieth century and continue to apply in the digital era. The main changes in the domestic protection for digital expression rights have not been driven by Article 10 or constitutional law, but have largely come about through piecemeal changes to the common law, statute and policy. Piecemeal change brings some advantages, allowing for flexibility and experimentation in the protection of expression alongside other rights and interests. However, this chapter will consider whether any changes to the general principles in the Article 10 jurisprudence are required in the light of the new communications environment.

9.2 Old principles in a digital world

In a chapter on internet expression and the ECtHR, Judge Nina Vajic and Panayotis Voyatzis noted that the Strasbourg Court 'seems reluctant to re-assess the basic principles concerning Article 10 that have been established in the relevant case law'.[9] When looking at the internet, the Court has tended to apply Article 10 with reference to the traditional principles. Under the traditional principles, heightened protection is given to political and public interest expression,[10] weight is given to the media in its role as a public watchdog[11] and certain duties and responsibilities are to be fulfilled when exercising expression rights.[12] There

6 Amongst the numerous contributions to this debate see Trevor Allan, 'Judicial deference and judicial review: legal doctrine and legal theory' (2011) 127 *Law Quarterly Review* 96; Aileen Kavanagh, 'Defending deference in public law and constitutional theory' (2010) 126 *Law Quarterly Review* 222; Jeff King, 'Institutional approaches to judicial restraint' (2008) 28(3) *Oxford Journal of Legal Studies* 409.

7 Human Rights Act 1998, s 2.

8 See for example *Rabone v Pennine Care NHS Foundation Trust* [2012] UKSC 2, [2012] 2 AC 72 and *R v Horncastle* [2009] UKSC 14, [2010] 2 AC 373.

9 Nina Vajic and Panayotis Voyatzis, 'The internet and freedom of expression: a "brave new world" and the ECtHR's evolving case-law' in Josep Casadevall (ed.), *Freedom of Expression: Essays in Honour of Nicolas Bratza, President of the European Court of Human Rights* (Wolf Legal Publishers 2012).

10 *Lingens v Austria* (1986) 8 EHRR 407, *Campbell v MGN* [2004] UKHL 22, [2004] 2 AC 406.

11 *The Observer v United Kingdom* (1991) 14 EHRR 153; *McCartan Turkington Breen (a firm) v Times Newspapers Ltd* [2001] 2 AC 277.

12 *Bladet Tromsø v Norway* (1999) 6 BHRC 599; *R v Shayler* [2002] UKHL 11, [2003] 1 AC 247.

is much to commend these principles and I do not call for a radical change within the Article 10 jurisprudence.

However, many of the basic principles of Article 10 were formulated when the mass media or organised protests provided the paradigm for free speech. That paradigm no longer reflects the range of speech cases that can come before courts. Some reassessment and refinement may be necessary in relation to some aspects of the digital media. In particular, there may be occasions where non-political speech, or speech that does not relate to matters of general interest, is deserving of greater protection. There are also occasions where the duties and responsibilities that condition Article 10 need to be reassessed in the light of the digital environment.

The outcome of such a reassessment is not obvious. At various times, different judges in the Strasbourg Court have given out different signals. In a dissent in *Mouvement raëlien suisse v Switzerland (2012)*, Judge Pinto de Albuquerque made some far-reaching comments calling for greater freedom on the internet.[13] Describing the internet as the 'global marketplace of ideas', he expressed support for a principle of internet neutrality under Article 10, argued that blocking content should be permitted only in very limited circumstances[14] and stated that domestic authorities have a narrow margin of appreciation with regard to information disseminated through the internet.[15]

The last of these points makes surprising claims, and does not seem consistent with the variable protection for different types of speech under the current Article 10 jurisprudence. Similar arguments about the benefits of internet expression were advanced in *Yildirim v Turkey*, in which the Court stated that the internet has now become one of 'the principal means by which individuals exercise their right to freedom of expression and information, providing as it does essential tools for participation in activities and discussions concerning political issues and issues of general interest'.[16] In that case, the Court recognised that Article 10 includes a right of internet access. Such observations suggest a more robust protection of expression rights in relation to digital communications.

However, in other cases the Strasbourg Court has emphasised the negative effects of the digital media. In *Editorial Board of Pravoye Delo and Shtekel v Ukraine*, the Court stated that the threat to private life on the internet 'is certainly higher than that posed by the press'.[17] Along these lines, Vajic and Voyatzis note that the Strasbourg Court has 'acknowledged the particular character of the internet' in several cases, such as the 'durability of information', the ability of users to access information at a time of their own choosing and the potential

13 *Mouvement raëlien suisse v Switzerland* (2012) 32 BHRC 646.

14 See also his concurring judgment in *Yildirim v Turkey* (Application no. 3111/10, 2012), arguing that the blocking of illegal content should be permitted only where the restriction is narrowly tailored.

15 *Mouvement raëlien suisse v Switzerland* (n 13).

16 *Yildirim v Turkey* (Application no. 3111/10, 2012) at [54].

17 *Editorial Board of Pravoye Delo and Shtekel v Ukraine* (2011) 58 EHRR 28.

to disseminate 'harmful' expression.[18] As a result, Vajic and Voyatzis suggest the greater power and impact afforded to speakers through the internet may warrant greater responsibilities in some cases.[19] For example, they argue that greater levels of care can be demanded in the case of internet archives, given the lack of urgency. From this perspective, the reach and impact of the new media suggests a need for more conditions upon or qualifications to expression rights.

Both of these perspectives have merit. The point in this chapter is not to choose between either, but to argue that the application of Article 10 needs to be sensitive to the context in which the expression takes place. This does not mean the internet is a 'wild west', but at the same time any restrictions need to be proportionate and provide space for casual and spontaneous conversations.

9.3 Abuse and vapid tittle-tattle

The tension between the potential benefits and harms relating to new communicative opportunities has been played out in the UK law.[20] In particular, much debate has focused on the proper response to online trolling. The digital media has given rise to new ways for people to send abuse, harass people, engage in hate speech, and to do so in ways that are deeply distressing to the targeted person.[21] A number of existing laws, both criminal and civil, can be used to curb such communications. Private law actions, including defamation and misuse of private information, are regularly invoked against speech on the internet and social media.

Private individuals can also apply for an injunction to restrain conduct that constitutes harassment. Criminal laws that were initially designed to preserve public order,[22] and to curb poison pen letters[23] and nuisance phone calls[24] have been applied to digital communications. Similarly, the Obscene Publications Act 1959 has been applied to a conversation between two individuals (both consenting participants) in an internet relay chat service.[25] New laws have also been enacted to respond to new problems involving digital expression, most notably in relation to 'revenge porn'[26] and to control the research activities of jurors.[27]

When faced with problems of abuse, harassment and other extreme content, it is a natural response for authorities to create new laws or to enforce old

18 Vajic and Voyatzis (n 9).

19 ibid.

20 This section draws on the argument made in J. Rowbottom, 'To rant, vent and converse' (2012) 71 *Cambridge Law Journal* 355.

21 For discussion of various examples see Danielle Keats Citron, *Hate Speech in Cyberspace* (Harvard University Press 2014).

22 Public Order Act 1986, s 4A.

23 Malicious Communications Act 1988.

24 Communications Act 2003, s 127.

25 *R v GS* [2012] EWCA Crim 398. For discussion see Alisdair Gillespie, 'Obscene conversations, the internet and the criminal law' (2014) *Crim LR* 350.

26 Criminal Justice and Courts Act 2015, s 33.

27 ibid, s 71 will insert a new offence into the Juries Act 1974.

ones to stop such abuses occurring. In some cases (such as calculated hate and harassment campaigns) the use of the criminal law is appropriate. However, many of these laws were drafted in broad terms and can potentially apply to a broader range of speech than one might imagine. For example, section 127 of the Communications Act 2003 provides that it is an offence to send or cause to be sent over a 'public electronic communications network' a message that is 'grossly offensive or of an indecent, obscene or menacing character'.[28]

At face value, such a provision could criminalise a wide range of content disseminated on the internet, social media and other digital communications. Whilst section 127 is the best known provision, the other laws mentioned can also have a broad application. With such tools at their disposal, there is a danger that authorities will cast the net widely.

A spate of cases in 2012 caused people to wonder whether the law was operating too harshly on some speakers. For example, a 21-year-old man, previously of good character, was sentenced to 56 days in prison after sending a drunken racist tweet about a footballer.[29] The spate of cases illustrated how a misguided or ill-judged message sent from a person's home, often whilst under the influence of alcohol, could trigger costly private law litigation or bring a speaker within the criminal justice system at the click of a button.

The features of digital expression that can make hate campaigns, harassment and abuse so harmful – namely the ease with which content can be located and accessed, alongside its durability – allow the law to regulate the type of comments and conversations to which it previously had only limited application. Prior to the internet, a foolish remark made amongst friends or within one's home would have attracted little comment. Now the online equivalent of such remarks can be monitored, policed and may change the course of a person's life.[30]

One of the functions of free speech protection is to curb overly broad applications of the law, even though the laws in question were enacted for perfectly good reasons. There are a number of reasons why the current protection for expression rights may fail to provide such a curb. Under the traditional Article 10 principles, trolling, abuse and insults attract minimal protection. Political speech is given heightened protection, whilst in the case of gratuitous insults the state has considerable leeway to use the criminal law. This approach values expression most when it will provide some benefit to the audience, such as when it informs people on matters of public importance. Under the current approach to article 10, idiotic, foolish, and bigoted remarks are seen to provide little value to the audience. Such trolling is not seen to be a contribution to a debate of public importance, and therefore falls outside the core of Article 10's concern.

28 See *Chambers v DPP* [2012] EWHC 2157 (Admin) [2013] 1 All ER 149, for a well-known case that was successful on appeal.

29 The crown court later rejected an appeal against the sentence; see *R v Stacey* (Appeal no. A20120033, 30 March 2012).

30 Rowbottom (n 20).

However, the courts should recognise that there can be a need to protect speech, even where it offers little in the way of quality or information. Contributing to a political debate may be of greatest concern under Article 10, but there should also be a freedom to converse, to take risks and make mistakes in everyday interactions. The traditional categories of political, artistic and commercial speech (and so on) should not be abandoned. However, the categories-based approach should be supplemented with an understanding that amateur, spontaneous and casual speech can be worthy protection (even if it is of low value to the audience) in order to allow the give and take of daily life to operate freely.

In some areas, domestic law is gradually recognising this point. Several years ago, in a defamation case, Sir David Eady ruled that certain comments in an online forum would not be regarded as defamatory, as no one would take such remarks so seriously.[31] Speech on an internet bulletin board are, he said, 'like contributions to a casual conversation . . . which people simply note before moving on; they are often uninhibited, casual and ill thought out; those who participate know this and expect a certain amount of repartee or "give and take"'.[32]

In other words, much of the casual, spontaneous content online should be taken with a pinch of salt, even if it could be seen to violate the strict letter of the law and might be actionable if published in the pages of a newspaper. Under this approach, a higher threshold of harm should be required to found a legal action. The point is underlined in the recent reforms enacted in the Defamation Act 2013, which requires a claimant to show that the statement 'caused or is likely to cause serious harm to the reputation of the claimant'. The online equivalents of a 'casual conversation' are less likely to cause such serious harm.[33]

In relation to the criminal law, the Director of Public Prosecutions has published guidelines as to when content on the social media should give rise to a criminal prosecution.[34] Under these guidelines, to justify a criminal prosecution the speech has to be more than '[o]ffensive, shocking or disturbing', '[s]atirical, iconoclastic or rude', or an 'expression of unpopular or unfashionable opinion about serious or trivial matters, or banter or humour, even if distasteful to some or painful to those subjected to it'.[35]

The guidelines also indicate that a prosecution is unlikely when the speaker 'has expressed genuine remorse', taken 'swift and effective action' to remove the content, where the message was 'not intended for a wide audience, nor was that the obvious consequence of sending the communication', and 'did not obviously go beyond what could conceivably be tolerable or acceptable in an open and diverse society which upholds and respects freedom of expression'.[36] These are, of course, just guidelines for prosecutors and do not change the substance

31 *Smith v ADVFN plc* [2008] EWHC 1797.

32 ibid at [14].

33 Defamation Act 2013, s 1.

34 Crown Prosecution Service, *Guidelines on Prosecuting Cases Involving Communications Sent via Social Media* (2013).

35 ibid.

36 ibid.

of the law. The guidelines, however, at least try to minimise the risk of everyday conversations on the digital media leading to a criminal conviction.

The developments in defamation law and prosecution policy, whilst still evolving, are important steps that carve out space for everyday exchanges, which will often not be high-minded, but which are a necessary part of communication. These developments have not come about as a result of constitutional law, but have independently arisen in defamation law and prosecution policy. However, these are just two developments and the controversies continue. Social media cases still come to court and the debate continues between those calling for tighter controls on certain types of message, and those who believe such controls infringe expression rights. As more harmful conduct on the digital media is identified, calls will come for further controls.

As a counterweight to such trends, the Article 10 principles could be developed as a reminder for the law to provide space for casual conversations. However, such a move would require a step away from the traditional framework for Article 10, which places much weight on the subject matter and quality of the expression. To supplement those traditional principles, weight should also be given to the context and setting of the expression, particularly looking at whether the speech is amateur, casual and spontaneous. As stated, this does not rule out measures to tackle certain harmful speech. The argument advanced here is that criminal cases and substantial private remedies should be reserved for the more extreme abuses. If less extreme casual content is to be regulated at all, it could be done through more proportionate regulatory approaches.[37]

9.4 Media protection, duties and responsibilities

Another basic principle of Article 10 is that heightened protection for expression is afforded to the media. An obvious question then arises as to what is meant by the 'media' or 'press'. The Strasbourg Court has rejected an institutional understanding of 'the press' and has made clear that the protection afforded to the media is not limited to professional institutions. The heightened protection can extend to an NGO that performs similar watchdog functions.[38] The definition of the press and media is therefore at least partly functional, insofar as it applies to those engaged in the function of journalism. Such journalistic activity is identified and protected by the Court when the speaker fulfils the various 'duties and responsibilities' that are expected of the media.

These 'duties and responsibilities' provide for heightened protection of the press, on the condition that it acts 'in good faith in order to provide accurate and reliable information in accordance with the ethics of journalism'.[39] In developing

37 See Rowbottom (n 20).

38 *Animal Defenders International v UK* (2013) 34 BHRC 137 at [103].

39 This section draws on the argument made in J. Rowbottom, 'In the shadow of the big media: freedom of expression, participation and the production of knowledge online' [2014] *Public Law* 491.

this approach, the Strasbourg Court has taken a close look at the practices undertaken by the press to check the accuracy of content, finding that 'special grounds are required before the media can be dispensed from their ordinary obligation to verify factual statements that are defamatory of private individuals'.[40] The Court has in some cases noted the 'irresponsible' and 'unprofessional' conduct of the press as factors when deciding that there has been no violation of Article 10.[41] In *Stoll v Switzerland*, the Grand Chamber looked at the selective and sensationalist tone of an article as a factor again in concluding that a restriction did not violate Article 10.[42]

How should these standards be applied in the digital era? Some judges have queried whether it still makes sense to talk of the 'press' as separate from individual speakers; after all, the tools of mass communication are no longer limited solely to a professional elite. For example, Judges Sajo and Vucinic in their concurring opinion in *Youth Initiative and Human Rights* stated that: 'In the world of the Internet the difference between journalists and other members of the public is rapidly disappearing.'[43] The significance and implications of such a brief statement are difficult to state, although it suggests a distinction between the media and other speakers will be difficult to sustain for some purposes at least. In a similar vein, Judge Wojtyczek in his dissenting opinion in *Guseva v Bulgaria* queried the significance of the speaker's status as a journalist or NGO in the context of a claim for access to information, and concluded that:

> The role of the press has evolved and its influence has declined considerably. It is no exaggeration to say that today we, the citizens of European States, are all journalists. We (at least many of us) directly access different sources of information, collect or request information from public authorities, impart information to other persons and publicly comment on matters of public interest. We directly participate in public debate through various channels, mainly through the Internet. We are all social watchdogs who oversee the action of the public authorities. Democratic society is – *inter alia* – a community of social watchdogs. The old distinction between journalists and other citizens is now obsolete. In this context, the case-law hitherto on the functions of the press seems out of date in 2015 and should be adapted to the latest social developments.[44]

The comments must, however, be viewed in the context of a claim for access to information. As such, Judge Wojtyczek suggests that access rights should not be limited to certain classes of person, but he does not reject the distinct position

40 Axel Springer (2012) 32 BHRC 493) at [82]. For discussion of this approach and some of the other cases cited in this section see Egbert Myjer 'About court jesters: freedom of expression and duties and responsibilities of journalists' in Casadevall (n 9).

41 *Flux v Moldova (No 6)* (Application no. 22824/04, 2008).

42 *Stoll v Switzerland* (2007) 24 BHRC 258.

43 *Youth Initiative for Human Rights v Serbia* (2013) 36 BHRC 687.

44 *Guseva v Bulgaria* [2015] ECHR 171 (Application no. 6987/07, 2015).

of the press for other purposes. Wojtyczek accepted that the press still plays an 'important role' and that 'their activity may require special regulations'.[45]

These statements should not, therefore, be read as an attempt to eradicate the distinctive position of the media in the Article 10 jurisprudence. The mass media and individual speakers should not be treated as equivalent for all purposes. Whilst such equivalence might initially seem more egalitarian, an adjustment to the Article 10 jurisprudence on such lines would misinterpret the changes in the digital media. The professional media still perform a distinctive function, which will be carried on by a relatively small group. For example, the production of original news reporting and investigative journalism requires considerable investment, which will be beyond the reach of most individuals. That the professional media can produce such content on a regular basis will help to ensure that it maintains a mass audience. In some cases, this might justify special protection for the press, but in other cases it might require special duties too.

A danger in treating individuals as equivalent to the media is that the same duties and responsibilities will be applied to all speakers. In *Steel & Morris v UK*, the Court stated that the same principles of journalism ethics 'must apply to others who engage in public debate'.[46] The problem then is that the standards set with the mass media in mind (such as methods of verification) are now being applied to other speakers as a condition of Article 10 protection. Treating every speaker as equivalent to the press might sound democratic, but the advantages are illusory. Most individuals will be unlikely to fulfil the professional standards that are a condition for heightened protection.

The problems were found in the old law of defamation in England and Wales. A defence was offered to those people publishing articles on matters in the public interest, as long as the defendant met the standards of responsible journalism.[47] In practice, attempts to rely on the defence by newspapers were rarely successful. One editor told a parliamentary committee about the painstaking preparation of news stories in order to rely on the defence, which required considerable investment before publication.[48]

If such standards were difficult for a smaller-scale professional newspaper to fulfil, then it was very unlikely that an amateur speaker online would be able to invoke the defence. For example, whilst we might expect the responsible professional journalist to call a person for comment before publishing a potentially defamatory article, the same would not be expected of a private individual making a statement on a social networking site. The problem with the old defence was that the balance between speech and reputation was struck by using the practices and ethics of the professional media to define the duties and responsibilities of the speaker.

45 ibid.

46 *Steel and Another v United Kingdom* (2005) 18 BHRC 545 at [90].

47 *Reynolds v Times Newspapers* [2001] 2 AC 127.

48 House of Commons Culture, Media and Sport Select Committee, *Second Report of 2009–10, Press standards, privacy and libel* (The Stationery Office 2010) HC Paper No. 362-II (Session 2009/10), evidence given on 5 May 2009, at Q897.

A statutory public interest test in the Defamation Act 2013 has now replaced the old common-law defence of responsible journalism. The new defence can be relied upon where the defamatory statement was on a matter in the public interest, and the defendant 'reasonably believed that publishing the statement complained of was in the public interest'. It remains to be seen how the courts will decide whether a belief was reasonable. They could revert to the old law, invoking professional standards as the touchstone of reasonableness. Alternatively, new standards may be developed in the light of the new media.

Rather than eradicating the difference between types of speaker, the developments in digital communications require recognition of differences between the media and other speakers. The professional media does not have a monopoly on public interest expression, but it is not appropriate to hold individual and amateur speakers to the professional standards of the media as a condition of Article 10 protection. The duties and responsibilities envisaged by the courts have been formulated with the professional media in mind. The emphasis on professional standards provided a way to strike a balance between rights of the media and other competing rights and interests.

If these standards are applied across the board, then the danger is that individual and amateurs will be less likely to avail themselves of Article 10's heightened protection, even when engaging in political speech. As a result, both the domestic and Strasbourg courts may need to rethink the duties and responsibilities, and strike a different balance when dealing with the speech of individuals online, than when dealing with the speech of media institutions.

Scope for such a rebalancing is already possible in the existing jurisprudence, in which the Strasbourg Court has emphasised that these standards are to be applied flexibly.[49] In *Stoll v Switzerland*, the Grand Chamber indicated that greater responsibilities are expected of those forms of media that have greater influence and impact.[50] Such flexibility and variation in standards may be developed further to reflect the various types of speaker and context found in the digital media.

9.5 Source protection and anonymity online

Some of the strongest statements in support of freedom of expression have been made in the context of protecting journalists' sources. In *Goodwin,* the Court stated:

> Protection of journalistic sources is one of the basic conditions for press freedom, as is reflected in the laws and the professional codes of conduct in a number of Contracting States and is affirmed in several international instruments on journalistic freedoms. Without such protection, sources may be deterred from assisting the press in informing the public on matters of public interest. As a result the vital public watchdog role of the press may

49 See *Bladet Tromsø v Norway* (n 12).

50 *Stoll v Switzerland* (n 42).

> be undermined and the ability of the press to provide accurate and reliable information may be adversely affected. Having regard to the importance of the protection of journalistic sources for press freedom in a democratic society and the potentially chilling effect an order of source disclosure has on the exercise of that freedom, such a measure cannot be compatible with Article 10 of the Convention unless it is justified by an overriding requirement in the public interest.[51]

The Court has also added that such protection is 'part and parcel of the right to information', which emphasises the audience's interest in receiving the content.[52] In the UK, the protection against the compelled disclosure of sources is provided for under section 10 of the Contempt of Court Act 1981. The protection afforded to journalists in domestic law is not restricted to the professional media, but applies to any 'publication'.[53]

However, the courts have interpreted section 10 to apply only where the publisher takes responsibility for what is published and exercises some 'editorial control'.[54] It is therefore not clear whether a website that, for example, automatically posts anonymously leaked information could benefit from that protection. If the website makes some assessment of the leaked information prior to publication, then it is more likely to constitute sufficient 'editorial control'.

Even when a publication falls within section 10, a court can still order disclosure of the source's identity if 'necessary in the interests of justice or national security or for the prevention of disorder or crime'.[55] In deciding what is necessary, the court takes into account a number of factors, which can include the journalist's role and 'history of acting responsibly'.[56] The reliance on that factor may mean, again, that whilst source protection is open to any publication, the professional media is more likely to have the credentials as a 'responsible journalist' that is given weight in the balancing process. However, this need not be a criticism, and a privilege against disclosure is arguably an area where the interests of the professional media are entitled to greater weight.

A broader question is whether the arguments for protecting journalists' sources justify the protection of anonymous speech.[57] The argument runs that if disclosing the identity of a source is likely to have a chilling effect on journalists' sources, then the same chilling effect can occur when the identity of a speaker is revealed. People may decide not to blog or comment if content will be connected to their

51 *Goodwin v UK* (1996) 22 EHRR 123.

52 *Tillack v Belgium* (2012) 55 EHRR 25 at [65].

53 Contempt of Court Act 1981, s 10.

54 *Totalise v Motley Fool* [2001] EMLR 29.

55 In some cases, the application of this standard by the domestic courts has been found to fall short of the requirements of Article 10; see *Goodwin v UK* (n 51) and *Financial Times Ltd v United Kingdom* (2009) 28 BHRC 616.

56 *Mersey Care NHS Trust v Ackroyd (No 2)* [2008] EMLR 1 at [67]–[68].

57 See Lord Neuberger, '"What's in a name?" Privacy and anonymous speech on the internet' Speech to Conference5RB on 30 September 2014.

real identity. If this view is taken, then the Article 10 jurisprudence may need to be adapted to protect anonymous speech that is made directly on the internet, rather than via a journalist.

This view should, however, be resisted, as there are a number of difficulties in relying on an analogy between anonymous speakers and journalists' sources. Whilst the language of the Court refers to the 'protection of journalistic sources', in reality Article 10 protects the position of the journalist, rather than the source. If someone discovers the identity of a source through other means and that source suffers adverse consequences (such as dismissal), then in most cases the source will have no protection.

The Article 10 jurisprudence explicitly relies on the presence of alternative means of discovering the source's identity as reason for protecting the journalist's professional obligation.[58] For example, in *John v Express Newspapers*, Lord Woolf stated that, 'Before the courts require journalists to break what a journalist regards as a most important professional obligation to protect a source, the minimum requirement is that other avenues should be explored', such as an internal investigation to determine who leaked the information.[59]

Of course, these principles need to be applied flexibly to adapt to new threats to the news-gathering process. For example, government surveillance and access to communications data has in some cases permitted authorities to identify journalists' informants.[60] Whilst such methods do not force the journalist to break a professional obligation, they still target the position of the journalist and can fall foul of the principles outlined in *Goodwin*.

A further difference between an anonymous speaker and a journalist's source is that the audience can more easily assess the credibility of the journalist, based on past record and reputation. If a reputable journalist known for breaking important stories refers to an 'inside source', that report may be given considerable weight. By contrast, with purely anonymous speech, there are fewer cues for the reader. Of course, there are difficulties with such generalisations and there may be cases where an anonymous blog or commenter establishes credibility, having had its claims verified and supported elsewhere. However, in many cases there will be little for the audience to rely on, save for a general attitude of scepticism.

Even if we reject the comparison between anonymous speakers and those communicating through a journalist, there are still free-standing arguments to protect the anonymity of speakers. To some commentators, anonymity should be protected as a way of ensuring that people are free to speak out without fear of adverse consequences. However, this is the subject of debate and, to others, anonymity allows people to engage in highly offensive, abusive and bullying

58 *Financial Times v UK* (n 55) at [69].

59 *John v Express Newspapers* [2000] 1 WLR 1931 at [27].

60 Interception of Communications Commissioner's Office, *IOCCO inquiry into the use of Chapter 2 of Part 1 of the Regulation of Investigatory Powers Act (RIPA) to identify journalistic sources* (February 2015).

activities, whilst avoiding any accountability. The general rule in the UK is that there is no general right to anonymity.

The point can be illustrated by the decision in the *Author of a Blog v Times Newspapers*, in which a policeman sought an injunction to prevent the *Times* newspaper revealing that he was the author of an anonymous award-winning blog.[61] The blogger brought the claim primarily on the basis that his identity was private information, but free-speech arguments were also advanced. Eady J rejected the claim, finding that the author had no reasonable expectation of privacy. According to Eady J, 'blogging is essentially a public rather than a private activity'[62] and, in any event, he found there was a public interest in revealing the author's identity.

The decision has been criticised for failing to give sufficient weight to the potential chilling effect that the disclosure of a speaker's identity might have.[63] Whilst there are dangers in chilling expression, it is also important to remember that in some cases knowing the identity of an author is an important piece of information. For example, if an anonymous website challenges the science on the health effects of obesity, it would be important for people to know if that site was funded or written by a food-industry insider. If a blogger gains a following writing about his own experiences of living with a terminal illness, it would similarly be important for the public to know if the author turned out to be healthy.

These are extreme cases, but the same can apply more generally. As Eady J noted, 'It is very often useful, in assessing the value of an opinion or argument, to know its source' and that 'one may wish to apply greater caution or scepticism in the case of a person with "an axe to grind"'.[64]

One response to this argument might be that audiences should simply treat any anonymous speaker with scepticism.[65] In other words, if the identity of the blogger is not known, readers should consider the possibility that the author might have a vested interest or conceal information about himself. The difficulty with this response is that readers will assume too much or too little credibility for the anonymous speaker.

Not all anonymous speakers are the same. In some cases the credibility discount will be warranted and in others it will not, but the audience will not be well placed to determine which is which. The response also undermines the public interest argument for protecting the anonymous speech. It is difficult to

61 *Author of a Blog v Times Newspapers* [2009] EWHC 1358 (QB). The case is complicated by the fact that, after the decision, it was revealed that the identity of the blogger had initially been discovered by gaining unauthorised access to an email account. See *Brett v Solicitors Regulation Authority* [2014] EWHC 2974. Such a method of obtaining the information changes the merits of the applicant's claim, but for the present purposes I focus only on the reasoning given by Eady J.

62 *Author of a Blog v Times Newspapers* (n 61) at [11].

63 For discussion of these arguments see Eric Barendt, 'Bad news for bloggers' (2009) 2 *Journal of Media Law* 141.

64 *Author of a Blog v Times Newspapers* (n 61) at [21].

65 Kirsty Hughes, 'No reasonable expectation of anonymity' (2010) 2 *Journal of Media Law* 169 at 180.

maintain that anonymous speakers should be protected to ensure audiences are well informed on matters of public interest, whilst at the same time arguing that readers should be aware that everything written by such a speaker might be made up, biased or lack any credibility.

None of this is to deny the need to protect a person's identity in certain situations. My point is that when looking at the issue generally, strong arguments lie on either side of the equation. A tentative view is that discussion of a broad 'right to anonymity' is not helpful. Much will depend on the circumstances and the way information about a speaker's identity is acquired and disclosed, as well as the way in which information is likely to be used. A claim for an injunction to restrain a private party revealing a speaker's identity (as in *The Author of a Blog* case) may prompt a different reaction from a proposal, say, for government to require every speaker on a certain platform to disclosure their identities.[66]

Similarly, one can reject a general right to anonymous expression and still object to the use of government surveillance to build a database of those holding certain political views, or to prevent people fully encrypting communications. Furthermore, if there are concerns that speakers will suffer adverse consequences, then there may be other solutions to guard against those consequences, such as stronger whistleblower protection. The issues are complex and I do not seek to resolve them here. The tentative view set out here is that we should be sceptical about arguments to adapt Article 10 and the principles outlined in *Goodwin* to give all speakers a prima facie legal right to anonymity.

9.6 Conclusion

The Article 10 jurisprudence has recognised the potential benefits and serious harms posed by communications in the digital media. So far, this has not led to a radical reformulation of the main Article 10 principles. Changes in the domestic criminal law and defamation law have been made not as a result of Article 10, but largely as a result of political pressures, policy changes and common-law adjudication. The approach under Article 10 has been to maintain the existing principles of freedom of expression. Such a position is understandable, given the difficulty in determining the free-speech implications of such fast-changing technology across so many different countries. There is, however, a case for Article 10 to adapt to the new communications system.

I do not suggest that the traditional principles should be abandoned, but that those principles may need to be supplemented when looking beyond the traditional mass-media paradigm. For example, sometimes speech may be deserving of protection not because it contributes to a debate on a matter in the public

66 This is not to say that all such proposals fall foul of Article 10. Compare the decision of the US Supreme Court in *McIntyre v Ohio Elections Commission* (1995) 514 US 334, where there was a requirement to include the speaker's name and address on electoral advocacy material, with the position in UK law, which requires names and addresses on election material; see Political Parties, Elections and Referendums Act 2000, s 143.

interest, but because it is part of the give and take of everyday life. Whilst the content of such expression may appear to have minimal informational value to the audience, there is value in preserving a freedom to engage in conversation, even when it strays into incivility.

Given that the Article 10 cases stress the importance of flexibility and the context of a case, there is scope for the approach discussed in this chapter to be accommodated within the existing jurisprudence. However, more could be done to make the various considerations an explicit part of the protection for freedom of expression. The principles of freedom of expression, if reassessed, could help to provide a firmer rationale for these developments, making it a clearer element of the constitutional protection of a fundamental right.

There is, however, a danger when reassessing the Article 10 jurisprudence of taking a wrong turning or misinterpreting the trends in digital communications. One such error would be to assume that the mass media and individuals are now equivalents. The digital media accommodates a full range of speakers in different settings, ranging from the professional media to casual conversations amongst a small group of people. That people rely on the same technology to distribute content does not mean that they are in an equivalent position. In fact, as more speech is digitised, more expression than before has the potential to be subject to legal controls and thereby rely on Article 10 for protection. This trend requires Article 10 to adapt its principles to accommodate the full range of speakers and contexts.

As I argued earlier, whilst developments in digital communications often seem to blur the distinction between the media and other speakers, it is in practice more important than ever to differentiate between the two when formulating the appropriate 'duties and responsibilities'. When looking at the duties and responsibilities of a speaker performing a watchdog function, there are dangers in demanding the fulfilment of standards that can reasonably be expected of the professional media, but not the individual and amateur.

Similarly, it was argued that the longstanding protection of journalists' sources should not simply be converted into a general right to speak anonymously online. Again, there are differences between the contexts. The discussion in this chapter is not exhaustive and there are many other issues that concern Article 10, such as the role and responsibilities of online intermediaries. However, the discussion has sought to highlight the importance and challenges of adapting Article 10 principles from an era when the mass media defined the paradigm speaker, to one where a wider range of speaker types increasingly rely on expression rights.

10 The constitutional ripeness of principles in internet law in the Netherlands

Gert-Jan Leenknegt

10.1 Introduction

The year 2014 marked the 200th anniversary of the Dutch Basic Law. It was formally adopted in 1814, it has been amended repeatedly since – rather fundamentally so in 1848 – and it was systematically modernised for the last time in 1983.[1] It has a number of typical characteristics which, taken together, set it apart from the constitutions of most modern liberal democracies. First, the procedure for constitutional amendment makes it a highly rigid constitution. Secondly, it explicitly forbids constitutional review by the courts. Thirdly, it is based on a strongly monistic perspective on the relationship between Dutch and international law, which allows and even obliges Dutch courts to apply human rights provisions in international treaties, setting aside Dutch law and even the Basic Law itself. These characteristics deserve attention here, as they are closely related to the constitutional discourse in the Netherlands – or rather, the apparent lack thereof.

Before addressing the process of constitutionalisation of internet law, I will briefly address the typical character of the constitutional structure of the Netherlands, and the general aspects of Dutch constitutional discourse. A crucial notion in those debates seems to be the rather elusive concept of 'constitutional ripeness'. I will then focus on the relevant fundamental rights provisions in the Dutch Constitution. The wordings of those provisions reflect the state of technology in the 1970s. I will pay attention to the role of ordinary legislation to protect fundamental rights relating to the internet, and on the (failed) attempts to amend the relevant constitutional provisions in the light of developments related to the internet.

In section 10.6, I will analyse the role of the European Convention on Human Rights (ECHR) as a 'substitute constitution', both in general and in relation to the protection of rights relating to the internet in particular. In recent years, the Charter of Fundamental Rights of the EU has acquired a similar function. I will

1 The 1983 general revision has been called the 'facelift of an elderly lady'; see A. W. Heringa and T. Zwart, Face-lift van een oude dame? De grondwet 1983' (1983) 58 *Nederlands Juristenblad* 233–47.

deal with relevant case law from Dutch courts, the European Court of Human Rights (ECtHR) and the Court of Justice of the European Union (CJEU).

10.2 General characteristics of the Dutch Basic Law

10.2.1 The notion of 'constitutional ripeness'

There seems to be a consensus in the constitutional debate – but no legally binding rule – that in order for legal rules or principles to be codified in the Basic Law, they must have reached *constitutional ripeness*.[2] The assumption behind this idea is that the Dutch Basic Law is basically a codification of generally accepted legal rules, and not a means to introduce new rules or principles into the constitutional system. Therefore, rules or principles must have been generally accepted and applied over a longer period of time before they may be considered for incorporation into the Basic Law. Such rules or principles may be found in legislation, or in unwritten – customary – constitutional law, or even in consistent case law. An example is the discussion on the possible codification in the Basic Law of a right to access to documents.[3]

Currently, the Basic Law only provides for the principle of open government (Article 110), but it contains no right to access to information; the rules that actually establish and protect that right are laid down in the Wet openbaarheid van bestuur (Act on Open Government), dating from 1991. The two Commissions that advised on the amendment of the Basic Law, in 2000 and 2010, discussed the necessity and 'constitutional ripeness' of a new provision in the Basic Law protecting the right to access information held by the authorities (see also section 10.5.1).[4]

10.2.2 Amendment of the Basic Law

According to Article 137 of the Basic Law, amendment thereof requires a bill which passes two readings in the States General (the Dutch Parliament), separated by general elections for the Second Chamber (the Dutch Lower House). The bill needs to be approved by a two-thirds majority in both chambers in the second reading in order to be enacted. As a result of this rigid character, very few significant amendments have been adopted since the last general revision (1983).

2 Franken Commission, *Report of the Commission on Fundamental Rights in a Digital Age* (The Hague 2000) 48; the report refers to an earlier statement of the government in *Kamerstukken II* (Parliamentary Proceedings, Second Chamber) 1997/98, 25 455, no. 5 at 2. The principle does not feature explicitly in the report of the Thomassen Commission; the Minister of Home Affairs does mention it in his memorandum on constitutional amendment of July 2013 (*Kamerstukken I* (Parliamentary Proceedings, First Chamber) 2012/13, 31 570, G at 2), and in the letter of 27 June 27 2014, sent to both Chambers of the States General, announcing a proposal to insert a general provision in the Basic Law protecting the Rule of Law, democracy and human rights.

3 Thomassen Commission, *Report of the Staatscommissie Grondwet* (November 2010) 69.

4 Franken Commission (n 2) 186 ff; Thomassen Commission (n 3) 90 ff.

Most of the amendments that have been adopted were of a technical nature, adding a sentence or a few words to existing provisions. They concerned mainly non-political issues, and enjoyed general support in both chambers of the States General. The most notable amendments during the last 20 years have been the modernisation of the provisions on the military and defence, the addition of a provision on temporary replacement of pregnant (or seriously ill) members of the States General and the insertion of a provision on the National Ombudsman institute. Repeated initiatives to amend the provisions on fundamental rights in relation to technological developments have failed so far, for various reasons (see section 10.5.1).

10.2.3 The prohibition of constitutional review by the courts

Article 120 of the Basic Law states that Dutch courts may not review the constitutionality of Acts of Parliament (or of treaties). This prohibition concerns both the substance of those Acts, and procedural aspects.[5] It dates back to 1848, when the Basic Law expressed that 'the laws are inviolable' for the first time. The aim of that statement was to make clear that Acts of Parliament would be binding for both the executive and the judicial power; interpretation of the Basic Law was reserved for the legislature. At the time, no need was felt for a form of constitutional review by the courts.[6] The provision was rephrased, and the prohibition concerning international treaties was added, but it was never abolished nor substantially amended, despite long debates and growing support for the introduction of some form of constitutional review by the courts.[7] In fact, an amendment of Article 120 was approved by the States General for the first time in 2008.[8] It was introduced in the States General for the second reading in March 2015, but it did not reach the required two-thirds majority in the Second Chamber. It seems, therefore, that Article 120 will yet remain a constitutional rarity.

Consequently, there is no case law regarding the constitutionality of Acts of Parliament.[9] In one rather exceptional case, however, the Supreme Court found that an Act of Parliament was blatantly contrary to the principle of legal certainty (although not to any of the provisions of the Basic Law). In the end it concluded that Article 120 of the Basic Law implied that it had no power to strike down the Act.[10] The effect, however, was that the legislature decided to amend the Act

5 HR (Supreme Court) (27 January 1961) *NJ* 1963, 248 (Van den Bergh/Staat).

6 C. J. Bax, 'Commentaar op artikel 120 van de Grondwet' in E. M. H. Hirsch Ballin and G. Leenknegt (eds), *Artikelsgewijs commentaar op de Grondwet, webeditie 2014* www.Nederlandrechtsstaat.nl (last accessed 24 August 2015).

7 For an overview see G. van der Schyff, *Judicial Review of Legislation: A Comparative Study of the United Kingdom, the Netherlands and South Africa* (Springer 2010).

8 Wet van 25 februari 2009, houdende verklaring dat er grond bestaat een voorstel in overweging te nemen tot verandering in de Grondwet, strekkende tot invoering van de bevoegdheid tot toetsing van wetten aan een aantal bepalingen van de Grondwet door de rechter (the so-called 'Halsema proposal'), *Stb.* 2009, 120.

9 There is some case law on the constitutionality of municipal regulations and by-laws, particularly concerning the freedom of the press; see section 10.4.2.

10 HR (14 April 1989) *NJ* 1989, 469 (Harmonisatiewet).

accordingly. That particular case has led to some debate amongst constitutional scholars.[11]

10.2.4 The monistic approach towards international law

In the Dutch constitutional system, international law is vastly more important than the Basic Law with respect to the protection of fundamental rights. The Basic Law implies a monistic perspective on the relation between national and international law.[12] According to Article 94 of the Basic Law, international law that is binding on all persons – treaties protecting fundamental rights and freedoms, in many cases – prevails over national law. The courts are thus not allowed to review Acts of Parliament against the constitution, but at the same time they are obliged to review any law, including Acts of Parliament, and even the Basic Law itself, against international law that is binding on all persons.

In case of a conflict between national and international law, they must apply international law, and not national law. As a consequence, the importance of international law, and especially of the European Convention on Human Rights, in Dutch legal debate and in legal practice has become enormous, putting the Basic Law almost completely in its shadow.

10.2.5 Dutch constitutional debate in general

The process of constitutionalisation of emerging legal principles requires constitutional debate. However, as we have seen, there is no constitutional review of Acts of Parliament in the Netherlands. As a result, court decisions that address constitutional issues are scarce; there is no dedicated Constitutional Court that could produce extensive case law on the exact meaning of the provisions of the Basic Law. Logically, there is hardly any legal or social debate on court decisions in relation to the Basic Law. Dutch courts have not developed a tradition of constitutional reasoning; or rather, they rarely decide cases from a constitutional point of view, even when they could. There seems to be a low 'constitutional consciousness' amongst judges. Furthermore, court decisions are hardly ever a motive for amendment of the Basic Law. A rare – and historic – example is a case dating from 1879, when the Supreme Court ruled that the king (which legally meant the government) had no power to issue royal decrees without explicit delegation by the legislature. That decision was partly codified in the Basic Law in 1887, to the extent that it now guarantees that punitive provisions may only be issued by royal decree pursuant to an Act of Parliament.[13]

Traditionally, there is also little public debate on constitutional issues in the

11 For an overview see J. Peters, 'Het Harmonisatiewet-arrest ofwel: de plaats van de rechter' in *Ars Aequi* (2010) 361.

12 The legal basis of that monistic view cannot be found in the Basic Law itself, but is a rule of unwritten constitutional law; see HR (3 March 1919) *NJ* 1919, 371 (Grenstractaat Aken).

13 HR (13 January 1879) *W* 4330 (Meerenberg). The decision was partly codified in art 89(2) of the Basic Law.

Netherlands. Even where the Basic Law could have a function in the debate on current social issues, it is hardly ever mentioned or considered in the media. In addition to the characteristics already mentioned above, a reason for that could be the rather technical, sober and uninspiring text of the Basic Law. Its provisions are brief, technical and sometimes rather enigmatic, and do not seem to address essential ideological issues or ethical or moral questions. It creates an open structure of basic legal rules, and relies to a large extent on the legislature to elaborate the general principles it lays down. As a result, it does not play a very prominent role in the public debate at all.[14] In other words, the Netherlands has a weak 'constitutional culture'.

However, Dutch constitutional debate can be found in several other places. The Council of State advises on all drafts for bills,[15] including amendments of the Basic Law, and bills for parliamentary approval of treaties; it pays specific attention to issues of constitutionality, whenever it is deemed relevant. The government is then expected to address those issues as it introduces the bill into the Second Chamber, together with the advice of the Council.

Furthermore, the First Chamber (the Dutch Senate) typically pays attention to questions of constitutionality whilst debating bills. In March 2014, the First Chamber organised a special debate on the 'Rechtsstaat', in which the modernisation of the Basic Law was a prominent subject. Since 2012, a College voor de Rechten van de Mens (Netherlands Institute for Human Rights) has been created, which advises on questions and conflicts that involve human rights, and conducts research in the area of human rights protection.[16]

Finally, there are various ad hoc commissions that advise on amendment of the Basic Law. In 2010, the Staatscommissie Grondwet (State Commission for the Basic Law; known as the Thomassen Commission) published an advisory report on amendment of the Basic Law; in 2006 the Nationale Conventie (National Convention), a forum composed of mainly legal and political scholars, was asked to draft a report on modernisation of the Basic Law. These commissions, and several others, have produced many interesting thoughts on the Dutch Basic Law and have also addressed developments in ICT in relation to the relevant provisions of the Basic Law. Disappointingly, these have had almost no impact.

10.2 6 Constitutionalisation through ordinary legislation

It is important to note that constitutionalisation, understood as the development and acceptance of new constitutional norms, takes place mostly through ordinary legislation in the Netherlands. New legal principles or rules that emerge can be enacted in ordinary law; some are deemed to be of such fundamental

14 Thomassen Commission (n 3) 26; E. M. H. Hirsch Ballin, L. H. J. Adams, G. Leenknegt and K. T. Meijer, 'De Grondwet is te belangrijk om aan specialisten over te laten' *Brabants Dagblad* (28 March 2014).

15 Basic Law art 74.

16 See www.mensenrechten.nl (last accessed 24 August 2015).

nature that they may attain a 'constitutional character'. For example, in 2012 the Netherlands was the second country in the world to enact the principle of net neutrality;[17] as I will demonstrate below (section 10.5.5.2), that principle is one of the foundations of the Dutch telecommunications legislation.

10.3 Issues of jurisdiction

10.3 1 Absolute and relative competence

I will only briefly describe the rules that determine the jurisdiction of Dutch courts and tribunals. I will focus on questions of jurisdiction with respect to conflicts concerning activities undertaken by persons or companies that reside outside the Netherlands, as the internet, email and social media may be used to offer products or services, or even to undertake criminal activities, from anywhere in the world. In that respect, two issues are relevant: the *absolute* and *relative* competence of Dutch courts and tribunals.

The rules concerning the *absolute* competence of the various courts and tribunals determine the scope of competence of each of them in relation to the others. In the Netherlands, ordinary district courts have the competence to deal with all civil and criminal cases, including fiscal cases.[18] They also serve as courts of first instance for administrative law cases. The courts of appeal deal with appeals in criminal, civil and fiscal cases, but not with administrative law cases. The Supreme Court is the top judicial institution in criminal, civil and fiscal cases.

The Administrative Jurisdiction Division of the Council of State is the appellate (and final) court in general administrative law cases. In addition, there are specialised tribunals in the area of socio-economic legislation (College van Beroep voor Bedrijfsleven – Trade and Industry Appeals Tribunal), and for cases involving the application of legislation concerning social security and the civil service (Centrale Raad van Beroep – Central Appeals Tribunal). All of these are considered to be 'supreme' courts in their respective areas of jurisdiction.

There is no dedicated constitutional court, nor a single supreme court. Therefore, any of these tribunals may be confronted with questions regarding the interpretation of the relevant provisions of the Basic Law. It is therefore possible that each of them could develop their own distinct interpretation of those provisions. Of course, all of them are bound by the prohibition of constitutional review of Acts of Parliament, laid down in Article 120 of the Basic Law.

The rules concerning the *relative* competence of courts and tribunals deal with territorial issues. Traditionally, in the field of administrative law, either the location of the administrative organ or the domicile of the plaintiff determines which court has jurisdiction, depending on the type of administrative organ.[19] Similarly, in most civil and criminal law cases, the domicile of the defendant is

17 Telecommunicatiewet (Telecommunications Act) art 7.4a.

18 Basic Law art 112; Wet op de rechterlijke organisatie (Judicial Organisation Act) arts 42–45.

19 Algemene wet bestuursrecht (General Administrative Law Act) art 8:7.

decisive.[20] The era of the internet, however, poses new questions with respect to the jurisdiction of Dutch courts and tribunals. Commercial or other activities, legal or illegal, may take effect in the Netherlands, whilst the person or company undertaking those activities is not domiciled in the Netherlands.

Within the EU, Article 5(3) of the EEX Regulation[21] provides that a person domiciled in a Member State may be sued in another Member State in matters relating to tort, delict or quasi-delict, in the courts for the place where the harmful event has occurred or may occur. According to the EU Court of Justice, that includes both the location where the harmful action is undertaken – the 'Handlungsort' – and the location where the harmful act has its effect – the 'Erfolgsort'.[22] Outside the scope of the EU, where the EEX Regulation is not applicable, Dutch civil and criminal procedural law provide for a similar arrangement.[23]

Dutch case law shows an example of a civil law case against Google, based in the USA;[24] several cases are related to companies based in other countries, offering products or services through the internet, violating relevant Dutch legislation,[25] and some examples involve international copyright issues.[26] These cases demonstrate that whenever the activities are carried out in the Netherlands (through the internet), or the victim is domiciled in the Netherlands or any harm caused by the activities takes effect in the Netherlands, the courts assume jurisdiction according to the rules of absolute and relative competence.

10.3.2 Influences of foreign domestic law and international law

As explained in section 10.2.4, Dutch courts are obliged to apply international law that is binding on all persons, setting aside Dutch law if necessary. Therefore,

20 Wetboek van Burgerlijke Rechtsvordering (Civil Procedure Code) art 99; Wetboek van Strafvordering (Criminal Procedure Code) art 2(1). See also art 17 of the Basic Law, which protects the *ius de non evocando*.

21 Council Regulation (EC) No. 44/2001 of 22 December 2000 on jurisdiction and the recognition and enforcement of judgments in civil and commercial matters.

22 ECJ (19 April 2012) C–523/10 (Wintersteiger). For an example under Dutch law see HR (7 December 2012) (G-Star/H&M), ECLI:NL:HR:2012:BX9018.

23 Wetboek van Burgerlijke Rechtsvordering (Civil Procedure Code) arts 2 and 3, 6(e), and 102; Wetboek van Strafrecht (Penal Code) arts 5 ff.

24 Rechtbank Amsterdam (9 October 2008) ECLI:NL:RBAMS:2008:BF7448.

25 Some examples: Rechtbank 's-Hertogenbosch (1 August 2012) (Nexpak), ECLI:NL:RBSHE:2012:BX3380; Voorzieningenrechter 's-Gravenhage (6 June 2011) (Yellow Pages), IEPT 20110606; Voorzieningenrechter Breda (8 February 2011) (Dahabshill), ECLI:NL:RBBRE:2011:BP3480; Rechtbank 's-Hertogenbosch (26 January 2011) (Mobilefencing), ECLI:NL:RBSHE:2011:BP3102; Rechtbank Rotterdam (3 February 2010) (OPTA vs DollarRevenu), ECLI:NL:RBROT:2010:BL2092; Voorzieningenrechter Amsterdam (1 October 2009) (Travelport), ECLI:NL:RBAMS:2009:BJ9179; Hof Amsterdam (22 September 2009) (Dimensione/Cassina) IEPT20090922; Voorzieningenrechter Amsterdam (30 July 2009) (The Pirate Bay), ECLI:NL:RBAMS:2009:BJ4298; Rechtbank Amsterdam (12 February 2009) (Dimensione), ECLI:NL:RBAMS:2009:BH6546.

26 For example Rechtbank Amsterdam (12 February 2009) 415634/KG ZA 08-2444 WT/CN, ECLI:NL:RBAMS:2009:BH6546.

international treaties such as the ECHR, the International Covenant on Civil and Political Rights (ICCPR)[27] and, more recently, the EU Charter of Fundamental Rights[28] have a strong influence on Dutch legal practice (see also section 10.6). Domestic foreign law, on the other hand, does not seem to play any role in legal practice. As far as fundamental rights protection is concerned, courts do not refer to foreign domestic law in their decisions and judgments.

In the political and scientific debate on fundamental rights protection in relation to the internet, foreign domestic law does play a role. The Commissie Grondrechten in het Digitale Tijdperk (Commission on Fundamental Rights in a Digital Age; known as the 'Franken Commission'), which advised the government on amendment of the Basic Law in 2000 (see section 10.5.1), based its conclusions partly on extensive comparative legal research. Its analysis and proposals were inspired by French, Belgian, German, Swedish, Canadian and American constitutional texts, as well as debates on internet law in those countries.[29]

10.4 Fundamental rights protection and the internet under the Dutch Basic Law

10.4.1 The fundamental rights system of the Dutch Basic Law

Chapter 1 (Articles 1–23) of the Dutch Basic Law constitutes the 'Bill of Rights', protecting both civil and political rights and freedoms, and socio-economic and cultural rights. Most of the provisions on civil and political rights and freedoms have specific limitation clauses; there is no general limitation clause. The limitation clauses mainly deal with issues of competence: they attribute the competence to impose limits on a certain right to the legislature, and in some cases they open the possibility of delegation of regulatory powers to other organs. Some clauses, but not all, specify goals or criteria to be pursued when limiting rights, and some prescribe a specific procedure to be followed. The limitation clauses do not contain the notion of proportionality,[30] nor any other substantive element to be

27 International Covenant on Civil and Political Rights, adopted and opened for signature, ratification and accession by General Assembly resolution 2200A (XXI) of 16 December 1966, entry into force 23 March 1976, in accordance with art 49 http://www.ohchr.org/en/professionalinterest/pages/ccpr.aspx (last accessed 24 August 2015).

28 European Union, *Charter of Fundamental Rights of the European Union* (26 October 2012) 2012/C 326/02 http://www.refworld.org/docid/3ae6b3b70.html (last accessed 24 August 2015) OJ 18 December 2000 (2000/C 364/01). The Charter became legally binding when the Treaty of Lisbon entered into force on 1 December 2009, as the Treaty confers on the Charter the same legal value as the Treaties.

29 A. K. Koekkoek and others, *Bescherming van grondrechten in het digitale tijdperk. Een rechtsvergelijkend onderzoek naar informatie- en communicatievrijheid en privacy in Zweden, Duitsland, Frankrijk, België, de Verenigde Staten en Canada* (Tilburg University 2000); Research Appendix to the report of the Franken Commission (n 2). This comparative research also features in the parliamentary debates on the report of the Commission: *Kamerstukken II* 2000/01, 27 460, no. 2.

30 The only exception is article 15(4), which deals with the limitation of rights of persons living

taken into account when limiting fundamental rights. The legislature thus enjoys a wide discretion in determining the scope and limits of fundamental rights; theoretically, it could impose very strict limitations (or delegate regulatory powers to other organs to do so). However, as I will demonstrate in section 10.5, Dutch courts tend to apply the notion of proportionality found in the ECtHR case law whenever they must decide on fundamental rights issues.

The provisions that are relevant for the protection of rights in relation to the internet (notably on freedom of expression, privacy in general and privacy of communications) were drafted in the 1970s, and reflect the state of technology in that era. Article 7 mentions the freedom of the expression through the 'printing press', 'radio' and 'television'; Article 13 mentions 'letter', 'telephone' and 'telegraph'. Those provisions do not fit current technological developments anymore; there is general agreement that they ought to be amended in order to render them 'technology neutral', but for various reasons they have not been amended yet (see section 10.5.1 below).

The Basic Law is silent with regard to the horizontal effect of civil and political rights and freedoms, but it is generally accepted that these rights and freedoms may be applied in horizontal relations.[31] The modes in which fundamental rights then apply vary; usually, they are applied in an indirect way in private law cases, for example in tort, or harmful publications, or in cases concerning conflicts between an employer and an employee. Fundamental rights are then understood as interests of the parties, and are balanced against other interests involved to determine if a certain action is to be considered as a wrongful act. Some examples are discussed in section 10.4.3.

10.4.2 Relevant provisions

The debate on protection of rights in relation to the internet in the Netherlands concentrates mainly on Articles 7 (freedom of expression), 10 (privacy in general, and protection of data) and 13 (privacy of communications) of the Basic Law. These provisions currently seem to raise the most urgent questions in the debate about protection of rights in relation to the internet.[32] Article 11 on the inviolability of the person has become urgently relevant in relation to developments in genetics, DNA testing, medical science and trade in human tissue and organs. However, these technological developments seem to be of a different nature, as communications technology or data protection are not necessarily at the core of these developments. Therefore, Article 11 will not be discussed further. Article 12 protects the inviolability of the home, and that provision does raise questions

in imprisonment. The rights of prisoners may only be limited 'to the extent' required by their imprisonment.

31 In the explanatory memorandum that accompanied the bill amending ch 1 of the Basic Law, which led to the 1983 general revision, the government explained its views on the various modes of horizontal effect that the fundamental rights in the Basic Law could have: *Kamerstukken II* 1975/76, 13 872, no. 3 at 15 ff.

32 The Thomassen Commission also claims this; see Thomassen Commission (n 3) 69.

in relation to technological developments, as these could enable 'virtual entering' into homes.[33]

Article 7[34] mentions a number of traditional means of expressing thoughts and opinions. The term 'other means' in the third section encompasses the use of the internet as a means to express thoughts and opinions. This seems inadequate, given the importance of the internet, including Facebook, Twitter and other social media, but amendment of Article 7 has proved difficult. A reason for this is that there is an established body of case law on municipal regulations concerning various means of distributing printed works, and on other means of disseminating thoughts.[35] Initiatives and proposals to amend this provision have been received with reluctance, because amendment could render that body of case law obsolete. The general opinion seems to be that the existing case law on Article 7 should retain its value, and codification of that case law would be too complicated because of all the nuances and exceptions.[36]

Article 10[37] is a general provision that protects the right to privacy, whilst Articles 11–13 deal with specific privacy issues. The scope of those specific privacy provisions is limited in some respects: Article 10 is applicable where Articles 11–13 are not. Consequently, the scope of Article 10 is very wide, which allows it to be applied in relation to new information and communication technologies. The second and third paragraphs instruct the legislature to regulate the use of data and the rights of persons whose data are recorded and processed. Amendment of this provision does not seem most urgent, although there is

33 E. J. Koops, E. J. H. van Schooten and M. M. Prinsen (eds), *Recht naar binnen kijken. Een toekomstverkenning van huisrecht, lichamelijke integriteit en nieuwe opsporingstechnieken* (Sdu Uitgevers 2004).

34 Article 7:

1. No one shall require prior permission to publish thoughts or opinions through the press, without prejudice to the responsibility of every person under the law.

2. Rules concerning radio and television shall be laid down by Act of Parliament. There shall be no prior supervision of the content of a radio or television broadcast.

3. No one shall be required to submit thoughts or opinions for prior approval in order to disseminate them by means other than those mentioned in the preceding paragraphs, without prejudice to the responsibility of every person under the law. The holding of performances open to persons younger than sixteen years of age may be regulated by Act of Parliament in order to protect good morals.

4. The preceding paragraphs do not apply to commercial advertising.

35 See B. P. Vermeulen, 'Commentaar op artikel 7 van de Grondwet' in Hirsch Ballin and Leenknegt (n 6) paras 8 and 9, which concern the body of case law on the means of dissemination.

36 See Thomassen Commission (n 3) 72–73.

37 Article 10:

1. Everyone shall have the right to respect for his privacy, without prejudice to restrictions laid down by or pursuant to Act of Parliament.

2. Rules to protect privacy shall be laid down by Act of Parliament in connection with the recording and dissemination of personal data.

3. Rules concerning the rights of persons to be informed of data recorded concerning them and of the use that is made thereof, and to have such data corrected shall be laid down by Act of Parliament.

debate about the need for a separate provision that explicitly protects the privacy of data.[38]

The right to inviolability of the home[39] traditionally encompasses the protection against a person *physically* entering a home against the will of the occupant.[40] The term 'home' is to be understood as any place a person regards as his home, whether he be the owner of his dwelling or not; it need not be a house in the traditional sense, but can also be a holiday home, a hotel room, a caravan, a tent or any other construction. Article 12 does not feature very prominently in the debate about fundamental rights in a digital age, but questions can be raised with respect to the 'virtual entering' of homes, using cameras or microphones, or by hacking PCs or hijacking webcams. Issues such as these now fall under the protection of Article 10; some argue that Article 12 itself should provide stronger protection in those cases.[41]

Although the official English translation of Article 13[42] of the Dutch Basic Law protects the privacy of 'correspondence', the Dutch text uses the term 'brief', which is actually a 'letter'. The second paragraph further mentions the telegraph and the telephone. This provision is to be amended most urgently, as the protection of privacy is based on specific and rather obsolete technologies. Communications using mobile phones, email, sharing and messaging on Facebook, Skype calls and numerous other means of communications through the internet no longer fit within the scope of Article 13.

Ordinary legislation in the field of telecommunications now provides protection for the privacy of all forms of communication; Article 8 of the ECHR, and

38 Thomassen Commision (n 3) 81 ff; G. Overkleeft-Verburg, 'Commentaar op artikel 10 van de Grondwet' in Hirsch Ballin and Leenknegt (n 6).

39 Article 12:

1. Entry into a home against the will of the occupant shall be permitted only in the cases laid down by or pursuant to Act of Parliament, by those designated for the purpose by or pursuant to Act of Parliament.

2. Prior identification and notice of purpose shall be required in order to enter a home under the preceding paragraph, subject to the exceptions prescribed by Act of Parliament.

3. A written report of the entry shall be issued to the occupant as soon as possible. If the entry was made in the interests of state security or criminal proceedings, the issue of the report may be postponed under rules to be laid down by Act of Parliament. A report need not be issued in cases, to be determined by Act of Parliament, where such issue would never be in the interests of state security.

40 S. S. Buisman and S. B. G. Kierkels, 'Commentaar op artikel 12 van de Grondwet' in Hirsch Ballin and Leenknegt (n 6).

41 Legally, structural observation of events taking place inside a home equals entering that home for observation purposes: see Criminal Procedure Act article 126l; *Kamerstukken II* 1996/97, 25 403, no. 3 at 79; Buisman and Kierkels (n 40) para. 1. See also Koops, Van Schooten and Prinsen (n 33).

42 Article 13:

1. The privacy of correspondence shall not be violated except in the cases laid down by Act of Parliament, by order of the courts.

2. The privacy of the telephone and telegraph shall not be violated except, in the cases laid down by Act of Parliament, by or with the authorisation of those designated for the purpose by Act of Parliament.

not Article 13, is the point of reference in debates about the right to privacy of communications. Various proposals for amendment of Article 13 have been put forward, in order to protect the privacy of communications, independently of the technologies used.[43] So far, none of those have been successful (section 10.5.1).

Recently, a debate arose on *traffic data*. Traffic data do not concern the content of, for example, a phone call or an email message, but provide information on issues such as 'who, when, how often, from what location' and so on. Currently, the privacy of these data is not protected by Article 13, but by Article 10 of the Basic Law. Again, some argue that the privacy of traffic data should be explicitly protected, preferably under Article 13.[44]

10.4.3 The application of the Dutch Basic Law in relation to the internet: relevant case law

The fact that the Basic Law forbids constitutional review of Acts of Parliament, combined with the circumstance that there is little constitutional debate and a low 'constitutional consciousness' in judicial reasoning, has consequences for the type of case law in relation to fundamental rights and the internet. There are, obviously, no cases on the constitutionality of Acts of Parliament; cases on the constitutionality of other regulatory instruments seem to be absent, too. Most cases involving fundamental rights protection in relation to the internet are private law cases, where those rights are applied in horizontal relations. In addition to that, there are several criminal law cases that involve fundamental rights. Below, I will briefly discuss the most important categories of cases.

One category of cases involves labour disputes, notably violation of the privacy of employees by an employer checking the content of their email correspondence without their consent. In all of these cases, the courts balance the interests of the employer and the employee in order to determine the lawfulness of a dismissal, taking the privacy of correspondence into account in rather general terms. Whilst doing this, the courts seldom make reference to the relevant provisions of the Basic Law, but occasionally do refer to Article 8 of the ECHR.[45]

In private law cases concerning unlawful or harmful publications on the internet or in emails that have become public, the right to privacy and the freedom of expression are balanced against each other, and against other interests involved, to determine the lawfulness of the publications. The Basic Law is usually not even mentioned in these cases.[46]

43 E. J. Koops, 'Commentaar op artikel 13 van de Grondwet' in Hirsch Ballin and Leenknegt (n 6).

44 Bert-Jaap Koops and Jan Smits, *Verkeersgegevens en artikel 13, Een technische en juridische analyse van het onderscheid tussen verkeersgegevens en inhoud van communicatie* (WLP 2014) 73 ff.

45 See e.g. Rechtbank Zwolle-Lelystad (28 April 2011) ECLI:NL:RBZLY:2011:BQ3287; Rechtbank Roermond (30 June 2009) ECLI:NL:RBROE:2009:BJ1615; Rechtbank Rotterdam (21 September 2011) ECLI:NL:RBROT:2011:BU4848; Rechtbank Midden-Nederland (11 April 2013) ECLI:NL:RBMNE:2013:BZ7178.

46 Rechtbank 's-Hertogenbosch (16 June 2010) ECLI:NL:RBSHE:2010:BM7956; Rechtbank Amsterdam (11 September 2009) ECLI:NL:RBAMS:2009:BK1859; Hof Amsterdam (23

Several cases concern the lawfulness of evidence that was acquired by monitoring correspondence using email or mobile phones. In one private law case, the court makes a brief reference to Articles 10 and 12 of the Basic Law and to the relevant provisions in the ECHR and the ICCPR, and then proceeds to determine the lawfulness of the way the evidence was collected by weighing the relevant interests against the violation of the right to privacy.[47]

One criminal law case concerns the lawfulness of evidence acquired with an IMSI-catcher, which is a technical device that scans the traffic data of mobile phones, as well as data on the movements of users thereof. The court makes a brief reference to the rights laid down in Articles 10 and 13 of the Basic Law, and to Article 8 of the ECHR, but then judges the case purely on the basis of the legislation on investigative instruments.[48] A third case is an administrative law case that involves the monitoring of email correspondence. The court judges the case on the basis of telecommunications legislation, but it does not mention the Basic Law in any way.[49]

Several cases concern the protection of privacy in relation to camera surveillance. One of those involves camera surveillance by municipal authorities. The court judges the proportionality of the violation of the right to privacy, referring to Article 8 of the ECHR, and not to the Basic Law.[50] In two private law cases, the court decides the case on the basis of privacy legislation, not on the right to privacy protected by the Basic Law.[51]

A further category of cases concerns the violation of copyrights through the internet. In most of these private law cases, the courts balance the relevant interests, including the freedom of expression, but the Basic Law is hardly ever explicitly mentioned by the courts. Occasionally, a reference to ECtHR case law is made.[52] In one case the freedom of expression is weighed against the right to privacy – again, without reference to the Basic Law.[53] In one case, one of the parties involved refers to the Basic Law in its arguments, but the court decides the case purely on the basis of the relevant copyright legislation.[54] In only one case does the court explicitly refer to Article 7 of the Basic Law: it involves the freedom of expression by publishing a book, using photographs freely available

February 2010) ECLI:NL:GHAMS:2010:BL6050; Rechtbank 's-Hertogenbosch (5 November 2010) ECLI:NL:RBSHE:2010:BO3655; Rechtbank Haarlem (18 January 2011) ECLI:NL:RBHAA:2011:BP1787; Rechtbank 's-Gragvenhage (21 November 2007) ECLI:NL:RBSGR:2007:BB8427; Rechtbank Gelderland (10 October 2013) ECLI:NL:RBGEL:2013:3801.

47 Rechtbank Rotterdam (3 September 2009) ECLI:NL:RBROT:2009:BJ7141.

48 Rechtbank Utrecht (23 January 2009) ECLI:NL:RBUTR:2009:BH0748.

49 Rechtbank Rotterdam (6 January 2011) ECLI:NL:RBROT:2011:BP0012.

50 Hof's-Hertogenbosch (11 December 2013) ECLI:NL:GHSHE:2013:5954.

51 Rechtbank Rotterdam (22 July 2010) ECLI:NL:RBROT:2010:BN3336; Rechtbank Amsterdam (17 March 2011) ECLI:NL:RBAMS:2011:BP8088.

52 Rechtbank 's-Gravenhage (10 May 2012) ECLI:NL:RBSGR:2012:BW5387.

53 Hof Amsterdam (22 May 2012) ECLI:NL:GHAMS:2012:BW6242.

54 Rechtbank Amsterdam (26 August 2004) ECLI:NL:RBAMS:2004:AQ7877.

on the internet. The court decides the case on the basis of the relevant copyright legislation.[55]

The general image that emerges from these examples seems clear. Dutch courts tend to solve issues involving fundamental rights by balancing the interests of the parties involved, taking into account all particular circumstances of each specific case. In most cases, the Basic Law is either not mentioned at all, or mentioned only in a 'matter of fact' sort of way, almost as a ritual statement that underlines the importance of the issue, but has no real or practical meaning. Fundamental rights and freedoms are seen as interests that must be weighed against other interests that are relevant in the case at hand, in order to determine the lawfulness of the actions of the parties in the case. The legal framework for balancing the interests involved is usually a rather general civil law notion, such as 'reason and equity' or 'due care'. Sometimes, the notion of proportionality can be recognised, when the court assesses the impact and necessity of a violation, or when it ponders less far-reaching alternatives.

Furthermore, courts appear to refer more frequently to the ECHR than to the Basic Law (see also sections 10.6 and 10.7, for further elaboration on this point).

10.5 Dutch constitutional debate in relation to the internet related rights

10.5.1 The debate on amendment of the Basic Law in relation to the digital era

As I explained earlier (section 10.2.2), the current text of the Basic Law was, for the most part, drafted in the 1970s and adopted in 1983. As early as 1995, Hofman pointed out that the existing provision on privacy of correspondence in the Basic Law had become inadequate in the light of technological developments.[56] As a reaction to this, the Dutch government drafted a bill in order to amend Article 13. In the Second Chamber, the bill was heavily debated and amended; the First Chamber was highly critical of the resulting bill and postponed the debates on it. In May 1999, the government withdrew the bill.[57] In February 1999 the government had already installed the Commissie Grondrechten in het Digitale Tijdperk (Commission on Fundamental Rights in a Digital Age; known as the 'Franken Commission'). It was asked to advise on amendment of the existing provisions of chapter 1 of the Basic Law in connection to the digital age, and on the desirability of adding new fundamental rights provisions.

The commission published its report in 2000.[58] It suggested that Articles 7, 10 and 13 needed to be amended, in order to make them resistant to the rapid technological developments, and to provide better protection for new questions

55 Rechtbank Breda (17 January 2011) ECLI:NL:RBBRE:2011:BP1094.

56 See amongst others J. A. Hofman, *Vertrouwelijke communicatie. Een rechtsvergelijkende studie over de geheimhouding van communicatie in grondrechtelijk perspectief naar internationaal, Nederlands en Duits recht* (Tjeenk Willink 1995).

57 For an overview see Koops (n 43) para. 2.

58 Franken Commission (n 2).

arising as a result of those developments. In relation to Article 7, it suggested that the Basic Law should contain an obligation for the government to ascertain pluralism of the media. Furthermore, it proposed the addition of a right to information held by the authorities. The Commission also explicitly mentioned the notion of 'constitutional ripeness' in order to determine whether certain legal rules or principles may be added to the Basic Law.[59]

Although the analysis of the problem made by the Franken Commission was accepted rather generally,[60] the solutions it proposed have led to a debate that continues to date. After the report was published, the government drafted new bills in order to amend Articles 7, 10 and 13 of the Basic Law, but after serious criticism by the Council of State the government decided not to submit the bills to the Second Chamber.

In 2009 the Staatscommissie Grondwet (State Commission for the Basic Law; known as the Thomassen Commission) was installed; it was asked to advise on the modernisation of the Basic Law, including the issue of fundamental rights protection in a digital age.[61] Its proposals for amendment of Articles 7, 10 and 13 closely resemble the suggestions of the Franken Commission, which received serious criticism. In its reaction to these proposals, the government deemed only the proposal for amendment of Article 13 to be 'constitutionally ripe'.

It has drafted a new proposal, which is different from that of the Thomassen Commission in various respects. It protects the privacy of correspondence and of telecommunications, and contains a rather complex limitation clause in order to enable the legislature to provide for the necessary measures in relation to national safety. In 2013, the Council of Ministers agreed on the text of the proposal, which was then sent to the Council of State for advice. The Council advised in January 2014, and the bill was sent to the Second Chamber for deliberation on 17 July 2014.[62]

The notion of 'constitutional ripeness' again seems important in these debates. In its official reaction on the report of the Thomassen Commission, the government stresses the need for 'constitutional ripeness' when amendment of the Basic Law is considered.[63] It seems to understand that notion in a rather stringent way, in the sense that an *urgent need* for amendment of the Basic Law is required. This seems to be a very conservative interpretation of the concept.[64]

59 ibid 48; see also section 10.2.6 below.

60 See e.g. L. F. Asscher, *Communicatiegrondrechten. Een onderzoek naar de constitutionele bescherming van het recht op vrijheid van meningsuiting en het communicatiegeheim in de informatiesamenleving* (Otto Cramwinkel Uitgever 2002).

61 Thomassen Commission (n 3) ch 8 http://www.rijksoverheid.nl/documenten-en-publicaties/rapporten/2010/11/11/rapport-staatscommissie-grondwet.html (last accessed 23 August 2015).

62 Advies W01.13.0179/I, *Kamerstukken II* 2013/14, 33 989, no. 4.

63 www.rijksoverheid.nl/bestanden/documenten-en-publicaties/kamerstukken/2011/10/24/kabinetsreactie-advies-staatscommissie-grondwet-11-november-2010/kabinetsreactie-advies-staatscommissie-grondwet-11-november-2010.pdf (last accessed 23 August 2015).

64 See *Kamerstukken I*, 2011/12, 31 570, A; see www.publiekrechtenpolitiek.nl/kabinetsreactie-staatscommissie-grondwet (last accessed 23 August 2015).

Why is amendment of the Basic Law so difficult, even when there is general agreement that certain provisions are outdated and should be amended? Several factors seem relevant here. As I have pointed out, the fact that there is general agreement on the nature of the problem does not mean that all actors involved agree on what is the best solution. The exact wording of the proposed new provisions is a cause for continuous political and scientific controversies. Furthermore, the fact that several consecutive governments had different political priorities and ideas about the proposed amendments was not very helpful either.

However, perhaps the most important factor is that there does not seem to be a very urgent *practical need* for amendment of the Basic Law. As I have demonstrated in section 10.4.3, courts that have to decide on cases involving fundamental rights in relation to the internet hardly ever refer to the Basic Law. In private law cases, they balance the relevant interests against a very general notion of privacy or freedom of expression; in other cases, they refer to Articles 8 and 10 of the ECHR, relying on a vast body of existing ECtHR case law (see also sections 10.6 and 10.7 below). It is not surprising that both the Franken Commission and the Thomassen Commission argue that amendment of the fundamental rights provisions in the Basic Law only makes sense when the prohibition of constitutional review of Acts of Parliament is (wholly or partly) abolished.

10.5.2 Discourse on principles governing the internet under Dutch constitutional law

In ordinary legislation, in the reports of the Franken Commission and the Thomassen Commission, and in the explanatory memoranda of several bills proposing amendments to the constitution, new principles are emerging in relation to fundamental rights protection in relation to the internet. These are not always mentioned in a very explicit way, but nonetheless seem to be part of the conceptual framework that shapes the discussions on amendment of the constitutional provisions concerning the freedom of expression and privacy in relation to the internet.

10.5.2.1 Access to the internet

In modern societies, access to the internet has become crucial. The internet is increasingly used to provide essential services, and public authorities increasingly communicate using websites, email, social media and so on. As a consequence, the right to access to the internet is clearly gaining constitutional value. Article 9(1) of the Telecommunications Act guarantees to everyone the access to essential services at an affordable price and of acceptable quality. Article 9(1) concerns mostly telephone services, but section 3 of the Article opens the possibility to extend that guarantee to other services. The Besluit universele dienstverlening en eindgebruikersbelangen (Decree on universal services and users' interests) extends the principle of Article 9(1) of the Telecommunications Act to data traffic with sufficient capacity to allow for functional internet access (Article

2(1)). This extension was actually motivated by two EU directives, dating from 2002.[65]

The Thomassen Commission, which advised the government on amendment of the Basic Law, repeatedly cites the principle of access to the internet in its analysis of Article 7 of the Basic Law (freedom of expression). According to the Commission, access to the internet has become an essential condition to gather information and to take part in the public debate, in order to express one's thoughts and opinions.[66] It proposes to add a provision to Article 7 that specifically guarantees the 'freedom to receive information' (in Dutch: 'het ontvangen van informatie is vrij'), which is to include information on the internet. Article 10 of the ECHR may very well have been a source of inspiration for this. However, as I have shown, the proposed amendment of Article 7 was not adopted by the government; in the opinion of the government, it lacks 'constitutional ripeness'.

10.5.2.2 Net neutrality

The Netherlands was the first country in Europe, and the second in the world, to enact the principle of net neutrality (June 2012). Article 7(4)(a) of the Telecommunications Act requires that providers of public electronic communication networks used to provide internet access services and providers of internet access services will not hinder or slow down services or the use of applications on the internet. The explanatory memorandum that accompanies the bill that added Article 7(4)(a) to the Telecommunications Act stresses the importance of the principle. Net neutrality and proper access to telecommunication services together are at the core of the telecommunications legislation; they are the central principles in the Act.[67] Again, reference is made to the EU Directive on Universal Service.[68] The principle of net neutrality does not feature explicitly in the report of the Thomassen Commission, which only underlines the importance of ordinary legislation in the protection of fundamental legal principles.

10.5.2.3 Access to documents

There is some debate about a new fundamental right relating to access to documents held by the authorities. Interestingly, the members of the Thomassen Commission could not agree on the issue, as the report explains.[69] As I mentioned

65 Notably Directive 2002/22/EC of the European Parliament and of the Council of 7 March 2002 on universal service and users' rights relating to electronic communications networks and services (Universal Service Directive) OJ L108, and Directive 2002/58/EC of the European Parliament and of the Council of 12 July 2002 concerning the processing of personal data and the protection of privacy in the electronic communications sector (Directive on privacy and electronic communications), OJ L201.

66 Thomassen Commission (n 3) 69, 70, 77.

67 *Kamerstukken II* 2010/11, 32 549, no. 3 at 14 ff.

68 ibid 64.

69 Thomassen Commission (n 3) 90 ff.

earlier (section 10.2.1), the right to access to information held by the authorities is now guaranteed by ordinary legislation, most importantly the Wet openbaarheid van bestuur (Act on Open Government). It contains general rules on the right to information laid down in documents – including electronic documents – held by administrative organs. The Act is limited in scope, as it does not apply to information held by the judiciary or the legislature. Moreover, it has become a rather complex and technical Act over the years.

Three members of the Thomassen Commission propose to add a new fundamental rights provision to the Basic Law that explicitly guarantees access to information held by the authorities. They refer to Articles 8 and 10 of the ECHR, and to the case law of the ECtHR regarding the right to access to information that is implied in those Articles. They also point out that the EU Charter of Fundamental Rights explicitly protects that right in Article 42 and, finally, they refer to the report of the Franken Commission, which had already proposed the addition of that right to the Basic Law.[70] The three members thought it was important to strike a balance in the Basic Law between the right to access to information and the rights protecting various aspects of privacy. The latter seem to have received most of the attention lately. However, the idea was not adopted by the other members of the Thomassen Commission, nor by the government.

10.5.2.4 Pluralism of the media

For an effective enjoyment of the freedom of expression it is crucial that everyone may peruse and consider all the relevant information, from various sources, without any interference. That presupposes the existence of a pluralist media landscape. Information should be provided and analysed from various perspectives, by autonomous media organisations. This is not only true for traditional media, but also for the internet. Currently, the guarantees for a pluralist media are to be found in ordinary legislation,[71] which concentrates mainly on rather traditional media (television and radio), and not specifically on the internet. The Commissariaat voor de Media (Dutch Media Authority) upholds the laws and regulations concerning traditional media, and the Act concerning fixed book prices. The Franken Commission had already concluded that a responsibility rests upon the state to protect pluralism in the media.[72]

In the debate about a possible amendment of Article 7 of the Basic Law, the Thomassen Commission again considered the role of the state with respect to pluralism of the media.[73] An important question is then, to what extent should the state intervene? How active should it be in stimulating or sanctioning media organisations? Is there a danger of state indoctrination? The Commission thought it unwise to oblige the state actively to protect pluralism of the media in

70 Franken Commission (n 2) 171 ff.
71 Most importantly, the Mediawet 2008 (Media Act 2008).
72 Franken Commission (n 2) 105 ff.
73 Thomassen Commission (n 3) 79.

any way; it proposed to add a new section to Article 7, stating that the authorities are to 'respect' pluralism of the media, in order to stress the importance of that principle.[74] The government, however, did not adopt the suggestion, as it did not consider the proposal for amendment of Article 7 to be 'constitutionally ripe'.

10.5.2.6 Privacy of personal data

In the digital era, the importance of personal data is enormous. However, at the same time, the threats to the privacy of personal data are enormous, too; both state institutions and private companies and organisations offering products and services make use of personal data, possibly in ways that threaten or violate the privacy of individual persons. Again, it is mostly ordinary legislation which protects the privacy of personal data in the Netherlands: mainly the Wet bescherming persoonsgegevens (Act on Protection of Personal Data), which provides general rules, and subordinate legislation, but also a large number of specific privacy arrangements in other legislation.[75]

Article 10 of the Basic Law protects privacy in general, and expressly leaves the regulation of privacy in relation to personal data to the legislature. The Thomassen Commission proposed to strengthen the protection of privacy of personal data, by formulating it as a fundamental right 'in se'. It refers to Articles 8 and 10 of the ECHR, and the case law of the ECtHR concerning those provisions, to the Data Protection Convention of 1981, to Article 8 of the EU Charter of Fundamental Rights and to relevant EU directives and regulations.[76] However, the Commission could not agree on the wording of a new provision; again, the government saw no need to introduce a bill that would amend the Basic Law accordingly.

10.6 The role of international and European human rights law

10.6.1 The ECHR as a 'substitute constitution'

The combination of Article 120 of the Basic Law, which prohibits constitutional review of Acts of Parliament, and Article 94 thereof, which obliges courts to apply international law that is binding on every person, reduces the importance of the Basic Law for Dutch legal practice greatly. The ECHR has become vastly more important in that respect. The ECHR does in fact serve as a 'bill of rights' in Dutch constitutional law, and is upheld as such by Dutch courts and tribunals. The fact that the ECtHR supervises the interpretation and application of the ECHR, which has produced a vast body of case law on which national courts can

74 ibid.

75 Some examples include: Telecommunicatiewet, Wet politiegegevens, Wet op de inlichtingen- en veiligheidsdiensten, Wet op de geneeskundige behandelingsovereenkomst, Gemeentwet, Provinciewet.

76 Thomassen Commission (n 3) 81–82.

rely, has certainly attributed to the status of the ECHR in Dutch legal practice, to such an extent that it may be called a 'substitute constitution'.[77]

More recently, the EU Charter of Fundamental Rights has acquired a similar status in Dutch case law relating to fundamental rights, but generally it is referred to by way of an additional argument, confirming the implications of the ECHR, but adding little legal value. Dutch courts generally perceive the Charter as equivalent to the ECHR as far as the scope and substance of the protected rights are concerned.[78]

In order to illustrate the importance of the ECHR in Dutch legal practice, two simple searches in the central database of the judiciary, www.rechtspraak.nl, will suffice. The database contains most of the case law of Dutch courts and tribunals since 1999 (although not all of it). In February 2015, a query using the term 'Grondwet' (the Dutch name for the Basic Law) yielded 3375 hits; the query 'EVRM' (ECHR) resulted in a little over 25,000 hits – about eight times as many.[79] To most Dutch constitutionalists, over 3000 cases on 'Grondwet' still seems to be an incredibly high number.

However, as became clear in section 10.4.3 above, the Basic Law is often only mentioned in the arguments of the courts as a 'ritual statement', meant to demonstrate the importance of the issue. In many cases, one of the parties involved briefly refers to the Basic Law, again mainly to state the importance of the issue, but the court does not even mention it in the arguments deciding the case. The ECHR is not only mentioned eight times more often, but also has more practical relevance. The notion of proportionality is actually applied by Dutch courts to decide cases relating to limitation of fundamental rights (see section 10.7).

Several other treaties also contain provisions that are binding on everyone. Most of the rights protected in the ICPPR[80] are considered to be binding on everyone, as well as provisions in various anti-discrimination treaties and some ILO conventions. The rights laid down in the EU Charter of Fundamental Rights[81] are considered to be binding on everyone, not on the basis of the relevant provisions of the Basic Law, but based on EU law itself. So far, none of these treaties has

77 M. Claes, G. Leenknegt, 'A Case of Constitutional Leapfrog: Fundamental Rights Protection under the Constitution, The ECHR and the EU Charter in the Netherlands' in P. Popelier (ed.), *The Interaction Between the European and the National Courts* (Intersentia 2011) 301 ff. See also leidenlawblog.nl/articles/on-the-lack-of-a-constitutional-court-and-the-constitutionalisation-of-the (last accessed 23 August 2015).

78 Claes and Leenknegt (n 77) 287–308.

79 Queries performed on 10 February 2015.

80 International Covenant on Civil and Political Rights, adopted and opened for signature, ratification and accession by General Assembly resolution 2200A (XXI) of 16 December 1966, entry into force 23 March 1976, in accordance with art 49 http://www.ohchr.org/en/professionalinterest/pages/ccpr.aspx (last accessed 24 August 2015).

81 European Union, *Charter of Fundamental Rights of the European Union* (26 October 2012) 2012/C 326/02 http://www.refworld.org/docid/3ae6b3b70.html (last accessed 24 August 2015) OJ 18 December 2000 (2000/C 364/01). The Charter became legally binding when the Treaty of Lisbon entered into force on 1 December 2009, as the Treaty confers on the Charter the same legal value as the Treaties.

acquired a status comparable to the ECHR in Dutch legal practice. With the exception of the EU Charter, which has only relatively recently acquired the status of binding EU law, this is probably caused by the absence of dedicated courts such as the ECtHR, and the obvious lack of an existing body of case law thereof.

10.6.2 The ECtHR, the CJEU and Dutch national courts: a 'constitutional dialogue'?

Together, Dutch national courts and European courts have to ensure a correct interpretation and application of national and European human rights law. Recently, the legal practice in the field of human rights protection has been characterised in terms of judicial or constitutional dialogues. Indeed, various forms of information exchange between courts exist, both institutionalised and informal – although not all of those may be called true dialogues.[82]

First of all, the preliminary ruling procedure with the EU context (Article 267 of the Treaty on the Functioning of the EU[83]) may be seen as the most important institutionalised dialogue between national courts and the CJEU. The procedure serves to ensure a correct and uniform interpretation and application of EU law by national courts. However, a true dialogue is characterised by reciprocity of communications and equality of participants. The preliminary rulings procedure does not fit these characteristics very well: a national court asks a question concerning the interpretation of EU law, and the CJEU answers that question. The ruling is a binding decision of the CJEU, which ends the discussion on the question that was asked (unless a new question is asked).[84] Whether the national court agrees or not is irrelevant. Therefore, the preliminary rulings procedure should rather be characterised as a 'prescriptive monologue'.[85]

A dialogue in the sense of an exchange of views and perspectives on the interpretation and application of national law, the ECHR and EU law can be found to some extent in the way national courts deal with the case law of both European

82 On this topic see A. S. Muller and M. A. Loth (eds), *Highest Courts and the Internationalisation of Law: Challenges and Changes* (Hague Academic Press 2009); Sam Muller and Sidney Richards (eds), *Highest Courts and Globalisation* (Hague Academic Press 2010); E. Mak, *Judicial Decision-making in a Globalized World: a Comparative Analysis of the Changing Practices of Western Highest Courts* (Hart Publishing 2013); Maartje de Visser, 'Changing the conversation in the Netherlands?' in M. Claes and others (eds), *Constitutional Conversations in Europe: Actors, Topics and Procedures* (Intersentia Publishing 2012) 343–45.

83 Formerly known as the EC Treaty, the Treaty of Rome or the Treaty establishing the European Community. The TFEU was given its name and amended by the Lisbon Treaty of 2009. The TFEU sets out organisational and functional details of the European Union.

84 Marc Loth, *De Hoge Raad in dialoog; over rechtsvorming in een gelaagde rechtsorde* (Tilburg University 2014) 25; M. Claes and M. de Visser, 'Are you networked yet? On dialogues in European judicial networks' (2012) 8(2) *Utrecht Law Review* 104 http://www.utrechtlawreview.org (last accessed 26 August 2015).

85 Elina Paunio, 'Conflict, power, and understanding: judicial dialogue between the ECJ and national courts' (2010) 7 *NoFo* 21 http://www.helsinki.fi/nofo/NoFo7Paunio.pdf (last accessed 26 August 2015).

courts. Loth distinguishes between a 'cooperative' and a 'competitive' position of national courts in the dialogue with European courts.[86] National constitutional courts, he argues, often tend to take a more competitive position towards European courts, as they perceive themselves as the 'guardians' of the domestic constitutional order, and consider it their task to protect that order against the influence of international and European law.

Dutch courts generally tend to take a more cooperative position, as they try to interpret Dutch law in accordance with the case law of European and international courts and tribunals, and to reconcile the domestic and European legal orders in their decisions. Gerards has found evidence that, whilst doing so, Dutch courts generally (although not specifically in relation to ICT-related issues) tend to interpret the fundamental rights provisions in the Basic Law in accordance with the corresponding provisions of the ECHR and the case law of the ECtHR, even where the Basic Law could theoretically provide additional protection.[87] In other words, when the Basic Law could provide a higher level of protection than the ECHR, the interpretation of the ECHR by the ECtHR is adopted by Dutch courts in the application of the Basic Law, which may then actually limit the scope of the potential fundamental rights protection under the Basic Law.

Furthermore, Dutch courts, tribunals and justices are active participants in various judicial network organisations, such as the European Judicial Network (EJN), Eurojust, the European Judicial Network in Civil and Commercial Matters (EJNCCM), the Association of the Councils of State and Supreme Administrative Jurisdictions of the European Union, the Conference of European Constitutional Courts (CECC; the Dutch Supreme Court is a member of this network, although it is not truly a constitutional court) and the Association of European Competition Law Judges (AECLJ).

Finally, there are, of course, many informal contacts between national and European justices, through *symposia*, academic conferences and other forums that provide opportunities to exchange information and perspectives. Informal judicial networks have emerged. However, these emerging networks of national and European courts seem to be hampered by the typical, generally somewhat conservative character of the judicial profession and of individual justices.

There seems to be a reluctance to share personal views on concrete cases or issues, and a reluctance to adopt perspectives or interpretations that are foreign to the national legal tradition and discourse. As Claes and De Visser put it, the notion of a judicial network itself is, at least to some extent, 'perceived to offend against traditional notions of judicial independence, legal order, hierarchy, ultimate authority and uniformity'.[88] As a result, the exact influence of these informal networks on the interpretation of domestic and European human rights law is unclear.

86 Loth (n 84) 17 ff.

87 J. Gerards, 'Samenloop van nationale en Europese grondrechtenbepalingen: hoe moet de rechter daarmee omgaan?' (2010) 3 *Tijdschrift voor Constitutioneel Recht* 224–55.

88 Claes andDe Visser (n 84) 113.

10.7 Application of the ECHR and the EU Charter by Dutch courts: relevant case law

As shown above, Dutch courts – including lower courts and courts of appeal – frequently refer to the ECHR in cases that involve fundamental rights. The EU Charter of Human Rights has gained importance for Dutch legal practice since 2009,[89] but still often only serves as an 'extra' reference, in order to underline the significance and importance of a right that is protected by the Basic Law and by the ECHR.[90] Usually, the arguments of Dutch courts focus on the application of the relevant ECHR provisions. The provisions of the Charter that correspond to rights protected in the ECHR are generally supposed to provide a level of protection that is equivalent to the ECHR.[91] Dutch courts tend to conclude this as they mention the Charter, and then focus on the ECHR, probably because the case law of the ECtHR provides them with a solid basis on which to build their arguments.

It is important to note that almost all of the Dutch case law related to the internet is about conflicts between natural or legal persons: in most cases, no state institution is directly involved. Conflicts in relation to the internet that involve fundamental rights are then framed and treated as 'standard' private law issues, such as questions regarding tort, wrongful acts, fairness, due care, proper employer/employee relationships or questions of property. Consequently, the rights laid down in the ECHR or the EU Charter are applied in an *indirect* way.

The Basic Law and the ECHR – and, increasingly, the EU Charter – mainly serve to label certain interests of the parties involved, and to stress the relative weight of those interests in relation to other factors or circumstances. Courts then balance all the interests involved to decide the case. This is generally not done in a very systematic way; the specific circumstances of each case may determine the balance that must be struck according to the court.

The notion of proportionality is sometimes used explicitly, but in other cases it seems to be used in a more implicit way. The proportionality principle does not feature in the Basic Law with respect to the limitation of fundamental rights. It is adopted from the ECHR context, often without an explicit reference, and it seems to have become part of the standard toolbox of Dutch courts. Some interesting examples of cases where the ECHR is applied in a more explicit fashion are discussed below.[92]

89 The EU Charter of Human Rights has become a legally binding instrument with the entry into force of the Lisbon Treaty, 1 December 2009. Before that date, it was sometimes referred to by Dutch courts, but only as a non-binding resolution, or a form of 'soft law' in the interpretation of EU law; see Claes/Leenknegt 2011.

90 For an example see Rechtbank Arnhem, 7 July 2011, http://uitspraken.rechtspraak.nl/inziendocument?id=ECLI:NL:RBARN:2011:BR0659 (last accessed 23 August 2015).

91 As expressed in art 52(3) of the EU Charter of fundamental rights. For an example, in Dutch case law see Afdeling bestuursrechtspraak Raad van State (17 April 2013) ECLI:NL:RVS:2013:BZ8388.

92 For an overview of ICT-related case law, arranged by subject (in Dutch) see http://internetrechtspraak.wikispaces.com/home (last accessed 26 August 2015).

10.7.1 'The right to be forgotten': application of the Google Spain case

In 2014, a Dutch national asked Google Search to remove links to websites containing data about a conviction for a serious crime, dating from 2012. He based his request on Articles 36 and 40 of the Dutch Data Protection Act (Wet bescherming persoonsgegevens). According to that Act, a person has the right to request correction or removal of data, when these data are incorrect, incomplete or irrelevant. The plaintiff also referred to the *Google Spain* case[93] of the CJEU, and the 'right to be forgotten' that was – arguably – established by that case. The Dutch court applied the *Google Spain* case, explicitly stating that the Data Protection Act is to be interpreted in accordance with the EU Privacy Directive, and with the judgment of the CJEU in the *Google Spain* case. It quoted the CJEU, arguing that one may request to remove or erase results that are 'inadequate, irrelevant, no longer relevant, or excessive in relation to the purpose of their processing'. The court further noted that in this case the right to privacy of the plaintiff is protected by Article 8 of the ECHR, whilst the freedom of speech of Google Inc. is protected by Article 10 of the ECHR and – lastly – by Article 7 of the Basic Law.

The Dutch court did not elaborate on the exact scope and meaning of these provisions; Articles 7 and 8 of the EU Charter, to which the CJEU referred in the *Google Spain* case, were not even mentioned. The Court then argued that, generally, negative publicity resulting from a serious crime committed by a person is relevant information, and will be so permanently. According to the court, the plaintiff had not proved that the information was excessively defamatory in this specific case; therefore, Google was not required to remove the data of the convicted man, or the links to those data.

Another interesting aspect of this case concerned the auto complete function Google Search provides when entering a query. According to the plaintiff, this function automatically linked his name to the name of a well-known Dutch crime fighter and private detective. He wanted that link to be removed, too. That request was also refused by the court. It argued that the combinations provided by the auto complete function do not constitute additional information on the person involved, but merely reflect connections between existing information that have already been made by others, whilst searching for information.[94]

10.7.2 Unlawful publications on the internet

The lawfulness of publications on the internet is frequently questioned before Dutch courts. In most cases, as mentioned above, the rights laid down in the Basic Law and the ECHR are applied by the courts in an indirect way. Courts

93 Case C–131/12 Google Spain SL and Google Inc v Agencia Española de Protección de Datos (AEPD) and Mario Costeja González CJEU (13 May 2014) http://eur-lex.europa.eu/legal-content/EN/TXT/?uri=CELEX:62012CJ0131 (last accessed 26 August 2015).

94 Rechtbank Amsterdam (18 September 2014) ECLI:NL:RBAMS:2014:6118.

generally treat these issues as typical private law cases of tort or wrongful act; courts balance the interests involved, including the freedom of expression and the right to privacy, and take into account all other circumstances specific to each case. Sometimes Articles 8 and 10 of the ECHR are explicitly mentioned; in other cases, the applicable rights and freedoms are quoted without reference to the ECHR.[95]

In one case, however, the court opted for a more explicit and direct application of the ECHR. It concerned the publication of a portrait without the permission of the person depicted. The photograph that was published in a newspaper, both on paper and in the web version, was actually a still taken from a documentary that had previously been broadcast on TV and on the internet. The court debated the balance that is to be struck between the right to privacy on the one hand, and the freedom of speech and the freedom of the press on the other; reference was made to Articles 8 and 10 of the ECHR.

The court noted that if one of these rights is to prevail, the other will be violated, and that this may be justified by the need to protect the rights of others, as is expressed in sub-section 2 of Articles 8 and 10. The courts then argued that, in the circumstances of this particular case, the publication of the photograph was unnecessary in relation to the aim thereof, and therefore it was not proportional. This is a rare example of a direct application of the limitation clauses of the ECHR in a private law case. Also notable is that the court reasoned fully in terms of the ECHR, whilst the Basic Law, which protects these very same rights, was not even mentioned.[96]

10.7.3 Criminal sanctions for offensive texts on the internet

A notable criminal case concerns an individual who published various offensive texts on a web forum, including discrimination of homosexuals, racial discrimination, anti-Semitism and Islamophobic texts. Publications of that sort are punishable under, inter alia, Articles 137c–e of the Dutch Criminal Code, and the author was prosecuted. The district court discussed Article 10 of the ECHR in order to establish the proportionality of a limitation in the form of a criminal sanction. Interestingly, the court distinguished between information on the internet that is 'forced' upon a person (through pop-ups, deceiving web links, etc.), and information one has to search for actively. As the information was published on a web forum with a semi-public character, taking notice of the offensive information could be avoided by simply not visiting that website. Therefore, the court decided that there was no 'pressing social need' in this case to impose a criminal sanction.[97]

95 Some examples include: Rechtbank Gelderland (21 October 2014) ECLI:NL:RBGEL:2014:6662; Rechtbank Rotterdam (20 August 2014) ECLI:NL:RBROT:2014:8043; Rechtbank Amsterdam (10 September 2014) ECLI:NL:RBAMS:2014:5809; and Rechtbank Haarlem (2 August 2012) ECLI:NL:RBHAA:2012:BX9028.

96 HR (4 October 2013) ECLI:NL:HR:2013:851.

97 Rechtbank Amsterdam (2 June 2008) ECLI:NL:RBAMS:2008:BD2977.

The Court of Appeal, however, took a different view: it stated that the internet is a medium that reaches a very broad audience. The fact that offensive information can only be found after an active search is irrelevant. The court focused purely on the content of the information. With reference to the ECtHR decisions in the *Gündüz*[98] and *Erbakan*[99] cases, it concluded that a criminal sanction was justified by the severely offensive character of the published texts.[100]

10.8 General conclusions

In the Netherlands, constitutionalisation of emerging principles in relation to the internet does not take place through judicial debate. Dutch courts do encounter issues related to the internet that may raise questions regarding the interpretation and application of fundamental rights provisions, both in the Basic Law and in international treaties, but that very seldom leads to a serious judicial debate on the significance of those rights and freedoms in relation to technological developments. Generally, there is a low 'constitutional consciousness' amongst Dutch courts and justices.

Questions that are essentially of a constitutional nature are dealt with by applying and interpreting the relevant ordinary legislation, or by balancing the interests of the parties involved within the framework of existing private law concepts, such as tort, wrongful act, fairness, due care, or reason and equity. This in fact comes down to the application and interpretation of open norms in the Dutch Civil Code. In other words, the protection of fundamental rights in relation to the internet, especially when new questions are raised and new solutions must be found, is first and foremost a task of the legislature. The debate on those issues is therefore mainly a political debate, taking place during the preparation of new legislative provisions, or is the process of proposing amendments to the Basic Law in the light of rapid technological developments.

The main reason for that is, of course, that Dutch courts have no constitutional jurisdiction with respect to Acts of Parliament: Article 120 of the Basic Law forbids the constitutional review of those Acts by the courts. Equally important is the fact that Article 94 obliges the courts to apply provisions of treaties that are binding on every person, and to set aside conflicting national law – including the Basic Law itself. As a consequence, the ECHR functions as a 'substitute constitution', or a 'Bill of Rights' in Dutch constitutional law; the EU Charter of Fundamental Rights is gaining importance in that respect, too.

Ordinary legislation and even the Basic Law itself are interpreted in accordance with the case law of the ECtHR and the CJEU. The ECHR has made the Basic

98 *Müslüm Gündüz v Turkey* Application no. 35071/97 of 4 December 2003, Judgment of the European Court of Human Rights (First Section) http://hudoc.echr.coe.int/sites/eng/pages/search.aspx?i=001-61522 (last accessed 26 August 2015).

99 *Erbakan v Turkey* Application no. 59405/00 of 6 July 2006, Judgment of the European Court of Human Rights (First Section) http://hudoc.echr.coe.int/sites/eng/pages/search.aspx?i=003-1728198-1812055 (last accessed 26 August 2015).

100 Hof Amsterdam (23 November 2009) ECLI:NL:GHAMS:2009:BK4139.

Law practically redundant in the legal debate on fundamental rights in relation to the internet. Dutch courts tend to take a cooperative position in relation to European courts, as they seem to be concerned mainly with a proper application of the ECHR and of EU law. Finally, Dutch courts seem to be reactive, not proactive, with regard to the development of new constitutional principles.

New technological developments may lead to changes in ordinary legislation, such as the codification of the principle of net neutrality, or guarantees for access to the internet. Or, if this legislative process is too slow to keep up with developments in the digital world, the courts interpret existing legislation in accordance with the case law of the ECtHR, and applicable EU law. Possibly, in due time, new principles may be deemed 'constitutionally ripe', which is a rather unclear and to some extent political concept. Constitutional ripeness seems to have become the most important criterion in order to determine whether new legal rules are to be constitutionalised. Principles that are deemed constitutionally ripe, may theoretically be codified in the Basic Law; but because it has a very rigid character, and because finding a broad agreement in Parliament on the exact wording of the provision that is to be added can prove very difficult, this seldom succeeds, and often takes years or even decades.

Concluding remarks

Internet law, protection of fundamental rights and the role of constitutional adjudication*

Oreste Pollicino and Graziella Romeo

1 Models of constitutional review and judicial law: making in comparative perspective

There are at least two reasons why this book chooses to resort to constitutional law in order to analyse contemporary developments of the internet regime, at both national and supranational levels. The first is the attempt to define a global regime of the internet at a time in which the World Wide Web continues to be an essentially state-dominated set of rules.[1] The second reason is the propagation of methods of constitutional adjudication[2] that makes the courts particularly fitting in the role of consolidators of transnational principles governing the internet, especially when those principles impact on the protection of fundamental rights. In other words, constitutional law doctrine, which maintains the proliferation of constitutional adjudication, supports the need for analysing the development of contemporary legal issues (such as the law of the internet) from the perspective of the judicial review performed by domestic constitutional courts, as well as by supranational courts.

Today, in fact more than ever, courts occupy a privileged position within their respective legal orders that enables them to identify the risk of potential collisions that may encroach upon the effective protection of fundamental rights between interconnected legal systems. Consequently, they can forge closer ties between different yet interacting systems. The crucial position of the courts is amplified even further with regard to the protection of fundamental rights in the digital age.

Indeed, the reluctance that courts have traditionally shown in addressing cases involving the technology issue – which probably depends on the difficulty of handling phenomena that alter the application of existing laws[3] – is somehow less

* Oreste Pollicino wrote sections 3 and 4; Graziella Romeo wrote sections 2 and 5. Section 1 is the result of thoughts shared by the two co-authors.

1 Gunther Teubner, 'Societal constitutionalism: alternatives to state-centred constitutional theory' *Storrs Lectures* 2003/04, Yale Law School.

2 Leonard Besselink, 'The proliferation of constitutional law and constitutional adjudication, or how American judicial review came to Europe after all' (2013) 9 *Utrecht Law Review* 19.

3 See Jane Bailey, 'Of mediums and metaphors: how a layered methodology might contribute to

strong in the case of the internet.[4] Looking at the case law, it seems that there are at least three distinct reasons why the World Wide Web is different from other technologies: the quantitative dimension of information that can be broadcast and accessed through the internet,[5] sometimes even anonymously; the aptitude of the internet technology for being combined with other technology amplifying the overall impact of their uses[6] and, finally, the 'fleeting nature' of internet disputes, which often raise problems of jurisdiction and urge the courts to fill in the gaps that might otherwise remain unregulated by both courts and legislatures.

The pivotal role of courts is the result of two peculiarities of the relationship between the internet phenomenon and law. The first peculiarity is substantive in nature and concerns the awareness that legal reforms tend to lag behind technological advances. The burden of making up for the legislative inertia falls heavily on the shoulders of the courts.

However, from our perspective, the novelty of the factual and legal context created by the internet is even more interesting. Indeed, this is the main reason explaining why the courts increasingly seek assistance and inspiration with counterparts of different, yet interconnected, legal orders when addressing the protection of fundamental rights on the internet, even more than they do in the analogue world.

The second reason underlying the choice to focus on interaction between courts is procedural in nature and is related to the jurisdictional issues brought about by the rise of the World Wide Web, which have had crucial implications for the protection of fundamental rights and led to a further amplification of the 'judicial dimension' in the field.

The attitude of both domestic and supranational courts towards the problem of jurisdiction confirms their role as pioneers in addressing internet issues. The recent developments in the Court of Justice of the European Union (CJEU) case law are a good example of that attitude. The CJEU developed a doctrine, which tends to affirm jurisdiction in a broad range of cases.[7] Leaning on an extensive interpretation of the notion of controller, which includes the search-engine operator, the judges of Luxembourg affirmed, de facto, even if formally the reference is still to the advertising EU-based activity performed by a non-EU company, to have jurisdiction in all cases in which data of an individual residing in the EU are processed, regardless of both the place in which the data processing server is located and the place in which the processing activity has been performed.

constitutional analysis of internet content regulation' (2003–2004) 30 *Manitoba Law Journal* 198–99.

4 See Lawrence Lessig, 'Reading the constitution in cyberspace' (1996) 45 *Emory Law Journal* 869.

5 See *Mouvement Raëlien Suisse v Switzerland* Application no. 16354/06 (ECtHR 2012) §§ 54–58. On the issue see also Caleb Mason, 'Framing context, anonymous internet speech, and intent: new uncertainty about the constitutional test for true threats' (2011) 41 *Southwestern Law Review* 43–118.

6 See *Riley v California* 134 S Ct 2473 (2014).

7 See Case C–131/12 Google Spain SL and Google Inc v Agencia Española de Protección de Datos (AEPD) and Mario Costeja González CJEU (13 May 2014) para. 4.

In other words, the Court has been able to expand to such a degree the notion of 'context of activity', related to the data processing, to find always a relevant context in the European Union to which the application of EU legislation could be connected.

Indeed, the trend towards a far-reaching concept of jurisdiction has never been so steady. However, other courts both in Europe and in the US have developed doctrines of jurisdiction, which require at least the relevant activity to be performed (even at a minimum level) in the territory whose jurisdiction is claimed. From this perspective, the CJEU's approach shows more judicial activism when compared with the other national and supranational jurisdictions.

Dealing with cases not specifically concerning the processing of data but rather e-commerce and the dissemination of obscene materials, other jurisdictions have applied slightly different approaches. In the US, as Land's chapter points out, the notion of personal jurisdiction implies that an action sufficiently purposeful toward a specific forum to establish a minimum contact enables US judges to affirm their jurisdiction if it would be consistent with traditional notions of fair play and substantial justice.

In the Council of Europe system, jurisdictional issues are even more complicated, especially in cybercrime cases, as Van de Heyning's chapter elucidates, also due to the wide margin of decision-making left to the Member States. Within this context, the European Court of Human Rights (ECtHR) clarified that the jurisdiction *ratione loci* is affirmed as regards ideas and information received through the internet in the territory of a contracting state, irrespective of the location from which they have been disseminated.[8] On the contrary, the Court of Strasbourg denied jurisdiction in those cases in which the receiving person showed no jurisdictional link with the territory of a Member State.[9]

Defining jurisdiction is a key issue in understanding how the protection of fundamental rights in the digital environment is performed in concrete terms. It is, however, a starting point. The trend towards the exercise of jurisdiction indeed is one of the indicators of the crucial relevance of courts, especially those vested with constitutional-like powers, in this field. The other indicators are connected to the courts' ability to frame the internet in a way that makes the use of legal categories feasible for a naturally anarchic medium.

2 'Framing', argumentation and legal categories in internet-related disputes

The conceptual path that has been followed throughout the book is shaped around the scheme of constitutional argumentation techniques. Identifying

8 See *Perrin v UK* Application no. 5446/03 (ECtHR 2005). See also Nina Vajić and Panayotis Vojatzis, 'The internet and freedom of expression: a "brave new world" and the ECtHR's evolving case law' in Josep Casadevall (ed.), *Freedom of Expression: Essays in Honour of Nicolas Bratza, President of the European Court of Human Rights* (Wolf Legal Publishers 2012) 402–03.

9 See *Ben El Mahi v Denmark* Application no. 5853/06 (ECtHR 2006).

models of constitutional adjudication for the purpose of carrying out this kind of analysis of the relevant case law has been interpreted as a necessary conceptual tool in a twofold perspective: on the one hand modelling constitutional adjudication explains the overall nature of the judicial approach[10] to internet issues; on the other it highlights the leading models in adjudication of fundamental rights in the digital era.

More specifically, the resort to a systematisation of constitutional adjudication models explains why the regulation of the internet follows a policy-centred approach in legal orders such as Italy or France, or a rights-centred approach in different cases, such as the UK one. As Paolo Passaglia argued, the structure of the constitutional adjudication in Italy has put the Constitutional Court in the position of adjudicating issues concerning the internet regulation at large (including the distribution of powers between territorial authorities), rather than issues directly related to the protection of fundamental rights. Moreover, the preference for regulating the internet through secondary legislation, which is excluded from constitutional review within the Italian system, prevented the development of a significant case law concerning the exercise of fundamental rights in the internet.

The courts' activism or deference can, however, affect the ability to develop a doctrine on fundamental rights, even where the system of constitutional adjudication does not help shaping issues around rights, as the French case – extensively discussed in Passaglia's chapter – clearly shows.

The assumption behind this book is that the analysis of the constitutional case law through judicial argumentation is capable of fully explaining and clarifying courts' reasoning in technological law cases only when combined with the analysis of judicial framing. Whenever judges are confronted with issues requiring a certain amount of technical expertise not specifically related to the law domain, judicial decision-making processes are influenced by the *contextualisation* of a given issue, arising from real life, in a legal frame.[11] As Sajó and Ryan have put it: 'There is nothing new in this act of judicial framing. The real challenge comes when judges (or legislators) are confronted with unexpected, unpleasant or ambiguous social and economic consequences of technology.'

This framing activity is crucial when it comes to shaping the legal argumentation. Authors addressing the framing in internet law generally refer to the cognitive activity of 'connecting outside context or cognitive structure to the context of the case through effective language, emphasis, and other techniques',[12] thus linking the framing with the recurrence of words, lemmas or rhetoric formulas. This approach seems to be capable of highlighting the ideological bias of some decisions: the use of the term 'piracy' in copyright infringement disputes related to the peer-to-peer exchange of data reveals a pro-corporation approach

10 On this issue see Michael Rosenfeld, 'Comparing constitutional review by the European Court of Justice and the Supreme Court' (2006) 4 *International Journal of Constitutional Law* 618.

11 See Chris Riley, 'The rite of rhetoric: cognitive framing in technology law' (2008–2009) 9 *Nevada Law Journal* 495.

12 See *Riley* (n 6) 502.

in the sense that it points out the illegal conduct of those who share files on the internet by referring to an activity that is typically classified as unlawful and prohibited.

Similarly, the insistent resort to the word 'privacy' in data-protection disputes refers to the need to protect against public intrusion and tends to assign prevalence to the individual interests rather than to the public ones. This method assumes the need to identify extremely significant words or lemmas that explain or clarify the hidden frame of judges.

Although this approach relies on an accurate and systematic analysis of the case law, it overestimates two components of the framing: the individual attitude (relying on a sort of 'radical subjectivism')[13] and the influence of parties' argumentations that inevitably contribute to shape the final argumentation developed by the courts. Inferring the framing from the use of specific words, that is, inferring contextualisation by the mere resort to rhetoric is somehow misleading to the extent to which such usage is not specifically connected with the overall argumentation.

The approach developed here follows a different path: it recognises the role of framing in internet disputes connecting the framing to the argumentation in a bi-directional fashion: starting from argumentation and extrapolating the framing with a view to understanding how the technology issue has been contextualised in constitutional adjudication, disregarding in principle the use of typical words or lemmas.

Framing is not necessarily linked to an ex ante option for a certain theory concerning law and technology. Courts do not necessarily support the instrumental theory or the substantive theory, which respectively conceive of technology as a tool with zero impact on the social community or, alternatively, as an instrument capable of controlling the social community, side-lining the 'human factor'.[14]

The Polish case can serve as a good example:[15] when the Constitutional Tribunal addressed the protection of personal data on the internet, it stated that the World Wide Web is 'a new form of human activity' connecting the use of the internet to one of the possible way in which an individual expresses himself. This statement represents the general frame within which the Polish Constitutional Tribunal places the decision over the constitutional protection of communication performed on the internet.

From this frame, the Polish judges have derived a principle of 'technological neutrality of the Constitution', which assumes that the internet does not deserve a brand new form of legal (or constitutional) protection, being no different from any other traditional form of communication for the purpose of the identification of applicable principles and norms. The Polish Constitutional Court echoes in

13 See Richard A. Posner, 'The law of the beholder' *New Republic* (16 October 2000) 49 and *Riley* (n 6) 501.

14 Arthur Cockfield and Jason Pridmore, 'A synthetic theory of law and technology' (2007) 8 *Minnesota Journal of Law, Science & Technology* 475.

15 See Krystyna Kowalik's chapter (ch 8).

this way the instrumental theories, which in principle do not assume that the use of technologies has significant social, cultural and political impact, even though this assumption is probably beyond the Polish judges' intent.

The same attitude to frame the internet essentially as a space in which individuals express themselves leads the German Constitutional Court to a different outcome,[16] acknowledging the distinctive features of the World Wide Web and elaborating a new category of right, that is the right to confidentiality and integrity of IT systems.[17]

Framing can easily change the outcome of a case: conceiving of the internet as primarily a medium to broadcast information lead Dutch courts to punish the author of offensive texts even in the case of a web forum with a semi-public character, that is even if the access to the violent content could have been easily avoided. On the contrary, when courts interpret internet as a communication and information tool in which users can freely choose the content they want to reach or use, the offensive nature of a publication does not raise personal responsibility insofar the search implies an active and voluntary (not forced) conduct.[18]

A similar dichotomy arises from the European Court of Human Rights' case law on the one hand and the US Supreme Court on the other. The latter, more precisely, seems to point out how this new medium opens up new forms of exercise of (traditional) freedoms.[19] This assumption bears consequences, as will be clarified later, on the standards of judicial scrutiny applied in an internet dispute. Indeed, the regulation of the internet deserves a kind of strict scrutiny as 'the interest in encouraging freedom of expression in a democratic society outweighs any theoretical but unproven benefit of censorship'.[20] The former, on the contrary, seems to endorse a view in which the underpinning frame is based on the risks related to the use of the new technologies.

In the next section the above-mentioned dichotomy will be addressed with specific reference to substantial issues emerging in the relevant case law. Eventually, the partially more nuanced position of the CJEU will be analysed.

16 See BVerfG, Urt (27 February 2008) BVerfGE 120, 274, see András Jori's chapter (ch 7).

17 The BVerfG specified that the inviolability of home (art 13(1) GG) covers surveillance 'inside' the dwelling, but 'insofar as the infiltration uses the connection of the computer concerned to form a computer network, it leaves the spatial privacy provided by delimitation of the dwelling unaffected'; see András Jori's chapter (ch 7).

18 See Rechtbank Amsterdam (18 September 2014) ECLI:NL:RBAMS:2014:6118; see Gert-Jan Leenknegt's chapter (ch 10).

19 See the well-known decision in *Reno v ACLU* 521 US 844 (1997). See also Oreste Pollicino, 'European judicial dialogue and the protection of fundamental rights in the new digital environment: an attempt at emancipation and reconciliation: the case of freedom of Speech' in Sonia Morando-Foadi and Lucy Vickers (eds), *Fundamental Rights in the EU: a Matter for Two Courts* (Hart 2015) 104.

20 See *Reno* (n 19) 885.

3 The framing in action: the case of freedom of expression in the internet

As emerges from Molly Land's chapter, the portrayal of the US situation reveals that the advent of the internet has resulted in a further enhancement of the already huge protection enjoyed by freedom of speech in the non-digital environment. Thus, the First Amendment has not only retained but even increased its value within the new digital context.

By contrast, in the most recent decisions adopted by ECtHR, it seems that the internet is seen (also) as a medium posing new potential risks to the protection of fundamental rights. In other words, the ECtHR seems to maintain – not univocally, as will be highlighted below – that the advent of the internet has further extended the ability to limit freedom of expression, provided that the conditions set out in Article 10(2) of the ECHR have been complied with by the national legislation.

The assumption that freedom of speech works as a watchdog for democracy appears to have been revisited or at least relativised, as the ECtHR seems to focus more on cases in which the internet is likely to pose new risks for the protection of fundamental rights (i.e. in which restrictions were then found to be justified) than to those in which the internet appeared as a new opportunity for the exercise of rights (i.e. in which free speech was thus to be upheld).

Even though the Court repeatedly held that the safe harbour entrusted to Article 10(2) must be construed strictly, the advent of the internet has resulted in greater consideration being paid to restrictions on free speech. Specifically, according to the ECtHR, the particular medium of the internet amplified threats to fundamental rights compared to the past. This point emerged, for the first time, in *Editorial Board of PravoyeDelo and Shtekel v Ukraine*,[21] a case concerning the particular segment of freedom of expression corresponding to freedom of the press:

> The risk of harm posed by content and communications on the internet to the exercise and enjoyment of human rights and freedoms, particularly the right to respect for private life, is certainly higher than that posed by the press. Therefore, the policies governing reproduction of material from the printed media and the internet may differ. The latter undeniably have to be adjusted according to technology's specific features in order to secure the protection and promotion of the rights and freedoms concerned.

The assumption behind the Court's reasoning is that the internet is likely to raise new problems for the protection of fundamental rights and that the measures applied to traditional media will not work effectively in the new digital environment. This means that a new balance must be struck between freedom of expression and other human rights. In a nutshell, since the internet is raising

21 *Editorial Board of PravoyeDelo and Shtekel v Ukraina* Application no. 33014/05 (ECtHR 2011).

unprecedented legal issues, restrictions on freedom of expression should be more broadly accepted.

This remark could per se be enough to describe how different the approach of the ECtHR is from that of the US Supreme Court, which expressed the completely opposite view in *Reno v ACLU*:[22]

> The record demonstrates that the growth of the Internet has been and continues to be phenomenal. As a matter of constitutional tradition, in the absence of evidence to the contrary, we presume that governmental regulation of the content of speech is more likely to interfere with the free exchange of ideas than to encourage it. The interest in encouraging freedom of expression in a democratic society outweighs any theoretical but unproven benefit of censorship.

In *KU v Finland*,[23] the Court also stressed the non-absolute nature of the protection of certain fundamental rights on the internet. The case concerned the dissemination of personal data relating to a child by an anonymous individual who had posted an online advertisement in which he claimed to be looking for a sexual relationship. When the applicant filed a complaint with the local court, there were no legal grounds under domestic law to force an ISP to disclose personal data in cases involving criminal conduct such as that at issue. In addition, the domestic legislation failed to strike a balance between the right to data protection and other interests. Although the complaint was not based on Article 10 of the ECHR, the ECtHR made significant remarks concerning the exercise of free speech on the internet:

> Although freedom of expression and confidentiality of communications are primary considerations and users of telecommunications and Internet services must have a guarantee that their own privacy and freedom of expression will be respected, such guarantee cannot be absolute and must yield on occasion to other legitimate imperatives, such as the prevention of disorder or crime or the protection of the rights and freedoms of others . . . [I]t is nonetheless the task of the legislator to provide the framework for reconciling the various claims which compete for protection in this context.

It is only when the limitations imposed on freedom of expression are excessive, compared with the aim pursued, that the Court has adopted a stricter approach. It did so for instance in *Ahmet Yildirim v Turkey*,[24] where the ECtHR concluded that Turkey had violated Article 10 of the Convention by imposing a disproportionate restriction on internet access. In criminal proceedings against the owner of a website on which expressions insulting Ataturk's memory had been posted,

22 See *Reno* (n 19) 885.
23 *KU v Finland* Application no. 2872/02 (ECtHR 2008).
24 *Ahmet Yildirim v Turkey* Application no. 3111/10 (ECtHR 2012).

an administrative authority had ordered that all Google sites be blocked in order to prevent access to the site in question, without ascertaining whether a less far-reaching measure could have been taken.

The applicant, who owned a website where his academic works were published and which was affected by the blocking order, alleged a violation of his right to freedom of expression. The Court noted that the blocking of a website is one of the legitimate restrictions that contracting states may adopt in accordance with Article 10(2) of the Convention, but only upon the condition that such a restriction meets the requirement referenced in that provision. In that case, there was neither a strict legal framework defining the scope of the ban nor any provision for judicial review.

The approach of the ECtHR has proved to be very cautious. On the one hand, it has concluded that Article 10 of the ECHR will be violated if the restrictions on freedom of expression do not comply with the conditions set out in Article 10(2). On the other hand, however, the Court has conceded that free speech is not an absolute, and does not enjoy greater protection compared with other fundamental rights: in fact, given the risks brought by the internet, it is more likely that freedom of expression may be limited than it would be in the non-digital context.

The same thinking lay behind the decision in the *Pirate Bay*[25] case, in which the ECtHR by contrast rejected an individual application based on Article 10 of the Convention. The applicants were the owners of a famous online platform, where users were provided with links enabling the illegal downloading of copyrighted materials through peer-to-peer systems. They had been convicted under the Swedish law forbidding copyright infringements, but complained that their right to freedom of expression had been violated. The Court ruled the complaint inadmissible, as the restriction imposed on free speech complied with the conditions set out in Article 10(2) of the Convention and which, in particular, was proportional to the legitimate aim pursued.[26]

Accordingly, the view taken by the Court of Strasbourg is that the advent of new technologies, and of the internet in particular, has not generally expanded the scope of freedom of expression. On the contrary, it has created more opportunities for this right to conflict with other interests protected under national constitutions.

This assertion can be confirmed, first, if we consider how the ECtHR reacted to the use of the internet with respect to the freedom of press, which is regarded as an essential pillar of freedom of speech and democracy. In the *Stoll* case,[27] the Court's reasoning was based on the assumption that new technologies have made the duties of journalists more demanding:

25 *Fredrik Neij and Peter SundeKolmisoppi (The Pirate Bay) v Sweden* Application no, 40397/12 (ECtHR 2013).

26 See also *Ashby Donald and Others v France* Application no. 36769/08 (ECtHR 2013).

27 *Stoll v Switzerland* Application no. 69698/01 (ECtHR 2007).

> [T]he safeguard afforded by Article 10 to journalists in relation to reporting on issues of general interest is subject to the proviso that they are acting in good faith and on an accurate factual basis and provide 'reliable and precise' information in accordance with the ethics of journalism . . . These considerations play a particularly important role nowadays, given the influence wielded by the media in contemporary society: not only do they inform, they can also suggest by the way in which they present the information how it is to be assessed. In a world in which the individual is confronted with vast quantities of information circulated via traditional and electronic media and involving an ever-growing number of players, monitoring compliance with journalistic ethics takes on added importance.

Furthermore, these observations are confirmed even if it is assumed that similar conduct also occurred in the non-digital realm. Recalling the case of *Yildirim v Turkey*, such a broad limitation of freedom of expression as that adopted by the Turkish authorities would not presumably have been necessary. If one single publication is found to be defamatory and there are legal grounds to prevent its circulation, the measures that must be adopted by the relevant authorities in the non-digital world must only relate to that particular publication, and not to others. In other words, there will be no reason to block additional online content – which is equivalent to offline seizure – instead of blocking only the content regarded as an unlawful exercise of freedom of expression.

Naturally, the issue of proportionality (which is the key factor here) is related to the nature of the technology. Moreover, it is one of the leading factors, which means that it is critical for the protection of freedom of expression on the internet.

The application of the proportionality principle was also crucial in the recent case of *Delfi v Estonia*,[28] in which the ECtHR was asked to consider whether fines imposed on an internet news portal for defamatory comments posted by users, which the website failed to remove promptly, amounted to a restriction of freedom of expression. The Strasbourg Court found that Article 10 of the Convention does not afford protection to freedom of expression in absolute terms. Rather, Article 10 allows Member States to interfere with the exercise of this right, provided that the said restrictions meet the conditions under Article 10(2), namely that: (i) they are prescribed by law; (ii) they have a legitimate aim; and (iii) they are necessary in a democratic society.

It is important to highlight that, whilst the Court held that the legislation at stake imposed a significant restriction, it nevertheless found that it did not violate Article 10 of the ECHR. Since, in the Court's view, the protection of individual reputations ranks amongst the objectives that may justify a limitation on freedom of expression, it held that there had been no infringement of Article 10 of the Convention because the interference was proportionate.

28 *Delfi v Estonia* Application no. 64569/09 (ECtHR 2013). It should be pointed out that the Chamber's decision in *Delfi* was appealed to the Grand Chamber, whose decision has recently been handed down.

The Grand Chamber, which has very recently[29] handed down its judgment in the *Delfi* case, confirmed the position of the Chamber: the national measure did not constitute a disproportionate restriction on the applicant company's right to freedom of expression. Accordingly, there has been no violation of Article 10 of the Convention.

The reasoning of the Court confirms the twofold characterisation that the Strasbourg judges seem to give to the internet, which is described at the same time as 'an unprecedented platform for the exercise of freedom of expression' and a medium posing 'certain danger'.[30] It should be also added that the overall perception from the judgment is that the latter perspective tends to prevail on the former one. It is noteworthy, in this regard, that the joint dissenting opinion of Judges Sajó and Tsotsoria critically focuses on this issue, namely that the result of the case has been quite clearly influenced by the overall framing of the specific technological medium at stake.

The assertion of civil liability of the intermediary rested upon the idea that the internet is uniquely dangerous. On the opposite side of the possible spectrum of ideas, the two dissenting judges argue that the internet is 'a sphere of robust public discourse with novel opportunities for enhanced democracy'.[31] Regarding the less restrictive alternative test, they added that: 'some justification is needed to explain why only the equivalent of prior restraint and absolute liability satisfies the non-specific duties and responsibilities of active intermediaries'.

The US Supreme Court's radically different approach cannot be explained simply on the basis of the well-known unique sensitivity that the common-law tradition has developed towards the issue of free speech. Even in the UK, judges seem to uphold a view that is similar to that of the Court of Strasbourg, although sometimes it is assertively connected to the body of common-law principles much more than to the influence of the ECtHR.[32] Rowbottom's chapter explains the relationship between Article 10 ECHR case law and the UK judges' approach to freedom of expression in digital communication, underlining a trend towards a double standard in the protection of free speech, largely owed to the influence of the ECtHR.

More precisely, speeches with an intrinsic public or political nature are valued, whilst remarks not providing benefits to the audience are interpreted as not worthy of the same level of protection. More recently, however, domestic courts are increasingly distancing themselves from Strasbourg case law, recognising the need to *contextualise* the speech in the specific medium of the internet and arguing for a higher threshold of harm that should be required to limit the exercise of the freedom of (digital) expression. Once again, where the internet phenomenon is concerned, framing activity plays an important role in judicial outcomes.

29 See *Delfi AS v Estonia* Application no. 64569/09 (ECtHR 2015).

30 ibid para. 110.

31 ibid para. 6, Joint dissenting opinion of Judges Sajó and Tsotsoria.

32 See *Kennedy v Charity Commission* [2014] UKSC 20, [2014] 2 WLR 808 at [46]; see Jacob Rombottom's chapter (ch 9).

4 A litmus test: balancing and fundamental rights-based approach in the EU

How would the CJEU have ruled in a case such as *Delfi*? This question, which has also been touched upon by Barata and Bassini, is crucial in introducing the European Union situation against the background that, as we have seen, characterises the ECtHR legal system and those jurisdictions that are more sensitive towards the Court of Strasbourg case law.

As noted in the previous section, the case involved a claim by the owner of an internet news portal company, which had been sentenced in relation to defamatory statements posted by users as comments to an article. The ECtHR held that there had been no violation of Article 10.

From a perspective other than scrutiny based on Article 10, the CJEU would have taken into account the e-Commerce Directive (Directive 2000/31/EC) when assessing whether Estonian legislation was compatible with the obligations imposed on and the liability exemptions accorded to internet service providers. Moreover, it would now in all likelihood also consider Article 11 of the Nice Charter.

This brief comparison provides an opportunity for stressing the differences between the ECtHR and EU systems, as well as the tasks of the respective courts.[33]

The Strasbourg Court handles complaints based – inter alia – on Article 10, with which the relevant provisions of national constitutions on freedom of expression should comply. Thus, the ECtHR acts as a pan-European constitutional court of fundamental rights. However, the parameter to be enforced was established in 1950, when the Convention came into force. This means that, when tackling cases involving new technologies, the Court has been required to conduct its review on the basis of a very long-standing parameter, which was designed to apply to a very different world. At the same time, however, Article 10 (as well as the other provisions of the Convention) does lend itself to very flexible interpretation.

It is no accident that the legislation which the CJEU must enforce, including in particular the e-Commerce Directive, appears in some senses to be more obsolete than Article 10 of the ECHR. In fact, the Court of Justice normally issues its decisions within proceedings relating to preliminary references. Since it is for the national courts of Member States to make a reference for preliminary ruling, the Court must remain within the limits of the question posed and cannot conduct a broader scrutiny.

That said, the parameters on which the Court of Justice issues preliminary rulings are less flexible than Article 10 of the ECHR. Nonetheless, they are more specific. As regards the protection of free speech, with the exception of a few

33 For more detail see Oreste Pollicino and Marco Bassini, 'Free speech, defamation and the limits to freedom of expression in the EU: a comparative analysis' in Andrej Savin and Jan Trzaskowski (eds), *Research Handbook on EU Internet Law* (Edward Elgar 2014) 508.

provisions contained in the Audiovisual Media Services Directive, there is no *hard law* at the EU level. The e-Commerce Directive regulates the responsibility of internet service providers, and is the sole legal framework that deals specifically with the internet. However, it is difficult to enforce these provisions since they have proved, albeit recently, to be obsolete compared with Article 10 of the Convention. The problem concerns in particular the liability exemptions set out in the e-Commerce Directive, which were adopted in relation to technology that was very different from today's. The rise, for instance, of user-generated content platforms or peer-to-peer systems has raised unprecedented issues, which Directive 2000/31 does not seem to be able to resolve satisfactorily.[34]

To return to our question, at the time, the *Delfi* case would most probably have been resolved on the basis of the liability exemptions. Rather than examining whether convicting the news portal for offensive comments violated freedom of expression, the CJEU would have focused – it may be supposed – on the absence of any control by the website's owner over the (unlawful) activity of users. In all likelihood, no consideration would have been paid to freedom of speech, since the Court's task is not to ascertain whether a violation has occurred but, rather, whether the provider can be held responsible for the conduct of users who have posted defamatory comments.

However, this does not mean that freedom of expression has not been considered in certain judgments of the Court of Justice. Even without a specific policy laying down substantive regulations, we can in fact assess how freedom of expression has been weighed against other fundamental rights in certain recent decisions involving the internet.[35]

First, the case law of the Luxembourg Court shows that freedom of expression has been considered in judgments concerning copyright protection. This is also a result of the incorporation of the Charter into EU law, which expressly protects intellectual property as a fundamental right under Article 17(2). The fact that intellectual property ranks among the rights protected under the Charter means that copyright is a competing interest with freedom of expression and is thus likely to be weighed against it.

This factor has an important consequence: whereas in the past freedom of expression – as an individual fundamental right – by no means competed with copyright, the latter having been regarded as a property right and subsequently as an economic interest, the position is completely different now. With the advent of the internet, this factor has escalated the conflict between copyright protection and freedom of expression. Thus, both the CJEU and the ECtHR have been faced with an increase in cases where these rights are in conflict.[36]

34 See, in this respect, Joined Cases C–236/08, C–237/08 and C–238/08 *Google France SARL and Google Inc. v Louis Vuitton Malletier SA, Google France SARL v Viaticum SA and Luteciel SARL, and Google France SARL v Centre national de recherche en relations humaines (CNRRH) SARL and others* [2010] ECR I–02417. See also Case C–324/09 *L'Oréal SA and Others v eBay International AG and Others* [2011] ECR I–06011.

35 See further Pollicino and Bassini (n 33).

36 *Ashby Donald and Others v France* (n 26).

Two almost identical cases (*Scarlet v SABAM* and *SABAM v Netlog*,[37] or the *SABAM* saga) addressed the issue as to whether the courts were entitled, as a matter of EU law, to subject internet service providers to an obligation to adopt a filtering system aimed at detecting potential copyright infringements on the assumption that the heavy use of an internet connection was indicative of the illegal downloading of content.[38]

Both cases questioned whether such injunctions were compatible with the relevant EU law, and specifically with: (i) users' rights to the protection of their personal data; (ii) ISPs' freedom to carry out economic activity; and, finally (iii) users' freedom of expression (as the filtering may not distinguish between illegal and legal content).

Surprisingly, the CJEU only considered the freedom of speech on a residual basis, having first examined the question with reference to the other two aspects. The CJEU found that the requirement to adopt a filtering system such as that at issue in this case was not proportionate with the objective of copyright protection. This is because it resulted in a restriction, first, of the ISP's right to engage in economic activity, which is protected under Article 16 of the Charter. Secondly, the Court held that the system also violated Articles 8 and 11 of the Charter, which refer, respectively, to the rights to personal data and freedom of expression.

Copyright is of course protected as a fundamental right under the Charter. However, it is significant that the compatibility of measures aimed at copyright protection has only been reviewed at a secondary stage after individual rights.

These decisions seem to downgrade the role of freedom of expression, which is considered as a fundamental right alongside others, especially entrepreneurial freedom. The fact that no particular prominence has been given to this right can perhaps be related to the emancipation of the EU from a predominantly economic dimension, which has still not been fully completed. The analysis of the CJEU case law concerning online copyright enforcement has revealed the emerging judicial tendency, in Luxembourg, to downgrade the role of freedom of expression within a digital context compared to the prominence afforded to that freedom in the analogue context.

Similar conclusions can be reached in relation to the very recent and already renowned judgment of the CJEU on the protection of the so-called 'right to be forgotten' on the internet,[39] in which the Court took the emergence of a digital right to privacy very seriously. Maybe, one could object, too seriously, especially if this judgment is read in conjunction with the no less famous[40] ruling that struck

37 Case C–70/10 *Scarlet Extended SA v SABAM* [2011] ECR I–11959 and Case C–360/10 *SABAM v Netlog NV* [2012] ECR–0000.

38 For a commentary see Stefan Kulk and Frederik Borgesius, 'Filtering for copyright enforcement in Europe after the SABAM cases' (2012) 11 *European Intellectual Property* Review 791 ff.

39 See Case C–131/12 *Google Spain SL* (n 7), Opinion of the Advocate General Niilo Jääskinen (25 June 2013).

40 Joined Cases C–293/12 and C–594/12 *Digital Rights Ireland and Seitlinger and Others* [2014].

down the data-retention directive a few weeks earlier[41] on the grounds that it breached, inter alia, Articles 7 and 8 of the Charter.[42] Such a radical privacy-based approach risks that the protection of the rights that may conflict with the new digital right to privacy may not be taken seriously.

Against this background, it must be pointed out that excessive protection for the right to be forgotten risks removing the necessary protection afforded to the right of expression, and particularly to the right of each internet user to be properly and fully informed. The CJEU does provide a few guidelines in its reasoning on how the balance may be struck between these conflicting rights. Moreover, the Court does make several references to Articles 7 and 8 of the Charter and to the relevant provisions of the directive. Nevertheless, in contrast with the much more balanced approach of the Advocate General,[43] Article 11 of the Charter – which protects freedom of expression – was not expressly mentioned in the judgment at any point. This does not seem to be a coincidence, but rather a confirmation of the asymmetrical balancing described above.

One can argue, as Fontanelli does in his chapter, that the CJEU is not performing a balancing test at all because balancing, and the related proportionality test, is not (at least at the present moment) appropriate in internet-related disputes. This conclusion rests upon the idea that internet is a highly technical and regulation-needing domain, which cannot be left to the courts' assessment. At least, one should consider the policy trade-off on which a facially proportional test of this kind is based. In Fontanelli's view, *Google Spain* is precisely the kind of case in which the flaws of the proportionality test become quite clear. The Court of Luxembourg asserted it was balancing at least three different values (the data subject's 'right to oblivion'; the operator's economic interest; and the public's right to impart and obtain information), whilst giving absolute prevalence to the first of these over the others, without providing a detailed assessment of the two main pillars of the proportionality test.

On the one hand, the judges did not spend many words on the intensity of the

41 Directive 2006/24/EC of the European Parliament and of the Council of 15 March 2006 on the retention of data generated or processed in connection with the provision of publicly available electronic communications services or of public communications networks and amending Directive 2002/58/EC, OJ L105 (13.4.2006) 54.

42 Such an approach has been confirmed, while this book is in its final stage of publication, by the Schrems judgment (Case C-362/14), in which the CJEU declared the Commission's US Safe Harbour Decision invalid on the ground that the US does not afford an adequate level of protection of pesonal data. From the CJEU's perspective the Commission failed to ascertain in substantial terms whether the US law ensures the level of protection required under EU law.

43 Opinion of Advocate General Jääskinen in Case C–131/12 (n 39). It is worth mentioning at least one passage of the opinion in which the Advocate General clearly considered, in contrast with the approach of the CJEU, the need to balance the enforcement of the right to privacy on the internet with the need to assure the protection of freedom of expression online. Specifically, as regards the possible implementation of a notice and take-down procedure based upon individual complaints, AG Jääskinen clearly noted that the imposition of such a system for the removal of the indexed content would undermine the freedom of expression of the owners of the websites, as it would amount to a private form of censorship.

proposed solution impact on the enjoyment of the other legal situations or on alternative means to protect the interests involved in the case. On the other hand, they did not add much to the reasons justifying the imposition of an obligation on the search engine.

Certainly, this case has broad implications on the 'web *status quo*'. The chilling effect of the decision on the business model and practical functioning of search engines should not be underestimated. If search engines want to avoid being overwhelmed by take-down requests, the only alternative is to decide, ex ante, only to publish news that could never be related to users' private lives. Thus, a tangible risk of self-censorship is immediately apparent.

If, however, search engines decide to wait for take-down requests to be submitted, it will be for the search engines themselves to strike the delicate balance between the individual right of being forgotten and the right of all the other users to be informed regarding facts or opinions of public interest. This is precisely the balancing test that is carried out by the courts or, in the worst-case situation, by the national data protection authorities and one that cannot be expected to be properly carried out by private actors. *Google Spain*, however, shows how much 'good reasoning' – as it may be called in legal argumentation scholarship – is needed to overcome the risk of leaving rights in a sort of digital jungle and, at the same time, of over-regulating the 'free market of ideas'.

5 Standards of scrutiny, courts and the internet: a tentative conclusion

What does the overall picture tell us about the influence of constitutional techniques on internet law?

First of all, courts, with sporadic exceptions,[44] do believe that the internet is not 'neutral' when it comes to the application of constitutional principles. Even if the elaboration of new legal categories tends to be 'left for another day' – in the most technology-sensitive jurisdictions as well[45] – or at most invoked by scholars more than by judges, courts connect consequences to the use of the internet as a peculiar medium. Whether it has something to do with its potential risks (as the ECtHR case law tends to reveal) or its potential benefits (as the US Supreme Court seems to believe), courts conceive of the web as a vehicle of information, data and expression that should be carefully weighted in judicial reasoning.

In most of the European (both domestic and supranational) courts' case law, the internet enters the balancing test as a medium that strengthens the proportionality test on the side of the reasons justifying the limitation of a fundamental right, such as the freedom of expression. In other cases, it offers justification to give way to one element of a balancing test in favour of the other – as is clear from

44 The Polish case (section 2) should be borne in mind here.

45 As Justice Scalia has maintained in at least two cases concerning new technologies and the application of traditional legal categories: see *City of Ontario v Quon* 130 S Ct 2635 (2010) and *Jones v United States* 132 S Ct 945 (2012).

the aforementioned *Google Spain* case – on the simple assumption that the use of an extraordinary powerful medium deserves a higher level of attention against potential misuses.

In the US, where the Supreme Court repeatedly maintained that the internet opens up new opportunities to exercise traditional freedoms, the attitude is completely the opposite as far as the judicial scrutiny in internet disputes is concerned. Acknowledging the peculiar nature of the medium reinforces the proportionality test, heightening the level of scrutiny deserved by the regulation of the internet. Indeed, the aforementioned Supreme Court's precedent *Reno* clarified that the interest in protecting and fostering freedom of expression in a democratic society 'outweighs any theoretical but unproven benefit of censorship'.[46] This sentence clearly recalls the outcome of a 'strict scrutiny' formula, which is normally used in freedom of expression cases. In the digital age, this may be read as the assumption that to conceive of a compelling interest weighted against the freedom of expression in the internet is almost impossible.

In both cases, constitutional or constitutional-like courts, in their privileged position, are no longer going to take a step backwards; that is, they are not likely to wait for legislators to occupy the gaps that the development of technology necessarily creates when it is applied or, more precisely, combined with the analogue world. Thus, if a news portal cannot control offensive comments that have been broadcast on it – not being in the position of acting as an ordinary newspaper with its employees – courts tend to impose obligations and establish responsibilities nonetheless. The courts seem to be increasingly in the position of not being willing to wait for the technology to elaborate more sophisticated mechanisms to prevent harmful actions and they tend not to wait for the legislators to decide where to place burdens as far as obligations are concerned. This is not always a sign of judicial activism; it is – to put it in simple terms – a sign of the inescapable need to address contemporary issues.

This attitude reinforces the need and the effort to place internet law in the realm of constitutional studies as this book project has intended to do.

46 See *Reno* (n 19).

Index

Table of cases

* Permanent Court of International Justice

* European Court of Human Rights

* Court of Justice of the European Union

* European domestic Courts

Austria

– Constitutional Court

Belgium

– Constitutional Court

– Court of Appeal

– *Court of Cassation*

Bulgaria

– *Supreme Administrative Court*

Czech Republic

– *Constitutional Court*

France

– *Conseil Constitutionnelle*

Italy

– *Constitutional Court*

The Netherlands

– *Supreme Court*

– *Rechtbank*

– *Voorzieningenrechter*

– *Hof*

Poland

– *Constitutional Tribunal*

– *Supreme Court*

– Court of Appeal

– Crown Court

** Canada*

– Supreme Court

** United States*

– Federal Supreme Court

– Federal Circuit Courts

– Federal District Courts

– State Supreme Courts

– Lower State Courts

For Product Safety Concerns and Information please contact our EU
representative GPSR@taylorandfrancis.com
Taylor & Francis Verlag GmbH, Kaufingerstraße 24, 80331 München, Germany

www.ingramcontent.com/pod-product-compliance
Ingram Content Group UK Ltd.
Pitfield, Milton Keynes, MK11 3LW, UK
UKHW020012200926
475702UK00014B/1848
* 9 7 8 0 3 6 7 5 9 7 1 5 3 *